THE CITY & GUILDS TEXTBOOK

LEVEL 3 DIPLOMA IN
PLUMBING STUDIES 6035
UNITS 302, 305, 307 AND 308

NEVILLE ATKINSON

MICHAEL B MASKREY

City&
Guilds

About City & Guilds

City & Guilds is the UK's leading provider of vocational qualifications, offering over 500 awards across a wide range of industries, and progressing from entry level to the highest levels of professional achievement. With over 8500 centres in 100 countries, City & Guilds is recognised by employers worldwide for providing qualifications that offer proof of the skills they need to get the job done.

Equal opportunities

City & Guilds fully supports the principle of equal opportunities and we are committed to satisfying this principle in all our activities and published material. A copy of our equal opportunities policy statement is available on the City & Guilds website.

First edition 2015

ISBN 9780851933023

Commissioning Manager Charlie Evans

Content Development Manager Hannah Cooper

Senior Production Editor Natalie Griffith

Cover design by Select Typesetters Ltd

Typeset by Palimpsest Book Production Ltd

Printed in UK by Cambrian Printers Ltd

British Library Cataloguing in Publication Data

A catalogue record is available from the British Library

Publications

For information about or to order City & Guilds support materials, contact 0844 534 0000 or centresupport@cityandguilds.com. You can find more information about the materials we have available at www.cityandguilds.com/publications.

Every effort has been made to ensure that the information contained in this publication is true and correct at the time of going to press. However, City & Guilds' products and services are subject to continuous development and improvement and the right is reserved to change products and services from time to time. City & Guilds cannot accept liability for loss or damage arising from the use of information in this publication.

City & Guilds

1 Giltspur Street

London EC1A 9DD

0844 543 0033

www.cityandguilds.com

publishingfeedback@cityandguilds.com

CONTENTS

ACKNOWLEDGEMENTS

City & Guilds would like to sincerely thank the following.

For invaluable plumbing knowledge and expertise:
John Hind

For their help with taking photos for use throughout the book:
Jules Selmes and Adam Giles (photographer and assistant); Jocelynne Rowan, Steve Owen, Diane Whinney and Dave Driver, Baxi Training Centre; Mykal Trim and Sam, CHS Gas Assessment Centre Norwich, and Anup Chudasama.

Picture credits
Every effort has been made to acknowledge all copyright holders as below and the publishers will, if notified, correct any errors in future editions.

Baxi p235; **City & Guilds/Jules Selmes/Hackney College** pp 160, 178; **City & Guilds/Jules Selmes/Baxi Training Centre** pp 176, 178, 179, 182, 185, 205, 253, 256, 258, 259, 260, 261, 277, 278, 282, 285, 286, 287, 288, 295, 296, 297; **CM Prestige** p208; **Gas Safe** pp 177, 204, 313; **Gas Measurement Instruments** p188; **Hot Notes (PO BOX 1023 Blofield Norwich NR13 5ZB)** p298; **HSE** p175; **Holland and Green**, p12; **Maxitrol** p290; **Monument** p233; **Neville Atkinson** pp 119, 129, 136, 138, 152, 157, 178, 180, 181, 182, 183, 192, 197, 199, 201, 202, 208, 162, 209, 214, 218, 219, 220, 221, 223, 224, 225, 229, 242, 250, 253, 254, 255, 256, 257, 263, 265, 269, 270, 271, 276, 277, 294; **Old Flames** p174; **Screwfix** p12; **Shutterstock** ©Kurhan p118, ©Artazum and Iriana Shiyan p120, ©Dmitry Kalinovsky p132, ©plumdesign p178, ©Risto Viita p189, ©Jon Le-Bon p205, ©Ivan Neru p214, ©Toenne p218, ©SGM p235, ©drpnncpptak p241, ©Photoseeker p242, ©Golf_chalermchai p247, ©Monkey Business Images p306; **Siemens** p181; **Stadium/ Flambeau (01843 854008)** pp 232, 240, 241; **Suggs Lighting** p189; **Talon** p248; **Tracpipe** p248.

Illustrations by William Padden.

It is usual, at this point in any book, to thank those people who have helped in some way in achieving the final product. The chapters of the book that I am responsible for have taken much research and many hours of writing. This has meant that I have not seen my family as much as I should have over the last year or so but they have never complained and their support has been unwavering.

And so, my dedication has been the easiest part of the book to write. I would simply like to thank my two sons Scott and Joseph who have encouraged me. I would also like to thank my partner Amanda for her patience and to wish her luck with her own forthcoming degree.

Mike Maskrey

NEVILLE ATKINSON

I was born in Gateshead in the valley of gasometers, coke ovens, steam engines and pylons. My father was an artist and he painted these industrial wonders and exhibited them around Britain and in France. I remember when I was still in a pushchair seeing my first view of overhead cables intersecting billowing steam from the locomotives, which tried to hide the great gasometers that seemed to get higher each time I returned to gaze at them.

As I grew up, I recall gas-fired wash boilers and zinc baths, ascot heaters and plumbers wiping lead water traps with a moleskin. I wondered if I would ever be able to do such a marvellous task. I still have the scar of dripping lead on my hand to confirm my initiation.

My first job was as an apprentice mechanical services engineer in a factory. Even before I could get my hands on a pipe I was given the baptism of sparks with three-phase circuitry, then the ultimate full immersion into water while maintaining huge process kettles and cisterns. Plumbing is such a diverse craft that my transferable skills eventually took me into the chemical industry and the shipyards.

I later took time out to be involved in the creative arts like my father. I travelled to Asia and studied music. I embodied this new learning into a modern contemporary format and was fortunate to have my work commercially published and recorded. Later on I was involved in several innovative technical ventures, one of which resulted in my first successful patent. I returned to applying my skills to pipework and decided to gain a specific City and Guilds Craft qualification in Plumbing. At the time CORGI was just being introduced to aid gas safety.

I spent a few years at Hackney College and benefitted from the excellent knowledge, guidance and support of master plumbing craftsmen and lecturers such as Ken Daniels, Jeff Hammond and Brian Ivemy, who opened my eyes to the wonders of the world of plumbing.

Several years were then spent with onsite training of apprentices. Eventually I became a lecturer at City College Norwich and then Great Yarmouth College, where I spent 11 years as a teacher and verifier.

I now run my own training solutions company called 'Atkinson Technical' (www.atkinsontechnical.co.uk).

MICHAEL B MASKREY

My father was quite simply the best plumber I have ever seen. It was his enthusiasm for the trade that he loved that rubbed off on me at a very early age. I was working with him at weekends and school holidays from the age of 10.

In 1977, aged 16, fresh from school and armed with the little knowledge I had gained from my father, I started as an apprentice at a local plumbing firm in my home city of Nottingham where I gained a superb background in plumbing, both industrial and domestic. In 1982, I joined my father's small plumbing firm where I stayed until his retirement in 1999 at the ripe old age of 73. He sadly passed away in 2006.

In 1988, I started teaching part-time at the Basford Hall College (now New College Nottingham), the same college where I did my own training, initially teaching Heating and Ventilation and, soon after, Plumbing at both Craft and Advanced Craft and later NVQ Level 2 and Level 3. My teaching career continued at Stockport College for 13 years. I now teach Building Services Engineering at HNC Level 4 and HND Level 5 (and occasionally plumbing!) at Doncaster College.

To the readers of this book, I say simply, you are beginning a journey into a trade that brings so much satisfaction when you get it right. To be a good plumber requires three Ds – Desire, Discipline and Dedication. Be the best plumber that you can possibly be and always strive to achieve excellence.

FOREWORD

I have been in the heating and plumbing industry all my working life, and was lucky enough to have an inspirational trainer when I first started out. That training set me on a career that has taken me through all sectors of the plumbing and heating industry.

Now, as a trainer myself, nothing gives me more pleasure than to witness what I call the 'light bulb' moment; that moment when, after drawing on many years of experience 'on the tools', after explaining how something works and the theory behind it, everything suddenly falls into place in a learner's mind. At that moment, they have learned something that will stay with them forever.

With this book, City & Guilds is providing an excellent foundation for a world-class skilled workforce. This will be an indispensable, comprehensive and relevant reference book for those entering today's plumbing trade and will help to inspire the next generation of heating engineers.

Steve Owen, National Training Manager, Baxi UK

Steve Owen was appointed National Training Manager for Baxi in 2006. He is responsible for all aspects of domestic technical training in the business, including internal and external customer training and partnerships with training centres and colleges. Steve first joined the company as a service engineer in 1990, moving into the training department in 2002. Prior to this, Steve completed an apprenticeship with British Gas before becoming self-employed.

HOW TO USE THIS TEXTBOOK

Welcome to your City & Guilds Level 3 Diploma in Plumbing Studies textbook. It is designed to guide you through your Level 3 qualification and be a useful reference for you throughout your career.

Each chapter covers a unit from the 6035 Level 3 qualification. Each chapter covers everything you will need to understand in order to complete your written or online tests and prepare for your practical assessments.

Throughout this textbook you will see the following features:

KEY POINT

U-values express the rate of heat transfer through any element of a building – walls, roofs, floors and windows.

KEY POINT These are particularly useful hints that may assist in you in revision for your tests or to help you remember something important.

British thermal units (BTU)

An imperial method of measuring energy. There are 1055.06 joules in a British thermal unit. To convert BTUs to kW divide by 3412.

DEFINITIONS Words in bold in the text are explained in the margin to aid your understanding. They also appear in the glossary at the back of the book.

SUGGESTED ACTIVITY

Using the techniques discussed above, complete the pipe-sizing table for the single-storey dwelling.

SUGGESTED ACTIVITY These hints suggest that you try an activity to help you practise and learn.

 SmartScreen Unit 305
Worksheet 5

SMARTSCREEN References to online SmartScreen resources to help you revise what you've learnt in the book.

At the end of each unit are some 'Test your knowledge' questions. These questions are designed to test your understanding of what you have learnt in that unit. This can help with identifying further training or revision needed. You will find the answers at the end of the book.

Also at the end of each unit is an assessment checklist, covering what you should know and be able to do on completing that unit. This checklist lists all Learning Outcomes and assessment criteria for the unit that you have just read, showing you where in the unit each outcome is covered. This enables you to understand what is required for your assessment and to go back and revise any area that you need a greater understanding of.

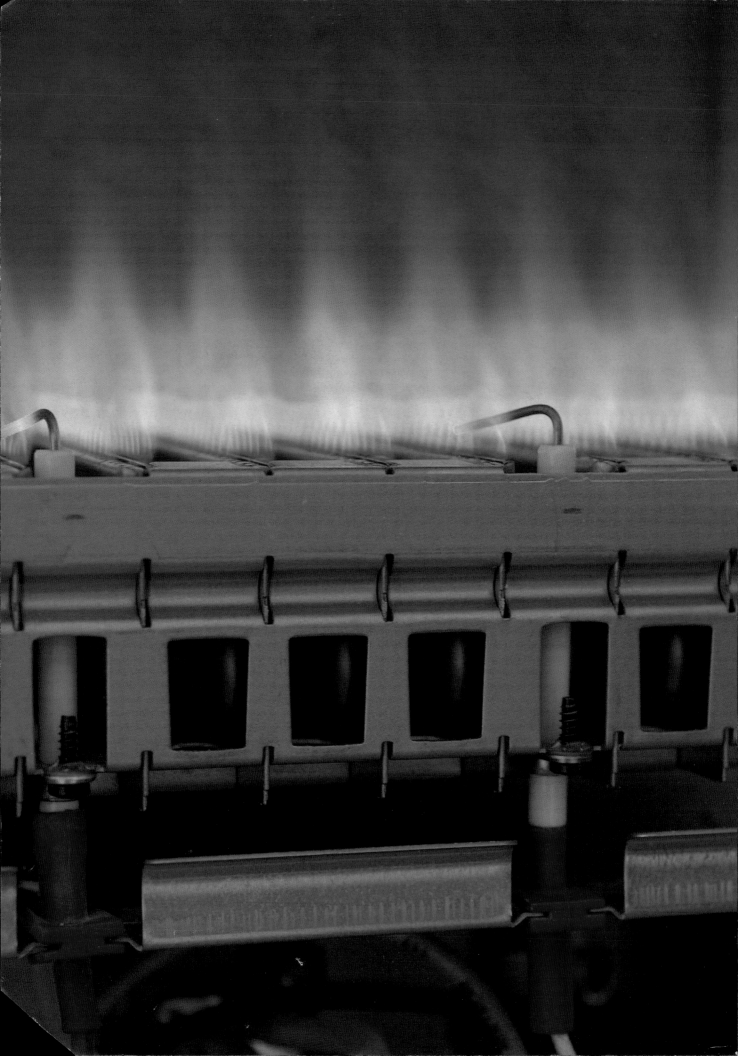

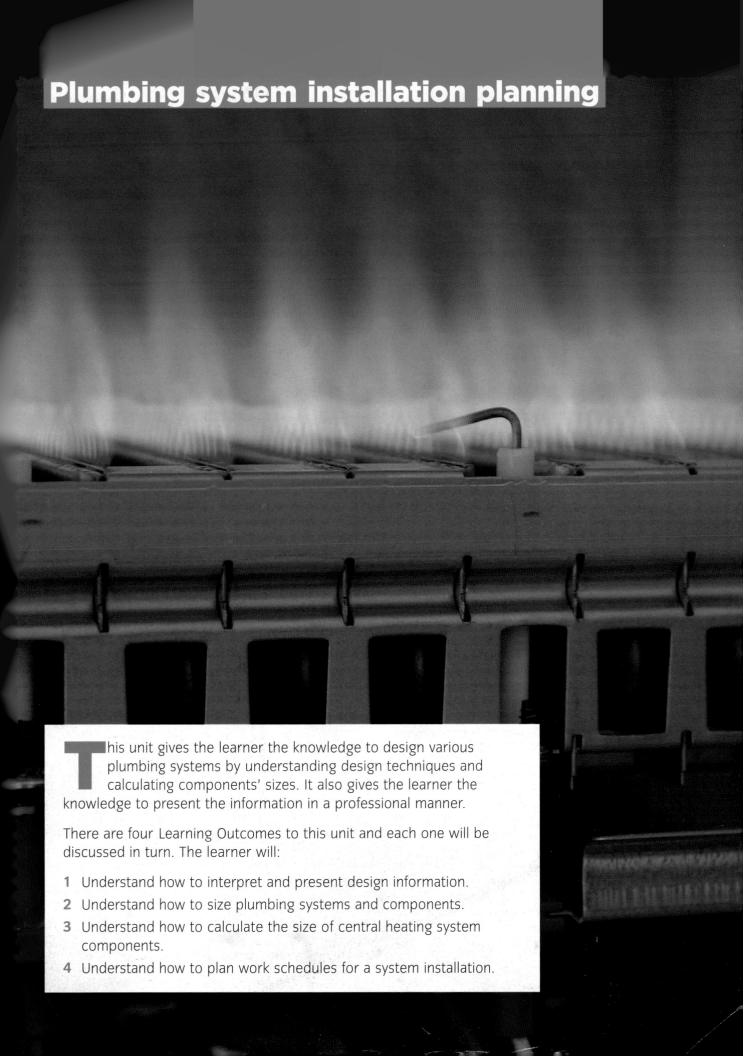

Plumbing system installation planning

This unit gives the learner the knowledge to design various plumbing systems by understanding design techniques and calculating components' sizes. It also gives the learner the knowledge to present the information in a professional manner.

There are four Learning Outcomes to this unit and each one will be discussed in turn. The learner will:

1 Understand how to interpret and present design information.
2 Understand how to size plumbing systems and components.
3 Understand how to calculate the size of central heating system components.
4 Understand how to plan work schedules for a system installation.

A plumber's job is to install the systems of hot and cold water, central heating, sanitation and gas, in a professional and workman-like manner, using materials safely, economically and correctly. This involves good calculation of systems, good planning and setting out the work and using installation techniques that not only satisfy the requirements of the customer and protect their property but that also comply with the relevant regulations, British Standards and codes of good practice.

In this unit, we will look at how we interpret information to enable systems to be designed and installed correctly. This involves methods of calculation of plumbing systems, sourcing and purchasing plumbing components and equipment, and methods of scheduling installation activities. We will also look at the effectiveness of relationships between the plumber and the client, the plumber and their suppliers and the plumbing team with other on-site trades, to enable the systems to be installed quickly, efficiently and with minimal problems.

Interpret and present design information (LO1)

There are nine assessment criteria for this Learning Outcome:

1 State the criteria used when selecting system and component types.
2 Explain positioning requirements when designing plumbing systems.
3 Describe the importance of sustainable design.
4 Interpret information for system plans for plumbing.
5 State additional considerations when carrying out systems planning.
6 Identify building measurements.
7 Identify methods for presenting system designs.
8 Identify cost of equipment used in plumbing systems using different sources.
9 Describe how to compile quotations and tenders.

SmartScreen Unit 302
PowerPoint 1

State the criteria used when selecting system and component types

There is no such thing as a generic plumbing system. Each system that we install is unique in some way. Before a system can be designed, priced and installed, we should consider:

- **Customer's needs** – This is arguably the most important part of any design as this is where we try to interpret exactly what the customer requires. There are certain questions we can ask to make the process easier:
  - What is it that they are trying to achieve?
  - Is it a simple installation or a replacement of an existing appliance?
  - Is it a new build or an existing property?
  - Is it an 'installation only' situation or will the customer require plastering, tiling or decoration?

It must be remembered that sometimes a customer will have no idea of what they want and will rely on us to give them inspiration and ideas. At other times, the customer will have researched the installation and will have ideas of their own and these, if practicable, should be considered wherever and whenever possible.

- **Building layout and features** – When the system is ready to be designed, looking around the building will give the installer an understanding of the:
  - type of building construction/building fabric, ie the type of outside walls – brick, block, concrete, timber framed
  - type of ground floor – solid or ventilated suspended floors
  - type of upper floors – timber, solid, block and beam
  - direction of joist run
  - layout of the existing services and their isolation points, ie gas, water, electricity, telecommunication, etc
  - additional work required
  - additional trades that may be needed such as an electrician, tiler, etc.

- **Suitability of system** – This is fundamental for any system. There are questions that we should be asking:
  - What are the pressure and flow rate of the existing water supplies?
  - Are there any system upgrades that need to be performed first such as the removal of old lead pipes or galvanised storage cisterns?
  - Is the pipework/cistern insulation adequate or will it require renewing?
  - Do any existing components such as taps or shower valves need replacing because of incompatibility with the new installation?
  - Will backflow protection be required and, if so, where?
  - Is the existing water storage sufficient?

Remember, the water supply (Water Fittings) Regulations are in force to prevent the following:

- wastage of water
- undue consumption of water
- misuse of water
- contamination of water
- erroneous metering of water.

■ **Energy efficiency** – New installations must be installed to the current regulations and, in the case of hot water and central heating systems, existing installations also must meet current regulation standards (Approved Document L1a and L1b) because the regulations apply retrospectively. This will need very careful explanation to the customer.

■ **Environmental impact** – It is a fact that the carbon footprint of today's modern plumbing installations must be considered. Installers can help to reduce the overall carbon footprint at the design stage:

- Suggest to the customer a system incorporating low-carbon, carbon-neutral or renewables technology.
- Design systems with low water usage in mind.
- Build in to the design a modern system of controls incorporating the latest energy-saving technology such as delayed start, night set-back and weather compensation.
- Use good insulation with low U-values on pipework and storage vessels.
- Consider the points raised on component and appliance benchmarking certificates.

■ **Fuel source** – Again, this is an important point to consider as it will have a bearing on the type of appliances that can be installed within the property. Consider the following:

- Is the property connected to the mains natural gas and electricity supplies?
- If not, which fuel does it use? Solid fuel? LPG?
- If so, is there access for fuel delivery tankers?

The type of fuel source, together with the type of system, will govern the installation regulations:

■ **Gas/LPG** – The Gas Safety (Installation and Use) Regulations 1998
■ **Electricity** – IET Wiring Regulations 17th edition
■ **Solid fuel** – Approved Building Regulation Document J: Combustion appliances and storage systems

- **Unvented hot water storage systems** – Building Regulations Approved Document G3
- **Hot and cold water installations** – The Water Supply (Water Fittings) Regulations 1999
- **Central heating systems/boilers** – Approved Building Regulation Document L: Conservation of fuel and power. These are also covered by Approved Document J mentioned earlier. Boilers must be installed by competent persons within each specialist area:
  - Gas Safe for gas installations
  - OFTEC for oil-fired appliances
  - HETAS for solid fuels
  - NICEIC for electrical installations.

Explain positioning requirements when designing plumbing systems

During the system design, due consideration should be given to the positioning requirements of pipework, components and appliances:

- **Clearances** – Space must be allowed for:
  - pipework
  - appliances
  - flue positioning
  - access for the customer
  - maintenance.

- **Disabled access** – Where bathrooms, shower rooms and WCs are installed, disabled access is a mandatory requirement under Approved Document M: Access to and use of buildings. At the design stage, we should ask:
  - Is there any need for disabled access?
  - Will disabled access be required in the future?

- **Legal** – The legal requirements of any installation must be completed. Reading the manufacturers' installation instructions will give a comprehensive interpretation of how the regulations can be complied with and those points that may need explaining to the customer.
- **Customer preference** – The make, type, colour and positioning of appliances must always be discussed with the customer before any installation takes place.
- **System performance** – When quoting for equipment, components or appliances, the performance criteria should be explained to the customer, such as a gravity shower against a pumped shower, a

combination boiler against a system boiler, panel radiators against convector radiators or renewable options against standard energy systems. The customer must be given the chance to make up their own mind about the equipment we quote for and any alternatives that may be available.

Describe the importance of sustainable design

In construction, sustainable design is the practice of increasing the efficiency of energy, water and materials usage of a building whilst reducing, over the life of the building, the impact of the building on the environment and human health.

New plumbing installations, whether within a new construction or an existing building, can make a very positive contribution to the sustainability of a building and the benefits can be explained to the customer. Consider the following example:

A customer is considering a complete renovation of a detached single-storey property built in the 1950s and this includes upgrading the central heating system. The installer has suggested that they have all panel radiators removed and an underfloor heating system installed throughout the property. The old gas fire/back boiler unit is to be removed and a new condensing system boiler installed, together with a full system of energy-reducing controls.

However, the customer has reservations about the possible benefits of making such drastic changes. They are happy with the system they have and question why a complete new system is needed.

What should the installer do?

First, the installer here has made a very good choice by suggesting an underfloor heating system linked to a new high-efficiency condensing boiler, complete with a comprehensive system of control. When outlining all of the considerations to the customer the installer should be able to outline the positive attributes of their design, for example:

- The installer can explain the cost-effectiveness of having a condensing boiler complete with its 90+% efficiency when compared with the 70+% efficiency of the existing appliance.
- The installer can outline that modern systems must conform to Approved Document L1 of the Building Regulations and that this will result in a lower carbon footprint for the property.

- The installer can advise of the increased comfort levels that will result from an underfloor heating system. They should explain how an underfloor heating system heats the building, the different kind of heat given off and how this would benefit the building's occupants.

- The installer can explain the benefits of an increased level of control to the heating system and how this will lead to significant savings on energy bills and increased system efficiency.

- The installer could also point out:
  - quicker heat recovery times
  - more heat retained within the building
  - better heating control
  - lower flue gas temperatures due to higher boiler efficiency
  - closer regulation of the temperature outputs.

In the example above, the installer quoted for a condensing boiler for use with an underfloor heating system but this could be improved on and further reductions in energy usage could be made by the customer.

SUGGESTED ACTIVITY

In small groups, discuss alternative methods of heating the water in the underfloor heating system that could lead to even more significant energy savings. Then produce a five-minute PowerPoint presentation of your findings to be delivered to the other groups at a time chosen by your tutor.

Interpret information for system plans for plumbing

The installation of plumbing and heating systems needs to comply with the regulations in force and we must always consider the recommendations of the British Standards wherever possible. Manufacturers' instructions have to be followed with regard to the appliances installed and materials used. Manufacturers' design flow rates and operating pressures will need to be considered at the system design stage for any installation to operate effectively.

Statutory regulations

Plumbing is one of the most regulated trades under the building services' engineering banner. We are governed by sets of regulations which tell us what we can and what we cannot do and what we must and what we must not do; failure to comply often results in prosecution. Regulations for plumbing systems include:

- Water Supply (Water Fittings) Regulations 1999
- Private Water Supply Regulations 2009
- Building Regulations
- The Gas (Installation and Use) Regulations 1998.

Aspects of these regulations are discussed throughout this unit.

British Standards, European Standards and Approved Codes of Practice (ACoPs)

The British Standards provide guidance on interpreting and following regulations, which are often written in language that is difficult to understand. They are not enforceable, but set out as a series of recommendations so that the minimum standard to comply with the regulations can be achieved. By adhering to the recommendations within the British Standards, the regulations will be seen to be satisfied. Often the regulations and the British Standards will make reference to one another and it may even be the case that the regulations make reference to more than one British Standard.

However important the regulations and the British Standards are, they are not our primary source of information when installing equipment and appliances. It must not be forgotten that the manufacturer's literature overrides both of these where a conflict arises.

Manufacturers' instructions

Manufacturers' installation, servicing/maintenance and user instructions are the most important of all documents you will have access to when installing, servicing and maintaining equipment and appliances. They tell us in basic installation language what we can and must do for correct and safe operation of their equipment and they must be followed, otherwise:

1 The terms of the warranty will be void.
2 The installation may be dangerous.
3 We may inadvertently be breaking the regulations.

In some instances, it may seem that the instructions contradict the regulations or the British Standards. This is because regulations are only reviewed periodically, whereas manufacturers are moving forward all the time with new, more efficient products, so their information may be more up to date. In these cases, follow a simple but effective rule: the manufacturer's literature must be followed at all times, even if it contradicts the regulations and British Standards.

Verbal and written communication with the customer

There are a number of ways that companies communicate with customers, such as:

Written communication	Letters
	Emails
	Faxes
Verbally (should always be backed up with written confirmation to prevent confusion)	Face to face
	Via the telephone

Written communication

Letters are an official method of communication and are usually easier to understand than verbal communication. Good written communication can help towards the success of any company by portraying a professional image and building goodwill. Official company business should always be in written form, usually on company headed paper and should have a clear layout. The content of the letter must be well written, using good English, correct grammar and be divided into logical paragraphs. Examples of business letters are sales letters, information letters, general enquiry and problem-solving letters.

Emails have emerged as a hugely popular form of communication because of the speed with which information can be transferred to the recipient. As with letters, they should be well written and laid out, using correct grammar and spelling to convey professionalism, whether the recipient is a client, customer or colleague.

Faxes are used mainly for conveying documents such as orders, invoices, statements and contracts where the recipient may wish to see an authorising signature. Again, the basic rules apply with regard to layout, grammar and content. Remember always to use a cover page that is appropriate for your company. This is an external communication that reflects the business and company image.

Communication between a company and a customer takes place at every stage of the contract from the initial contact to customer care at the contract completion. Written communication can take the form of:

- **Quotations and estimates** – Both of these are written prices as to how much the work will cost to complete. A quotation is a fixed price and cannot vary. An estimate, by comparison, is not a fixed price but can go up or down if the estimate is not accurate or the work is completed ahead of schedule. Most contractors opt for estimates because of this flexibility. Wherever possible, the estimate/quotation should be accompanied by detailed scale drawings to help the customer understand the work that is to be completed.

- **Invoices/statements** – Documents that are issued at the end of any contract as a demand for final payment for services rendered. Usually a period of time is allowed for the payment to be made.

- **Statutory cancellation rights** – A number of laws give the customer the legal right to cancel contracts after signing, providing work has not already started. There is usually no penalty for cancellation providing the cancellation is confirmed in writing within a specific timeframe. Most cancellation periods start when the customer receives notification of their right to cancel, which should be at least seven days before work commences.

- **Handover information** – At the end of any contract, the customer must be given certain information. For large contracts, this includes a health and safety file. For small domestic contracts, a file should be made which contains any manufacturer's information, installation, servicing and user instructions, the appliance warranty information, contact numbers of key personnel within the company and a letter of thanks for their custom. During the handover process, the customer should be shown where all control valves are and how to use any appliances and controls that have been installed.

Verbal communication

The spoken word is, more often than not, our main method of communication, especially in a work context. In order to present a professional image and communicate effectively, you must consider what you are saying, your tone of voice, your body language, and the response of your listener. Good verbal communication involves listening carefully as well as speaking clearly.

- **Feedback** – Often, verbal discussions with a customer help us to understand the following points:
  - details of ways in which the service to the customer could be improved
  - details of any faults that have developed in relation to the work completed; discussions with the customer can help us to diagnose and identify these faults and, therefore, complete any rectification work quickly and efficiently.

State additional considerations when carrying out systems planning

When planning an installation, consideration should be given to work outside of the scope of plumbing. It should be remembered that those regulations that may not be directly related to the plumbing trade must be followed, such as:

- Gas work must follow the Gas Safety (Installation and Use) Regulations 1998.
- Electrical work must comply with the IET Wiring Regulations (17th edition) BS 7671:2008 (2011).
- Unvented hot water installations must follow the guidelines in Approved Document G3 of the Building Regulations 2010.

Identify building measurements

Before design calculations can be made of an installation, measurements from the building must first be taken. This can be done in two ways:

- direct from the architect's scale drawings
- by visiting the site and taking measurements in situ.

Identifying measurements from architects' scale drawings

Architects' working drawings are drawn to scale. The scale is necessary because it would be totally impractical to draw at full size (1:1) for the entire building. The scale resembles a ruler with one exception; the markings represent proportionally smaller or larger distances with the millimeter as its base measurement.

Typically, architects' scale drawings use a variety of scales and this can be determined by looking at the drawing legend, which is usually situated to the right of the drawing. The legend is the information that the drawing contains, ie the architect who drew it, the scale, the name of the drawing, what the drawing shows and any notes that should be considered by the person using the drawing.

Typical drawing scales are:

- 1:1000 for site plans (10mm = 10m)
- 1:500 for site plans (10mm = 5m)
- 1:100 for plans and elevations (10mm = 1m)
- 1:50 for plans, sections and elevations (10mm = 500mm)
- 1:20 for part plans, sections and internal elevations (10mm = 200mm)
- 1:10 for details and joinery (10mm = 100mm)
- 1:5 for details (10mm = 50mm).

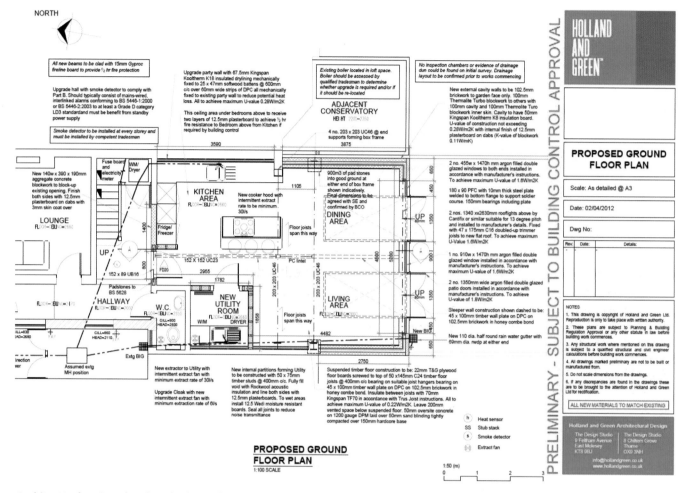

Architect's drawing showing the legend on the right of the drawing

Architect's scale rules

Taking measurements using a scale rule

1 Ensure that the drawing is lying flat so that there is no distortion of the drawing. Mistakes in measuring are easy to make when the drawing is not on a flat surface.

2 Identify the scale of the drawing from the legend.

3 Identify the part of the drawing that you wish to measure. This may be a wall, room or a pipe run.

4 Identify the correct scale on the rule that corresponds with the scale on the drawing.

5 Place the zero mark of the rule against the start of the line you wish to measure and read the length. Care must be taken here as it is very easy to misinterpret the length by reading along the wrong scale. Most scale rules have two different scales along each edge and it is important that the correct scale is used.

6 Note the length you have measured.

Taking measurements on site

Quite often, especially when dealing with existing properties, it may be necessary to visit the site and take measurements directly from the building. This can be done in several ways:

- **By using an architects' tape measure** – This is an extra long tape measure often used by site engineers to plot out a building. Requires two people for accurate measuring of buildings and can be inaccurate if care is not taken to prevent the tape bending and distorting.

- **By using a standard tape measure** – Requires two people for accurate measuring of buildings and can be inaccurate if care is not taken to prevent the tape bending and distorting.

- **By using a laser measure** – By far the most accurate method as these will not bend like a flexible tape or be affected by obstacles in the way. They use a pulse of laser light to measure the distance and are accurate to ± 3mm. A single person can operate them quickly and effectively without distortion.

- **By using an ultrasonic measure** – This uses an ultrasonic wave to judge the distance but can be affected by obstacles and obstructions that interrupt the wave.

Area, volume and weight

Being able to calculate the area, volume and weight of a component such as a cold water storage cistern is an important part of the design process. Plumbers are often faced with questions such as:

- Will the cistern fit through the roof space hatch?
- Will the roof trusses take the strain of the mass (weight) of water?
- What is the capacity of the cistern?

The table below shows the basic formulae for area, volume and capacity. These were discussed in detail at Level 2.

Measure of	Unit	Symbol
Area (length × width)	square metre	m^2
Volume (length × width × height)	cubic metre	m^3
Volume of liquid (length × width × height × 1000)	litre	l

Weight (and therefore mass) must be thought of in terms of pressure. Consider the following:

Pressure

In physics, the weight of an object is measured in newtons per square metre (N/m^2) and its mass is measured in kilograms. The way a cistern is positioned will determine the pressure it exerts on, say, a roof truss. In different orientations it might have a different area in contact with the roof trusses and will therefore exert a different pressure. For example, if a cistern measuring 1m long × 0.5m wide × 0.7m high was placed in a roof space, what pressure would it exert if:

- it were placed on its bottom?
- it were placed on its side?
- it were placed on its end?

Before we can attempt these calculations, we must first find the mass of the cistern in kg. The formula for this is:

Length × width × height = volume in m^3.

$1 \times 0.5 \times 0.7 = 0.35m^3$

Volume × 1000 = litres

$0.35 \times 1000 = 350l$

Since 1 litre of water has a mass of 1kg

$350l = 350kg$

From calculations at Level 2, we know that to find the force of an object:

Kg × gravity = N

$350 \times 9.81 = 3433.5N$

Therefore a cistern measuring 1m × 0.5m × 0.7m has a force of **3433.5N**.

The formula for finding pressure is: force ÷ area = N/m^2

- Area of cistern on its bottom = $1 \times 0.5 = 0.5$
  $3433.5 \div 0.5$ = **6867N/m^2 pressure**

- Area of cistern on its side = $1 \times 0.7 = 0.7$
  $3433.5 \div 0.7$ = **4905N/m^2 pressure**

- Area of cistern on its end = $0.5 \times 0.7 = 0.35$
  $3433.5 \div 0.35$ = **9810N/m^2 pressure**

From these calculations we can see that the greater the surface area for a given mass the less force will be exerted by that mass. This is of particular importance when placing large cisterns in roof spaces since the greater the surface area we can rest the cistern on, the more we will spread the load of the cistern.

Identify methods for presenting system designs

The calculation, design and estimation processes for plumbing systems take time to complete and unless these are set out correctly, mistakes are often made. The use of spreadsheets and tables when completing design calculations, especially for pipe sizing, is commonplace amongst most professional installers and designers. These are excellent for including with any quotation or design specification that the company wishes to present to the customer.

Scale drawings and schematic drawings help to show the customer what you are proposing to install to fulfill their requirement. This is especially important when a large installation is to be completed as it helps the customer to keep a track of what is being installed and where. Many companies now also provide three-dimensional and computer-aided design (CAD) drawings and artistic impressions of what the installation will look like when completed.

The use of computer software

Computer design programs have become more widespread over the last few years as they offer not only an accurate sizing method, but also the ability to print out the finished design complete with calculations for presentation to the customer. Programmes such as Hevacomp are widely used by building services engineers for the design of heating, air conditioning, lighting and hot and cold water services.

Applications (apps)

A more modern way of using technology is by the use of applications or 'apps' of the kind found on most modern mobile phones and tablets. Apps are available for heat loss calculations, radiator sizing and a host of other uses, such as pricing components and appliances. Many manufacturers and merchants have apps to assist in the design and estimation process.

Identify cost of equipment used in plumbing systems using different sources

Plumbing equipment, components and appliances are available from a wide range of outlets. No longer is purchasing the appliances strictly tied to a plumbers' or builders' merchant. In many cases, the internet will provide a better deal than those available from the regular outlets. Some of the many outlet types are shown on the next page:

- **Manufacturers** – These are often reluctant to supply appliances etc direct to the installer, especially in the case of bathroom and boiler manufacturers, as this can often cause contractual problems with merchants and other contracted outlets. However, parts for repairs are generally available from most manufacturers.

- **Merchants** – Historically, these were the most recognised method of purchasing equipment, components and appliances. Many merchants are now part of a national chain of merchants, with very few small independent merchants still trading.

- **Independent suppliers** – Usually small companies used by a regular clientele base. These will often be very competitive on price for everyday items such as tubes and fittings.

- **Catalogues** – These are becoming increasingly popular, especially for items such as tools, sundry items and tubes and fittings. Usually very competitive with the high-street merchant. Most offer same-day or next-day delivery times.

- **Internet and websites** – These are the fastest growing sector for the sale of large items such as boilers, convector radiators and bathroom suites. Most websites are extremely competitive on price offering multi-discounts to secure the sale. Many of the large chain merchants sell online and offer a wider range of materials than is available in their national branches with many items being website- or catalogue-sale-only items.

Describe how to compile quotations and tenders

An estimate/quote should contain the customers' details/address and a brief description of the work you are quoting for. It is not necessary to detail the cost of every item of equipment or the materials that are being used as this often leads the customer to check up on the items and the price you are charging for them. The quote should simply say what you are proposing to install and the total price you are charging for your services. Any VAT on either materials or labour should be shown.

Please note that VAT on labour charges should not be charged unless the company is VAT registered.

SmartScreen Unit 302
Worksheets 1 and 2

Size plumbing systems and components (LO2)

There are four assessment criteria for this Learning Outcome:

1 Calculate the size of system pipework.

2 Calculate the size of system components.

3 Select the size of sanitary pipework using manufacturers' specifications.

4 Select the size of rainwater system components using manufacturers' specifications.

Calculate the size of system pipework

SmartScreen Unit 302
PowerPoint 2

Pipework-sizing of hot and cold water systems is probably the most important part of any good plumbing design. When considering pipe size, there are a number of factors that must be taken into account if the volume flow rate required is to be delivered to the outlets without oversizing the pipework. The factors that need to be considered are:

- the volume flow rate required
- the pressure of the incoming supply
- the length of the pipework run
- the number of changes of direction and valves to be included in the design.

The flow rate

The British Standards differ slightly on the recommended flow velocities depending on which British Standard is being used. The flow velocity is the speed at which the water is moving through the pipework. This needs to be kept to minimum to prohibit excessive noise within the system:

- BS 6700 recommends that flow velocities should not exceed 3m/s.
- BS EN 805 recommends flow velocities between 0.5m/s to 2m/s with a maximum of 3.5m/s only in exceptional circumstances.

The pipework of any plumbing system must be designed so that the flow rates of the individual appliances and draw-offs are at least equal to those shown in the British Standards or the manufacturer's literature.

KEY POINT

Remember, excessive velocity + excessive pressure = excessive noise!

Table 1

Outlet	Design flow rate (l/s)	Minimum flow rate (l/s)	Loading units
WC flushing cistern (single or dual flush) to fill in 2 minutes	0.13	0.05	2
WC trough cistern	0.15 per WC	0.10	2
Washbasin with ½" – DN15 tap	0.15 per tap	0.10	1.5 to 3
Spray tap or spray mixer	0.05 per tap	0.03	–
Bidet	0.20 per tap	0.10	1
Bath with ¾" – DN 20 tap	0.30	0.20	10
Bath with 1" – DN 25 tap	0.60	0.40	22
Shower head (will vary with the type of head used)	0.2 hot or cold	0.10	3
Sink top with ½" – DN15 tap	0.20	0.10	3
Sink top with ¾" – DN20 tap	0.30	0.20	5
Sink top with 1" – DN25 tap	0.60	0.40	–
Clothes washing machine with ½" – DN15 tap	0.2 hot or cold	0.15	3
Dish washing machine with ½" – DN15 tap	0.15	0.10	3
Urinal flushing cistern	0.004 per bowl	0.002	–
Urinal pressure flushing valve	1.5	1.2	–

Notes:

1. Flushing troughs are advisable where the likely use of WCs is more than once per minute.

2. Mixer fittings use less water than individual taps, but this can be disregarded in sizing.

3. Flow rates to shower mixer valves vary according to the type fitted. Manufacturers should be consulted.

4. Manufacturers should be consulted for flow rates to washing machines and dishwashers for any building other than a dwelling.

5. The demand for cistern-fed urinals is usually very low and can be ignored. Alternatively, use continuous flow.

6. Loading units should not be used for outlet fittings which have high peak demands, ie those in industrial installations. In these cases, use continuous flow.

7. BS 6700 does not give loading units for a sink top with a DN20 tap or pressure flushing valves for urinals.

Calculating the correct pipe size will ensure that the flow rate at the appliances is adequate and meets the design specification.

Assessing the likely demand

The more outlets and appliances there are on an installation, the fewer of them will generally be used at any one time. The system in use to estimate the likely demand and therefore pipe size is based on loading units.

Table 1 shows the anticipated flow rates and the loading units for the common appliances that are fitted to domestic installations. These can be found in BS 6700. Let's see how this is used.

KEY POINT
What is a loading unit (LU)? A loading unit is a number or a factor which is allocated to an appliance. It relates to the flow rate at the terminal fitting, the length of time in use and the frequency of use.

Example

Let's assume that an installation fed via the mains cold water supply contains the following:

1 kitchen sink with ½" high neck pillar taps
1 wash basin with ½" pillar taps
1 WC
1 bath with ¾" bath taps
1 washing machine with ½" taps

Once we have listed the appliances, we can apply the loading units by looking at Table 2 and multiplying by the number of appliances. This is easier in a simple table. Remember, this is just the cold water supply.

Table 2: Loading units for a simple domestic cold water system

Appliance	Number	Loading units	Total
Kitchen sink with ½" high neck pillar taps	1	3	3
Wash basin with ½" pillar taps	1	1.5	1.5
WC	1	2	2
Bath with ¾" bath taps	1	10	10
Washing machine with ½" taps	1	3	3
		Total loading units	19.5

Before we can begin pipe-sizing activities, the need for hot water should also be considered. Obviously, if the system is to be a mains-fed, unvented hot water system, then the manufacturer's data should be consulted with regards to flow rate required. If the system is to be a combination boiler or an instantaneous multipoint hot water heater, then the loading units can be added to the table shown because the cold water supply would also have to serve these outlets. If, however, the hot water is to be supplied via a vented hot water cylinder, then the capacity of the cistern feeding it will have to be taken into account. From this, we can calculate the required flow for the cistern.

British Standard 6700 no longer states a minimum capacity for cisterns but does recommend a minimum of 230 litres' storage where the cistern is supplying both cold water outlets via a cold distribution pipe and cold water to a hot water storage vessel. In the past, it has always been the case that where the cistern is supplying cold water to a hot water storage vessel only, the capacity of any cistern should be at least equal to the hot water vessel/cylinder it is supplying. This concept will suffice for this exercise.

The average hot water storage cylinder contains around 140 litres of water. We will assume therefore that the storage cistern for the system will also have a capacity of 140 litres. The flow rate for the float-operated valve in the cistern can be calculated by dividing the cistern capacity by the required filling time in seconds. The filling time should not exceed one hour. Assuming, therefore, a filling time of, say, 15 minutes:

140 (litres) ÷ 900 (seconds in 15 mins) = 0.15l/s flow rate

Because the flow rate is small, no loading unit exists for it so once we have worked out the flow rate of the loading units, the flow rate for the cistern can be added on.

The loading unit total is 19.5. By looking at Chart 1 we can determine the flow rate.

From the chart we can see that the flow rate for 19.5 loading units is approximately 0.45l/s. Add to this the 0.15l/s for the storage cistern and we have a total flow rate of 0.6l/s.

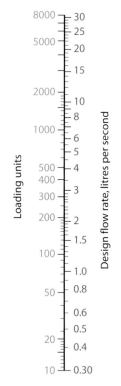

Chart 1: Litres/second to loading units conversion chart

The available pressure (head)

Systems that use the water undertaker's mains pressure need to be checked to ascertain the minimum available pressure during times of peak demand. This can either be done on site or alternatively, the water undertaker should be contacted for this information. With cistern-fed supplies, the head of pressure can be determined by measuring the distance from the base of the cistern to the outlet. Low pressure supplies generally require an increase in pipe size to compensate for the lack of pressure.

The pipe-sizing procedure

Pipe-sizing small systems is not a difficult task and in many cases follows a known convention based upon knowledge and experience. Most plumbers can estimate successfully the pipe sizes for simple domestic systems whilst on site. For larger domestic systems, however, it is always a good idea to formally calculate the pipe sizes from a drawing beforehand rather than trusting to experience. This is usually done using a tabular method. By completing a table from a drawing, the system pipe sizes can be calculated easily and relatively quickly. BS 6700 gives examples of this procedure. For the purpose of this book, a simplified tabular method will be used.

The tabular method uses a work sheet that is completed at each stage of the design process. It follows a fairly logical step-by-step approach, which can be applied to hot or cold water pipework design.

The tabular method explained

Make a drawing of the system and enter the flow rates and loading units. The system that we will be working through is shown below complete with flow rates and loading units.

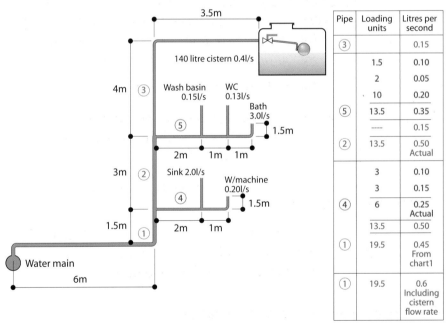

System drawing with flow rates and loading units

Before we can begin pipe sizing, a table is required. This shows numbered columns, 1 to 14, and an example is shown below with a brief description of what each column does:

1	2	3	4	5	6	7	8	9	10	11	12	13	14
Pipe reference	Loading units	Minimum flow rate (l/s)	Assumed pipe size (mm)	Head loss (m/m run)	Velocity of flow (m/s)	Actual pipe length (m)	Equivalent pipe length (m)	Effective pipe length (m) add columns 7 and 8	Vertical rise (deduct) or drop (add)	Head used (m) column 5 × column 9 + head loss of outlets	Residual head (m) column 13 – column 11	Head available (m) column 12 ± column 10	Final pipe size (mm)
1													
4													
2													
5													
3													
The pipe reference number from the drawing is entered into this column.	The loading units for each section are entered here. These can be found on the drawing or by using Chart 1.	The flow rate in l/s is entered here. Again these can be found on the drawing or by using Chart 1.	Enter the assumed/estimated pipe size here.	Calculate the frictional resistance using the chart provided.	Using the chart provided, determine the velocity of flow.	Total the amount of pipework in each section. Use the pipe reference numbers as a guide.	Calculate the length of pipe offered by the fittings and changes of direction in the system. Enter the equivalent pipe length in this column.	Enter the effective pipe length here. This is the total of columns 7 and 8 added together.	Any vertical rise must be deducted from column 13 and any drop added to it. A rise decreases pressure available but a drop increases it.	Multiply columns 5 and 9 and add the head loss of outlets.	Add the head used in column 10 to the previous progressive head in.	Record the head available at the point of delivery to the section.	Compare the residual head to the head available. If the residual head is less than the available head, the pipe size is good.

Step-by-step

1 **Pipework drawing:**

   a Make a drawing, not necessarily to scale, of the system. The drawing must show pipe lengths and appliances. The flow rates can also be included for every appliance.

   b Number the pipes beginning with the section that has the greatest flow rate requirement. The main pipe run should be numbered first, followed by the branch pipes.

   c Make a table showing the loading units and the flow rates at each stage of the main pipe run. The LU and flow rates can then be calculated.

2 **Determine the loading units:**

   a Calculate the maximum flow demand for each section of the drawing by using the method previously used in Example 1. This is done by:

      i.   adding up the loading units (LU) for each stage
      ii. converting the LU into flow rates
      iii. adding up the LU for all stages
      iv. converting the LU to flow rates.

3 **Add the figures to the table:**

| Initial mains head = 30m (3 bar) | | | | | | | | | | | | | |
1	2	3	4	5	6	7	8	9	10	11	12	13	14
Pipe reference	Loading units	Minimum flow rate (l/s)	Assumed pipe size (mm)	Head loss (m/m run)	Velocity of flow (m/s)	Actual pipe length (m)	Equivalent pipe length (m)	Effective pipe length (m) column 7 + column 8	Vertical rise or drop	Head used (m) column 5 × column 9 + head loss of outlets	Residual head (m) column 13 − column 11	Head available (m) column 12 ± column 10	Final pipe size (mm)
1	19.5	0.6											
4	6	0.25											
2	13.5	0.51											
5	13.5	0.35											
3	--	0.15											

Looking at the table, it should be noted that the pipe references are entered by order on the drawing and not numerical order.

4 **Make an assumption of the pipe size** – When calculating the size of pipework for a cold water system, it is usual to make an initial assumption about the size you think will be required. It is then down to the calculations to prove or disprove whether the initial pipe size estimation will deliver the required flow rate to ALL of the outlets. The estimated pipe sizes for the purpose of the pipe sizing example are noted on the table:

Initial mains head = 30m (3 bar)

1	2	3	4	5	6	7	8	9	10	11	12	13	14
Pipe reference	Loading units	Minimum flow rate (l/s)	Assumed pipe size (mm)	Head loss (m/m run)	Velocity of flow (m/s)	Actual pipe length (m)	Equivalent pipe length (m)	Effective pipe length (m) column 7 + column 8	Vertical rise or drop	Head used (m) column 5 × column 9 + head loss of outlets	Residual head (m) column 13 − column 11	Head available (m) column 12 ± column 10	Final pipe size (mm)
1	19.5	0.6	22										
4	6	0.25	15										
2	13.5	0.51	22										
5	13.5	0.35	15										
3	--	0.15	15										

We will assume that the system is going to be installed in copper pipe. In some cases, designers use the internal bore size of the pipe when calculating pipe size as this is the actual part of the pipe that carries the water. However, for the purpose of this example, the sizes shown are external diameters as this is what we are most familiar with.

5 **Calculate the length of the pipe runs** – Total the amount of pipe that is going to be installed on the system and enter it into column 7. This must be done for every section. Again, look at the drawing, calculate the pipe lengths and enter them into the table. This is shown as follows:

Initial mains head = 30m (3 bar)

1	2	3	4	5	6	7	8	9	10	11	12	13	14
Pipe reference	Loading units	Minimum flow rate (l/s)	Assumed pipe size (mm)	Head loss (m/m run)	Velocity of flow (m/s)	Actual pipe length (m)	Equivalent pipe length (m)	Effective pipe length (m) Column 7 + column 8	Vertical rise or drop	Head used (m) column 5 × column 9 + head loss of outlets	Residual head (m) column 13 – column 11	Head available (m) column 12 ± column 10	Final pipe size (mm)
1	19.5	0.6	22			7.5							
4	6	0.25	15			3.5							
2	13.5	0.51	22			3							
5	13.5	0.35	15			4.5							
3	--	0.15	15			6.5							

6 **Calculate the equivalent lengths of pipe** – Every fitting, valve and change of direction offers a resistance to the flow of water. Simply put, the water cannot flow through an elbow, for example, at the same velocity as it would through a straight piece of pipe. As the water hits the elbow, it creates turbulence, which has the effect of slowing the water down momentarily. The slowing of the water, whether through turbulence or resistance, can be expressed as distance added and this needs to be taken into account in the calculations. For example, a 15mm elbow offers the same resistance as a piece of 15mm pipe 0.5m long, so if the pipe run contains three elbows, we would need to add 1.5m of pipe to the overall actual pipe run length.

The table below shows how much pipe needs to be added to the actual pipe runs to compensate for the fittings and valves.

Table 3: Equivalent lengths of pipe for fittings (copper, stainless steel and plastics only)

Pipe size (mm)	Elbow (m)	Tee (m)	Stop valve (m)	Check valve (m)
15	0.5	0.6	4.0	2.5
22	0.8	1.0	7.0	4.3
28	1.0	1.5	10.0	5.6
35	1.4	2.0	13.0	6.0
42	1.7	2.5	16.0	7.9
54	2.3	3.5	22.0	11.5

Notes:
1. For tees, consider the branch only.
2. Gate valve resistance is insignificant and will not affect flow rate.
3. For fittings not shown, consult manufacturers' literature.

KEY POINT

Flow can be expressed in two ways:

Laminar flow – This is where a fluid, such as water, travels in regular paths. Often called streamline flow, the velocity and pressures at each point remain fairly constant. Laminar flow over a parallel surface such as the internal bore of a pipe consists of layers that are all parallel to each other. The fluid that is in contact with the pipe surface moves only very slowly because of the resistance offered by the pipe material and all other layers slide over it with varying degrees of velocity. The fluid moves at its fastest in the centre of the pipe because there is little or no resistance to flow.

Fluid moves in parallel layers of differing velocity and resistance

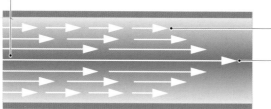

Fluid has greatest resistance and moves with the least velocity

Fluid has least resistance and moves with the greatest velocity

Laminar flow

Turbulent flow – This is flow that undergoes irregular fluctuations. The fluid continuously changes direction and velocity. The water swirls and creates eddies whilst the bulk of the water generally flows in one direction. In a pipe, turbulent flow can be caused by many factors including the internal roughness of the pipe bore or sudden changes in direction, such as an elbow or a tee piece.

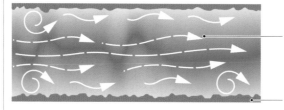

Fluid undergoes irregular fluctuations causing a reduction in velocity

The internal bore of the pipe

Turbulent flow

The pipe itself also offers resistance to flow. The smoother the internal bore, the better the flow rate will be. Plastic pipe has a slightly smoother bore than copper and so the flow rate is marginally better. Of all of the common pipe materials, galvanised pipe offers the greatest resistance to flow because its internal bore is not smooth.

So, with this in mind, let's look at how we calculate equivalent lengths. This is easier done in table format. Take a look at the system drawing and note down in the table the drawing sections and the fittings they contain, then add to this the equivalent lengths from Table 4. Now calculate the total equivalent lengths for each section by multiplying the number of each fitting by the equivalent length and adding them together:

Table 4: Equivalent lengths by section of the system

Drawing section	Fitting	Number	Size (mm)	Equivalent length (m)	Total (m)
1	Elbow	3	22mm	0.8	2.4
	Tee	2	22mm	1	2
	Stop valve	1	22mm	7	7
				Total	**11.4**
4	Elbow	1	15mm	0.5	0.5
	Tee	1	15mm	0.6	0.6
				Total	**1.1**
2	Tee	1	22mm	1	1
				Total	**1**
5	Elbow	1	22mm	0.8	1.6
	Tee	2	22mm	1	2
				Total	**3.6**
3	Elbow	1	15mm	0.8	0.8
	Stop valve	1	15mm	7.0	7.0
				Total	**7.8**

These can now be entered into the table and the effective pipework length calculated.

Initial mains head = 30m (3 bar)

1	2	3	4	5	6	7	8	9	10	11	12	13	14
Pipe reference	Loading units	Minimum flow rate (l/s)	Assumed pipe size (mm)	Head loss (m/m run)	Velocity of flow (m/s)	Actual pipe length (m)	Equivalent pipe length (m)	Effective pipe length (m) column 7 + column 8	Vertical rise or drop	Head used (m) column 5 × column 9 + head loss of outlets	Residual head (m) column 13 – column 11	Head available (m) column 12 ± column 10	Final pipe size (mm)
1	19.5	0.6	22			7.5	11.4	18.9					
4	6	0.25	15			3.5	1.1	4.6					
2	13.5	0.51	22			3	1	4					
5	13.5	0.35	15			4.5	3.6	8.1					
3	--	0.15	15			6.5	7.8	14.3					

Note: Where the fittings to be used are not known, a percentage of the pipework can be added to each section to compensate. This can be between 10% and 40% of the pipe run depending on the complexity of the system.

7 **Determine the head of pressure available** – Head of pressure can be given in any one of four ways:

   a **In pascals (Pa)** – This is the SI unit for pressure.

   b **In newtons per metre squared (N/m²)** – This is force per unit area. $1N/m^2$ = 1 pascal.

   c **In bar pressure** – This is the usual notation of water pressure in the UK. It is more correctly termed 'atmospheric pressure'. $1bar = 100kPa = 100kN/m^2$.

   d **In metres head** – This refers to the pressure exerted by a column of water in relation to its height from the water source to the point of draw-off. 1m head = 0.1 bar. 10m head = 1 bar $= 100kPa = 100kN/m^2$.

When pipe sizing water systems, any of these units can be used. For the purpose of this unit, metres head will be used as it provides a visual reference to pressure that can be compared with the height of the building and the position of storage vessels and draw-offs to be installed on the system.

Available head (column 13) – This is the head (or pressure) at the outlet or fitting and is measured vertically in metres head. For example, looking at the system drawing, it will be seen that section 1 finishes at the junction between section 2 and section 4. The mains pressure available is 30m head (or 3 bar). The distance from the cold water mains to the end of section 1 measured vertically is 1.5m. This means that at the junction between section 2 and section 4, the head of pressure available is 28.5m head (or 2.85 bar). At this first point, the vertical distance has simply been deducted from the mains pressure because there are no draw-offs to reduce it further. We must, however, deduct the head loss due the frictional resistance of the pipe and the stop valve. From this point forward, all other sections will need to be calculated because each draw-off will reduce further the available head.

Head loss through the pipework – As we have already seen, the internal roughness of the pipe will cause frictional resistance to the flow of water. The frictional resistance leads to a loss of pressure which is directly related to the length of the pipe run under consideration.

Head loss through fittings, valve and outlets – Table 5 shows the head loss through taps and outlets. Some designers find it more desirable to subtract the likely resistances for taps and outlets directly from the available head rather than converting the head loss into effective pipe lengths and this is the method used here. The head loss for the taps must be added to the head used in column 11.

Table 5: Equivalent lengths of pipe and head loss for taps

Size of tap	Flow rate (l/s)	Head loss (m)	Equivalent length (m)
½" DN15	0.15	0.5	3.7
½" DN15	0.20	0.8	3.7
¾" DN20	0.30	0.8	11.8
1" DN25	0.60	1.5	22.0

If a water meter is to be installed on the system, then the head loss through the meter should also be added to the head used.

To determine the head loss through stop valves and float-operated valves, Charts 2 and 3 can be used.

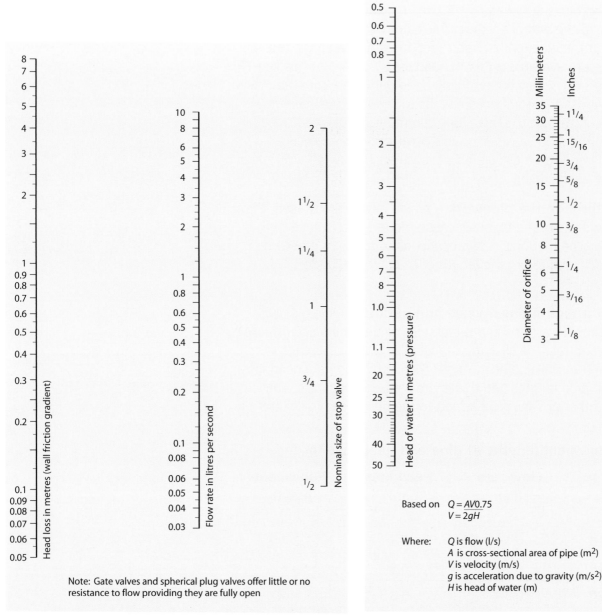

Note: Gate valves and spherical plug valves offer little or no resistance to flow providing they are fully open

Based on $Q = \underline{AV}0.75$
            $V = 2gH$

Where: Q is flow (l/s)
          A is cross-sectional area of pipe (m²)
          V is velocity (m/s)
          g is acceleration due to gravity (m/s²)
          H is head of water (m)

Chart 2: Head loss through stop valves

Chart 3: Head loss through float-operated valves

Permissible head loss – This is available head taking into account the frictional resistances in the pipework for each section. This can be calculated using the following formula:

$$\text{Permissible head loss} = \frac{\text{available head}}{\text{effective pipe length}} = \text{m/m}$$

This formula is used to determine if the frictional resistance in the pipework will allow the required flow rate at the outlets without excessive loss of head (or pressure). Each section of pipework must be calculated.

Example

Section 1

$$\text{Permissible head loss} = \frac{\text{available head}}{\text{effective pipe length}} = \frac{28.5m}{16m} = 1.78m/m$$

This means that the head loss for section 1 must not exceed 1.78m/m. To check the head loss, we must use Chart 4.

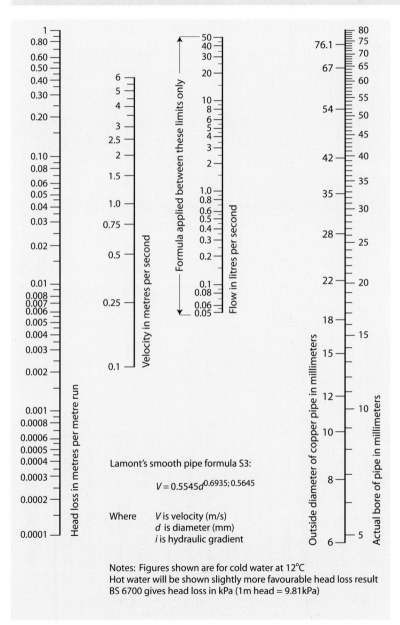

Lamont's smooth pipe formula S3:

$$V = 0.5545d^{0.6935}; 0.5645$$

Where V is velocity (m/s)
         d is diameter (mm)
         i is hydraulic gradient

Notes: Figures shown are for cold water at 12°C
Hot water will be shown slightly more favourable head loss result
BS 6700 gives head loss in kPa (1m head = 9.81kPa)

Chart 4: Determining correct pipe size

Method of reading Chart 4:

Using a straight edge, align the outside diameter of the tube with the flow rate for that section of pipe.

Read the head loss on the extreme left of the chart and the velocity flow rate on the centre left.

Remember, the velocity flow rate should not exceed 3m/s and the head loss should not exceed the figure that has been previously calculated.

In the case of section 1 of the example pipe sizing exercise, the head loss is 0.19m/m and the velocity flow rate is 1.8m/s. Both of these figures are within the tolerances allowed and can now be entered into columns 5 and 6 of the pipe-sizing table.

Now calculate the head used by multiplying columns 5 and 9 and adding any head losses through outlets on the section of pipe. Enter the result into column 11.

Column 12 is the residual head or the remaining head. In the following sections, the head used (column 11) must be deducted from the available head (column 13) and the result entered in column 12.

Column 10 is the vertical distance between the sections and equates to a loss of metres head. This must be deducted from the residual head in column 12 and the result entered in column 13 on the section below the one being worked on, eg from section 1: residual head 24.9 − 0.5 = 24.4 (entered into column 13 of section 4). This becomes the available head for section 4.

Initial mains head = 30m (3 bar)													
1	2	3	4	5	6	7	8	9	10	11	12	13	14
Pipe reference	Loading units	Minimum flow rate (l/s)	Assumed pipe size (mm)	Head loss (m/m run)	Velocity of flow (m/s)	Actual pipe length (m)	Equivalent pipe length (m)	Effective pipe length (m) column 7 + column 8	Vertical rise or drop	Head used (m) column 5 × column 9 + head loss of outlets	Residual head (m) column 13 − column 11	Head available (m) column 12 ± column 10	Final pipe size (mm)
1	19.5	0.6	22	**0.19**	**1.8**	7.5	11.4	18.9	**−1.5**	**3.6**	**24.9**	**28.5**	22
4	6	0.25	15	**0.24**	**1.6**	3.5	1.1	4.6	**−0.5**	**1.9**	**22.5**	**24.4**	15
2	13.5	0.51	22	**0.15**	**1.6**	3	1	4	**−3.0**	**0.6**	**18.9**	**19.5**	22
5	13.5	0.35	15	**0.43**	**2.25**	4.5	3.6	8.1	**−0.5**	**4.8**	**13.6**	**18.4**	15
3	--	0.15	15	**0.10**	**0.9**	7.5	7.8	15.3	**−3.0**	**1.53**	**9.07**	**10.6**	15

8 **Determining the correct pipe size** – If the residual head of each section is the same or above that required by the outlet(s), then the pipe sizing is correct. If, however, the residual head is less than that required or a negative head exists, then the pipe sizes will need to be increased and the process restarted afresh. The residual head for the example calculation for section 3 is 9.07m or 0.907 bar pressure. The last outlet is a float-operated valve with a 5mm orifice, which requires 6.6m or 0.66 bar pressure to deliver the required flow rate of 0.15l/s, so the pipe sizing is adequate. The figures for float-operated valves can be checked using Chart 3.

Pipe sizing – learner exercise

Now that you have seen the process, attempt to pipe size the system in the diagram below. The difference with this system is that the water supply is cistern-fed rather than mains-fed. This means that you should begin at section 1, which is closest to the cistern. There are no deductions in column 10 of the table. Instead, the vertical distance is *added* to each successive section, which will increase the system pressure and possibly reduce the pipe size.

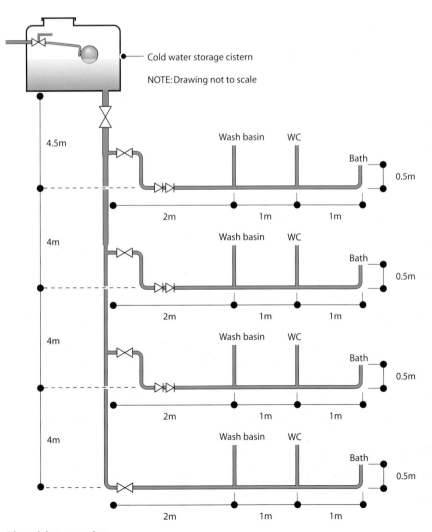

Pipe-sizing exercise

Pipe sizing – an alternative method using Thomas Box's formula

An alternative method of pipe sizing can be found using Thomas Box's pipe-sizing formula. Although not as accurate as the loading unit method, it offers a quicker solution to pipe-sizing problems. The formula is shown below:

$$d = \sqrt[5]{\frac{q^2 \times 25 \times L \times 10^5}{H}}$$

Where:

d = diameter of the pipe

q = flow rate in litres/second (l/s)

H = height (or head of pressure) in metres (m)

L = length of pipe, including allowances for bends, branches, valves etc in metres (m)

Let's look at our example pipe-sizing exercise again. If we look at section 1 of the pipe sizing drawing, we can see that the information we need to size the pipework in section 1 using Box's formula is present:

q = 0.6l/s

H = 24.9m

L = 18.9m

We can now enter this information directly into Box's formula as follows:

$$d = \sqrt[5]{\frac{0.6^2 \times 25 \times 18.9 \times 10^5}{24.9}}$$

$$d = \sqrt[5]{\frac{0.36 \times 25 \times 18.9 \times 100{,}000}{24.9}}$$

$$d = \sqrt[5]{683{,}132.5301}$$

d = 14.7mm

This shows that, in fact, we could have used 15mm pipe for section 1 but this would leave no room for error and would use all available head with none in reserve and so the next pipe size up (22mm) was chosen.

To check to see whether a 15mm pipe will deliver 0.6l/s flow rate, we can transpose the formula thus:

SmartScreen Unit 302
Worksheet 3

$$q = \sqrt{\dfrac{d^5 \times H}{25 \times L \times 10^5}}$$

$$q = \sqrt[5]{\dfrac{18{,}908{,}437.5}{47{,}250{,}000}}$$

$$q = \sqrt[5]{0.40018}$$

$$q = 0.63l/s$$

This shows that a 15mm pipe will, indeed, give 0.6l/s flow rate.

Calculate the size of system components

Modern plumbing systems have seen an increase in the use of direct cold water systems whereby all the outlets within a building are supplied with water direct from a water undertaker's cold water supply. However, there are situations where the use of cold water storage cisterns is unavoidable, especially in areas where the mains pressure is low. Storing cold water also has the advantage of a reserve supply of water being available should the mains be isolated for any period of time.

British Standard BS 6700 no longer gives storage capacities for domestic dwellings but, in clause 5.3.9.4, recommends a minimum of 230 litres in systems that are supplying cold water to both cold and hot water systems.

For larger buildings, the capacity of any cistern supplying cold water depends upon:

- the type and use of the building
- the number of occupants
- the type and number of the appliances
- the frequency of use
- the likelihood of a breakdown of the supply.

Most capacities are calculated to provide a 24-hour supply should mains failure occur. Table 6 provides a reference for cistern capacities based on the type of building and number of occupants. The table also includes hot water supply storage requirements.

Table 6: Recommended minimum storage of hot and cold water for domestic installations

Type of building	Minimum cold water storage (l)	Minimum hot water storage (l)
Hostel	90 per bed space	32 per bed space
Hotel	200 per bed space	45 per bed space
Office premises: With canteen facilities	45 per employee	4.5 per employee
Without canteen facilities	40 per employee	4.0 per employee
Restaurant	7 per meal	3.5 per meal
Day school: Nursery } Primary }	15 per pupil	4.5 per pupil
Secondary } Technical }	20 per pupil	5.0 per pupil
Boarding school	90 per pupil	23 per pupil
Children's home/residential nursery	135 per bed space	25 per bed space
Nurses' accommodation	120 per bed space	45 per bed space
Nursing/convalescent home	135 per bed space	45 per bed space

This table can be used in the calculation of cistern capacity.

Calculation of cistern capacities

Calculating cistern capacity is quite straightforward providing that the correct information is to hand. To determine cistern capacities, the following calculation should be used:

Litres of storage required (from Table 6) × number of people/guests

Consider the following example:

A hotel has 25 beds and 50 restaurant guests. Calculate the amount of cold water storage required.

200 × 25	=	5000 litres for hotel guests
7 × 50	=	350 litres for restaurant guests
5000 + 350	=	5350 litres total cold water storage

Assuming the cistern will have a 6-hour fill time, the design flow rate required to fill the cistern will be as follows:

Design flow rate = litres required ÷ time in seconds
= 5350 ÷ (6 × 3600)
= 0.247 litres/second (l/s)

This shows that it will require a flow rate of 0.25l/s (answer rounded up) to fill a cistern with a capacity of 5350 litres in 6 hours.

Calculation of pump power

Calculation of pump power is usually performed to ascertain the power of the pump needed to lift a certain quantity of water at a certain pressure. It is based on the physics of work done relative to time. Work done is the applied force through distance moved and the unit of measurement is the joule (J). It is thus explained as the work done when a 1 newton force acts through 1 metre distance or:

1 joule = 1N × 1m

The time must be expressed as a period of seconds, which can be combined with work done to become work done over a period of time. It is expressed in the following way:

Power = work done ÷ time

= (force × distance) ÷ seconds

= (newtons × metres) ÷ seconds (J/s) where: 1J/s = 1 watt

Force in newtons = kg mass × acceleration due to gravity (9.81m/s^2)

Power (watts) = (mass × 9.81 × distance) ÷ time

Consider the example below:

SUGGESTED ACTIVITY

A small primary school is to be built accommodating 350 pupils. Calculate the cold water storage required and the design flow rate to fill the cistern within a 4 hours fill time.

Delivery at 4kg/s

1 litre of water has a mass of 1kg

Length of pipe = 45m
(actual length + allowance
for fittings, bends and valves)

Break cistern

Centifugal pump
at 75% efficiency

Pump-rating exercise

As can be seen from the drawing, a delivery rate of 4kg/s is required to fill the cistern. 1kg = 1l, therefore 4kg/s = 4l/s. The total length of pipework when all bends, valves and fittings is 45m.

$$\text{Power} = (\text{mass} \times 9.81 \times \text{distance}) \div \text{time}$$

$$= (4 \times 9.81 \times 45) \div 1$$

$$= 1765.8W$$

Allowance for pump efficiency:

$$= 1765.8 \times (100 \div 75)$$

$$= 2354.4W$$

Therefore:

Pump rating (including 75% efficiency allowance) = **2500W** or **2.5kW** (rating rounded up to the nearest ½kW)

Pump laws

A pump is manufactured with an impeller of constant diameter. This will have the following characteristics:

- Quantity of water delivered (Q) will vary according to the rotational speed of the impeller (N). This is expressed as:

$(Q_2 \div Q_1) = (N_2 \div N_1)$

- Pressure produced (P) will vary with the square of the rotational speed of the impeller (N). This is expressed as:

$(P_2 \div P_1) = (N_2)^2 \div (N_1)^2$

- Power (W) required will vary with the cube of the rotational speed of the impeller (N). This is expressed as:

$(W_2 \div W_1) = (N_2)^3 \div (N_1)^3$

Where:

Q_2 and Q_1 = discharge of water delivered (l/s)

N_2 and N_1 = rotational speed of the impeller (rpm or rps)

P_2 and P_1 = pressure produced (kPa or kN/m^2)

W_2 and W_1 = power required (W)

Example

A 25kW pump discharges 4kg/s when the pump impeller rotational speed is 1000rpm. If the impeller speed is increased to 1200rpm, what effect will this have on the power required, pressure produced and water delivered?

To calculate these changes, a transposition of the known formula is required.

- Quantity of water delivered $= (Q_2 \div Q_1) - (N_2 \div N_1)$
  When transposed, this becomes:
  $Q_2 = (N_2 \times Q_1) \div N_1$
  $Q_2 = (1200 \times 4) \div 1000$
  Q2 = 4.8kg/s = 4.8l/s

- Power required $= (W_2 \div W_1) = (N_2)^3 \div (N_1)^3$
  When transposed, this becomes:
  $W_2 = (N_2)^3 \times W_1 \div (N_1)^3$
  $W_2 = (1200)^3 \times 2500 \div (1000)^3$
  W2 = 4320W or 4.32kW

- Pressure produced $= (P_2 \div P_1) = (N_2)^2 \div (N_1)^2$
  When transposed, this becomes:
  $P_2 = (N_2)^2 \times P_1 \div (N_1)^2$
  45kPa pressure is produced 1000rpm. When increased to 1200rpm, this will produce:
  $P_2 = (1200)^2 \times 45 \div (1000)^2$
  P2 = 64.8kPa

If the water pump will accept component change or upgrade and the impeller can be changed with an impeller of a different diameter, then the following formulae will apply:

- At a constant rotation speed (N), the quantity of water delivered (Q) will vary according to the cube of impeller diameter (D). This is expressed as:
  $(Q_2 \div Q_1) = (D_2)^3 \div (D_1)^3$

- Pressure produced (P) will vary with the square of the diameter (D) of the impeller (N). This is expressed as:
  $(P_2 \div P_1) = (D_2)^2 \div (D_1)^2$

- Power (W) required will vary as the fifth of the diameter of the impeller (D). This is expressed as:
  $(W_2 \div W_1) = (D_2)^5 \div (D_1)^5$

Assessment of accumulator capacity

Most accumulators are installed in domestic situations because the water supply entering the property suffers from either low pressure, poor flow rate or a combination of both. Accumulators, when fitted correctly, will boost flow rate and pressure to an acceptable level. It must be remembered, however, that to avoid problems with over-pressurisation during off-peak periods, a pressure-reducing valve

> **SUGGESTED ACTIVITY**
>
> A cistern requires a delivery rate of 0.36kg/s. 1kg = 1l, therefore 0.36 kg/s = 0.36l/s. The total length of pipework when all bends, valves and fittings have been taken into account is 60m. Calculate the pump rating in kW including a pump efficiency of 75%.

should be fitted on the mains supply. This will ensure a constant pressure entering the accumulator and prevent bursting of the internal bladder.

Although calculations exist to determine the size of accumulator required, most manufacturers of accumulators work on a fairly accurate rule of thumb. The calculation is based around the incoming pressure and flow rate of the water main. There are several factors, which will need to be taken into account:

- the pressure of the water supply
- the flow rate into the property
- the number of occupants and their water usage requirements
- the proposed location of the accumulator.

Accumulators work on the principle of Boyle's Law, which states that the absolute pressure and volume of a given mass of confined gas (in this case air) are inversely proportional, if the temperature remains unchanged within a closed system. If the space inside the closed system reduces, then the pressure within the system will rise accordingly:

- A balloon when inflated contains 4 litres of air at 0.5 bar pressure. If the balloon is squeezed to half its original size, the pressure inside will double to 1 bar pressure because the same amount of air is being forced to occupy only 50% of the space. In other words, it is being compressed.

With this theory in mind, look at the following example.

The rule of thumb

A property, occupied by two people, has an incoming mains supply pressure of 2 bar. The flow rate of the incoming supply is low at 10 litres per minute (0.1666 litres per second). The property also has a shower fitted delivering a flow rate of approximately 15 litres per minute. Calculate:

- the amount of storage for a given accumulator size
- the air charge required
- the length of time of storage usage
- the length of time required to replenish the accumulator.

The pressure charge in the accumulator needs to be half that of the incoming water supply if it is to fill sufficiently. In this case, if a 2-bar charge was used inside the accumulator, then, because the incoming supply is also 2 bar, the accumulator would not fill at all. Therefore, a lower accumulator charge of 1 bar is required to allow it to fill satisfactorily. This means that if the accumulator has a capacity of

300 litres with a charge of 1 bar pressure of air and an incoming supply pressure of 2 bar, then the accumulator would store 150 litres of water, half of the actual capacity.

If the shower flow rate is 15 litres per minute, then:

Litres ÷ flow rate of the shower = length of time of storage usage

150 ÷ 15 = 10 minutes

The accumulator has a storage capacity that will allow 10 minutes of shower use.

If the incoming supply flow rate is 10 litres per minute, then:

10 ÷ 60 (seconds in 1 minute) = 0.1666 litres/second

150 (litres) ÷ 0.1666 (l/s) ÷ 60 (seconds in 1 minute) = 15 minutes' accumulator replenishing time

Location of the accumulator

Accumulators can be situated anywhere within a property but it must be remembered that the higher the accumulator is positioned above the incoming supply the lower the pressure will be. The pressure will drop by 0.1 bar for every metre the accumulator is raised. Delivery pressure to the outlets, however, will increase by 0.1 bar.

Calculation of hot water storage vessel capacity

The minimum storage requirements of a hot water storage vessel are given in BS 6700 as:

- 35 litres to 45 litres per occupant unless the hot water storage vessel provides a quick reheat of stored water
- 100 litres for systems that use solid fuel as a heat source
- 200 litres for systems that use off-peak electricity as the main heat source.

There are two methods for calculating the capacity of a hot water storage vessel. The first method is based, in part, on information contained within the Chartered Institute of Plumbing and Heating Engineers (CIPHE) Design Guide. The second method takes a slightly different approach and is shown in detail in BS 6700. This is the method we will look at here.

The BS 6700 method of hot water storage capacity calculation takes into account the following factors:

- the pattern of use
- the rate of heat input to the stored water
- the recovery period for the hot water storage vessel
- the stratification (if any) of the vessel.

Accumulator sizing
A house with a low flow rate of 7 litres per minute and an incoming water supply pressure of 2 bar is occupied by three persons. There are two showers in the property, each with a maximum flow rate of 10 litres per minute each. The accumulator size is to be 400 litres. Calculate:

1 the charge in bar pressure required at the accumulator

2 the storage capacity of the accumulator

3 the amount of showering time available when both showers are running

4 the time needed to replenish the accumulator to full capacity.

Below is a table of typical heat inputs.

Table 7: Typical heat inputs

Appliance	Heat input (kW)
Electric immersion heater	3
Gas-fired circulator	3
Small boiler with direct cylinder	6
Medium boiler and indirect cylinder	10
Large domestic boiler with indirect cylinder	15
Directly fired gas hot water storage heater	10

A brief overview of stratification

Stratification is where the hot water 'floats' on the layer of colder water entering the storage vessel. The hot water sits in temperature layers with the hottest water at the top of the storage cylinder, gradually cooling towards the bottom.

Stratification is necessary if the cylinder is to perform to its maximum efficiency and manufacturers will purposely design storage vessels and cylinders with stratification in mind. Designers generally design:

- a vessel that is cylindrical in shape
- a vessel that is designed to be installed upright rather than horizontally
- with the cold feed entering the cylinder horizontally.

It is generally accepted that stratification occurs more readily in vertical rather than horizontal cylinders.

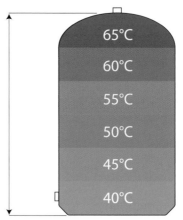

In a hot water storage cylinder, water forms in layers of temperature from the top of the cylinder, where the water is at its hottest, to the base, where it is at its coolest

Stratification of hot water storage vessels

Calculation of heat input

In Table 7, we saw some of the more common heat inputs. However, heat input can be calculated based upon the efficiency of the heat source. If a boiler is the main source of heat for the generation of hot water, then the efficiency of the boiler is required. This is one of the most important factors for improving energy efficiency for the selection of a hot water storage vessel. The formula for calculating heat input is as follows:

$$\frac{\text{SHC} \times \text{litres of water} \times \text{temp. difference } (\Delta t) \times \text{boiler efficiency}}{\text{time in seconds} \times 100} = \text{kW}$$

Where:

SHC = specific heat capacity of water. This is taken as being 4.19kj/kg/°C

Litres of water = the storage of water in the hot water storage vessel

Temp. difference = the difference in temperature between the incoming cold supply and the required temperature of the stored hot water

Boiler efficiency = usually taken as 93% for a condensing boiler

Time in seconds = the time limit for the water to get hot in seconds

Example

A hot water storage cylinder has a capacity of 210 litres. The cylinder is required to be at 65°C within 2 hours. The temperature of the incoming water is 4°C. What is the kW required?

$$\frac{\text{SHC} \times \text{litres of water} \times \text{temp. difference } (\Delta t) \times \text{boiler efficiency}}{\text{time in seconds} \times 100} = \text{kW}$$

SHC = 4.19

Litres of water = 210

Δt = 61

time in seconds = 7200 (2hrs)

$$\frac{4.19 \times 210 \times 61 \times 93}{7200 \times 100} = \frac{4,991,672.7}{720,000} = \textbf{6.93kW}$$

SUGGESTED ACTIVITY

A hot water storage cylinder has a capacity of 140 litres. The cylinder is required to reach 60°C in 2 hours. The temperature of the incoming water is 4°C. What is the kW required?

Calculating capacity based on recovery time

The capacity of the hot water storage vessel depends upon the rate of heat input to the stored water and the pattern of use. The calculation used for this takes into account the time M (in minutes as the previous calculation) taken to heat a specific quantity of water through a specific temperature rise. The formula is as follows:

M = VT/(14.3P)

Where:

V = volume of water heated (l)

T = temperature of water (°C)

P = rate of heat input into the water (kW)

The above formula ignores any heat loss from the cylinder as this is likely to be negligible over a short period of time and the formula can be applied to any hot water storage situation whether stratification occurs or not.

So, how does the formula work?

The following examples, taken from BS 6700 Annex C, assume that a small domestic dwelling has 1 bath installed and assumptions on pattern of usage have been made. The maximum requirements:

1 bath using 60 litres of hot water at 60°C + 40 litres of cold water + 10 litres of hot water at 60°C for kitchen use followed by a second bath fill 25 minutes later.

Totals are 70 litres of hot water at 60°C followed 25 minutes later by 100 litres for a second bath fill, which may be achieved by mixing hot water at 60°C with cold water at 10°C.

Example 1 – Assuming good stratification

If the water in the cylinder is heated via a top-entry 3kW immersion heater then good stratification is likely to occur. The time needed to heat 60 litres of water from 10°C to 60°C for the second bath is therefore:

M = VT/(14.3P)

$60 \times 50 \div (14.3 \times 3) = 3000 \div 42.9 = 69.93$ minutes (rounded up to 70 minutes)

However, the second bath is required within 25 minutes of the first and so this water must come from the storage cylinder. To calculate this the original formula must be transposed to:

V = M(14.3P)/T

The volume of water heated in 25 minutes is then as follows:

V = M(14.3P)/T

$V = (25 \times 14.3 \times 3)/50$

V = 21.45 litres rounded to 21 litres

Total minimum storage requirement is calculated as:

70 litres + 60 litres − 21 litres = **109 litres**

SUGGESTED ACTIVITY

A small dwelling has the following hot water requirements:

1 bath using 55 litres of hot water at 65°C + 45 litres of cold water + 10 litres of hot water at 65°C for kitchen use followed by a second bath fill 30 minutes later.

Totals are 65 litres of hot water at 65°C followed 30 minutes later by 100 litres for a second bath fill, which may be achieved by mixing hot water at 65°C with cold water at 10°C.

Calculate the minimum hot water capacity required assuming good stratification using a 3kW top-entry immersion heater.

The total of 109 litres is shown in the table below from BS 6700 as the minimum storage capacity of a hot water storage vessel with stratification for a small domestic dwelling.

Table 8: Minimum hot water storage capacity

Heat input to the water	Small dwelling with one bath		Large dwelling with two baths	
	With stratification (l)	With mixing – indirect type (l)	With stratification (l)	With mixing – indirect type (l)
3	109	122	165	250
6	88	88	140	200
10	70	70	130	130
15	70	70	120	130

Example 2 – Assuming good mixing

Good water mixing occurs when the hot water storage vessel is heated by a primary heat exchanger coil of the type found in a double-feed indirect open-vented hot water storage cylinder (or the equivalent unvented type storage cylinder).

Because mixing is occurring, as soon as hot water is drawn off, to be replaced by colder water, mixing takes place and the whole of the cylinder becomes cooler. If 70 litres of hot water are used (60 litres for the first bath and 10 litres for kitchen use), then the remaining hot water in the cylinder and the 70 litres of cold water at 10°C replacing the used hot water will equal the heat energy of the entire contents simply because mixing has taken place.

The heat energy in the cylinder is the product of the volume of the hot water storage vessel and its resultant temperature.

A further transposition of the original formula is necessary.

Therefore, if V is the storage vessel volume and T is its temperature after being refilled with 70 litres of water at 10°C:

70 litres (storage vessel volume) × 60°C + (70 litres replacement × 10°C) = VT

4200 + 700 = VT

Therefore:

T = 60V (volume of bath) − (4200 − 700) ÷ V

T = (60V − 3500) ÷ V

T = 60 − 3500 ÷ V

From the original requirement, a second bath is required after 25 minutes. Therefore, with a heat input of 3kW:

$$25 = VT \div (14.3 \times 3)$$

$$T = (25 \times 14.3 \times 3) \div V$$

$$T = 1072.5 \div V$$

The temperature required for the second bath is 40°C. Therefore, after the first draw-off of 70 litres and its subsequent replenishment with 70 litres of water at 10°C, the temperature must be at least 40°C (or above) after 25 minutes. To achieve this, the minimum storage capacity must be:

$$60 - (3500 \div V) + (1072.5 \div V) = 40°C$$

$$60 - 2427.5 \div V = 40°C$$

When the calculation is transposed:

$$2427.5 \div (60 - 40) = \textbf{121.375 rounded up to 122 litres}$$

Sizing a secondary circulation circulating pump

Sizing a hot water secondary circulation circulating pump involves the calculation of the mass flow rate of the circuit based upon the heat loss from the circuit and the temperature difference between the flow and the return. Take a look at the drawing on the next page.

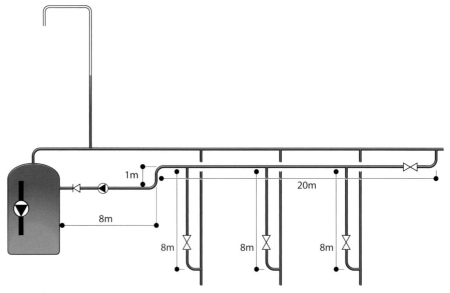

Secondary circulation sizing

From the drawing, we can see that the length of the return pipe is 53m. From this, we can calculate the size of the return pipe and the size of the pump. The data we need for this is as follows:

Length of pipe $= 53m$

Temperature of the secondary flow (t_f) $= 65°C$

Temperature of the secondary return (t_r) $= 55°C$

Specific heat capacity of water (SHC) $= 4.19kj/kg$

Heat loss from the insulated pipe $= 8w/m^2/C$

By calculating the mass flow rate of the return pipe in kg/s, the size of the return pipe and the circulating pump size (in pascals pressure drop – Pa/m) can be calculated by using the reference data for copper tubes from CIBSE Guide C. First, however, the mass flow rate must be calculated by using the following formula:

$$Ma = \frac{kW}{SHC \times \Delta t \, (t_f - t_r)} = kg/s$$

To find the kW:

$kW = length \times w/m^2/C$

$kW = 53 \times 8 = 424W = 0.424kW$

Therefore:

$$Ma = \frac{kW}{SHC \times \Delta t \, (t_f - t_r)} = kg/s$$

$$Ma = \frac{0.424}{4.19 \times (65 - 55)}$$

$$Ma = \frac{0.424}{4.19 \times 10}$$

$$Ma = \frac{0.424}{41.90}$$

Ma = **0.010kg/s**

Looking at CIBSE guide C for copper tube, it can be seen that the nearest mass flow rate to the calculated figure is boxed in red:

Pipe sizing tables 1

qm = mass flow rate   kg/s
c = velocity   m/s
Δp/l = pressure loss per unit length   pa/m

Copper tubes BS 2871 Table X
Water at 75°C

Δp/l	c	10 mm		12mm		15mm		22mm		28mm		35mm		42mm		c	Δp/l
		qm	c	qm	c	qm	c	qm	c	qm	c	qm	c	qm	c		
0.1								0.001	0.00	0.000	0.00	0.007	0.01	0.015	0.01		0.1
0.2								0.002	0.01	0.005	0.01	0.014	0.02	0.023	0.02		0.2
0.3								0.003	0.01	0.008	0.02	0.019	0.02	0.026	0.02		0.3
0.4								0.004	0.01	0.011	0.02	0.019	0.02	0.032	0.03		0.4
0.5						0.001	0.01	0.005	0.02	0.014	0.03	0.021	0.03	0.036	0.03		0.5
0.6						0.001	0.01	0.006	0.02	0.015	0.03	0.023	0.03	0.040	0.03		0.6
0.7						0.001	0.01	0.007	0.02	0.015	0.03	0.026	0.03	0.044	0.04		0.7
0.8						0.001	0.01	0.008	0.03	0.015	0.03	0.028	0.03	0.048	0.04		0.8
0.9						0.001	0.01	0.009	0.03	0.016	0.03	0.030	0.04	0.051	0.04		0.9
1.0						0.002	0.01	0.010	0.03	0.017	0.03	0.032	0.04	0.055	0.05	0.05	1.0
1.5				0.001	0.01	0.003	0.02	0.012	0.04	0.022	0.04	0.040	0.05	0.070	0.06		1.5
2.0				0.001	0.01	0.004	0.03	0.012	0.04	0.026	0.05	0.048	0.06	0.083	0.07		2.0
2.5				0.002	0.02	0.005	0.04	0.014	0.04	0.030	0.06	0.055	0.07	0.094	0.08		2.5
3.0		0.001	0.02	0.002	0.02	0.006	0.04	0.016	0.05	0.033	0.06	0.061	0.07	0.105	0.09		3.0
3.5		0.001	0.02	0.003	0.03	0.007	0.05	0.017	0.05	0.036	0.07	0.067	0.08	0.114	0.09		3.5
4.0		0.001	0.02	0.003	0.03	0.008	0.06	0.019	0.06	0.039	0.07	0.072	0.09	0.124	0.10		4.0
4.5		0.001	0.02	0.003	0.03	0.008	0.06	0.020	0.06	0.042	0.08	0.078	0.10	0.132	0.11		4.5
5.0		0.001	0.02	0.004	0.04	0.008	0.06	0.022	0.07	0.045	0.09	0.083	0.10	0.141	0.12		5.0
5.5		0.002	0.03	0.004	0.04	0.008	0.06	0.023	0.07	0.048	0.09	0.087	0.11	0.149	0.12		5.5
6.0		0.002	0.03	0.005	0.06	0.008	0.06	0.024	0.08	0.050	0.09	0.092	0.11	0.156	0.13		6.0
6.5		0.002	0.03	0.005	0.06	0.008	0.06	0.025	0.08	0.053	0.10	0.096	0.12	0.164	0.14		6.5
7.0		0.002	0.03	0.006	0.07	0.008	0.06	0.027	0.09	0.055	0.10	0.100	0.12	0.171	0.14		7.0
7.5		0.002	0.03	0.006	0.07	0.009	0.06	0.028	0.09	0.057	0.11	0.105	0.13	0.178	0.15	0.15	7.5
8.0		0.003	0.05	0.006	0.07	0.009	0.06	0.029	0.09	0.059	0.11	0.108	0.13	0.185	0.15		8.0
8.5		0.003	0.05	0.006	0.07	0.010	0.07	0.030	0.10	0.061	0.12	0.112	0.14	0.191	0.16		8.5
9.0		0.003	0.05	0.006	0.07	0.010	0.07	0.031	0.10	0.064	0.12	0.116	0.14	0.198	0.16		9.0
9.5		0.003	0.05	0.006	0.07	0.010	0.07	0.032	0.10	0.066	0.13	0.120	0.15	0.204	0.17		9.5
10.0	0.05	0.003	0.05	0.006	0.07	0.011	0.08	0.033	0.11	0.068	0.13	0.123	0.15	0.210	0.17		10.0
12.5		0.004	0.07	0.006	0.07	0.012	0.08	0.037	0.12	0.077	0.15	0.140	0.17	0.239	0.20		12.5
15.0		0.005	0.08	0.007	0.08	0.014	0.10	0.042	0.13	0.086	0.16	0.156	0.19	0.265	0.22		15.0
17.5		0.005	0.08	0.008	0.09	0.015	0.11	0.046	0.15	0.094	0.18	0.170	0.21	0.289	0.24		17.5
20.0		0.005	0.08	0.008	0.09	0.016	0.11	0.049	0.16	0.101	0.19	0.184	0.23	0.312	0.26		20.0
22.5		0.005	0.08	0.009	0.10	0.017	0.12	0.053	0.17	0.108	0.21	0.197	0.24	0.334	0.28		22.5
25.0		0.005	0.08	0.010	0.11	0.019	0.13	0.056	0.18	0.115	0.22	0.209	0.26	0.354	0.29	0.30	25.0
27.5		0.005	0.08	0.010	0.11	0.020	0.14	0.060	0.19	0.122	0.23	0.221	0.27	0.374	0.31		27.5

This shows that a 15mm copper pipe will deliver 0.010 kilograms per second (kg/s) at a velocity of 0.07 litres per second (l/s) with a pressure loss of 9.5 pascals per metre (Pa/m). In this case, the mass flow rate matches perfectly. In most instances, the nearest figure up would be chosen. However, there may be instances where there is more than one alternative. Look at the table again and it will be seen that 12mm pipe will also deliver 0.010kg/s but the pascals per metre is 27.5 with a velocity of 0.11 litres per second. This means that the pump power will have to be over twice the size than for 15mm to deliver the same flow rate, so in this case 15mm would be chosen.

Now the pump size can be calculated. To do this, the frictional resistance of the return pipe must be found taking into account the fittings and valves.

Each change of direction and each valve offer resistance to flow. This is measured in length of pipe. In other words, the resistance of an elbow or bend will have the same resistance as a specific amount of pipe. Consider the table below.

Table 9: Typical equivalent lengths for copper tube

Bore of pipe	Equivalent length			
	Elbow (m)	Tee (m)	Stop valve (m)	Check valve (m)
15	0.5	0.6	4.0	2.5
22	0.8	1.0	7.0	4.3
28	1.0	1.5	10.0	5.6
35	1.4	2.0	13.0	6.0
42	1.7	2.5	16.0	7.9
54	2.3	3.5	22.0	11.5

The return pipe has been calculated to 15mm pipe. Looking at the system drawing, it will be seen that there are:

6 elbows at 0.5m   = 3m

3 tees at 0.6m   = 1.8m

1 check valve at 2.5m = 2.5m
_____
= 7.3m

So, the resistance in the fittings totals another 7.3m of pipe. When this is added to the actual length of pipe, it totals:

53 + 7.3 = 60.3m

Looking at the CIBSE table again, the pascals pressure drop was 9.5. This is now multiplied by the length of pipe:

$9.5 \times 60.3 = 572.85$Pa

So, the circulating pump must have at least 572.85 pascals of pressure to circulate the return water through 15mm copper pipe at 0.07l/s to guarantee the temperature of the return water is 55°C when it reaches the hot water storage cylinder.

Sizing a hot water shower-boosting pump

A shower-boosting pump is designed to boost water at low pressure and flow rate to a higher pressure and flow rate to give a better showering experience. Calculation of the size of a shower-boosting pump is based upon the pressure and flow rate that the pump is designed to deliver at the showerhead and the height of the column of water that pump has to move.

Pump duty is calculated in kilopascals, the pascal being the unit of pressure:

1bar pressure = 10m head = 100kPa

Flow rate is calculated in litres per second. Shower pumps can deliver between 11 and 25 litres per minute (l/m) or 0.41 litres per second (l/s) depending on the type and its application.

To correctly size a shower pump, we must find the pump duty. The pump duty is the ability of a pump to overcome frictional resistances and the additional static head to displace water from one point, eg the cistern in an open-vented hot water storage system, to another, often higher, point, eg the shower head. When calculating the pump duty, both the desired flow rate and head (pressure) must be taken into account. Once this has been calculated then the correct pump can be chosen from the duty point on the manufacturer's design charts.

The duty point is defined as that point on the H–Q system curve where the actual pump performance is in line with the calculated design criteria. The drawing below illustrates a typical duty point where the design criteria and the pump performance coincide.

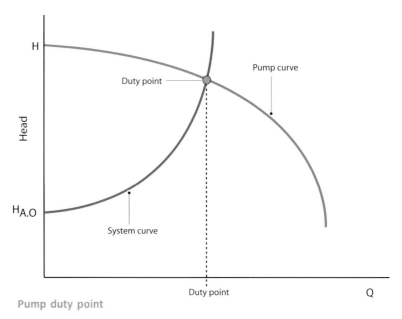

Pump duty point

The actual duty point is always at the point where the pump H–Q and the system H–Q points intersect.

Calculating pump duty

A shower-boosting pump is required to deliver 15 litres per minute at a pressure of 2 bar to a shower head 3m higher than the pump itself. Frictional losses in the system due to pipework, valves and fittings can be calculated as static head × 0.05.

Static head from the pump to the shower head = 3m or 0.3bar or 30kPa

Frictional losses = 30 × 0.05 = 1.5kPa

Design head = 2bar or 200kPa

Therefore, the pump duty is:

30 + 200 − 1.5 = **228.5kPa**

Now, a pump can be chosen from the manufacturer's literature with a duty of 228.5 kPa that will deliver 15l/m or 0.25l/s flow rate.

Sizing an expansion vessel

There are several methods for sizing expansion vessels. All methods must take into account the volume of cold water in the system and the amount by which it will expand in order to reach its design temperature. The CIBSE method is shown below.

If the system volume is known, expansion vessels can be sized with the following formula:

$$V = \frac{eC}{1 - \dfrac{p_1}{p_2}}$$

V = The total volume of the expansion vessel

C = The total volume of water in the system in litres

P_1 = The fill pressure in bars absolute (gauge pressure + 1bar)

P_2 = The setting of the pressure relief valve + 1bar

e = The expansion factor that relates to the maximum system requirements.

Expansion factor 'e'	Temperature °C
0.0324	85
0.0359	90
0.0396	95
0.0434	100

'e' can be found from the formula:

$$e = \frac{d_1 - d_2}{d_2}$$

Where:

d_1 = density of water at filling temperature kg/m^3

d_2 = density of water at operating temperature kg/m^3

Example 1

A sealed central heating system has a total water volume of 600 litres. The pressure of the water main is 1.5 bar and the pressure relief maximum pressure is 6 bar. The system is designed to operate at a maximum temperature of 80°C, which means the expansion factor will have to be calculated. The fill temperature of the water is 10°C.

Calculate the expansion factor using:

$$e = \frac{d_1 - d_2}{d_2}$$

Calculate the expansion vessel volume using:

$$V = \frac{eC}{1 - \frac{p_1}{p_2}}$$

1 Calculate the expansion factor 'e'

The temperature of the fill water is 10°C with a density of 999.8kg/m³. The maximum operating temperature is 80°C with a density of 972kg/m³. Therefore the 'e' factor is:

$$\frac{999.8 - 972}{972} = 0.0286$$

2 Calculate the expansion vessel volume

V   = The total volume of the expansion vessel

C   = 600 litres

P_1 = 1.5 + 1

P_2 = 6 + 1

e   = 0.0286

$$V = \frac{eC}{1 - \frac{p_1}{p_2}}$$

Therefore, the expansion vessel volume is:

$$\frac{0.0286 \times 600}{1 - 2.57} = \frac{17.16}{1 - 0.357} = \frac{17.16}{1 - 0.643} = 26.68l \text{ or } 4.44\%$$

So, the expansion vessel volume is: **26.68 litres or 4.44% of total system volume.**

Select the size of sanitary pipework using manufacturers' specifications

When sizing sanitary pipework, BS EN 12056-2 NC.2.2 explains that water flowing into discharge stacks will cause air pressure fluctuations and suction can occur below discharging branch connections and offsets which can cause water seal loss by induced siphonage from the appliances connected to the stack. Back pressure or positive pressure can occur above bends and offsets in the stack which can cause foul air to be blown through the trap water seal and potential loss of seal.

The following identifies some causes for loss of seal:

a   the flow load which relates to the total number of appliances connected to a stack, how they are distributed on each floor and their frequency of use

b   the height and diameter of the stack; the stack size not being calculated to accommodate the height of a building and the number of appliances connected to it

c   the design of pipe fittings, the shape and size of branch inlets and the radius of the bend at the base of the stack connecting the system to the drain

d   changes in direction in the wet portion of the stack

e   provision, or lack, of a ventilating pipe

f   surcharging of a drain

g   provision, or lack, of an interceptor trap.

When sizing drainage systems we must therefore refer to BS EN 12056 and the following pipework dimensions relate to appliances in the UK.

- 32mm – wash basin, bidet, drinking fountain
- 40mm – sink, bath, shower, urinal, sanitary towel macerator
- 50mm – food waste disposal unit or dual appliance branch
- 100mm – WC (90mm with 80mm outlet pan).

Houses of single occupancy rarely need sizing as a 100mm stack is required for one WC. Even 50 houses with one WC can be connected to a 100mm vertical stack.

Sizing is however required for flats, halls of residence, commercial and public entertainment places and **discharge units** are used to help calculate a stack size for a specific installation.

Discharge units

Discharge units are used to calculate the size of a soil stack.

The following step-by-step example will help to show how stack sizes can be calculated. By referring to the tables and formulas extracted from BS EN 12056-2 discharge units (DU), flow rates (Qww), frequency factors (K) and hydraulic capacities (Q^{max}) can be calculated and in the end the correct size of discharge stack selected.

Table 10: Discharge units based on system III used in the UK

Appliance	System III
	DU (l/s)
Wash basin, bidet	0.3
Shower without plug	0.4
Shower with plug	1.3
Single urinal with cistern	0.4
Urinal with flushing valve	–
Slab urinal	0.2*
Bath	1.3
Kitchen sink	1.3
Dishwasher (household)	0.2
Washing machine up to 6kg	0.6
Washing machine up to 12kg	1.2
WC with 4.0l cistern	**
WC with 6.0l cistern	1.2 to 1.7***
WC with 7.5l cistern	1.4 to 1.8***
WC with 9.0l cistern	1.6 to 2.0
Floor gully DN50	
Floor gully DN70	
Floor gully DN100	

*   Per person
**   Not permitted
*** Depending on type (valid for WCs with siphon flush cisterns only)
*** Not used or no data

1 Use Table 10 to select the total number of appliances running into the stack. System III is based on the British above-ground sanitation system.

2 The next stage is to add up the discharge units (DU) for these appliances.

3 Use Table 11 below to select the frequency factor for the use of the appliances.

Table 11: Frequency factors

Usage of appliances	K
Intermittent use, eg in dwelling, guesthouse, office	0.5
Frequent use, eg in hospital, school, restaurant, hotel	0.7
Congested use, eg in toilets and/or showers open to public	1.0
Special use, eg laboratory	1.2

4 The formula to work out the waste water flow rate is shown below.

Qww is the expected flow rate of waste water in a part or in the whole drainage system where only domestic sanitary appliances are connected to the system.

Where:

Qww: waste water flow rate (l/s)

K: frequency factor

ΣDU: sum of the discharge units

5 Use Table 12: Q^{max} (litres per second) to size the pipe. We tend to use swept entry fittings in the UK but as you can see there is also a column for sizing square entry.

Table 12: Hydraulic capacity (Q^{max}) and nominal diameter (DN)

Stack and stack vent	Systems I, II, III, IV Q^{max} (L/s)	
DN	Square entries	Swept entries
60	0.5	0.7
70	1.5	2.0
80*	2.0	2.6
90	2.7	3.5
100**	4.0	5.2
125	5.8	7.6
150	9.5	12.4
200	16.0	21.0

* Minimum size where WCs are connected in system II

** Minimum size where WCs are connected in systems I, III, IV

6 If the soil and waste system includes secondary ventilation then Table 13 is to be referred to.

Table 13: Hydraulic capacity (Q^{max}) and nominal diameter (DN)

Stack and stack vent	Second vent	Systems I, II, III, IV Q^{max} (L/s)	
DN	DN	Square entries	Swept entries
60	50	0.7	0.9
70	50	2.0	2.6
80*	50	2.6	3.4
90	50	3.5	4.6
100**	50	5.6	7.3
125	70	7.6	10.0
150	80	12.4	18.3
200	100	21.0	27.3

* Minimum size where WCs are connected in system II

** Minimum size where WCs are connected in systems I, III, IV

How to calculate the size of a discharge stack

If a congested football stadium with 50 6-litre WCs and 100 wash basins is used as an example then we may end up with a calculation as shown below. Once the total discharge units are added then the square root of that number is applied and multiplied by the frequency factor.

Discharge units for WCs = 50 × 1.7 = 85

(The figure 1.7 is taken from Table 10 as the discharge unit for a 6-litre WC on a **system III** installation is between 1.2 and 1.7.)

Discharge units for wash basins = 100 × 0.3 = 30

Total discharge units   = 115
The square root of 115   = 10.7
Frequency factor   = 1.0 ——————————→

(The frequency factor is taken from Table 11 and relates to installations with congested use.)

Calculated flow rate   = 10.7 × 1.0
                            = **10.7l/s**

Stack and stack vent	Systems I, II, III, IV Q^{max} (L/s)	
DN	Square entries	Swept entries
60	0.5	0.7
70	1.5	2.0
80*	2.0	2.6
90	2.7	3.5
100**	4.0	5.2
125	5.8	7.6
150	9.5	12.4
200	16.0	21.0

 * Minimum size where WCs are connected in system II
 ** Minimum size where WCs are connected in systems I, III, IV

10.7l/s is the calculated flow rate and because swept entries are used, by referring to the appropriate column it can be seen that the flow rate is less than 12.4l/s; therefore a 150mm diameter soil stack is required.

Calculating the size of a discharge stack for a single occupancy dwelling

The previous example related to a commercial installation but the same process can be applied to a domestic dwelling. A qualified Level 3 apprentice should be able to apply these methods to achieve a well-designed sanitary pipework installation.

For example a dwelling may contain the following appliances with discharge units taken from Table 10.

Appliances	Discharge units
2 × 6l WCs	1.7 × 2 = 3.4
2 × baths	1.3 × 2 = 2.6
2 × wash basins	0.6 × 2 = 1.2
1 shower with plug	1.3
1 × bidet	0.3
1 × kitchen sink	1.3
1 × 6kg washing machine	0.6
1 × domestic dishwasher	0.2
TOTAL	**11.2**

SmartScreen Unit 302
Worksheet 5

SUGGESTED ACTIVITY

Calculate the size of a discharge stack serving two flats each containing 1 × 6-litre WC, 1 × bath, 1 × shower without a plug, a 6-litre washing machine and a dishwasher.

The square root of 11.2 is 3.35 and the frequency factor for a dwelling is 0.5. Therefore 3.35 × 0.5 = 1.75l/s and if we refer to the previous table which relates to swept entries, it can be seen that a typical 100mm-diameter soil discharge stack would be more than adequate.

Select the size of rainwater system components using manufacturers' specifications

A guttering system should have sufficient capacity to carry the expected flow of water at any point on the system. When designing a guttering system for a dwelling, there are factors that must be considered if the system is to comfortably cope with the rain that falls on the roof surface. The actual flow in the system depends upon the area to be drained, the rainfall intensity and the position of the rainwater outlets.

Rainfall intensity

In the introduction to this chapter, it was mentioned that the amount of rainfall throughout the UK differs greatly with the south-east being considerably dryer than the north-west. In England, the county of Cumbria has the greatest total rainfall at around 1.8m per year with Essex and Kent being considerably less at around 500mm.

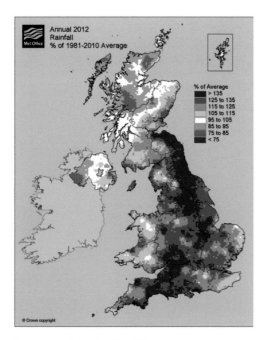

Average rainfall in the UK

Average rainfall, however, is only half of the story. While it may rain much more in Cumbria than in Essex over a 12-month period, the number of litres discharged in a single two-minute rainstorm is greater in Essex at $0.022l/s/m^2$ (litres per second per square metre) compared with Cumbria at $0.014l/s/m^2$. This is called rainfall intensity and must be factored into any guttering system design because the guttering system must be able to cope with a sudden, intense downpour.

BS EN 12056-3:2000 gives rainfall intensity in litres per second per square metre ($l/s/m^2$) for a two-minute storm event. The maps in the British Standard show the intensity for various periods from 1 year to 500 years. Rainfall intensity is divided into four categories, the different categories relating to the types of building. Domestic dwellings are category 1.

Cat 1	Return period of 1 year	Eaves gutters and flat roofs
Cat 2	Return period of 1.5 × design life of the building	Valley and parapet gutters for normal buildings
Cat 3	Return period of 4.5 × design life of the building	Valley and parapet gutters for higher-risk buildings
Cat 4	Maximum probable rainfall	Highest-risk buildings

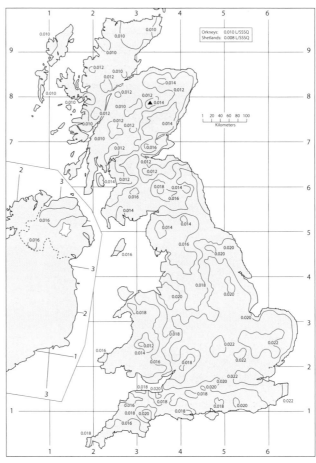

Rainfall intensity in the UK

Roof area

The angle and area of the roof are a key part of any guttering system design. Take a look at the diagram below.

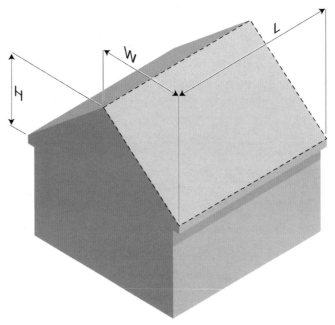

Roof angle and area

The illustration shows the roof of a dwelling. If the area of the roof increases, the amount of water collected and discharged from it also increases. Similarly, if the angle of the roof increases then the area will increase, the amount of water will increase and the velocity at which the water enters the gutter will increase also.

The area of a roof can be calculated by using the following formula in accordance with BS EN 12056-3:2000.

Effective max. roof area (allowance for wind)

$$W + \frac{H}{2} \times L = \text{area in m}^2$$

Where:

W = horizontal span of slope

H = height of roof pitch

L = length of roof

Example 1

A roof has a length of 10m, a width of 6m and a height of 3m. Calculate the effective area of the roof.

$$6 + \frac{3}{2} \times 10 = \textbf{75m}^2$$

The area of a flat roof should be regarded as the total plan area. If the roof has a complex layout with different spans and pitches, each area should be calculated separately.

The Approved Building Regulation Document H3 gives an acceptable alternative for the calculation of roof area where the area of the roof is multiplied by a pitch factor. These are detailed in the table below. For this calculation, only the length of the roof and the span are required.

Type of surface	Design area (m^2)
1. Flat roof	Plan area of relevant portion
2. Pitched roof at 30°	Plan area of portion × 1.29
Pitched roof at 45°	Plan area of portion × 1.50
Pitched roof at 60°	Plan area of portion × 1.87
3. Pitched roof over 70° or any wall	Elevational area × 0.5

Note: To calculate flow in litres/second for 75mm/hour intensity, multiply effective roof area in m^2 by 0.0208.

SUGGESTED ACTIVITY

Calculation of effective roof area

Using the formula given in the text, calculate the following effective roof areas:

1. A roof which has a length of 12m, a width of 7m and a height of 3m.
2. A roof which has a length of 8m, a width of 8m and a height of 4m.
3. A roof which has a length of 10m, a width of 8m and a height of 4m.

In this instance, if the angle of the pitch of the roof is known, the calculation is simplified. For example, if we use the data from the previous scanario, we arrive at the following example.

Example 2

A roof has a length of 10m and a width of 6m. Calculate the effective area of the roof if the pitch of the roof is 300:

Length of roof	= 10m
Width of roof	= 6m
The pitch factor from the table	= 1.29
10 × 6 × 1.29	= **77.4m²**

We can now calculate the amount of rainwater to be expected on any given roof area in a sudden storm deluge of 75mm rainfall per hour. To convert the area to litres per second (l/s), multiply the roof area (m²) by 0.0208.

Example 3

The area of the roof in Example 1 is 75m². What is the expected rainfall in l/s?

75 × 0.0208 = **1.56l/s**

Running outlet position

The image below shows a running outlet. It is the connection between the guttering and the rainwater pipe.

A running outlet

The position of the running outlets is usually based upon the position of the gullies for the surface water sewer/drain to the property. These can be found on the building layout drawing.

The more outlets there are on a gutter system, the shorter distance the water has to travel and the more effective the system is at discharging the rainwater. Consider the drawing on the next page:

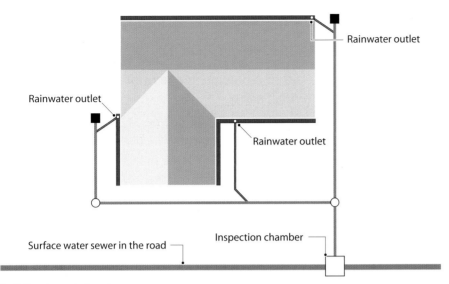

Building layout drawing

In drawing 1, the outlet has to be able to cope with the total rainwater run-off from the whole roof area. The outlet in this situation could be positioned at either end of the roof but the total flow rate would be the same. Running outlets are designed to cope with rainwater from two directions, so the outlet at either end can only cope with half the flow rate. Only half the capacity of the outlet can effectively be used. Placing the outlet centrally would increase the total area of roof that the gutter can serve.

The outlet position in drawing 2 is more effective than drawing 1 simply because there are now two outlets and each outlet is coping with half the expected rainwater run-off. Again, an alternative but equally effective layout would be one outlet placed in the centre of the gutter run.

With outlets placed as in drawing 3, each half of the outlet has only a quarter of the flow rate to cope with and so layout 3 is much more effective at discharging the rainfall without the risk of flooding because both outlets are being used to their full flow rate capacity.

Each manufacturer will have different rainwater flow rates for their running outlet designs. It should not be assumed that all manufacturers' flow rates will be equal. Therefore, manufacturers' data should be considered before the installation begins.

To find out how many outlets are required on a rainwater system design, simply divide the expected flow rate of the roof area by the flow rate for the outlet, given in the manufacturer's technical literature.

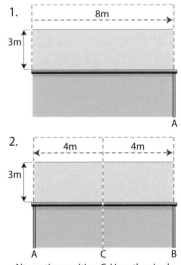

Alternative position C: Here the single outlet is equal to two outlets either end because of the outlet design

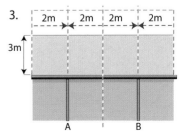

Outlet positions

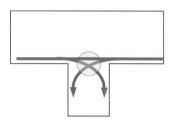
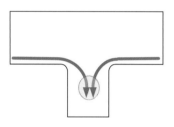
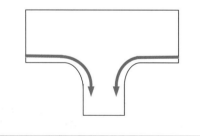

The fall of the gutter

BS EN 12056 – 3: 2000, section 7.2.1 and NE.2.1 state that:

1 Gutters should be laid to a nominal gradient of between 1mm/m and 3mm/m where practicable.
2 The gradient of an eaves gutter shall not be so steep that the gutter drops below the level of the roof to such an extent that water discharging from the roof will pass over the front edge of the gutter.

In most cases, manufacturers interpret these two points as a slight fall of 1:600 (25mm in 15m). Laying a gutter with a fall greatly increases the flow capacity and, therefore, the area of roof that can be drained. It also ensures that silting of the gutter does not occur. However, manufacturers design guttering systems in such a way that the performance of the gutter is not compromised if it is laid level with little or no fall. A fall of 1:600 ensures that the gutter will not fall so low as to be below the discharge point of the roof.

Changes of direction in the gutter run

In most domestic gutter systems, changes of direction cannot be avoided. Where changes in direction greater than 100 occur within a guttering system, they restrict the flow of water through the system. A 900 gutter angle reduces the effectiveness of the run of gutter where the angle is situated by 15%, effectively reducing the roof area that the gutter can usefully serve. Each subsequent change of direction reduces the gutter's effectiveness still further. A gutter angle that is placed near an outlet will also reduce the effectiveness of the outlet.

Calculate the size of central heating system components (LO3)

There are four assessment criteria for this Learning Outcome:

1 Explain how heat loss from a building occurs.
2 State methods for calculating heat loss for buildings.
3 Calculate heat loss for rooms.
4 Calculate the size of central heating components.

Explain how heat loss from a building occurs

SmartScreen Unit 302
PowerPoint 3

In this section, we will investigate the heat loss and heat gain of a building. Both principles rely on the steady state transfer of heat through the fabric of the building itself.

Heat loss

Heat loss from a building is the reason why we need central heating systems in our homes, offices, shops and factories. The heat the building loses will have to be replaced with more heat to maintain a comfortable temperature within the building itself. The principles of heat loss are known as the 'steady state thermal characteristics' of a building. Heat loss from a building is measured in watts and occurs in two ways:

- through the building fabric
- due to ventilation.

Heat loss through the fabric of the building

The thermal transmittance of heat from a building to the outside is given in U-values. U-values express, for the purposes of calculation, the rate of heat transfer through the building structure, ie its walls, floors, ceilings, roofs and windows. Because the construction of buildings varies so much owing to different materials and construction methods, the U-values vary too. This means that on occasion the U-value for a particular building will need to be calculated from scratch.

The calculation of a U-value for, say, an outside wall, is based upon the heat loss of each element or material used in the wall. Each element will have its own heat loss measured in watts per metre Kelvin (w/mK) known as a K-value.

The units used to express U-values are watts per m^2 Kelvin (W/m²K). This means that if a wall, for example, had a U-value of 1.0 W/m²K, for every degree of temperature difference between the air on the surface inside the wall and the air on the surface outside, 1 watt of heat would pass through any m^2. So, it follows that the smaller the U-value, the better the wall is at keeping the heat in.

KEY POINT

U-values express the rate of heat transfer through any element of a building – walls, roofs, floors and windows.

Most materials have published K-values for the rate of thermal conductance through them and this is measured under specific conditions. These are then subdivided into the required thickness of the material being used to obtain its R-value. This can be very confusing so let's take a look more closely:

K-value = The thermal conductivity of a material per metre (W/mK)

$$\text{R-value} = \frac{\text{thickness of the material (mm)}}{\text{K-value (W/mK)}}$$

$$\text{U-value} = \frac{1}{\text{total of all R-values for the wall (W/m}^2\text{K)}}$$

So, if an outside wall were constructed from 100mm brick with 50mm of cavity, 100mm of thermalite block, 50mm of mineral wool and finished with 12.5mm plasterboard, to calculate the U-value of the wall, the procedure would be as follows.

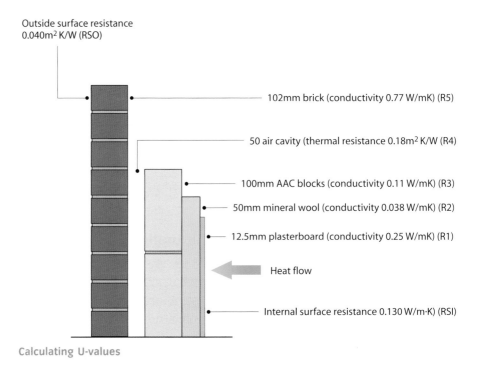

Outside surface resistance
0.040m^2 K/W (RSO)

102mm brick (conductivity 0.77 W/mK) (R5)

50 air cavity (thermal resistance 0.18m^2 K/W (R4)

100mm AAC blocks (conductivity 0.11 W/mK) (R3)

50mm mineral wool (conductivity 0.038 W/mK) (R2)

12.5mm plasterboard (conductivity 0.25 W/mK) (R1)

Heat flow

Internal surface resistance 0.130 W/m·K) (RSI)

Calculating U-values

K-values for the wall construction:

Brick	= 0.77 W/mK
Cavity	= 0.18 W/mK
Thermalite block	= 0.11 W/mK
Mineral wool insulation	= 0.38 W/mK
Plasterboard	= 0.25 W/mK

Because each material is of a specific thickness, eg 102mm brick, the thickness of the material must be divided by the K-value to obtain the R-value:

Brick	= 0.102m ÷ 0.77 W/mK	= 0.132 (R5)
Cavity	= 0.050m ÷ 0.18 W/mK	= 0.277 (R4)
Thermalite block	= 0.100m ÷ 0.11 W/mK	= 0.909 (R3)
Mineral wool insulation	= 0.050m ÷ 0.038 W/mK	= 1.315 (R2)
Plasterboard	= 0.0125m ÷ 0.25 W/mK	= 0.050 (R1)

There are two other elements that need to be added to the list. These are constants and never change. These are air resistances to heat loss and are different for the inside and outside faces of the building.

Outside air resistance	= 0.040 W/mK (RSO)	
Inside air resistance	= 0.130 W/mK (RSI)	

The calculation of the U-value now looks like this:

$$\frac{1}{RSI + R_1 + R_2 + R_3 + R_4 + R_5 + RSO} = W/m^2K \text{ (U-value)}$$

$$\frac{1}{0.130 + \frac{0.0125}{0.25} + \frac{0.050}{0.038} + \frac{0.100}{0.11} + \frac{0.050}{0.18} + \frac{0.102}{0.77} + 0.040} = W/m^2K$$

$$\frac{1}{0.130 + 0.05 + 1.31 + 0.909 + 0.277 + 0.132 + 0.040} = \frac{1}{2.848} = 0.35 W/m^2K$$

$$\therefore \mathbf{0.35W/m^2K} = \text{U-value}$$

So, the U-value for the outside wall is 0.35. This can now be used in heat loss calculations for the building.

Fortunately, some U-values are published so this rather long calculation is not often needed. Approved Document L1A/B 2010 of the Building Regulations: Conservation of fuel and power has traditionally set U-values and this is still the case where extensions to existing properties are concerned. For new buildings, however, a more holistic approach has been taken to improve energy efficiency. Whole building calculations that take a detailed look at the carbon emissions now have to be conducted. U-values are still included but they form only a small part. For new dwellings up to 450m² Standard Assessment Procedures (SAPs) are used to perform these calculations. For larger buildings the Simplified Building Energy Model (SBEM) is used.

Table 14: Current U-values

Element	U-value (W/m²K)
Walls	0.30
Party walls	0.20

Element	U-value (W/m^{2}K)
Studded internal walls with plasterboard	1.72
Roof — Flat	0.25
Roof — Pitched with insulation between joists	0.16
Roof — Pitched with insulation between rafters	0.20
Floor – Ground and other floors	0.25
Window	2.0
Roof-light	2.2
Vehicle access or similar large door	0.7

Glass and glazing

Glass has a fairly high thermal conductivity of around 1.05W/mK but the reason why so much heat is lost through glass is that it is the thinnest part of a building. Therefore heat loss can only be reduced by increasing the thickness of the glass or using it to form cavities like double and triple glazing. Below are the U-values for glazing as given in the Chartered Institute of Building Services (CIBSE) Engineers Guide:

Table 15: CIBSE guide to glazing U-values

Construction	U-value for stated exposure		
	Sheltered	Normal	Severe
Single window glazing	5.0	5.6	6.7
Double window glazing with air space			
25mm or more	2.8	2.9	3.2
12mm or more	2.8	3.0	3.3
6mm or more	3.2	3.4	3.8
3mm or more	3.6	4.0	4.4
Triple window glazing with air space			
25mm or more	1.9	2.0	2.1
12mm or more	2.0	2.1	2.2
6mm or more	2.3	2.5	2.6
3mm or more	2.8	3.0	3.3
Roof glazing light	5.7	6.6	7.9

Heat gain

Just as buildings lose heat during the winter months, they can also gain heat when the surrounding temperature is higher than that inside.

During the summer months, when the outside temperature is higher, a building will gain heat in two ways:

- from direct solar radiation, in other words direct sunlight
- from the surrounding warm air.

The passage of heat from outside to inside operates by almost exactly the same principle as heat loss. The difference is that it is not uniform. Different parts of the building will gain more heat due to the length of exposure to the sun's solar radiation. In simple terms, the sun rises in the east, swings out to the south during the day whilst gaining height until it reaches a peak height at 12.00 noon, before slowly setting in the west. This height-to-angle ratio is called an 'azimuth' and is crucial when calculating solar gain for air conditioning and cooling purposes. The solar effect even exists in the winter when the angle of the sun is much lower. On average, a south-facing wall in London will gain about 900 watts of heat per square metre (m^2) every hour during the summer and around 300 watts in the winter. This reduces for east and west-facing walls as they are not exposed to the sun for as long a period. A north-facing wall will gain very little solar radiation because it never feels the heat of the sun.

> **KEY POINT**
>
> The intensity of the sun during the summer explains why solar hot water heating works so well in the summer months. Solar hot water panels can give as much as 60% of a household's yearly hot water needs, free of charge, just from the heat of the sun.

Heat gain also occurs because of the warmth of the air. This is known as sol–air temperature and occurs because the sun has warmed the air surrounding the dwelling. The same principle occurs inside the dwelling when heat is transferred from one room to another when the two rooms have different internal temperatures. If one room is at 21°C and an adjoining room is at 18°C then heat will be gained by one and lost by the other. The rate at which this heat transfer takes place and the amount of heat lost or gained will depend on the U-value of the wall.

Dwellings also gain heat from other sources such as electrical equipment and lighting as these give off heat when they are on. A 150-watt bulb, for instance will give off just that –150 watts of heat. Human beings too contribute to heat gains in a building. A human will emit around 115 watts of sensible heat and around 50 watts of latent heat when at rest. This increases with physical exercise.

> **KEY POINT**
>
> Sensible and latent heat were discussed in the sister publication *The City and Guilds Textbook: Level 2 Diploma for Plumbing and Heating*, written by the author.

Heat loss due to ventilation – air change rate

Approved Document F of the Building Regulations sets the provisions for the ventilation of a building. They set out the regulations required to restrict the build-up of moisture and pollutants that would otherwise present a danger to health. The flow of air through the building results in heat loss, the lost heat having to be replaced. Ventilation rates are usually quoted as 'air changes per hour', which are defined as the volume of air moving through a room every hour divided by the volume of the room itself. The replacement air will be heated by the central heating system and is calculated by multiplying the volume of the room by the air change rate by the temperature rise and by the ventilation factor. Thus the loss of heat due to air change can be calculated by:

$$\begin{matrix} \text{ventilation} & & \text{room} & & \text{air change} & & \text{temperature} & & \text{ventilation} \\ \text{heat loss} & = & \text{volume} & \times & \text{rate} & \times & \text{difference} & \times & \text{factor} \\ \text{(watts)} & & \text{(m}^3\text{)} & & \text{(qty)} & & \text{(°c)} & & \text{(w/m}^3\text{k)} \end{matrix}$$

The ventilation factor is taken as the specific heat of air at 20°C, which is 0.33 W/m^{3}K and is used to calculate the heat loss to the air changing within the rooms due to infiltration or mechanical ventilation.

The specific mass (density of air) at 20°C is 1.205kg/m^3 and the specific heat capacity of air at 20°C is 1.012kJ/kgK. Therefore, the quantity of heat required to raise unit volume through 1 Kelvin is:

$1.012 \times 1.205 = 1.219kJ/m^3$

In order to be able to apply this heat loss of air by volume, the unit of kilojoules needs to be converted to joules and unit of time should be in seconds (not hours) because 1 watt is equal to 1 joule per second. Therefore:

$\dfrac{1.219 \times 1000}{3600} = 0.3386j/s/m^3K$ or $0.3386W/m^3K$

Hence the air change U-value of **0.33W/m³K.**

State methods for calculating heat loss for buildings

There are three very different methods for sizing the pipework and circulators for central heating systems and each one has its advantages and disadvantages. These are:

1 **Longhand calculations** – This is by far the most accurate of all heating design methods as U-values can be calculated to suit the building structure where the installation is to take place. This ensures that an economical and environmentally friendly design of the building heating system can be guaranteed. Longhand calculations involve the use of external data such as the tables for flow rate and resistance published by the Chartered Institute of Building Services Engineers in the CIBSE Design Guide C.

Circulating pump size is fairly simple to calculate as most of the work is done during the pipe sizing calculation. It should be remembered that the size of the circulator will be based around the resistance in the index circuit. This will be discussed later in the unit.

2 **Computer-aided central heating design programs** – Computer design programs have become more widespread over the last few years as they offer not only an accurate sizing method, but also the ability to print out the finished design complete with calculations for presentation to the customer. Programs such as Hevacomp are widely used by building services engineers for the design of heating, air conditioning, lighting and hot and cold water services.

3 **Mears calculator** – The Mears calculator is a circular slide rule that enables the calculation of central heating systems. The key functions of the calculator are:

- calculation of heat loss
- calculation of heat emitter size and output
- calculation of hot water load
- calculation of boiler size
- calculation of heating pipework size.

The calculator is usually used as an onsite tool because it allows the quick calculation of heat losses and heat emitter size but it can be a little inaccurate for modern dwellings as the U-values it uses are higher than modern U-values.

The different models available allow the calculation of single dwelling heat losses, conservatory heat losses and the heat loss from industrial heating systems.

> **KEY POINT**
>
> The index circuit of a central heating system is the circuit that has the biggest resistance to flow and *not* the circuit with the biggest heat load. The index circuit is always taken as the circuit with the longest run of pipework because the circulating pump will have to overcome the resistance due to length of pipe.

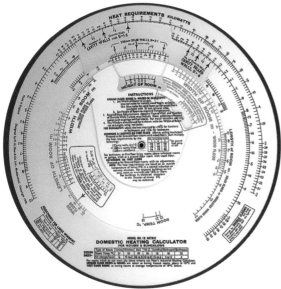
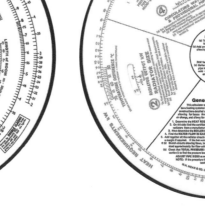

The Mears calculator

SmartScreen Unit 302
Worksheet 6

Calculate heat loss for rooms

Now that the U-values have been determined for the heat loss calculations, the information needed can be collated to allow the calculations to be performed. The information that is required is listed below:

- room size
- temperature required – indoor to outdoor
- air change rate.

The room size

The size of the room may seem like an obvious piece of information but if the room is measured inaccurately then the calculations will be also be inaccurate. It follows that the bigger the room, the greater the heat loss. The heat emitter positioning also becomes troublesome as the room size increases. In most cases it is better to consider the use of two or more strategically positioned heat emitters in larger rooms rather than using just one large one. This subject will be discussed later in the unit.

Key information is required about each room before heat loss calculations can be performed, such as:

1 the length, width and height of the room
2 the number of external and internal walls and their construction
3 the number and type of party walls
4 the type of floor and ceiling
5 the type and size of the windows and doors.

The information required may be taken during a site visit and noted down or it may be taken from working drawings and plans.

The room temperature and the outside temperature

Internal design temperatures

The design temperatures within dwellings are based upon the type and usage of the room. Internal design temperatures should be chosen to ensure satisfactory comfort conditions. In order to achieve a comfortable living condition within the room and to enable the heat loss calculations to be completed, it is necessary to select a design room temperature that needs to be achieved when the central heating system is operating. There are three aspects that must be considered to achieve a comfortable condition in a room:

- temperature
- humidity
- ventilation rate.

The temperature of the heated space during the winter at which humans feel comfortable falls within a certain temperature range. Temperatures between 19°C and 23°C are generally considered acceptable when wearing normal clothing, although some people may disagree when subjected to temperatures at the lower or higher end of the range. The exact comfortable temperature often varies with the physical condition of the individual and so is quite subjective. Because of these varying temperature ranges, exact room temperatures need to be discussed and agreed with the customer before any design work commences. Too much heat in a room can be controlled by thermostatic means but a shortfall in temperature is rather more difficult to assess and may result in a costly re-design of the heat losses. Design temperatures become even more critical if the customer is to be the permanent resident within the dwelling, as is the case with domestic dwellings. If the customer is an architect or a developer, temperatures may have been specified as part of the design brief or specification.

Special considerations may be needed where the customer is elderly or infirm. The table below illustrates the risk that elderly and infirm face during the winter months.

Table 16: The effects of low temperatures on the elderly and infirm

Temperature	Effects
24°C	Top end of the thermal comfort zone
21°C	Recommended living temperature
<20°C	Below 20°C, the risk of death begins to increase
18°C	Recommended bedroom temperature
16°C	Resistance to respiratory diseases is weakened
12°C	After more than two hours at this temperature, the risk of raised blood pressure, heart attack and strokes increases
5°C	Significant risk of hypothermia

For normal circumstances recommended temperatures are given in the table below.

Table 17: Design room temperatures

	Lounge/sitting room	Living room	Dining room	Kitchen	Breakfast room	Kitchen/breakfast	Hall	Cloak room	Toilet	Utility room	Study	Games room	Bedroom	Bedroom/en-suite	Bed sitting room	Bedroom/study	Landing	Bathroom	Dressing room	Storeroom
Design temperature (°C)	21	21	21	18	21	21	18	18	18	18	21	21	18	18	21	21	18	22	21	16

The temperatures listed in the table represent normal living conditions and working conditions. For properties that are designed for the elderly or the infirm, these temperatures should be increased by one or two degrees for each given application and usage. It will also be seen that the temperatures vary depending on the intended use of the room. This is simply because the body temperature of an individual and their subsequent comfort levels will vary depending on their activity, ie resting, sleeping, bathing, etc – hence the wide range of temperatures quoted.

Some building services engineers design heating systems for residential buildings with a constant temperature throughout, irrespective of the room type or usage. This single temperature approach reduces the number of calculations required, as it uses the 'whole house' assessment method but this can lead to over-sizing of the heating system and an unnecessary increase in overall energy usage.

External design temperatures

The successful design of any central heating system is based on the fact that the dwelling is maintained at a certain specified temperature based upon the prevailing external temperature. It follows that calculations must be based on a realistic external temperature that can be expected for the region during the coldest months. Research shows that the temperatures vary greatly in the UK with the south-eastern corner being the mildest throughout the year and the north of Scotland being the coldest.

The UK often sees temperatures between −2°C and −6°C during the winter and, on occasions, it has been known to drop as low as −15°C or lower. However, it would be uneconomical to design a central heating system using a low of −15°C as it occurs so infrequently. The resultant over-sizing would encourage the boiler to **hunt** on its thermostat and increase the risk of boiler breakdown. Therefore, a more suitable, logical external design temperature should be used

KEY POINT

For further information on climatic conditions in the UK, reference should be made to CIBSE guides A and J, and local meteorological data.

Hunt

To cycle on and off unnecessarily with even a slight drop in temperature.

based upon the lowest average temperature for the location. Another possibility for determining the external design temperature is to use the lowest two-day mean temperature that has been registered ten times over a 20-year period.

Table 18 shows the recommended base temperatures for the UK but local knowledge can also be applied, as severe exposure conditions are not always obvious.

Table 18: Recommended UK base temperatures

Type of building	Exposure	Base design temperature
House and multi-storey buildings with solid intermediate floors up to and including the 4th floor – England and Wales	Normal, sheltered in towns and cities surrounded by other buildings	−1°C
House and multi-storey buildings with solid intermediate floors up to and including the 4th floor – Scotland, Northern England and Northern Ireland	Normal, sheltered in towns and cities surrounded by other buildings	−3°C
Single-storey houses	Normal	−3°C
Houses in coastal areas or at high altitude including exposed rural areas	Exposed	−4°C
Multi-storey buildings with solid intermediate floors up to and including the 4th floor and single-storey in coastal or exposed rural areas	Exposed	−5°C

Air change rates

The air change rate is a measure of how many times the air within a defined space (normally a room or a house) is replaced per hour, usually through natural ventilation. It is necessary to prevent the air in a room from becoming stale and to prevent the onset of moisture problems and mould growth. As the air change occurs, the heat in the room is lost by warm air leaving the room and cold air entering.

Air enters the building because of the poor seal in the building structure, usually through airbricks, ventilators, flues and chimneys. Flues and chimneys often cause excessive air change because warm air escapes up the flue, due to the fact it is less dense. As cold air enters, it forces out more warm air. This effect is known as the stack effect.

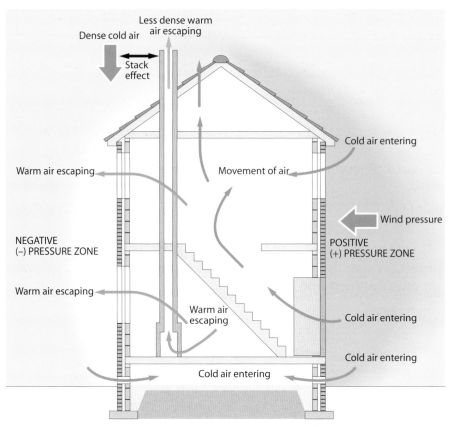

The stack effect

The air change rates listed below in Table 19 are for modern buildings. When calculating heat losses for older dwellings, there is a case for increasing the rates to allow for ill-fitting doors and windows because these will affect the heat loss from the building.

The exact amount of air infiltration is difficult to assess and because of this, exact design temperatures are often difficult to predict. The air changes listed below are arrived at by empirical means and can be considered accurate for new and well-maintained buildings.

Table 19: Air change rates

	Lounge/sitting room	Living room	Dining room	Kitchen	Breakfast room	Kitchen/breakfast	Hall	Cloak room	Toilet	Utility room	Study	Games room	Bedroom	Bedroom/en-suite	Bed sitting room	Bedroom/study	Landing	Bathroom	Dressing room	Storeroom
Air change rate	1.5	1.5	1.5	2.0	2.0	2.0	2.0	2.0	2.0	1.5	1.5	1.5	1.0	2.0	1.5	1.5	2.0	2.0	1.5	1.0

Where mechanical ventilation is installed in a room, it is advisable to allow for the increased air change rate in the heat loss calculations. This should be allowed for not just in the room where the mechanical ventilation system is fitted but also any connecting rooms such as an en suite bathroom with an extractor fan and a bedroom.

Calculating the heat loss from a dwelling – the tabulation method

The easiest and quickest way to conduct heat loss calculations is by using a table to record all of the figures. Each room needs to be dealt with separately and requires its own table. Take a look at the example table on page 80 which should help in understanding how the heat losses are put together. You will see that it is divided into various columns. Not all of these columns will be used for every room.

The simple room has four outside walls and heat loss through both the floor and roof. Intermediate rooms in a large building may not have these losses unless there is a temperature difference between the rooms.

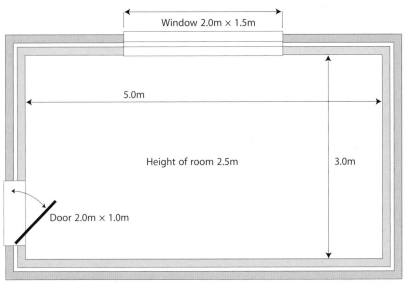

Sample heat loss room

The U-values required are as follows:

External walls: 0.35

Floor: 0.25

Roof: 0.25 (flat roof)

Windows: 2.9

Ext. door: 2.9 (the same as the windows)

Air change factor: 0.33

Temperature difference: 21 (int. temperature) – –3 (ext. temperature) = 24°C

The first point is that there are no internal walls to worry about. As all walls are external the calculation is quite straightforward. So, the calculations revolve around the following elements:

1 Calculate the air change heat loss.
2 Calculate the external wall heat loss.
3 Calculate the glazing heat loss.
4 Calculate the floor and roof heat loss.
5 Calculate any adjustments due to exposure and intermittent heating loads.

Let's concentrate on point 1.

Air change heat loss

The room is 5m × 3m × 2.5m. This gives a volume of $37.5m^3$. When this figure is multiplied by the temperature difference (24°C), the number of air changes (2) and the air change factor (0.33), the total becomes 594 watts. This means that because there are two air changes every hour, the room will lose 594 watts of heat during these changes:

$37.5 \times 24 \times 2 \times 0.33$ = **594W**

Now look at point 2.

External wall heat loss

This can be a little involved. If we laid all of the external walls flat, we would end up with the following:

$5 + 5 + 3 + 3 = 16m$

This figure must now be multiplied by the height of the wall:

$16 \times 2.5 = 40m^2$

But this figure is not much use to us as it is. There are windows and doors that have a greater heat loss than the wall so these must be deducted before we calculate the external wall heat loss. The window and door heat loss will be dealt with separately. So first calculate the area of the windows and doors:

Window: 2m × 1.5m = 3
Door: 2m × 1m $^+$ = 2
                                    = $5m^2$

This figure can now be deducted from the external wall total:

$40 - 5 = 35m^2$

So, the heat loss from the external walls is:

$35 \times 24 \times 0.35 =$ **294W**

Progress to point 3.

Glazing heat loss

This part of the calculation is made easy by the fact that we have already calculated the areas of the glazing, so it's a straightforward calculation. Also the same U-value is used for both window and door because they are made from the same material. This isn't always the case and you must check before doing the calculation:

Window heat loss: $3 \times 24 \times 2.9 = $ **208.8W**
Door heat loss: $2 \times 24 \times 2.9 = $ **139.2W**

The penultimate stage, point 4.

Heat loss from the floor and roof/ceiling

Because these use the same area, the calculation, again, becomes very straightforward. The area of the room is:

$5m \times 3m = 15m^2$

So, now multiply all of the figures together for both floor and ceiling:

Floor: $15 \times 24 \times 0.25 = $ **90W**
Ceiling/roof: $15 \times 24 \times 0.25 = $ **90W**

So, the total heat loss for the room is a sum of all of the calculated elements:

$594 + 294 + 208.8 + 139.2 + 90 + 90 = $ **1416W**

Calculation of any adjustments

We are assuming that the room is in an exposed location. This would mean an increase in the total of 10% in case of severe weather. Furthermore, we are also assuming that the heating will be on intermittently. In other words, it will only be on at certain times of the day or when external controls call for heat such as a frost stat. This will result in an extra 15% increase in the total to cope with the intermittent heating patterns:

Exposed location at 10% $= 1416 \times 0.10 = 141.6W$
Intermittent heating load at 15% $= 1416 \times 0.15 = 212.4W$
                                    $= 354W$
                                  $+ 1416W$
                                    $= $ **1770W**

Therefore, the heat loss from the room when all adjustments have been made is **1770W.**

The calculation is probably more understandable when viewed in a table format. Take a look at the table below. It must be realised, however, that because all of the walls were external and the structure was a single storey, there is no data for internal wall structures or where there is another room above. This will be dealt with next.

Room	Example 1							
Design temp. °C	21		Outside temp °C		−3	Design temp difference °C		24
Room volume	Room dimensions			Volume of room (m³)	Air change factor (W/m³K)	Temp. difference	Air changes per hour	Total heat loss (W)
	Length	Width	Height					
Total room	5m	3m	2.5m	37.5	**0.33**	24	2	594
Fabric heat loss	Length (m)	Width (m)	Height (m)	Fabric area	U-value W/m³K	Temp. difference	Gain	Loss
Floor	5m	3m		15	0.25	24		90
Ceiling/roof	5m	3m		15	0.25	24		90
External glazing	2m		1.5m	3	2.9	24		208.8
External doors	1m		2.0m	2	2.9	24		139.2
Ext. wall	16m		2.5m	40				
Ext. wall (minus glazing)	40 − (3.0 + 2.0) = **35**			35	0.35	24		294
Internal wall 1								
Internal wall 2								
Internal wall 3								
Internal wall 4								
Party wall								
Design heat loss (total watts for all elements)								1416

Additional factors	Y/N	% add	Total
Exposed location	Y	10	141.6
Intermittent heating	Y	15	212.4
Grand total heat loss for room (W)			1770

Heat loss and heat gain from the internal walls and rooms above and below

The first example we looked at was a building with four external walls. Now we must advance to a room that contains both external and internal walls.

The method of calculation is exactly the same but with the addition of extra walls that may mean a loss of heat from our example rooms or, indeed, may give a heat gain!

Take a look at the example rooms shown on the next page.

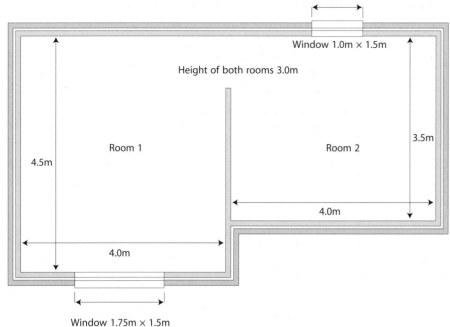

Example heat loss room 2

The data for both rooms is listed below.

Table 20: Room data for rooms 1 and 2

Element	Room 1	Room 2
Temperature	18°C	21°C
Outside temperature	–3°C	–3°C
Temperature difference	21°C	24°C
Number of ext. walls	4	3
Number of int. walls	1	1
U-value of ext. walls	0.35	0.35
U-value of int. walls	1.72	1.72
U-value of the glazing	2.9	2.9
U-value of the floor	0.25	0.25
U-value of the roof/ceiling	0.16	0.16
Number of air changes	1	2
The rooms are of normal exposure		
The heating is intermittent		

We will deal with room 1 first. The first thing to note is that the data states that there are 4 outside walls and 1 internal wall. This is due to the fact that room 2 is slightly shorter in length than room 1 and leaves a small amount of wall as an external structure. We cannot ignore this and so it must be treated as a small external wall.

The dimensions for the external wall of room 1 are:

4.5 + 4 + 4 + 1 = 13.5m

Multiply by the height of the room: $13.5 \times 3 = 40.5m^2$

The window size is: $1.75 \times 1.5 = 2.625m^2$

Deduct the window from the wall: $40.5 - 2.625 = 37.875m^2$

Now using the formula previously shown, we can enter the details on the table and calculate the external wall heat loss (see table for room 1 below). We can also calculate the heat loss for the glazing.

Look at the internal wall dimensions. The wall is 3.5m in length including the door opening and 3m high. Some designers will work out the heat loss for the door but for the purposes of this unit, it will be treated as part of the wall for simplification. The most important factor here is that the room temperatures are different. The adjoining room requires a warmer temperature at 21°C. This means that room 1, at 18°C, will *gain* heat from the room 2 next door and so any heat gain must be *deducted* from our calculation and *not* added. The temperature difference between room 1 and room 2 is 3°C. Take a look at the table.

Room	Example 2 – ROOM 1							
Design temp. °C	18		Outside temp. °C		−3	Design temp. difference °C		21
Room volume	Room dimensions			Volume of room (m³)	Air change factor (W/m³K)	Temp. difference	Air changes per hour	Total heat loss (W)
	Length	Width	Height					
Total room	4.5	4	3	54	0.33	21	1	374.22
Fabric heat loss	Length (m)	Width (m)	Height (m)	Fabric area	U-value W/m³K	Temp. difference	Gain	Loss
Floor	4.5	4		18	0.25	21		94.5
Ceiling/roof	4.5	4		18	0.16	21		60.48
External glazing	1.75		1.5	2.625	2.9	21		159.86
External doors								
Ext. wall	13.5		3	40.5				
Ext. wall (minus glazing)	40.5 – 2.625			37.875	0.35	21		278.38
Internal wall 1	3.5		3	10.5	1.72	3	54.18	−54.18
Internal wall 2								
Internal wall 3								
Internal wall 4								
Party wall								
Design heat loss (total watts for all elements)								913.26

Additional factors	Y/N	% add	Total
Exposed location	Y	10	
Intermittent heating	Y	15	136.99
Grand total heat loss for room (W)			1050.25

When the calculation for the internal walls is conducted, it will be seen that there is a gain of 54.18 watts. This is highlighted in red to remind us to deduct it and not add it. If the temperatures were the same, then the internal wall would be ignored purely because there is neither a heat loss nor a heat gain. The rest of the table can now be completed.

Now look at room 2. The heat gain that was seen in room 1 now becomes a heat loss in room 2 because room 1 is a cooler 18°C and so this must be allowed for in the heat loss calculations. All other factors remain the same and so the heat loss for the room can be calculated in the normal way.

Room	Example 2 – ROOM 2							
Design temp. °C	21		Outside temp. °C		–3	Design temp. difference °C		24
Room volume	Room dimensions			Volume of room (m³)	Air change factor W/m³K	Temp. difference	Air changes per hour	Total heat loss (W)
	Length	Width	Height					
Total room	4.0	3.5	3	42	0.33	24	2	665.28
Fabric heat loss	Length (m)	Width (m)	Height (m)	Fabric area	U-value W/m³K	Temp. difference	Gain	Loss
Floor	4.0	3.5		14.0	0.25	24		84
Ceiling/roof	4.0	3.5		14.0	0.16	24		53.76
External glazing	1.0		1.5	1.5	2.9	24		104.4
External doors								
Ext. wall	11.5		3	34.5				
Ext. wall (minus glazing)	34.5 – 1.5 = 33.0			33.0	0.35	24		277.2
Internal wall 1	3.5		3.0	10.5	1.72	3		54.18
Internal wall 2								
Internal wall 3								
Internal wall 4								
Party wall								
Design heat loss (total watts for all elements)								1238.82

Additional factors	Y/N	% add	Total
Exposed location	Y	10	
Intermittent heating	Y	15	185.82
Grand total heat loss for room (W)			1424.64

From the table, it will be seen that the heat gain from room 1 is exactly the same as the heat loss in room 2. The total heat loss for the room is greater simply because the air change rate was doubled in room 2 and the temperature difference between the internal temperature and external temperature was higher.

SUGGESTED ACTIVITY

The diagram below shows the floor plan for a simple single-storey dwelling situated in an exposed location. Using the knowledge you have gained, calculate the heat losses for each room when the external temperature is –5. All other factors and U-values remain as the examples previously shown.

These two examples show only heat loss. They do not tell us the size of heat emitter each room requires. The totals here require further work to convert them into heat emitter emissions and these will be discussed later in the unit.

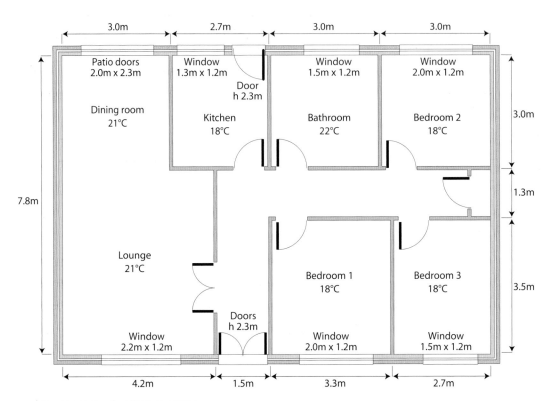

Single-storey dwelling exercise

Key:

1 All outside walls to be of brick construction with a 50mm cavity. Thermalite aerated block internally with 50mm of mineral wool insulation and 12.5mm plasterboard face.

2 All internal walls to be 75mm insulated studding with 12.5mm plasterboard face.

3 All floors to be of concrete construction with 100mm of semi-dry screed.

4 The roof to be of pitched construction with 150mm of insulation between the joists.

5 The windows are to be of PVCu material with double glazed units and 25mm air gap.

6 All rooms are to be 2.3m from finished floor level to ceiling.

A blank table is shown below for you to copy. You will need one table for every room.

Room								
Design temp. °C			**Outside temp. °C**			**Design temp. difference °C**		
Room volume	**Room dimensions**			**Volume of room (m³)**	**Air change factor W/m³K**	**Temp. difference**	**Air changes per hour**	**Total heat loss (W)**
	Length	**Width**	**Height**					
Total room								
Fabric heat loss	**Length (m)**	**Width (m)**	**Height (m)**	**Fabric area**	**U-Value W/m³K**	**Temp. difference**	**Gain**	**Loss**
Floor								
Ceiling/roof								
External glazing								
External doors								
Ext. wall								
Ext. wall (minus glazing)								
Internal wall 1								
Internal wall 2								
Internal wall 3								
Internal wall 4								
Party wall								
Design heat loss (total watts for all elements)								

Additional factors	Y/N	% add	Total
Exposed location	Y	10	
Intermittent heating	Y	15	
Grand total heat loss for room (W)			

Calculate the size of central heating components

Earlier in this section we looked at how to calculate the heat loss from a dwelling. This was only the first step in designing a successful heating system. Further calculations are required and these are listed below:

- heat emitter size
- hot water heating load
- boiler size
- pipe size
- pump size.

These follow a logical pattern and will be discussed in turn.

Calculating heat emitter size

Calculating the size of the heat emitter is not just a case of performing the heat loss calculations and selecting a heat emitter size. Adjustments have to be made using correction factors. Radiator catalogues list radiator outputs but these outputs were obtained in a controlled laboratory environment using tests laid down by various British Standards. Whilst these tests give accurate outputs in laboratory conditions, the requirement for the designer is to adjust these figures based upon BS EN 442.

In July 1997, according to BS EN 442, all radiators manufactured in the EU had to undergo specific tests based upon a flow temperature of 75°C and a return of 65°C in a test room with a temperature of 20°C. In addition, the flow and return connections were at the same end. This is known as top, bottom, same end, or TBSE. The pipe arrangements that are common are:

- top, bottom, same end or TBSE
- top, bottom, opposite end or TBOE
- bottom, bottom, opposite end or BBOE (the most common arrangement in domestic heating systems).

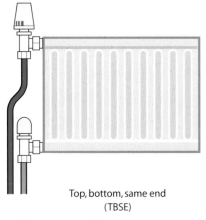

Top, bottom, same end
(TBSE)

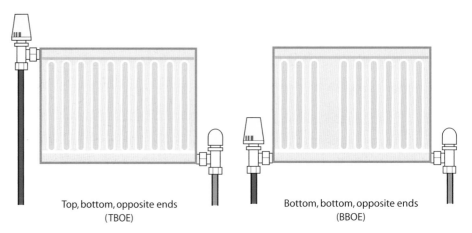

Top, bottom, opposite ends
(TBOE)

Bottom, bottom, opposite ends
(BBOE)

Radiator connections

Most domestic systems in the UK are designed with flow and return temperatures and pipework arrangements that are different from those that were used under the test conditions of BS EN 442. This means that to obtain the correct output, correction factors have to be applied.

The correction factor is based upon the mean water temperature or MWT. The MWT is half of the sum of the flow and return temperatures added together. For example:

If a condensing boiler is fitted to a central heating system with a flow temperature of 82°C and a return of 60°C, then the MWT is:

82 + 60 ÷ 2 = 142 ÷ 2 = 71°C MWT

From this, we now deduct the temperature of the room, say a lounge at 21°C:

71 − 21 = 50°CΔt

In Table 21 it can be seen that an adjustment factor of 0.798 must be applied to all radiators installed in rooms that require 21°C. Similarly, a factor of 0.858 must be applied to all radiators to rooms of 18°C and a factor of 0.778 to those rooms that require 22°C.

Table 21: Δt adjustment factors

°C	Factor	°C	Factor
45	0.700	56	0.918
46	0.719	57	0.938
47	0.739	58	0.959
48	0.758	59	0.979
49	0.778	60	1.000
50	0.798	61	1.021
51	0.818	62	1.041
52	0.838	63	1.062
53	0.858	64	1.083
54	0.878	65	1.104
55	0.898		

A further adjustment factor is required because the radiators are connected BBOE. The BBOE factor is 0.98.

Therefore the calculation of the output from the radiator looks like this:

2400 ÷ 0.898 ÷ 0.98 = 2727W

Below is a diagram of a simple single-storey dwelling. The heat loss calculations were performed using a Mears calculator, model number 15: Domestic Central Heating Calculator.

Lounge: L6m x W5m
21°C
2 air changes
Window: H1.5m x W2m
Heat loss: 2400 watts

Bathroom: L4m x W3m
22°C
2 air changes
Window: H1.5m x W1.7m
Heat loss: 2400 watts

Bed 1: L4.5m x W4.5m
18°C
1 air change
Window: H1.5m x W2m
Heat loss: 1400 watts

Hall: L6m x W1.5m
18°C
1 air change
Door: H2.2m x W1.2m
Heat loss: 960 watts

Bed 2: L6m x W4m
18°C
1 air change
Window: H1.5m x W2m
Heat loss: 1700 watts

Cloaks: L2m x W2m
18°C
1 air change
Heat loss: 460 watts

Kitchen: L3m x W3m
18°C
2 air changes
Door: H2.2m x W1.2m
Heat loss: 860 watts

Heat loss bungalow

The heat losses from the dwelling are as follows.

Lounge: 2400W
Bedroom 1:   1400W
Bedroom 2:   1700W
Kitchen: 860W
Bathroom: 1300W
Cloakroom: 460W
Hall: 960W

The lounge at 21°C has a heat loss of 2400 watts so, if the factors are applied:

2400 ÷ 0.798 ÷ 0.98 = 3069W.

Therefore, a radiator with an output of 3069 watts is required and *not* 2400. If a radiator of 2400 watts were chosen, with a Δt of 50°C, the radiator would only give out the following.

2400 × 0.798 × 0.98 = 1867.89W

What this means is that even though the manufacturer's data states that the output of the radiator is 2400 watts, this is with water with a Δt of 75°C and *not* 50°C as is required, so the radiator would be only 88% of the required size.

The final heat emitter sizes can now be calculated:

Table 22: Heat emitter final sizes

Room	Watts + adjustment factors	Final emitter size
Lounge at 21°C	2400 ÷ 0.798 ÷ 0.98 = 3069	3069
Bedroom 1 at 18°C	1400 ÷ 0.858 ÷ 0.98 = 1665	1665
Bedroom 2 at 18°C	1700 ÷ 0.858 ÷ 0.98 = 2021	2021
Kitchen at 18°C	860 ÷ 0.858 ÷ 0.98 = 1022	1022
Bathroom at 22°C	1300 ÷ 0.778 ÷ 0.98 = 1705	1705
Cloakroom at 18°C	460 ÷ 0.858 ÷ 0.98 = 547	547
Hall at 18°C	960 ÷ 0.858 ÷ 0.98 = 1141	1141
Total for the entire system		**11,170**

SUGGESTED ACTIVITY

You should have, by now, calculated the heat loss for the single-storey building previously shown. Calculate the heat emitter/radiator sizes for the building from the heat losses previously calculated.

Calculating hot water heating load

The heat input into a hot water storage cylinder can be calculated based upon the efficiency of the heat source. If a boiler is the main source of heat for the generation of hot water, then the efficiency of the boiler is required. This is one of the most important factors for improving energy efficiency for the selection of a hot water storage vessel.

The formula for calculating heat input is as follows.

$$\frac{\text{SHC} \times \text{litres of water} \times \text{temp. diff } (\Delta t) \times \text{boiler effi.}}{\text{time in seconds} \times 100}$$

Where:

SHC	=	specific heat capacity of water. This is taken as being 4.19kJ/kg/°C
Litres of water	=	the storage of water in the hot water storage vessel
Temperature difference (Δt)	=	the difference in temperature between the incoming cold supply and the required temperature of the stored hot water
Boiler efficiency	=	usually taken as 93% for a condensing boiler
Time in seconds	=	the time limit for the water to get hot in seconds

SUGGESTED ACTIVITY

A hot water storage cylinder has a capacity of 190 litres. The cylinder is required to be at 65°C within 2 hours. The temperature of the incoming water is 5°C. What is the kW required?

$$\frac{\text{SHC} \times \text{litres of water} \times \text{temp. diff } (\Delta t) \times \text{boiler effi.}}{\text{time in seconds} \times 100}$$

SHC = 4.19

Litres of water = 190

$\Delta t = 60$

Time in seconds = 7200 (2hrs)

Example

A hot water storage cylinder has a capacity of 240 litres. The cylinder is required to be at 60°C within 2 hours. The temperature of the incoming water is 5°C. What is the kW required?

$$\frac{\text{SHC} \times \text{litres of water} \times \text{temp. diff } (\Delta t) \times \text{boiler effi.}}{\text{time in seconds} \times 100}$$

SHC = 4.19

Litres of water = 240

$\Delta t = 55$

Time in seconds = 7200 (2hrs)

$$\frac{4.19 \times 240 \times 55 \times 93}{7200 \times 100} = \mathbf{7.14kW}$$

Calculating total boiler size

In the previous two sections, the totals for both heat emitter output and hot water input were calculated. Now, these must be added together to find out what the boiler size will be.

Radiator output: 11,170W or 11.170kW
Hot water input: 7.14 kW

When these are added together a total of 18.310kW is obtained. However, this does not take into account the fact that there will be heat loss from the pipework. If all of the pipework is to be surface-mounted in the rooms on walls and skirting boards, then no allowance need be made because the heat loss will contribute directly to the heating of the room, but, typically, much of the pipework will be under floors and in roof spaces. In this instance it is usual to allow around 10% to 15% extra to take into account heat loss from pipework and further extensions to the system. The extra percentage of heat allowance will also ensure a quick water heat-up but caution must be exercised if boiler oversizing is to be avoided.

So, taking the 18.310kW and adding 15% will give:

$18.310 \times 0.15 = 2.75$
$18.310 + 2.75 = 21.06\text{kW}$

This can be rounded up to 22kW. A suitable boiler can now be sourced from the various manufacturers' literature.

Calculating central heating pipe sizes

Pipe-sizing central heating systems is not calculated on the amount of heat required by any one room in kW. It is calculated on the amount of water containing heat that will flow down a pipe in kilograms per second or kg/s.

As the heated water moves along the pipe, it will encounter frictional resistance. In other words, the movement of water will be slowed by the size of the pipe, the roughness of the internal surface of the pipe, the number of changes of direction and restrictions, such as radiator valves and other fittings. To counteract the resistance to flow, a central heating circulating pump is used to force the water around the system. In any system, the resistance will always be greater at the beginning of the circuit than at the end because the resistance, measured in pascals, diminishes with length. The greatest resistance to flow will be in the longest circuit. If the pump used will overcome the resistance in the longest circuit, it will always circulate around any other circuit, simply because the resistance is less. For this reason, pump-sizing is always calculated from the longest circuit. This is known as the index circuit. This will be discussed in the next section.

So, let us work through the pipe-sizing process. Take a look at the drawing below.

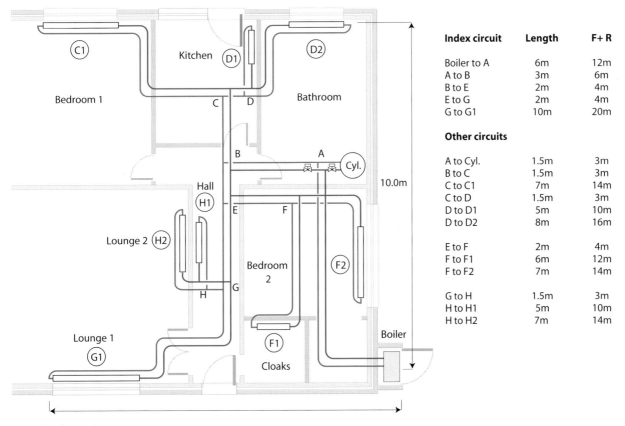

Index circuit	Length	F+ R
Boiler to A	6m	12m
A to B	3m	6m
B to E	2m	4m
E to G	2m	4m
G to G1	10m	20m

Other circuits

A to Cyl.	1.5m	3m
B to C	1.5m	3m
C to C1	7m	14m
C to D	1.5m	3m
D to D1	5m	10m
D to D2	8m	16m
E to F	2m	4m
F to F1	6m	12m
F to F2	7m	14m
G to H	1.5m	3m
H to H1	5m	10m
H to H2	7m	14m

Pipe size bungalow

The illustration shows a heating system that has been designed to heat the radiators from the heat losses of the single-storey dwelling in the section 'Calculating the heat loss from a dwelling – the tabulation method' on page 77. As can be seen, the pipework has been split into sections with each section being given a letter or letter–number combination. This is so that pipe-sizing can be calculated by section. These sections are then entered on to a table to simplify the pipe-sizing process and to provide a visual reminder of progress. You will see that the table overleaf is divided into various columns.

1	2	3	4	5	6	7	8	9	10	11	12
Section	Heat required (kW)	Mains loss (%)	Total heat required (kW)	Flow rate (kg/s)	Pipe size (mm)	Length of pipe run (m)	Fittings resistance (m)	Effective length of pipework	Velocity	Pressure loss (pa/m)	Total pascals by section

Column 1: This is the section of pipe that is being sized.

Column 2: This is the total heat requirement for the section.

Column 3: This is the percentage of the heat required being allowed for heat loss from the pipe. Typically this is between 5% and 20% depending on the length of the pipe run. As a rough guide, add 10% for every 20m but never less than 5% for any section.

Column 4: This is the total heat requirement with the heat allowance added.

Column 5: This is the flow rate through the pipe in kg/s and needs to be calculated.

Column 6: The pipe size.

Column 7: The actual length of pipe from the drawing.

Column 8: This is the allowance made for fittings and changes of direction, usually around 33% of the actual pipe length.

Column 9: The presumed length of pipe once the resistance from column 8 has been added. This will be used to calculate the total resistance to flow so that the pump can be sized correctly.

Column 10: The velocity of the water through the pipe. This should not be greater than 1.5 metres per second (m/s) or the system may be noisy. A typical velocity of between 0.5m/s and 1m/s should be adequate.

Column 11: This is the resistance per metre of the size of pipe chosen and will be used to calculate the pump size.

Column 12: The total pascals per section is calculated by multiplying columns 9 and 11. This is used for pump sizing.

The pipe-sizing procedure

Because the pump size is calculated from the index circuit, this is what we will be concentrating on. The index circuit is the longest circuit and follows the sections of pipework shown in the table below.

Table 23: The index circuit

Section	Heat required (kW)
Boiler to A	18.310
A to B	11.170
B to E	6.436
E to G	3.868
G to G1	1.364

A provisional pipe size can be estimated by looking at how much heat a pipe will carry:

28mm = 22kW
22mm = 12kW
15mm = 6kW
10mm = 3kW

Stage 1 – Look at section Boiler to A on the drawing. The total boiler load is 18.310kW and so the pipe size from Boiler to A will need to carry all of that heat. A 5% margin for heat loss from the pipe is being added and the length of the pipe run is 12m.

18.310 × 1.05 (5%) = 19.23kW

If you look at the table on page 97 you will see that these figures have been added.

As was discussed earlier, the heat required is converted from kilowatts to kg/s. The method is as follows:

$$\text{Flow rate} = \frac{\text{kW}}{\text{SHC} \times \Delta t} = \text{kg/s}$$

Where:

kW = total heat carried by the pipe
SHC = specific heat capacity of water taken as 4.19 kJ/kg°C
Δt = flow and return temperature difference

The boiler is to be a condensing boiler with a 20°C temperature difference across the flow and return. Therefore, the calculation looks like this:

$$\frac{19.23}{4.19 \times 20} = 0.225 \text{ kg/s}$$

Now, we must look at the CIBSE copper pipe sizing tables for water at 75°C:

Pipe sizing tables   1

qm	=	mass flow rate	kg/s
c	=	velocity	m/s
Δp/l	=	pressure loss per unit length	pa/m

Copper tubes BS EN 1057 R250

Water at 75°C

Δp/l	c	10 mm qm	c	12mm qm	c	15mm qm	c	22mm qm	c	28mm qm	c	35mm qm	c	42mm qm	c	c	Δp/l
0.1								0.001	0.00	0.00	0.00	0.007	0.01	0.015	0.01		0.1
0.2								0.002	0.01	0.005	0.01	0.014	0.02	0.023	0.02		0.2
0.3								0.003	0.01	0.008	0.02	0.019	0.02	0.026	0.02		0.3
0.4								0.004	0.01	0.011	0.02	0.019	0.02	0.032	0.03		0.4
0.5						0.001	0.01	0.005	0.02	0.014	0.03	0.021	0.03	0.036	0.03		0.5
0.6						0.001	0.01	0.006	0.02	0.015	0.03	0.023	0.03	0.040	0.03		0.6
0.7						0.001	0.01	0.007	0.02	0.015	0.03	0.026	0.03	0.044	0.04		0.7
0.8						0.001	0.01	0.008	0.03	0.015	0.03	0.028	0.03	0.048	0.04		0.8
0.9						0.001	0.01	0.009	0.03	0.016	0.03	0.030	0.04	0.051	0.04		0.9
1.0						0.002	0.01	0.010	0.03	0.017	0.03	0.032	0.04	0.055	0.05	0.05	1.0
1.5				0.001	0.01	0.003	0.02	0.012	0.04	0.022	0.04	0.040	0.05	0.070	0.06		1.5
2.0				0.001	0.01	0.004	0.03	0.012	0.04	0.026	0.05	0.048	0.06	0.083	0.07		2.0
2.5				0.002	0.02	0.005	0.04	0.014	0.04	0.030	0.06	0.055	0.07	0.094	0.08		2.5
3.0		0.001	0.02	0.002	0.02	0.006	0.04	0.016	0.05	0.033	0.06	0.061	0.07	0.105	0.09		3.0
3.5		0.001	0.02	0.003	0.03	0.007	0.05	0.017	0.05	0.036	0.07	0.067	0.08	0.114	0.09		3.5
4.0		0.001	0.02	0.003	0.03	0.008	0.06	0.019	0.06	0.039	0.07	0.072	0.09	0.124	0.10		4.0
4.5		0.001	0.02	0.003	0.03	0.008	0.06	0.020	0.06	0.042	0.08	0.078	0.10	0.132	0.11		4.5
5.0		0.001	0.02	0.004	0.04	0.008	0.06	0.022	0.07	0.045	0.09	0.083	0.10	0.141	0.12		5.0
5.5		0.002	0.03	0.004	0.04	0.008	0.06	0.023	0.07	0.048	0.09	0.087	0.11	0.149	0.12		5.5
6.0		0.002	0.03	0.005	0.06	0.008	0.06	0.024	0.08	0.050	0.09	0.092	0.11	0.156	0.13		6.0
6.5		0.002	0.03	0.005	0.06	0.008	0.06	0.025	0.08	0.053	0.10	0.096	0.12	0.164	0.14		6.5
7.0		0.002	0.03	0.006	0.07	0.008	0.06	0.027	0.09	0.055	0.10	0.100	0.12	0.171	0.14		7.0
7.5		0.002	0.03	0.006	0.07	0.009	0.06	0.028	0.09	0.057	0.11	0.105	0.13	0.178	0.15	0.15	7.5
8.0		0.003	0.05	0.006	0.07	0.009	0.06	0.029	0.09	0.059	0.11	0.108	0.13	0.185	0.15		8.0
8.5		0.003	0.05	0.006	0.07	0.010	0.07	0.030	0.10	0.061	0.12	0.112	0.14	0.191	0.16		8.5
9.0		0.003	0.05	0.006	0.07	0.010	0.07	0.031	0.10	0.064	0.12	0.116	0.14	0.198	0.16		9.0
9.5		0.003	0.05	0.006	0.07	0.010	0.07	0.032	0.10	0.066	0.13	0.120	0.15	0.204	0.17		9.5
10.0	0.05	0.003	0.05	0.006	0.07	0.011	0.08	0.033	0.11	0.068	0.13	0.123	0.15	0.210	0.17		10.0
12.5		0.004	0.07	0.006	0.07	0.012	0.08	0.037	0.12	0.077	0.15	0.140	0.17	0.239	0.20		12.5
15.0		0.005	0.08	0.007	0.08	0.014	0.10	0.042	0.13	0.086	0.16	0.156	0.19	0.265	0.22		15.0
17.5		0.005	0.08	0.008	0.09	0.015	0.11	0.046	0.15	0.094	0.18	0.170	0.21	0.289	0.24		17.5
20.0		0.005	0.08	0.008	0.09	0.016	0.11	0.049	0.16	0.101	0.19	0.184	0.23	0.312	0.26		20.0
22.5		0.005	0.08	0.009	0.10	0.017	0.12	0.053	0.17	0.108	0.21	0.197	0.24	0.334	0.28		22.5
25.0		0.005	0.08	0.010	0.11	0.019	0.13	0.056	0.18	0.115	0.22	0.209	0.26	0.354	0.29	0.30	25.0
27.5		0.005	0.08	0.010	0.11	0.020	0.14	0.060	0.19	0.122	0.23	0.221	0.27	0.374	0.31		27.5
30.0		0.006	0.10	0.011	0.12	0.021	0.15	0.063	0.20	0.128	0.24	0.232	0.28	0.393	0.33		30.0
32.5		0.006	0.10	0.011	0.12	0.022	0.16	0.066	0.21	0.134	0.25	0.243	0.30	0.411	0.34		32.5
35.0		0.006	0.10	0.012	0.13	0.023	0.16	0.069	0.22	0.140	0.27	0.253	0.31	0.429	0.36		35.0
37.5		0.007	0.12	0.012	0.13	0.024	0.17	0.071	0.23	0.145	0.28	0.263	0.32	0.446	0.37		37.5
40.0		0.007	0.12	0.013	0.15	0.025	0.18	0.074	0.24	0.151	0.29	0.273	0.33	0.462	0.38		40.0
42.5		0.007	0.12	0.013	0.15	0.026	0.18	0.077	0.25	0.156	0.30	0.283	0.35	0.478	0.40		42.5
45.0		0.008	0.13	0.014	0.16	0.026	0.18	0.079	0.25	0.161	0.31	0.292	0.36	0.494	0.41		45.0
47.5		0.008	0.13	0.014	0.16	0.027	0.19	0.082	0.26	0.166	0.32	0.301	0.37	0.509	0.42		47.5
50.0		0.008	0.13	0.015	0.17	0.028	0.20	0.084	0.27	0.171	0.32	0.310	0.38	0.524	0.44		50.0
52.5	0.15	0.008	0.13	0.015	0.17	0.029	0.20	0.087	0.28	0.176	0.33	0.319	0.39	0.539	0.45		52.5
55.0		0.009	0.15	0.016	0.18	0.030	0.21	0.089	0.28	0.181	0.34	0.327	0.40	0.553	0.46		55.0
57.5		0.009	0.15	0.016	0.18	0.031	0.22	0.091	0.29	0.186	0.35	0.336	0.41	0.567	0.47		57.5
60.0		0.009	0.15	0.016	0.18	0.031	0.22	0.094	0.30	0.190	0.36	0.344	0.42	0.581	0.48		60.0
62.5		0.009	0.15	0.017	0.19	0.032	0.23	0.096	0.31	0.195	0.37	0.352	0.43	0.594	0.49	0.50	62.5
65.0		0.010	0.17	0.017	0.19	0.033	0.23	0.098	0.31	0.199	0.38	0.360	0.44	0.608	0.51		65.0
67.5		0.010	0.17	0.018	0.20	0.034	0.24	0.100	0.32	0.203	0.39	0.368	0.45	0.621	0.52		67.5
70.0		0.010	0.17	0.018	0.20	0.034	0.24	0.102	0.33	0.208	0.40	0.375	0.46	0.634	0.53		70.0
72.5		0.010	0.17	0.018	0.20	0.035	0.25	0.104	0.33	0.212	0.40	0.383	0.47	0.646	0.54		72.5
75.0		0.010	0.17	0.019	0.21	0.036	0.25	0.107	0.34	0.216	0.41	0.390	0.48	0.659	0.55		75.0
77.5		0.011	0.19	0.019	0.21	0.036	0.25	0.109	0.35	0.220	0.42	0.398	0.49	0.671	0.56		77.5
80.0		0.011	0.19	0.019	0.21	0.037	0.26	0.111	0.35	0.224	0.43	0.405	0.50	0.683	0.57		80.0
82.5		0.011	0.19	0.020	0.22	0.038	0.27	0.113	0.36	0.228	0.43	0.412	0.51	0.695	0.58		82.5
85.0		0.011	0.19	0.020	0.22	0.038	0.27	0.114	0.36	0.232	0.44	0.419	0.51	0.707	0.59		85.0
87.5		0.011	0.19	0.021	0.24	0.039	0.28	0.116	0.37	0.236	0.45	0.426	0.52	0.718	0.60		87.5
90.0		0.012	0.20	0.021	0.24	0.040	0.28	0.118	0.38	0.240	0.46	0.432	0.53	0.730	0.61		90.0

CIBSE Sheet 1

Pipe sizing tables   2

qm	=	mass flow rate kg/s
c	=	velocity m/s
Δp/l	=	pressure loss per unit length pa/m

Copper tubes BS EN 1057 R250
Water at 75°C

Δp/l	c	10 mm		12mm		15mm		22mm		28mm		35mm		42mm		c	Δp/l
		qm	c	qm	c	qm	c	qm	c	qm	c	qm	c	qm	c		
92.5		0.012	0.20	0.021	0.24	0.040	0.28	0.120	0.38	0.243	0.46	0.439	0.54	0.741	0.62		92.5
95.0		0.012	0.20	0.022	0.25	0.041	0.29	0.122	0.39	0.247	0.47	0.446	0.55	0.752	0.63		95.0
97.5		0.012	0.20	0.022	0.25	0.042	0.30	0.124	0.40	0.251	0.48	0.452	0.55	0.763	0.63		97.5
100		0.012	0.20	0.022	0.25	0.042	0.30	0.126	0.40	0.254	0.48	0.459	0.56	0.774	0.64		100
120		0.014	0.24	0.025	0.28	0.047	0.33	0.139	0.44	0.282	0.54	0.508	0.62	0.857	0.71		120
140		0.015	0.25	0.027	0.30	0.051	0.36	0.152	0.49	0.308	0.59	0.554	0.68	0.934	0.78		140
160		0.017	0.29	0.029	0.32	0.056	0.40	0.164	0.52	0.332	0.63	0.598	0.73	1.000	0.83		160
180	0.30	0.018	0.30	0.032	0.36	0.060	0.42	0.176	0.56	0.354	0.67	0.638	0.78	1.070	0.89		180
200		0.019	0.32	0.034	0.38	0.063	0.44	0.186	0.59	0.376	0.71	0.677	0.83	1.130	0.94		200
220		0.020	0.34	0.035	0.39	0.067	0.47	0.197	0.63	0.397	0.75	0.714	0.88	1.200	1.00	1.00	220
240		0.021	0.35	0.037	0.41	0.070	0.49	0.207	0.66	0.417	0.79	0.750	0.92	1.260	1.05		240
260		0.022	0.37	0.039	0.44	0.074	0.52	0.216	0.69	0.436	0.83	0.784	0.96	1.310	1.09		260
280		0.023	0.39	0.041	0.46	0.077	0.54	0.226	0.72	0.454	0.86	0.817	1.00	1.370	1.14		280
300		0.024	0.40	0.042	0.47	0.080	0.56	0.235	0.75	0.472	0.90	0.849	1.04	1.420	1.18		300
320		0.025	0.42	0.044	0.49	0.083	0.59	0.243	0.78	0.490	0.93	0.880	1.08	1.470	1.22		320
340		0.026	0.44	0.046	0.52	0.086	0.61	0.252	0.81	0.506	0.96	0.910	1.12	1.530	1.27		340
360		0.027	0.46	0.047	0.53	0.089	0.63	0.260	0.83	0.523	0.99	0.940	1.15	1.570	1.31		360
380		0.028	0.47	0.049	0.55	0.092	0.65	0.268	0.86	0.539	1.02	0.968	1.19	1.620	1.35		380
400		0.028	0.47	0.050	0.56	0.094	0.66	0.276	0.88	0.555	1.05	0.996	1.22	1.670	1.39		400
420		0.029	0.49	0.052	0.58	0.097	0.68	0.283	0.90	0.570	1.08	1.020	1.25	1.720	1.43		420
440	0.50	0.030	0.51	0.053	0.59	0.099	0.70	0.291	0.93	0.585	1.11	1.050	1.29	1.760	1.46		440
460		0.031	0.52	0.054	0.60	0.102	0.72	0.298	0.95	0.600	1.14	1.070	1.31	1.800	1.50	1.50	460
480		0.032	0.54	0.056	0.63	0.105	0.74	0.306	0.98	0.614	1.17	1.100	1.35	1.850	1.54		480
500		0.032	0.54	0.057	0.64	0.107	0.76	0.313	1.00	0.628	1.19	1.120	1.37	1.890	1.57		500
520		0.033	0.56	0.058	0.65	0.109	0.77	0.320	1.02	0.642	1.22	1.150	1.41	1.930	1.61		520
540		0.034	0.57	0.060	0.67	0.112	0.79	0.326	1.04	0.656	1.25	1.170	1.44	1.970	1.64		540
560		0.035	0.59	0.061	0.68	0.114	0.81	0.333	1.06	0.669	1.27	1.200	1.47	2.010	1.67		560
580		0.035	0.59	0.062	0.69	0.116	0.82	0.340	1.09	0.682	1.30	1.220	1.50	2.050	1.70		580
600		0.036	0.61	0.063	0.71	0.119	0.84	0.346	1.11	0.695	1.32	1.240	1.52	2.090	1.74		600
620		0.037	0.62	0.065	0.73	0.121	0.85	0.353	1.13	0.708	1.35	1.270	1.56	2.130	1.77		620
640		0.037	0.62	0.066	0.74	0.123	0.87	0.359	1.15	0.721	1.37	1.290	1.58	2.160	1.80		640
660		0.038	0.64	0.067	0.75	0.125	0.88	0.365	1.17	0.733	1.39	1.310	1.61	2.200	1.83		660
680		0.039	0.66	0.068	0.76	0.127	0.90	0.371	1.19	0.745	1.42	1.330	1.63	2.240	1.86		680
700		0.039	0.66	0.069	0.77	0.130	0.92	0.378	1.21	0.757	1.44	1.350	1.66	2.270	1.89		700
720		0.040	0.67	0.070	0.78	0.132	0.93	0.383	1.22	0.769	1.46	1.380	1.69	2.310	1.92		720
740		0.041	0.69	0.071	0.80	0.134	0.95	0.389	1.24	0.781	1.48	1.400	1.72	2.350	1.95		740
760		0.041	0.69	0.073	0.82	0.136	0.96	0.395	1.26	0.793	1.51	1.420	1.74	2.380	1.98	2.00	760
780		0.042	0.71	0.074	0.83	0.138	0.97	0.401	1.28	0.804	1.53	1.440	1.77	2.410	2.00		780
800		0.043	0.73	0.075	0.84	0.140	0.99	0.407	1.30	0.816	1.55	1.460	1.79	2.450	2.04		800
820		0.043	0.73	0.076	0.85	0.142	1.00	0.412	1.32	0.827	1.57	1.480	1.82	2.480	2.06		820
840		0.044	0.74	0.077	0.86	0.144	1.02	0.418	1.34	0.838	1.59	1.500	1.84	2.510	2.09		840
860		0.044	0.74	0.078	0.87	0.146	1.03	0.423	1.35	0.849	1.61	1.520	1.86	2.550	2.12		860
880		0.045	0.76	0.079	0.88	0.147	1.04	0.429	1.37	0.860	1.63	1.540	1.89	2.580	2.15		880
900		0.046	0.78	0.080	0.90	0.149	1.05	0.434	1.39	0.871	1.65	1.560	1.91	2.610	2.17		900
920		0.046	0.78	0.081	0.91	0.151	1.07	0.440	1.41	0.881	1.67	1.570	1.93	2.640	2.20		920
940		0.047	0.79	0.082	0.92	0.153	1.08	0.445	1.42	0.892	1.69	1.590	1.95	2.680	2.23		940
960		0.047	0.79	0.083	0.93	0.155	1.09	0.450	1.44	0.902	1.71	1.610	1.97	2.710	2.25		960
980		0.048	0.81	0.084	0.94	0.157	1.11	0.455	1.45	0.913	1.73	1.630	2.00	2.740	2.28		980
1000		0.048	0.81	0.085	0.95	0.158	1.12	0.461	1.47	0.923	1.75	1.650	2.02	2.770	2.30		1000
1100		0.051	0.86	0.090	1.01	0.167	1.18	0.486	1.55	0.973	1.85	1.740	2.13	2.920	2.43		1100
1200		0.054	0.91	0.094	1.05	0.176	1.24	0.510	1.63	1.020	1.94	1.820	2.23	3.060	2.54		1200
1300		0.056	0.94	0.098	1.10	0.184	1.30	0.533	1.70	1.060	2.01	1.910	2.34	3.200	2.66		1300
1400	1.00	0.059	1.00	0.103	1.15	0.191	1.35	0.555	1.77	1.110	2.11	1.980	2.43	3.330	2.77		1400
1500		0.061	1.03	0.107	1.20	0.199	1.41	0.577	1.84	1.150	2.18	2.060	2.53	3.460	2.88		1500
1600		0.063	1.06	0.111	1.24	0.206	1.45	0.598	1.91	1.190	2.26	2.140	2.63	3.580	2.98	3.00	1600
1700		0.066	1.11	0.115	1.29	0.214	1.51	0.618	1.97	1.230	2.34	2.210	2.71	3.700	3.08		1700
1800		0.068	1.15	0.118	1.32	0.220	1.55	0.638	2.04	1.270	2.41	2.280	2.80	3.820	3.18		1800
1900		0.070	1.18	0.122	1.37	0.227	1.60	0.658	2.10	1.310	2.49	2.350	2.88	3.930	3.27		1900
2000		0.072	1.21	0.126	1.41	0.234	1.65	0.677	2.16	1.350	2.56	2.410	2.96	4.040	3.36		2000

CIBSE Sheet 2

As you can see, the CIBSE tables are divided into columns. To the far left and the far right are columns with the heading Δp/l. This is the resistance and is measured in pascals, the unit of pressure. This is a vital piece of data as we cannot calculate the pump size without it and so must be entered on our table in column 11. Across the top of the tables are the various pipe sizes. Below each pipe size are two columns. The left column is marked qm and is the flow rate that we have calculated. The flow rates calculated and the flow rate on the table may not be identical. In this instance, the nearest flow rate *above* the calculated flow rate should be used and *never* below or the pipe will not deliver enough heat. To the right is a column marked *c.* This is the water velocity and should not exceed 1m/s for small-bore systems and 1.5m/s for micro-bore systems. The maximum velocity is 1.5m/s across all systems. The velocity must be entered on to our table in column 10. The zig-zag line also relates to velocity. To read it, follow the line upwards until you find the velocity in m/s. Remember, the flow rate we require is 0.229kg/s.

Now look at the chart and find the flow rate, which either matches or is slightly above, *but* also keep an eye on the left/right columns as the pascals should not exceed 300Pa/m for any one section or the pump, when its size is calculated, will need a large head of pressure and this could possibly create noise in the system. Below is a snapshot of CIBSE Table 1. The nearest flow rate is boxed for identification.

Pipe sizing tables   1

qm	=	mass flow rate	kg/s
c	=	velocity	m/s
Δp/l	=	pressure loss per unit length	pa/m

Copper tubes BS EN 1057 R250 — Water at 75°C

Δp/l	c	10 mm qm	10 mm c	12mm qm	12mm c	15mm qm	15mm c	22mm qm	22mm c	28mm qm	28mm c	35mm qm	35mm c	42mm qm	42mm c	c	Δp/l
52.5	0.15	0.008	0.13	0.015	0.17	0.029	0.20	0.087	0.28	0.176	0.33	0.319	0.39	0.539	0.45		52.5
55.0		0.009	0.15	0.016	0.18	0.030	0.21	0.089	0.28	0.181	0.34	0.327	0.40	0.553	0.46		55.0
57.5		0.009	0.15	0.016	0.18	0.031	0.22	0.091	0.29	0.186	0.35	0.336	0.41	0.567	0.47		57.5
60.0		0.009	0.15	0.016	0.18	0.031	0.22	0.094	0.30	0.190	0.36	0.344	0.42	0.581	0.48		60.0
62.5		0.009	0.15	0.017	0.19	0.032	0.23	0.096	0.31	0.195	0.37	0.352	0.43	0.594	0.49	0.50	62.5
65.0		0.010	0.17	0.017	0.19	0.033	0.23	0.098	0.31	0.199	0.38	0.360	0.44	0.608	0.51		65.0
67.5		0.010	0.17	0.018	0.20	0.034	0.24	0.100	0.32	0.203	0.39	0.368	0.45	0.621	0.52		67.5
70.0		0.010	0.17	0.018	0.20	0.034	0.24	0.102	0.33	0.208	0.40	0.375	0.46	0.634	0.53		70.0
72.5		0.010	0.17	0.018	0.20	0.035	0.25	0.104	0.33	0.212	0.40	0.383	0.47	0.646	0.54		72.5
75.0		0.010	0.17	0.019	0.21	0.036	0.25	0.107	0.34	0.216	0.41	0.390	0.48	0.659	0.55		75.0
77.5		0.011	0.19	0.019	0.21	0.036	0.25	0.109	0.35	0.220	0.42	0.398	0.49	0.671	0.56		77.5
80.0		0.011	0.19	0.019	0.21	0.037	0.26	0.111	0.35	0.224	0.43	0.405	0.50	0.683	0.57		80.0
82.5		0.011	0.19	0.020	0.22	0.038	0.27	0.113	0.36	0.228	0.43	0.412	0.51	0.695	0.58		82.5
85.0		0.011	0.19	0.020	0.22	0.038	0.27	0.114	0.36	0.232	0.44	0.419	0.51	0.707	0.59		85.0
87.5		0.011	0.19	0.021	0.24	0.039	0.28	0.116	0.37	0.236	0.45	0.426	0.52	0.718	0.60		87.5
90.0		0.012	0.20	0.021	0.24	0.040	0.28	0.118	0.38	0.240	0.46	0.432	0.53	0.730	0.61		90.0

This shows that the nearest flow rate is slightly above 0.229 at 0.232 with a pipe size of 28mm. The velocity 0.44 m/s and the pascals are 85.0Pa/m pressure drop. On the face of it this looks good *but* are there any alternative pipe sizes? Look at sheet 2.

Pipe sizing tables   2

qm	=	mass flow rate	kg/s
c	=	velocity	m/s
Δp/l	=	pressure loss per unit length	pa/m

Copper tubes BS EN 1057 R250 — Water at 75°C

Δp/l	c	10 mm qm	10 mm c	12mm qm	12mm c	15mm qm	15mm c	22mm qm	22mm c	28mm qm	28mm c	35mm qm	35mm c	42mm qm	42mm c	c	Δp/l
92.5		0.012	0.20	0.021	0.24	0.040	0.28	0.120	0.38	0.243	0.46	0.439	0.54	0.741	0.62		92.5
95.0		0.012	0.20	0.022	0.25	0.041	0.29	0.122	0.39	0.247	0.47	0.446	0.55	0.752	0.63		95.0
97.5		0.012	0.20	0.022	0.25	0.042	0.30	0.124	0.40	0.251	0.48	0.452	0.55	0.763	0.63		97.5
100		0.012	0.20	0.022	0.25	0.042	0.30	0.126	0.40	0.254	0.48	0.459	0.56	0.774	0.64		100
120		0.014	0.24	0.025	0.28	0.047	0.33	0.139	0.44	0.282	0.54	0.508	0.62	0.857	0.71		120
140		0.015	0.25	0.027	0.30	0.051	0.36	0.152	0.49	0.308	0.59	0.554	0.68	0.934	0.78		140
160		0.017	0.29	0.029	0.32	0.056	0.40	0.164	0.52	0.332	0.63	0.598	0.73	1.000	0.83		160
180	0.30	0.018	0.30	0.032	0.36	0.060	0.42	0.176	0.56	0.354	0.67	0.638	0.78	1.070	0.89		180
200		0.019	0.32	0.034	0.38	0.063	0.44	0.186	0.59	0.376	0.71	0.677	0.83	1.130	0.94		200
220		0.020	0.34	0.035	0.39	0.067	0.47	0.197	0.63	0.397	0.75	0.714	0.88	1.200	1.00	1.00	220
240		0.021	0.35	0.037	0.41	0.070	0.49	0.207	0.66	0.417	0.79	0.750	0.92	1.260	1.05		240
260		0.022	0.37	0.039	0.44	0.074	0.52	0.216	0.69	0.436	0.83	0.784	0.96	1.310	1.09		260
280		0.023	0.39	0.041	0.46	0.077	0.54	0.226	0.72	0.454	0.86	0.817	1.00	1.370	1.14		280
300		0.024	0.40	0.042	0.47	0.080	0.56	0.235	0.75	0.472	0.90	0.849	1.04	1.420	1.18		300

There is an alternative pipe size because a 22mm pipe will also deliver the required flow rate with a velocity of 0.72m/s (nearer to the ideal 1m/s) but take a look at the pascals per metre. At 280Pa/m it is near to the 300Pa/m maximum pascals limit. There are several advantages to using 22mm. It's cheaper to buy, which keeps the cost of the installation down and it is easier to work with and install. However, the pascals may present a problem later but this will not be known until the rest of the index circuit is calculated. For the purpose of this example, 22mm pipe will be chosen. The data can be entered onto the table.

1	2	3	4	5	6	7	8	9	10	11	12
Section	Heat required (kW)	Mains loss (%)	Total heat required (kW)	Flow rate (kg/s)	Pipe size (mm)	Length of pipe run (m)	Fittings resistance (33%)	Effective length of pipework	Velocity (m/s)	Pressure loss (Pa/m)	Total pascals by section
Boiler to A	18.310	5	19.23	0.229	22	12	1.33	15.96	0.75	300	4788
A to B	11.170	5	11.37	0.135	22	6	1.33	7.98	0.44	120	957.6
B to E	6.436	5	6.75	0.080	22	4	1.33	5.32	0.26	47.5	252.7
E to G	3.868	6	4.10	0.049	15	4	1.33	5.32	0.36	140	744.8
G to G1	1.364	10	1.50	0.017	10	20	1.33	26.6	0.29	160	4256
						Total pascals for pump sizing from the index circuit					10,999.1
A to Cly	7.140	5				3	1.33				
B to C	4.392	5				3	1.33				
C to C1	1.665	7				14	1.33				
C to D	2.727	5				3	1.33				
D to D1	1.022	5				10	1.33				
D to D2	1.705	7				16	1.33				
E to F	2.568	5				4	1.33				
F to F1	0.547	6				12	1.33				
F to F2	2.021	7				14	1.33				
G to H	2.505	5				3	1.33				
H to H1	1.141	5				10	1.33				
H to H2	1.364	7				14	1.33				

Stage 2 – At the beginning of the process we allowed a percentage of the total kW for the section for heat loss from the pipe. This can now be checked to see if it is adequate.

To check to see if the 5% we added to the heat required is sufficient, we perform another calculation. If the room is to be maintained at 21°C and the flow pipe is at 80°C, this gives a temperature difference of 59°C, which falls between 55°C and 60°C (see Table 23). This means that the exact figure will have to be calculated.

Table 23: Heat emission in watts per metre of pipe run

Nominal pipe size (mm)	Temperature difference of surface to surroundings (°C)				
	40	45	50	55	60
8	28	32	35	39	43
10	33	37	41	46	50
15	40	46	53	59	66
22	48	56	62	70	78
28	58	68	78	88	98
35	71	82	93	110	120
42	78	92	105	110	130
54	96	112	130	150	170
66.7	120	140	160	180	200
76.1	140	160	180	211	230

Therefore:

$60 - 55 = 5$

The heat emission at these temperatures is 78°C and 70°C respectively. So:

$78 - 70 = 8$

$8 \div 5 = 1.6$

This shows that there is 1.6W emission for every 1°C rise.

There is 4°C difference between 55°C and 59°C. Therefore:

$4 \times 1.6 = 6.4$

70 (at 55°C from the table above) + 6.4 = 76.4

Length of run × 76.4

$12 \times 76.4 = 916.8W$

$$\text{Percentage emission} = \frac{\text{total watts of run}}{\text{total heat emission in watts}} \times 100$$

$$\text{Percentage emission} = \frac{91,680}{18,310} = \mathbf{5.0\%}$$

So, the estimation of 5% heat loss from the pipework was correct; therefore the pipe size is also correct.

Stages 1 and 2 can now be performed for the entire index circuit.

The index circuit

A to B = 11.170 + 5% = 11.7285kW

Flow rate = $\dfrac{11.7285}{4.19 \times 20}$ = 0.139kg/s

Pipe size = 22mm

Velocity = 0.44m/s

Pascals = 120Pa/m

Percentage check

Length of run × 76.4

6 × 76.4 = 458.4W

Percentage emission = $\dfrac{\text{total watts of run}}{\text{total heat emission in watts}} \times 100$

Percentage emission = $\dfrac{45,840}{18,310}$ = **2.5%**

B to E = 6.436 + 5% = 6.75kW

Flow rate = $\dfrac{6.75}{4.19 \times 20}$ = 0.080kg/s

Pipe size = 22mm

Velocity = 0.44m/s

Pascals = 120Pa/m

Percentage check

Length of run × 76.4

6 × 76.4 = 458.4W

Percentage emission = $\dfrac{\text{total watts of run}}{\text{total heat emission in watts}} \times 100$

Percentage emission = $\dfrac{45,840}{18,310}$ = **2.5%**

E to G = 3.868 + 6% = 4.10kW

Flow rate $= \dfrac{4.10}{4.19 \times 20} = 0.049$kg/s

Pipe size = 15mm

Velocity = 0.36m/s

Pascals = 140Pa/m

Percentage check

Length of run × 63

4 × 63 = 252 watts

Percentage emission $= \dfrac{\text{total watts of run}}{\text{total heat emission in watts}} \times 100$

Percentage emission $= \dfrac{25,200}{18,310} = $ **1.37%**

G to G1 = 1.364 + 10% = 1.50kW

Flow rate $= \dfrac{1.50}{4.19 \times 20} = 0.017$kg/s

Pipe size = 10mm

Velocity = 0.29m/s

Pascals = 160Pa/m

Percentage check

Length of run × 49.2

20 × 49.2 = 984 watts

Percentage emission $= \dfrac{\text{total watts of run}}{\text{total heat emission in watts}} \times 100$

Percentage emission $= \dfrac{98,400}{18,310} = $ **5.37%**

Using the techniques discussed above, complete the pipe-sizing table for the single-storey dwelling.

Sizing the circulating pump

Before we can size the circulating pump, we must calculate the total pascals per section of pipe. This is completed by first finding out the effective length of pipe in column 9. It is usual to allow a 33% increase in the pipework to allow for fittings resistance. This is a fairly simple task that involves multiplying the pipe length by 1.33 as shown in the index circuit table below. This will give the effective pipe length. Now, multiply the effective length by the pascals for the section. Then when all of the total pascals per section have been calculated, add the totals together as shown.

1	2	3	4	5	6	7	8	9	10	11	12
Section	Heat required (kW)	Mains loss (%)	Total heat required (kW)	Flow rate (kg/s)	Pipe size (mm)	Length of pipe run (m)	Fittings resistance (33%)	Effective length of pipework	Velocity (m/s)	Pressure loss (Pa/m)	Total pascals by section
Boiler to A	17.968	5	18.866	0.225	22	12	1.33	15.96	0.72	280	4788
A to B	10.828	5	11.37	0.135	22	6	1.33	7.98	0.44	120	957.6
B to E	6.436	5	6.75	0.080	22	4	1.33	5.32	0.26	47.5	252.7
E to G	3.868	6	4.10	0.049	15	4	1.33	5.32	0.36	140	744.8
G to G1	1.364	10	1.50	0.017	10	20	1.33	26.6	0.29	160	4256
							Total pascals for pump sizing from the index circuit				10,999.1

The total needs to be converted to metres head. If 1 pascal is equal to 0.0001019977334 metres head then:

$10,999.1 \times 0.0001019977334 = 1.12$ metres head

You can see that the index circuit has a pressure loss of 1.12 metres head.

The next step is to find out if the boiler creates a significant pressure drop. Some low water content boilers generate a high resistance to flow through the heat exchanger and this results in a drop in pressure. This, too, is measured in metres head. Consulting the boiler manufacturer's instructions will indicate if this is the case. Any pressure drop at the boiler will also need to be added to the pressure drop across the index circuit.

Assuming there is a pressure drop at the boiler of 2m head, then the total for the system will be:

$2 + 1.12 = 3.12$m head pressure drop

This must be converted to kilopascals (kPa). To convert metres head to kPa simply multiply the metres head by 9.81:

$3.12 \times 9.81 = 30.61$ kPa

You must now consult the pump manufacturer's literature to select a pump and pump speed based on your calculation. From the diagram below, it will be seen that a Grundfos UPS-15/50 pump will give 30.61kPa on both speed 2 at 0.28l/s and speed 3 at 0.38l/s.

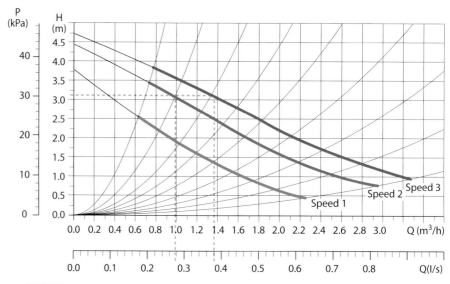

30.36kPa

@ speed 2 = 0.28l/s
@ speed 3 = 0.38l/s

Pump flow chart

Plan work schedules for a system installation (LO4)

There are six assessment criteria for this Learning Outcome:

1 Identify other trades involved in the installation process.
2 Describe effective working relationships between trades.
3 Describe the elements of a plumbing system installation schedule for a domestic dwelling.
4 Explain the sequence of work in a domestic dwelling plumbing system installation.
5 Describe difficulties that may arise when supervising system installations.
6 Describe handover procedures.

SmartScreen Unit 302

PowerPoint 4

Identify other trades involved in the installation process

- **Carpenters/joiners** – The wood trades provide a vital function on site during the initial building phase, fitting door and window frames, floor joists and roof trusses. During the second phase they will fix internal doors, skirting boards, architraves, etc.

- **Electricians** – Install and test all electrical installation work on site, including power, lighting, fire and smoke alarms and security systems, usually running the cables in trunking or conduits for neatness.

- **Gas fitters** - Install natural gas lines in domestic properties and in commercial or industrial buildings. On some sites they may also install large appliances and pipelines.

- **Plasterers** – Responsible for wall and ceiling finishing, dry lining and external rendering, if required, using a mixture of both modern and traditional techniques.

- **Painters and decorators** – Responsible for wall and ceiling finishing, including painting skirting boards, architraves and any specialist decorating such as murals, frescos, etc.

- **Tilers** – Responsible for internal and external tiling of walls and floors and specialist tiling such as swimming pools and wet rooms.

Describe effective working relationships between trades

Communication between the various trades on site

We have now identified some of the trades that have a direct involvement with plumbing installations whether it is an electrician completing the wiring to a central heating system or a tiler completing the tiling to a bathroom prior to the installation of a wash basin or WC.

The diverse nature of the construction industry brings together these individual, very different trades with the sole aim of successfully completing the request of the customer, on time and to an acceptable standard.

Plumbing installations on a construction site rely on the cooperation, communication and coordination between various trades to ensure that the installation is completed as smoothly as possible. Consideration of customer requirements is vital and can often mean that specifications and plans have to be altered and amended to suit their wishes. This can involve negotiation between the trades to accommodate the alterations to planned schedules of work and timings. It must be remembered, however, that there are no set rules and different companies and construction sites will approach these problems in a number of ways.

More often than not, a schedule of work will have been drawn up which highlights the timings of such items like first fix and second fix operations and the trades that are involved. Careful planning and verbal communication is paramount to ensure that the schedules do not go astray.

Communication between the company and the customer

Communication between the company and the customer takes place at every stage of the contract from the initial contact to customer care at the contract completion. Written communication can take the form of:

- **Quotations and estimates** – Both of these are written prices as to how much the work will cost to complete. A quotation is a fixed price and cannot vary. An estimate, by comparison, is not a fixed price but can go up or down if the estimate is not accurate or the work is completed ahead of schedule. Most contractors opt for estimates because of this flexibility.

- **Invoices/statements** – Documents that are issued at the end of any contract as a demand for final payment. Invoices and statements can be from the supplier to the contractor for payment for materials supplied or from the contractor to the customer for services rendered. Usually a period of time is allowed for the payment to be made.

- **Statutory cancellation rights** – A number of laws give the customer the legal right to cancel contracts after the customer signs a contract. There is usually no penalty for cancellation providing the cancellation is confirmed in writing within a specific timeframe. Most cancellation periods start when the customer receives notification of their right to cancel up to seven days before work commences.

Communication between the employer and the employee

One of the key points about running a successful business is the relationship between the employer and the employee. Businesses are successful when the management and staff work together, are motivated and engage in constructive dialogue.

Whereas in the past, pay and working conditions varied from employee to employee and the employer had the power to 'hire and fire' as they saw fit, today employers and employees are actively encouraged to engage in discussions about matters across the whole spectrum of a business including their respective rights.

Types of communication

There are a number of ways that companies communicate with customers, staff and suppliers, and other companies, such as:

Written communication	Letters
	Emails
	Faxes
Verbally (should always be backed up with written confirmation to prevent confusion)	Face to face
	Via the telephone

Written communication

Letters are an official method of communication and are usually easier to understand than verbal communication. Good written communication can help towards the success of any company by portraying a professional image and building goodwill. Official company business should always be in written form, usually on company headed paper and should have a clear layout. The content of the letter must be well written, using good English, correct grammar and be divided into logical paragraphs. Examples of business letters are sales letters, information letters, general enquiry and problem-solving letters.

Emails have emerged as a hugely popular form of communication because of the speed with which information can be transferred. As with letters, they should be well written and laid out, using correct grammar and spelling to convey professionalism, whether the recipient is a client, customer or colleague.

Faxes are another useful form of communication for businesses. They are used mainly for conveying documents such as orders, invoices, statements and contracts where the recipient may wish to see an authorising signature. Again, the basic rules apply with regard to layout, grammar and content. Remember always to use a cover page that is appropriate for your company. This is an external communication that reflects the business and company image.

Oral communication

The spoken word is, more often than not, our main method of communication, especially in a work context. In order to present a professional image and communicate effectively, you must consider what you are saying, your tone of voice, your body language, and the response of your listener.

Describe the elements of a plumbing system installation schedule for a domestic dwelling

Plumbing installations have a finite timescale in which they must be completed. An estimate for a complete plumbing installation in, say, a new-build property that includes hot and cold water supplies, central heating installations and sanitation pipework will include a timeline that the installer will need to work to if the company is to make a profit from the installation. In many cases, the installation can be plotted on a schedule of work or a Gantt chart so that time is allotted to each phase of the installation. By using a Gantt chart, material deliveries can be planned for a certain day and staff loadings for the job can be calculated.

Task	Duration (Days)	Time												
		Week 1	Week 2	Week 3	Week 4	Week 5	Week 6	Week 7	Week 8	Week 9	Week 10	Week 11	Week 12	Week 13
		01 Jun	08 Jun	15 Jun	22 Jun	29 Jun	06 July	13 July	20 July	27 July	03 Aug	10 Aug	17 Aug	25 Aug
Clear oversite	1													
Excavate foundations	3													
Concrete foundations	1													
Footings to DPC	4													
Drainage/ services	4													
Backfill	2													
Ground floor	2													
Walls to first floor	14													
First floor carcass	3													
First floor deck	2													
Walls to wall plate	15													
Roof structure	5													
Roof covering	10													
Rainwater gear	2													
Windows	4													
External doors	1													

A Gantt chart

Staffing an installation is a delicate matter as too few plumbers on site will quickly lead to a job falling behind schedule. Similarly, too many plumbers on a job can sometimes have the same result as the presence of more installers leads to greater organisational problems. There is often a fine line between getting enough people on site and making a profit.

Explain the sequence of work in a domestic dwelling plumbing system installation

A well-functioning plumbing system that meets or exceeds the customer's requirements is the result of a number of important aspects:

- good design
- good planning
- good installation
- correct commissioning and setting up procedures.

Planning a plumbing installation

Planning a plumbing installation involves:

- designing the system
- coordinating the availability of staff to undertake the installation
- ordering and coordinating the delivery of the materials
- installing the first fix
- installing the second fix
- filling and commissioning the system
- completing the benchmarking paperwork
- handover to customer
- removing all scrap and unused materials from site.

Planning a plumbing installation is often completed using a Gantt chart, as described in the previous section.

Designing a plumbing installation

Designing a plumbing installation will involve taking measurements from site drawings or visiting the site in person and taking measurements from the building so that pipework sizes, heat losses and heat emitter outputs, flow rates, hot water temperatures etc can be calculated. The layout of a building is instrumental in how we design the systems for it. In many cases, the position of appliances, such as bathroom suites, has already been dictated by the architect's drawings and our job is to design a functioning system based upon these predetermined positions. Where central heating is concerned, positioning components, such as radiators, may be a little more flexible and consultation with the customer is needed to ensure that the position of radiators, the boiler and so on is satisfactory. It is here that the designer/installer will get a feel for where pipework runs can be installed and a decision made about the system type and the materials that will be used. Many installers now favour polybutylene pipe over copper tubes and fittings because of the benefits it offers in installation time.

Once the design is completed, an estimated cost of the installation can be prepared.

Ordering and storing the materials

When a customer has accepted an estimate, ordering of the materials can take place. Most plumbing companies shop around for the best deals on boilers and radiators and will not be dependent on one sole supplier. Alternatively, a company might have favourable contract rates with its supplier which will supply all the items needed, including tubes and fittings, at discounted rates.

The materials, obviously, must arrive early either before the job is started or on the day that the installation is to begin. A phased delivery is often the best method to use, as delivery of key items and appliances can be planned to coincide with the progression of the installation.

Materials that arrive on site must be stored in a secure and safe lock-up to prevent theft and to ensure that a check can be made of the materials in stock at any one time. Fragile materials such as sanitary ware should be kept separate and stored so as to prevent breakages.

Installation planning

Once the system has been designed in accordance with the customer's wishes, the installation planning can take place. Installation can be divided into five separate and distinct phases:

- **First fix** – Usually the first fix phase is where the installer will get their first look at the property. They will walk the job and plan the pipework routes, marking any floorboards that require lifting. On new build installations, the plumber will arrive before any ceilings are fixed and often before the upper floors are down. Marking and notching/drilling of the joists will take place in accordance with the Building Regulations and the pipework for the hot and cold water, the central heating, any gas pipework and sanitary pipework, waste pipes and so on will be installed. At this stage, because there are no appliances or components installed, the plumber will position the pipework tails to where the appliances will eventually be fitted, using the working drawings of the building to position the pipework correctly. Any pipework that is to be positioned behind plasterboard walls, such as droppers for central heating behind the dot and dab plasterboards, will be installed. This phase of pipework is often called 'carcassing'. Once the carcassing has been completed, it must be fully pressure tested to 1.5 times the normal operating pressure, in accordance with BS EN 806 and BS 6700.

- **Second fix** – The second fix takes place after all of the internal work, such as fitting plastering, skirting boards and internal doors, has been done. Where bathroom suites are installed, the bath is fitted first so that the tiler can tile around the bath and any areas where the wash basin and WCs are to be fitted. These can then be completed once the tiler has finished. Boilers, radiators and any central heating electrical controls can be installed and any hot water storage vessels, cold water cisterns fitted and connected. Once the second fix has been completed, commissioning can begin.

- **Commissioning and testing** – Commissioning and testing procedures depend upon the system being commissioned. It is at this point that the system is filled up with water to full operating pressures and the systems are run for the first time. Any leaks must be cured and flow rates and pressures checked to ensure that the installation meets the design specification. Central heating systems can be balanced and the temperatures checked against the design specification. Benchmarking the system can take place during this stage of the installation.

- **Snagging** – Snagging is the term used to describe the curing of minor problems that have emerged during the commissioning and testing process.

- **Signing off** – Commonly called 'handover', this is where we present the customer with all of the system documentation, including benchmarking certificates, building regulation compliance certificates, manufacturers' instructions and commissioning documentation. This is often presented in a system folder together with any emergency contact details for use in the event of a problem. The customer should be instructed in the use of all system controls and shown where isolation points for the water, gas and electricity are. Any system servicing requirements, such as annual boiler servicing, should also be pointed out.

Describe difficulties that may arise when supervising system installations

Conflicts in the workplace

When people work together in groups, there will be occasions when individuals disagree and conflicts occur. Whether these disagreements become full-blown feuds or instead fuel creative problem-solving is, in large part, up to the person in charge. Conflicts can occur for many reasons, such as:

- unfair working conditions
- unfair pay structures
- clash of personalities
- language differences
- attitudes towards ethnic differences.

It is important to deal with workplace conflicts quickly and effectively, as if left unchecked they can affect morale, motivation and productivity, and potentially cause stress and even serious accidents. Conflicts may occur between:

- **Employer and employee** – May need union involvement or some form of mediation
- **Two or more employees** – Will need employer intervention
- **Customer and employer** – May need intervention by a professional body
- **Customer and employee** – Will need employer intervention.

Dealing with workplace conflicts

There are several ways that your employer may deal with disagreements. They should:

- Identify the problem. Make sure everyone involved knows exactly what the issue is, and why they are arguing. Talking through the problem helps everyone to understand that there is a problem, and what the issues are.
- Allow every person involved to clarify their perspectives and opinions about the problem. They should make sure that everyone has an opportunity to express their opinion. They may even establish a time limit for each person to state their case. All participants should feel safe and supported.
- Identify and clarify the ideal end result from each person's point of view.
- Work out what can reasonably be done to achieve each person's objectives.
- Find an area of compromise to see if there some part of the issue on which everyone agrees. If not, they may try to identify long-term goals that mean something to all parties.

Informal counseling is one method that helps managers and supervisors to address and manage conflict in the workplace. This may be in the form of:

- meetings
- negotiation/mediation sessions
- other dispute-resolving methods.

It is important that employees know that there is someone to go to if a conflict develops. If an employee has a conflict with another member of staff, then they should first discuss the problem with their immediate supervisor. In extreme cases where the matter cannot be resolved, then mediation or union involvement may be required (see table from ACAS below).

Type of help	Mutually agreed solutions	Recommendations by an expert	Legally binding decisions	Key features
Mediation (sometimes referred to as 'collective conciliation' when used with a group of employees)	✓	Not usually, but parties can ask for them		• Helps to maintain ongoing working relationships • Develops problem-solving skills • Tackles conflict early
Arbitration		✓	✓	• Simpler, faster alternative to tribunal hearing • Only available for cases involving unfair dismissal or flexible working
Individual conciliation	✓		✓	• Success rate of ACAS service: 70% cases settled or withdrawn before cases get to a tribunal hearing • Often conducted on the phone: parties may not talk to each other.

In the plumbing industry, workplace conflicts can usually be resolved by the Joint Industry Board (JIB) thus avoiding the need to approach ACAS in all but the most severe disputes.

The effects of poor communication at work

The effects of poor communications can be extremely harmful to both businesses and personnel. If poor communication exists then goals will not be achieved and this could develop into problems within the company. It can lead to demotivation of the workforce and the business will not function as a cohesive unit. The effects are obviously negative:

- Employees become mistrustful of management and, often, of each other.
- Employees argue and reject their manager's opinions and input.
- Employees file more grievances related to performance issues.
- Employees don't keep their manager informed and avoid talking to management.
- Employees do their best to hide their deficiencies or performance problems.
- Employees refuse to take responsibility.

Poor communication in the workplace can disrupt the organisation and cause strained employee relations and lower productivity which can often result in the following issues.

- Time may be lost as instructions may be misunderstood and jobs may have to be repeated.
- Frustration may develop, as people are not sure of what to do or how to carry out a task.
- Materials may be wasted.
- People may feel left out if communication is not open and effective.
- Messages may be misinterpreted or misunderstood causing bad feelings.
- People's safety may be put at risk.

All of these problems will eventually filter down to existing and potential customers, and when that happens, customer confidence will disappear leading to a possible collapse of the company.

Problems arising from the delivery of materials

Occasionally, problems can arise with the suppliers that deliver plumbing equipment, appliances and materials to site:

- **Resource shortages** – Lack of materials is a big contributing factor when jobs and contracts are not completed on time. When delivery dates are missed, it has a knock-on effect:
  - Operatives are left standing idle.
  - Jobs get behind on time.
  - Completion dates are missed.
  - Customers become annoyed at the lack of progress.

- **Poor quality components** – Many of the components, fittings and appliances used in the plumbing industry are mass-produced. Occasionally, fittings and appliances are delivered to site that have not undergone quality checks and arrive not fit for purpose. This can cost time and money in seeking replacements. Common problems include the following.
  - Appliances such as boilers arrive with faulty components that are only discovered when the appliance is commissioned.
  - Delays occur because bathroom suites often arrive with damage that has occurred during transit or poor quality components or parts missing.
  - Fittings occasionally arrive either of the wrong type or the wrong size.

There are a number of *dos* and *don'ts* to observe when parts, appliances, components and equipment are delivered to site:

- DO check all materials that are delivered whilst the delivery driver is present. Any items that are found that are incorrect can be sent back with the driver and replacements requested immediately.
- DO check ALL items and not just the large ones.
- DO count all items and tick them off against the delivery note.
- DO check all sanitary items for damage. It is very difficult to request replacements after the delivery driver has left site.
- DO keep the delivery note in a safe place.
- DO NOT sign for anything that hasn't been checked against the delivery note.
- DO sign the advice note 'unchecked' if you do not have the time to check all items whilst the delivery driver is present.

Describe handover procedures

When the system has been tested and commissioned, it can then be handed over to the customer. The customer will require all documentation regarding the installation and this should be presented to the customer in a file, which should contain:

- All manufacturers' installation, operation and servicing manuals for the boilers, heat emitters and any other external controls such as motorised zone valves, pumps and temperature/timing controls fitted to the installation.
- The commissioning records and certificates.
- The Building Regulations Compliance certificate.
- An 'as fitted' drawing showing the position of all isolation valves, drain-off valves, strainers, etc and all electrical controls.

The customer must be shown around the system and shown the operating principles of any controls, time clocks and thermostats. Emergency isolation points on the system should be pointed out and a demonstration of the correct isolation procedure in the event of an emergency. Explain to the customer how the systems work and ask if they have any questions. Finally, point out the need for regular servicing of the appliances and leave emergency contact numbers.

Conclusion

A company that employs a plumber of Level 3 standard expects them to be able to undertake at least minor estimation and design techniques and to be able to communicate their findings to the customer. It is also a fact that at some point, a large majority of plumbers will try their hand at self-employment.

During this unit, we have investigated many of the aspects of good system design, estimation and installation that are essential for a Level 3 plumber to have at least a basic knowledge of, as well as discussing good communication techniques.

These are hugely important skills if a plumber is to succeed in business.

Test your knowledge questions

1   What should a plumber consider before designing a plumbing installation?

2   Disabled access is covered by which Approved Document?

3   Briefly describe 'sustainable design'.

4   Briefly describe the aim of British Standards.

5   Which three methods of communication are all written forms?

6   What is the difference between a quotation and an estimate?

7   A hotel has 20 beds and 30 restaurant guests. Calculate the amount of cold water storage required.

8   Where should an accumulator be installed on a cold water system?

9   What is stratification?

10 A roof has a length of 12m, a width of 8m and a height of 4m. Calculate the effective area of the roof.

11 In which two ways can a building gain heat?

12 What are the common pipe arrangements for radiator connections?

13 A hot water storage cylinder has a capacity of 200 litres. The cylinder is required to be at 60°C within 2 hours. The temperature of the incoming water is 4°C. What is the kW required?

14 What are 'statutory cancellation rights'?

15 A well-functioning plumbing system that meets or exceeds the customer's requirements is the result of a number of important aspects. What are they?

16 What scale of drawing is generally used for plans and elevations?

17 Calculate the capacity of a cistern measuring 0.75m × 0.5m × 0.6m.

18 What does excessive velocity + excessive pressure generally create?

19 Calculate the loading units of a cold water installation that contain the following appliances: 2 wash basins, 2 baths, 1 kitchen sink, 2 WCs.

20 If a cistern contains 230 litres and is required to fill in 10 minutes, what is the minimum flow rate through the float-operated valve?

Assessment checklist

What you now know (Learning Outcome)	What you can do (Assessment criteria)	Where this is found (page numbers)
1. Understand how to interpret and present design information	1.1 State the criteria used when selecting system and component types.	2
	1.2 Explain positioning requirements when designing plumbing systems.	5
	1.3 Describe the importance of sustainable design.	6
	1.4 Interpret information for system plans for plumbing.	7
	1.5 State additional considerations when carrying out systems planning.	10
	1.6 Identify measurements from design plans.	11
	1.7 Identify methods for presenting system designs.	15
	1.8 Identify cost of equipment used in plumbing systems using different sources.	15
	1.9 Describe how to compile quotations and tenders.	16
2. Understand how to size plumbing systems and components	2.1 Calculate the size of system pipework.	17
	2.2 Calculate the size of system components.	35
	2.3 Select the size of sanitary pipework using manufacturers' specifications.	53
	2.4 Select the size of rainwater system components using manufacturers' specifications.	58
3. Understand how to calculate the size of central heating system components	3.1 Explain how heat loss from a building occurs.	65
	3.2 State methods for calculating heat loss for buildings.	70
	3.3 Calculate heat loss for rooms.	72
	3.4 Calculate the size of central heating components.	86
4. Understand how to plan work schedules for a system installation	4.1 Identify other trades involved in the installation process.	102
	4.2 Describe effective working relationships between trades.	103
	4.3 Describe the elements of a plumbing system installation schedule for a domestic dwelling.	106
	4.4 Explain the sequence of work in a domestic dwelling plumbing system installation.	106
	4.5 Describe difficulties that may arise when supervising system installations.	109
	4.6 Describe handover procedures.	113

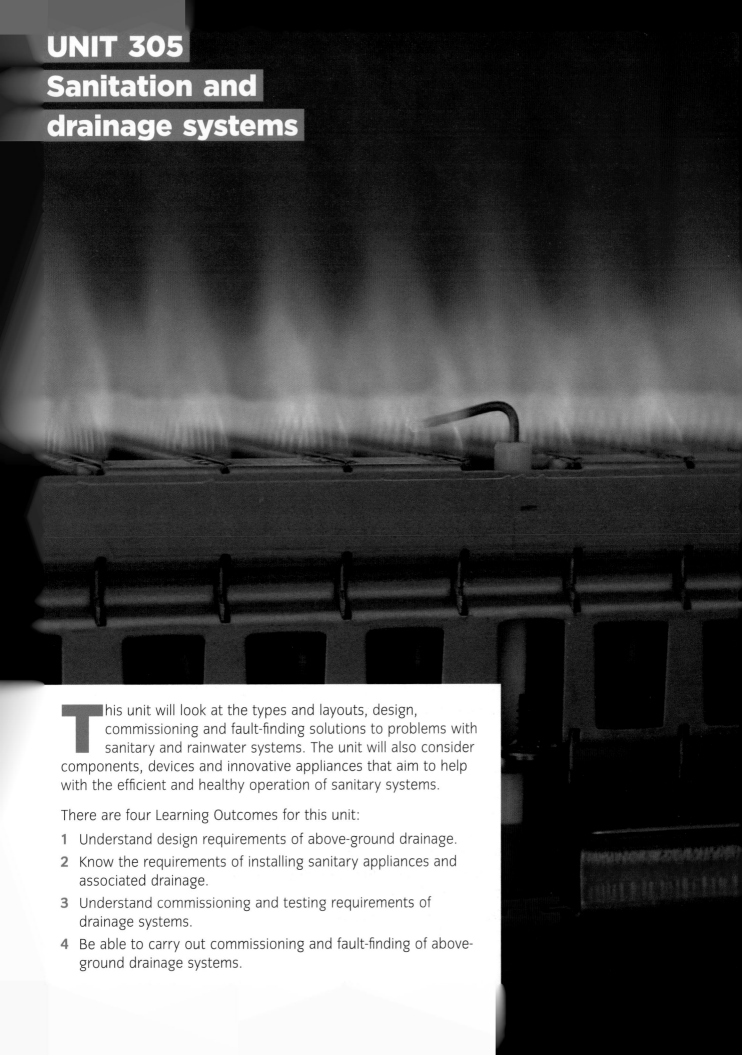

UNIT 305
Sanitation and drainage systems

This unit will look at the types and layouts, design, commissioning and fault-finding solutions to problems with sanitary and rainwater systems. The unit will also consider components, devices and innovative appliances that aim to help with the efficient and healthy operation of sanitary systems.

There are four Learning Outcomes for this unit:

1 Understand design requirements of above-ground drainage.
2 Know the requirements of installing sanitary appliances and associated drainage.
3 Understand commissioning and testing requirements of drainage systems.
4 Be able to carry out commissioning and fault-finding of above-ground drainage systems.

Design requirements of above-ground drainage systems (LO1)

There are seven assessment criteria for these outcomes:

1 State documents relating to sanitation and above-ground drainage systems and components.
2 Identify different types of above-ground drainage system types.
3 Explain the reasons for selecting above-ground drainage system types.
4 Describe design specifications of waste pipes.
5 Describe the design considerations of stub stacks.
6 Describe the operation of an air admittance valve.
7 Explain the benefits of waste valves (mechanical traps) compared with traditional water seal traps.

Drainage design to the European Code of BS EN 12056

Equilibrium

In this instance, this term relates to keeping the air pressure even within a sanitary system so that any negative pressure or pressure fluctuation does not cause the trap seal to be lost and allow the ingress of foul air into a building.

SmartScreen Unit 305

PowerPoint 1

A plumber talking with a customer

The daily work of plumbers can involve work on both domestic and commercial sanitary installations and the correct sizing of discharge pipework is essential to maintain the **equilibrium** of the traps within the building and prevent the ingress of foul smells through loss of trap seals. When designing a sanitary system it is important to discuss the customer's needs to try to find ways to incorporate them into the pipework installation. The building layout may pose problems with the customer's design proposals, but usually these can be overcome with careful planning in accordance with the current standards and regulations. Feedback to the customer about proposed options or variations to the original design at the outset of any work is essential, as changes later can be costly and could lead to disputes.

A full survey of a proposed job is essential to ascertain what type of system would be suitable. A visual check to establish the condition and design of an existing system may show that it does not comply with the current standards. For example, if a waste pipe discharged into a hopper that was located under a kitchen window then new pipework would have to be installed and then rerouted. In addition, there could be problems with the previous workmanship, such as poor gradients from appliances causing backflow or loss of trap seal because of very long pipe runs. All remedial work must be carried out along with any new installations so that the system complies with the standards and regulations.

An example of poor practice of pipework installation

Presenting design calculations and quotes

When a Level 3 plumber is qualified they may be given the opportunity to discuss pricing for jobs in more detail. In addition, if they had to supplement a basic written quotation for work with drawings, they would take the form of well drawn but not-to-scale drawings, unless the customer specifically requested more specific to-scale drawings.

The name, address and contact details of the company proposing to do the work should be clearly stated on any quotation as well as the customer's name and address. If the company is part of any trade specification professional bodies such as the Chartered Institute of Plumbing and Heating Engineering (CIPHE) then this should be included in the quote.

The make and model of the appliances and the fittings should be clearly identified on a quotation. The start and end dates for a quoted job could be attached in writing along with any advance warnings of when appliances are likely to be out of service and for how long.

It is advisable for a plumber to be part of a certification scheme when installing new sanitary systems or when extending an existing system, eg a bathroom. If they are not a member then they will have to inform the local authority before they begin their work.

Regulations and standards

Each part of the Building Regulations is identified by a letter and sometimes by the addition of a number after the letter.

- **The Building Regulations Approved Document H** – Deals with the following:

    H1 Foul water drainage

    H2 Waste water treatment systems

    H3 Rainwater drainage

    H4 Building over sewers

    H5 Separate systems of drainage

    H6 Solid waste storage.

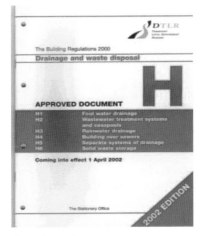

Document H

- **Approved Document F** – Gives information on ventilation requirements for dwellings and states that there shall be an intermittent rate of extraction of 15l/s for a bathroom. It also gives guidance on ventilation requirements for walk-in wetrooms.

- **Approved Document G** – Covers hygiene for sanitary conveniences and washing facilities. It also includes bathrooms and section three deals with hot water.

There are five parts to this British Standard which offer guidance and advice:

Part 1   General information and performance requirements

Part 2   Sanitary pipework including layout calculations

Part 3   Roof drainage and layout calculations

Part 4   Waste water lifting plant

Part 5   Installation and testing, instructions for operation maintenance and use.

The different types of systems (BS EN 12056 Part 2)

Soil stack systems re BS EN 12056

SmartScreen Unit 305

Outcome 1 PowerPoints

System I – Single stack system with partly filled branch discharge pipes

This means the sanitary appliances are connected to partly filled branch discharge pipes which are designed with a filling degree of 0.5 (50%) and are connected to a single discharge stack. **System I is based on German, Swiss and Austrian practice.**

System II – Single discharge stack with small-bore discharge branch pipes

This is where sanitary appliances are connected to small discharge pipes. The small-bore discharge pipes are designed with a filling degree of 0.7 (70%) and are then connected to a single discharge stack. **System II is based on Scandinavian practice.**

System III – Single stack system with full-bore branch discharge pipes

Here sanitary appliances are connected to full-bore discharge pipes. The full-bore branch discharge pipes are designed with a filling degree of 1.0 (100%) and each branch discharge pipe is separately connected to a single discharge stack. **System III is based on UK practice.**

System IV – Separate discharge stack system

Drainage systems types I, II and III may also be divided into a black water stack serving WCs and urinals and a grey water stack serving other appliances. **System IV is based on French practice.**

Ventilation of sanitary systems

For any sanitary system to work efficiently the equilibrium of the trap seal must be maintained to prevent trap seals being lost due to negative pressure or pressure fluctuations.

There are four types of sanitation system used in the UK:

- Primary ventilated stack system
- Secondary ventilated stack system
- Ventilated branch discharge system
- Stub stack.

> **KEY POINT**
>
> On a primary ventilated stack system the soil pipe also acts as the ventilation pipe, hence the name soil and vent pipe (SVP).

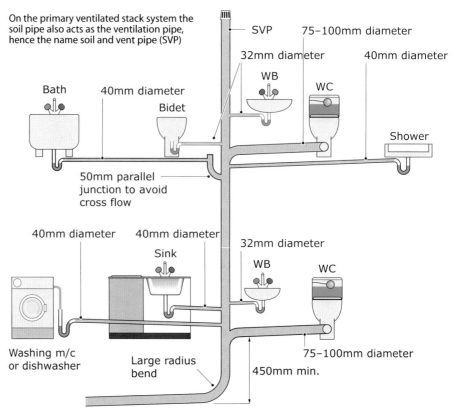

On the primary ventilated stack system the soil pipe also acts as the ventilation pipe, hence the name soil and vent pipe (SVP)

SVP

75–100mm diameter

32mm diameter

40mm diameter

Bath

WB

WC

40mm diameter

Bidet

Shower

50mm parallel junction to avoid cross flow

40mm diameter

40mm diameter

32mm diameter

Sink

WB

WC

Washing m/c or dishwasher

Large radius bend

75–100mm diameter

450mm min.

Primary ventilated stack system

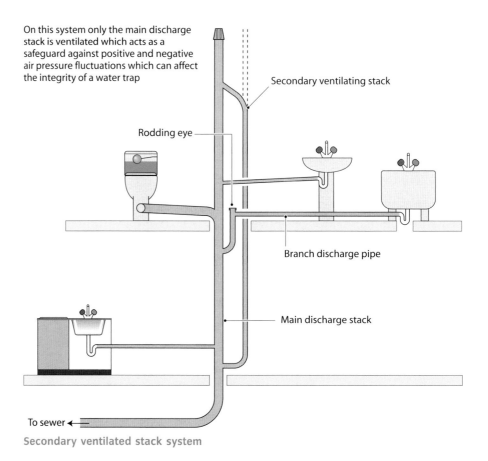

On this system only the main discharge stack is ventilated which acts as a safeguard against positive and negative air pressure fluctuations which can affect the integrity of a water trap

Secondary ventilating stack

Rodding eye

Branch discharge pipe

Main discharge stack

To sewer

Secondary ventilated stack system

Water trap seals are protected from induced or self-siphonage because a branch ventlating branch pipe is located not more than 750mm from any appliance

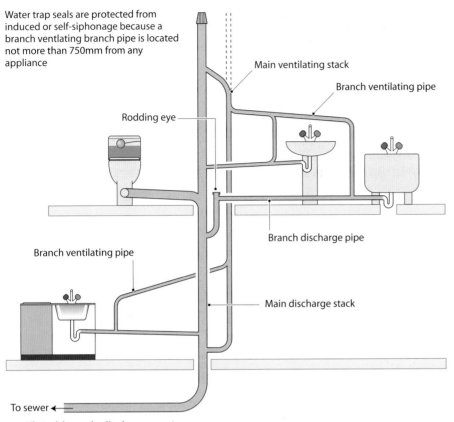

Main ventilating stack

Branch ventilating pipe

Rodding eye

Branch discharge pipe

Branch ventilating pipe

Main discharge stack

To sewer ◄

Ventilated branch discharge system

Ventilation is required if the highest connection of an appliance from the invert from the drain exceeds 2 metres or if the distance between the crown of the WC connection and the drain inverts exceeds 1.3 metres

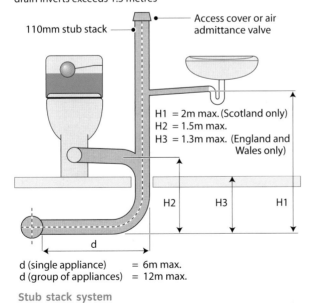

Access cover or air admittance valve

110mm stub stack

H1 = 2m max. (Scotland only)
H2 = 1.5m max.
H3 = 1.3m max. (England and Wales only)

H2   H3   H1

d

d (single appliance)   = 6m max.
d (group of appliances) = 12m max.

Stub stack system

Primary ventilated stack system

The design of this system means that no separate ventilation pipes are required, but this can only be achieved by following the guidelines laid down in BS EN 12056:

- All sanitary appliances must be closely grouped to the discharge stack.

- All appliances, as far as possible, should be fitted with a P trap or a waste pipe valve, with a discharge pipe diameter equal to that of the trap. Bends and branches should be avoided and the gradient must be kept to a minimum, normally 5° per metre is sufficient.

- The vertical discharge stack must be installed as straight as possible and incorporate 2 × 45° bends or a long radius bend at its base, with a radius twice the diameter of the pipe. It is important that knuckle bends should not be used as they can cause compression.

Close grouping of appliances is achieved by adhering to the pipework dimensions and distances from appliance to soil stack

Dimensions and distances of appliances and waste pipework from the soil stack	
32mm waste	1.7m
40mm waste	3.0m
50mm waste	4.0m
100mm waste	6.0m

Waste pipes
All of the measurements above will be drastically reduced if bends are introduced to change direction or the gradient on the branch discharge pipework is too steep

When designing remember that for every 1m³ of water utilised 30m³ of air is required to maintain equilibrium within the system

Primary ventilated stack system

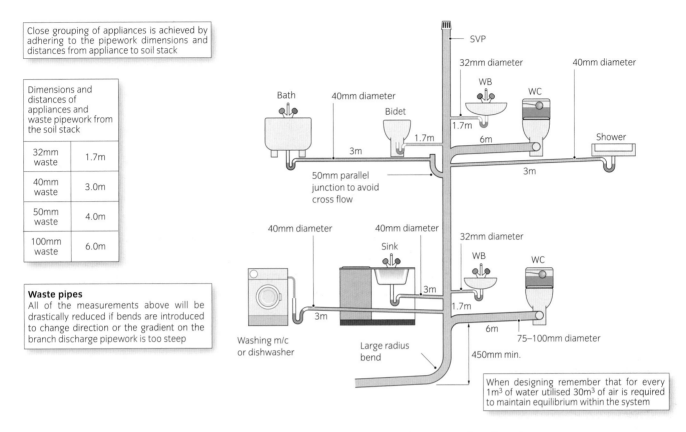

Close grouping of appliances is achieved by adhering to the pipework dimensions and distances from appliance to soil stack

Dimensions and distances of appliances and waste pipework from the soil stack	
32mm waste	1.7m
40mm waste	3.0m
50mm waste	4.0m
100mm waste	6.0m

Waste pipes
All of the measurements above will be drastically reduced if bends are introduced to change direction or the gradient on the branch discharge pipework is too steep

When designing remember that for every 1m³ of water utilised 30m³ of air is required to maintain equilibrium within the system

The maximum branch pipework diameters, lengths, gradients and trap seals on a ventilated stack system

Whenever the pipe lengths shown in the table below are exceeded the waste pipe diameter should be increased to the next size up.

Branch connections

Pipe size	Maximum length	Approximate gradient
32mm	1.7 m	22mm/m
32mm	1.1 m	44mm/m
32mm	0.7 m	87mm/m
40mm	3.0 m	18–80mm/m
50mm	4.0 m	18–80mm/m
100mm	6.0 m	mimimum 18mm/m

The effects of gradient on sanitary pipework

By using the graph it can be seen that the gradient changes to 44mm corresponds with reduced branch pipework length.

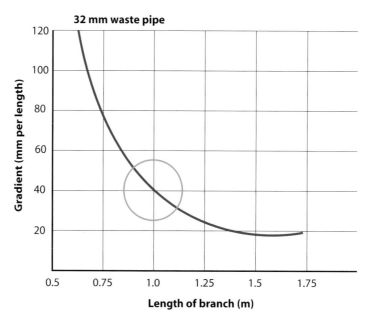

Gradient graph for wash basin

The graph above shows that whenever the fall (gradient) of the pipe is increased then the length of the waste pipe is reduced accordingly.

Appliance	Diameter (mm)	Max. pipe length (m)	Pipe gradient mm per m run	Max. number of bends	Max. drop (m) vertical pipe
Wash basin or bidet	32	1.7	18–22	None[1]	None
	32	1.1	18–44	None[1]	None
	32	0.7	18–87	None[1]	None
	40	3.0	18–44	2[1]	None
Bath or shower	40	3.0[2]	18–90	No limit	1.5
Kitchen sink	40	3.0[2]	18–90	No limit	1.5
Domestic washing m/c or dishwasher	40	3.0	18–44	No limit	1.5
WC with outlet up to 80mm diameter	75	No limit	18 min.	No limit[4]	1.5
WC with outlet over 80mm diameter	100	No limit	18 min.	No limit[4]	1.5
Bowl urinal [4]	40	3.0[3]	18–90	No limit[4]	1.5
Trough urinal	50	3.0[3]	18–90	No limit[4]	1.5
Slab urinal [5]	65	3.0[3]	18–90	No limit[4]	1.5
Food waste disposal unit [6]	40 min.	3.0[3]	135 min.	No limit[4]	1.5
Sanitary towel disposal unit	40 min.	3.0[3]	54 min·	No limit[4]	1.5
Floor drain	50–100	3.0[3]	18 min.	No limit	1.5
Branch serving 2 to 4 wash basins	50	4.0	18–44	None	None
Branch serving several bowl urinals[4]	50	3.0[3]	18–90	No limit[4]	1.5
Branch serving 2 to 8 WCs	100	15.0	9–90 (21.5)	2	1.5
Up to 5 wash basins with spray taps[7]	32	4.5[3]	18–44	No limit[4]	None

Notes:
1. Excluding the 'connection bend' fitted directly or close to the trap outlet.
2. If no longer than 3m, this may result in noisy discharge, and there will be an increased risk of blockage.
3. Should ideally be as short as possible to limit deposition problems.
4. Sweep bends should be used: not 'knuckle' bends.
5. For up to 7 people: longer slabs should have more than one outlet.
6. Includes small potato-peeling machines.
7. Wash basins must not be fitted with outlet plugs.

BS EN 12056 – maximum permissible pipe lengths

Calculating the size of sanitary pipework in accordance with BS EN 12056

See pages 53–58 in Unit 302.

Self-sealing waterless waste valves

A self-sealing valve is a waterless valve that uses a thin neoprene rubber membrane to create an airtight seal, stopping foul air from entering the dwelling and maintaining equal pressure within the soil and vent systems.

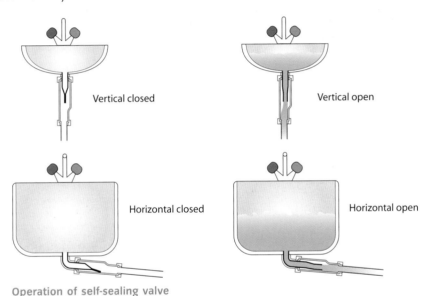

Vertical closed

Vertical open

Horizontal closed

Horizontal open

Operation of self-sealing valve

Self-sealing valve

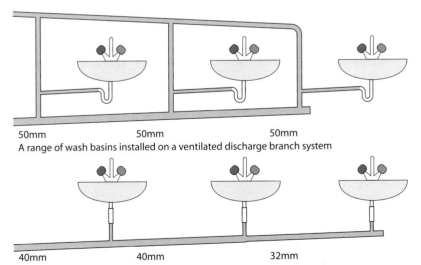

50mm   50mm   50mm
A range of wash basins installed on a ventilated discharge branch system

40mm   40mm   32mm
The same installation using self-sealing valves
There are no ventilation pipes and the main waste pipe is of smaller diameter

Multiple installations of self-sealing valves

The membrane opens under the pressure of water from an appliance, closing again when the water discharge has finished.

It is so effective that it can be used safely on primary ventilated stack systems and ventilated discharge branch systems. A self-sealing valve has certain advantages over a conventional trap:

SmartScreen Unit 305
Worksheet 1

- The valve removes the problems associated with negative pressure within a system by opening to allow air in, in much the same way as an air admittance valve. This creates a state of equilibrium within the system and means that air admittance valves and extra vent pipes are not required.

- Because there is no water in the valve, the problems of self-siphonage and induced siphonage are eliminated.

- The valve operates silently. This eliminates the noises generally associated with water-filled traps.

Requirements of installing sanitary appliances and associated drainage (LO2)

There are seven assessment criteria for this outcome:

1 Identify types of urinals.
2 Describe installation considerations of urinals.
3 Explain the spacing requirements of sanitary appliances.
4 Interpret documents relating to disabled accommodation.
5 Explain the importance of ventilation in bathrooms.
6 Describe design considerations of macerators.
7 Explain installation considerations of sink waste disposal units.

SmartScreen Unit 305
PowerPoint 2

Air admittance valves and their importance in above ground pipework systems

There are alternative ways to allow air into a system and devices called air admittance valves are installed on various systems to achieve this. The British Standard for air admittance valves is BS EN 12380.

An air admittance valve (AAV) is a device fitted to the top of sanitary pipework which allows air into a system but does not allow foul smells to escape. Its purpose is to keep the equilibrium of the water trap's seal and balance out of any suction effects, which could draw the water out of the trap. The mechanism of the AAV returns to the closed position after it has been opened by negative pressure created within the stack.

An AAV enables ventilating pipes to be terminated inside the building which eliminates the need for a vent pipe to penetrate a roof and therefore allows flexibility in the design of new installations and when adding to existing drainage systems. AAVs are not a substitute for a ventilation stack. Wherever an AAV is installed, the system at some stage must also have a vent stack to outside air.

There are some points to consider when installing AAVs, such as ensuring that underground foul drainage is always ventilated and that a ventilating pipe is provided at or near the head of each main drain.

In addition, an open ventilating pipe without any AAV should always be provided on any drain fitted with an intercepting trap, especially on a sealed system or on any drain that could be subject to surcharge.

Ventilating pipe in situ

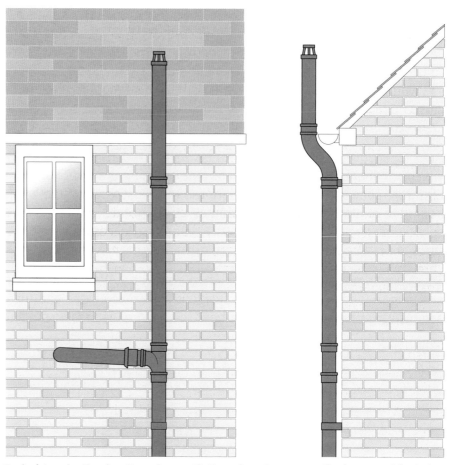

Typical termination locations for ventilating pipes to prevent the ingress of foul air into a building

AAVs should not be used when a soil stack provides the only ventilation to a septic tank or to a cesspool. An air admittance valve should not be considered where there is no open ventilation on an existing drainage system or through any connected drains. In this situation the plumber should research other ways to relieve positive pressures.

Air admittance valves should not usually be used outside because of the risk of moisture in the air settling on the unit and freezing, causing the components to stick in either the open or closed position. However, companies are now developing products that can be used externally. Because the world of plumbing is constantly evolving, and building designs and costs drive the need for new solutions in new and existing installations, there are always new ideas and products on the market. The company FloPlast™ has created an air admittance valve which can be installed externally and has been designed for push-fit installation directly into 110mm UK designated pipe. An EDPM finned seal makes up a push-fit connection and it can be removed to provide a secondary **rodding point**. These units are designed for use on discharge stacks up to 45 metres or 10 storeys high with an airflow capacity that equals 43 litres/sec. As with most AAVs, the AX110 must be installed in a vertical position and with the usual minimum of 200mm above the highest branch connection. Preferably, it should be located in a non-habitable space, such as a duct or roof. The space should have adequate ventilation and be accessible for maintenance.

Air admittance valves should be removable to give access for clearance of blockages. It is therefore important that if an AAV is boxed in, it must be installed in a way that allows access. In addition, vents should be included in the design, as well as an access port. Care should be taken to ensure that AAVs are not installed in dust-laden atmospheres as fibres and lint in the atmosphere could block up air filters and cause the unit to fail.

These valves can also help indicate the probability of blockages within the drainage system by showing evidence of high water levels in WC bowls following flushing and the consequent slow drainage of appliances located upstream from the suspected blockage. An AAV should therefore always be installed above the flood level of the highest appliance in an installation.

Kinetic ram guns should not be used to remove blockages on sanitary pipework where air admittance valves are fitted. The excessive pressure created by the action of the gun and the resulting back pressure could cause a malfunction with the mechanism of the AAV.

Rodding point

A place where the drain or section of drain can be accessed to clear blockages.

Kinetic ram guns

A device that uses a pump action to create compressed air which is discharged down sanitary pipework to remove blockages.

A kinetic ram gun

At the design and installation stage it is worth noting that sizes, limitations and the use of air admittance valves are subject to national and local regulations and practice. It is good practice to consult in advance with the building control officer (BCO) at the local authority building control office.

Plumber in discussion with building control officer on site

The BS EN 12380 A1 rating of the valve means that it can be located below the flood level of the appliances being vented. It is important to note that this component should not be used as the sole ventilation to a septic tank or cesspool.

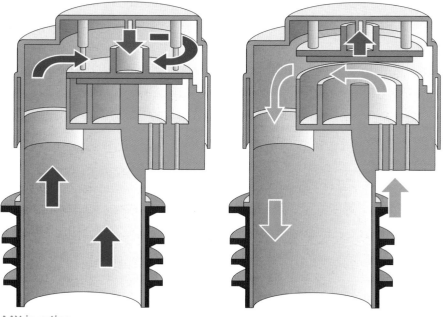

AAV in action

An air admittance valve provides a means of ventilation to the drainage system under conditions of reduced pressure when ventilating pipes are terminated inside buildings in accordance with BS EN 12056-2:2000.

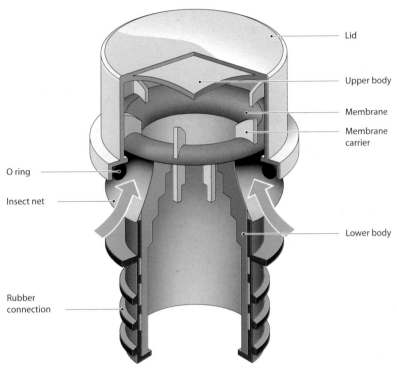

Lid

Upper body

Membrane

Membrane carrier

O ring

Insect net

Lower body

Rubber connection

Cutaway of AAV

The image above shows how an AAV functions and the arrows show the flow of air.

The valve incorporates a sealing diaphragm which lifts and allows air to be drawn into the system when it is subjected to negative pressure. Once the negative pressure has ceased, the diaphragm returns to the closed position thereby preventing the escape of foul air into the building. Some AAVs have a spring to return the diaphragm to the closed position. The valve is designed to open and close spontaneously when required thereby allowing a supply of air to adequately ventilate the system to ensure a smooth discharge.

AAV installation in multi-dwelling houses

If AAVs are to be fitted then the following rules apply:

1 One stack in five must be ventilated to the atmosphere and this should be located at the head or at the start of the drain run.

2 Up to four properties of up to three storeys can use AAVs.

3 Where a drain serves more than four properties with AAVs, such as on a multi-dwelling housing estate, then the following applies:

- If there are 5–10 buildings then ventilation is required at the head and the foot of the drain.

- If there are 11–20 buildings then ventilation is required at the head and at the midpoint of the drain.

4 All multi-storey buildings will require additional ventilation if more than one property is connected to a drain which is not ventilated by a conventional discharge stack.

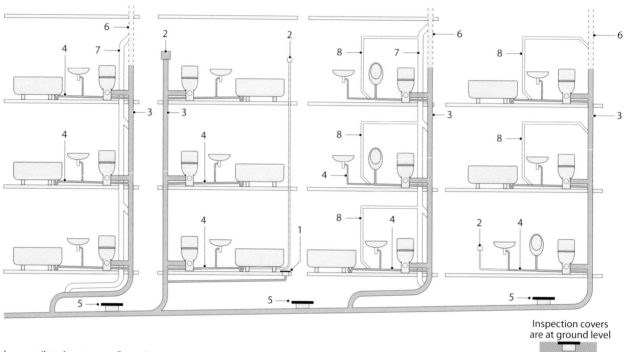

Inspection covers are at ground level

Secondary ventilated system configuration

1. Floor gully	2. Air admittance valve	3. Stack	4. Branch discharge pipe
5. Drain lid (mid and ground level)	6. Stack vent	7. Ventilating stack	8. Branch ventilating pipe

Illustrations demonstrating the installation variations for air admittance valves

Control of pressure in the discharge stack is achieved by use of separate ventilating stacks and/or secondary branch ventilating pipes in connection with stack vents. Alternatively, air admittance valves may be used.

The different types of AAV and their applications

There are many different applications and pipe sizes for AAVs which give the plumber a variety of options when specifying and installing. The following images and descriptions show the variety of options.

Type of AAV	Application
	This type of AAV will typically be located at the top of a vertical soil and vent pipe. A 110mm soil pipe with dual-fit synthetic rubber finger seal outlet for 3" /75mm or 4" /110mm pipe, 4" /110mm pipe-push over rubber seal, 3" /75mm pipe-push into rubber seal.

Type of AAV	Application
	An AAV with solvent weld outlet for 4" /110mm pipe.
	This versatile type of AAV is fitted with a dual-fit synthetic rubber finger seal outlet for 3" /75mm or 4" /110mm pipe. Also, it incorporates a 2" universal outlet 4" /110mm pipe-push over rubber seal 3" /75mm pipe.
	This unit has a 2" compression outlet.
	A solvent weld outlet for 1½" or 2" BS EN 1329-1:2000 solvent weld waste pipe.
	The screw thread on the outlet for this device allows a connection to a BSP 1½" socket.
	A compression tee incorporating a small AAV.

URINALS

Urinals are fitted in non-domestic buildings and come in three different styles:

■ **Bowl urinals** – Usually made of vitreous china and stainless steel, these are the most commonly used urinal type and the easiest to install. Dividers may be placed between the urinal bowls to give a little privacy. The bowl should be fixed at around 600mm from the floor to the front lip. This can be reduced for urinals installed in schools.

Bowl urinal

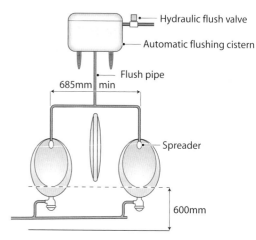

Bowl urinal layout

Stainless steel trough urinal

Slab urinal

■ **Trough urinals** – These are generally made from stainless steel and installed where the risk of vandalism is high. The trough should be sized according to the number of people that are expected to use it and they are, therefore, available in different lengths. The trough has a waste connection, and the trough floor has a built-in slight fall to allow the urinal to be installed level.

■ **Slab urinals** – This type of urinal is manufactured from fireclay and is assembled on site. The channel in the base of the urinal is laid to a slight fall and the waste connection is made directly to the drain via the channel into a trapped gully.

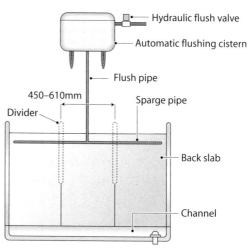

Slab urinal layout

Flushing the urinal

The Water Regulations state that urinals may be flushed with either:

- a manual or automatically operated cistern
- a pressure flushing valve directly connected to a supply or distributing pipe, which is designed to flush the urinal either directly (manually) or automatically, provided that the flushing arrangement incorporates a backflow arrangement or device appropriate to fluid category 5 (see Schedule 2, Paragraph 15).

Clause G25.13 states:

'Where manually or automatically operated pressure flushing valves are used for flushing urinals, the flushing valve should deliver a flush volume not exceeding 1.5 litres per bowl per position each time the device is operated.'

The automatic flushing cistern

As the name suggests, automatic flushing cisterns use an automatic flushing siphon to flush the urinals automatically when the water reaches a predetermined level in the cistern. The Water Regulations stipulate that any auto-flushing cistern must not exceed the following water volumes:

- 10 litres per hour for a single bowl or stall
- 7.5 litres per hour per urinal position for a cistern serving two or more urinal bowls or 700mm of slab.

The maximum flow rate from any automatic flushing cistern must be regulated by the inflow of water from the cold supply. This can be done quite easily by the use of urinal flush control valves such as a hydraulic flush control valve fitted to the incoming water supply. The hydraulic flush control valve allows a certain amount of water through to the cistern when other appliances like taps and WCs are used, rather than have a constant supply of water dripping into the cistern. The sudden reduction in pressure on the mains supply opens the valve to allow a certain amount of water through. The amount of water can be varied depending on the installation requirements and number of urinals. The idea is to prevent the urinals flushing when the building is not being used, thus saving on wasted water.

The flushing valve

This is a new method of flushing a urinal that involves the use of a valve, which can either be manual or automatic, that delivers a short 1.5-litre flush to an individual urinal bowl. The water can be supplied either direct from the water main, from a boosted cold water system or at low pressure from a cistern supplied by a distribution pipe.

KEY POINT

When the level of the water reaches the top of the dome, the head of water at point A becomes greater than the pressure at point B. The water pressure in the trap (point C) overcomes the air pressure inside the siphon and this initiates siphonic action, emptying the cistern.

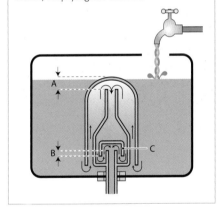

Hydraulic flush control valve

Manual flushing valve

Manual valves are lever-operated and are located just above the urinal bowl. Automatic valves are activated via an infrared sensor, which senses the presence of a person. The sensor must 'see' the person for at least 10 seconds to prevent accidental activation by someone walking by. The sensor activates a solenoid valve and this allows the minimum short flush. Automatic flushing valves require a backflow prevention device to be included, which prevents backflow of a fluid category 5 contaminated water.

The statutory requirements for the provision of sanitary facilities and equipment in dwellings for the disabled

Section 0 of the Approved Building Regulation Document M's aim is to ensure that buildings are accessible to and usable by everyone, regardless of disability, age or gender. Everyone should be able to gain access to buildings and use their facilities, both as visitors and as people who live and work in them. In addition everyone should be able to use sanitary conveniences in the principal storey of a new building.

The application of Document M relates to a non-domestic building or a dwelling that is newly erected, when an existing non-domestic building is extended or undergoes a material alteration or if an existing building or part of an existing building undergoes a material change of use. This includes a hotel, boarding house, institution, public building or shop.

Plumbers will often be asked to install a Doc M pack into a building, which means that by the addition of bars and levers the sanitary equipment can easily be used by people with physical impairments.

Spacing requirements in bathrooms

When installing bathroom appliances, consideration must be made to allow for the minimum space requirements for each appliance for personal use and to supervise the bathing of children. British Standard BS 6456-2:1996 gives advice on these space requirements.

There must also be a minimum number of appliances within a dwelling based on the number of people occupying the property and this information is detailed in BS 6465-1:2006+A1:2009.

Sanitary appliances	Number per dwelling	Additional notes
WC	1 for up to 4 people 2 for 5 people or more	There should be a wash basin adjacent to every WC in every property
Wash basin	1	
Bath or shower	1 for every 4 people	
Kitchen sink	1	

Chart to show appliances required per dwelling

It is not always possible to achieve the recommended dimensions especially when dealing with small bathrooms. The British Standards have therefore made allowances for overlaps of the appliance space. These overlaps also apply to a cloakroom and a downstairs WC.

SmartScreen Unit 305

Worksheet 4

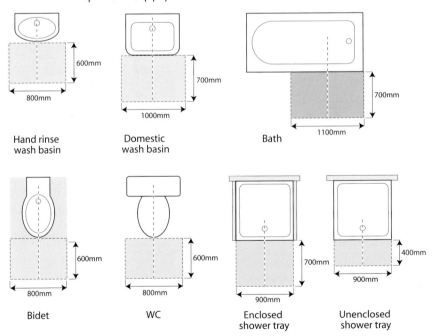

Diagram to show provision of space in sanitary installations

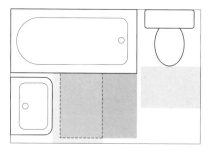

In this layout, the activity space of both the bath and the wash basin overlap. The space for the WC usage is not affected.

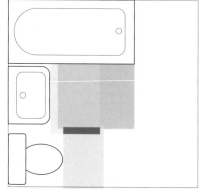

In this layout, the activity space of the bath, wash hand basin and WC all overlap. The overlap is shown by the red rectangle on the drawing.

This one is the most common of all bathroom layouts.

Overlap – provision in bathrooms

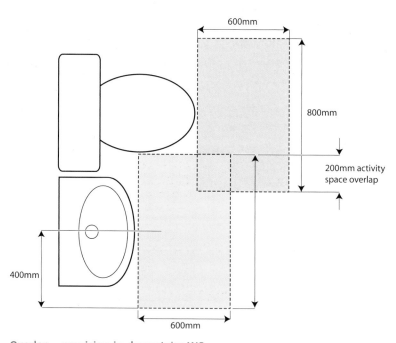

Overlap – provision in downstairs WC

Ventilation in bathrooms

It is important when designing bathroom or toilet accommodation that Building Regulation Approved Document Part F (Scottish Government Building Regulations Guide to Ventilation in Scotland) should be complied with. Part F refers to the ventilation of sanitary accommodation which is a necessity for all rooms containing a sanitary appliance. Ventilation helps prevent damp and bacteria growth and ensures air quality. It may be provided naturally through an opening window, or by mechanical means. Any window in toilet accommodation should have an opening of ⅟₂₀ of the floor area of the room, with at least some part of the ventilation being 1.75m above floor level. Windows should also be able to provide background ventilation such as trickle ventilators.

WC macerators

Macerators offer the plumber many options when installing sanitary appliances in remote locations. They also offer a solution where access to the main soil stack is not practical from a conventional gravity outlet appliance. However, if a WC macerator is installed Building Regulation Part G requires that there must also be a gravity WC located in the same building.

WC macerator

G1

Section 1

SANITARY CONVENIENCES AND WASHING FACILITIES

Number, type and siting of appliances

1.1 Any dwelling (house, flat or maisonette) should have at least one closet and one wash-basin. A house in multi-occupation (a house in which the occupants do not form part of a single household) should have at least the same provision as a dwelling and the provision should be accessible to all the occupants.

1.2 A space containing a closet or urinal should be separated by a door from a space used for the preparation of food (including a kitchen and any space in which washing up is done).

1.3 Washbasins should be located in the room containing the closet, or in a room or space giving direct access to the room containing the closet (provided it is not used for the preparation of food) or in a room adjacent to the room containing the closet in the case of a dwelling.

a branch pipe to a discharge stack or a drain (see Approved Document for requirement H1 Sanitary pipework and drainage for guidance on provision for traps, branch discharge pipes, discharge stacks and foul drains).

1.10 A closet fitted with a macerator and pump may be connected to a small bore branch discharge pipe discharging to a discharge stack if:

a. there is also access to a closet discharging directly to a gravity system, and

b. the macerator and pump small bore drainage system is the subject of a current European Technical Approval issued by a member body of the European Organisation for Technical Approvals e.g. the British Board of Agrément and the conditions of use are in accordance with the terms of that document.

1.11 A washbasin should discharge through a grating, a trap and a branch discharge pipe to a discharge stack or may, where the washbasin is located on the ground floor, discharge into a gully or direct to a drain.

Building Regulation Part G

Building Regulation Part G

Gravity fall from appliances

A pump/macerator unit does not suck in the incoming waste, which means that the waste water has to enter the unit by gravity. This is especially important when installing a low trap item such as a shower. If, for example, the fall from the inlet pipe into the Saniflo macerator unit is not sufficient, less than 1:40, then problems such as backing up of soil water could occur in the shower tray. It is therefore important to check the installation instructions for each unit for the minimum height of shower traps above the floor level.

Vertical rise of outlet pipework

It is important always to run any vertical outlet pipe as near as possible to the Saniflo macerator unit outlet connection. This is to ensure the optimum discharge capability through the outlet pipework. This is important because a long horizontal run adds unwanted frictional loss and resistance to the mechanical pumping operation of the appliance.

The outlet pipework must rise at least 300mm before any horizontal pipework is fitted.

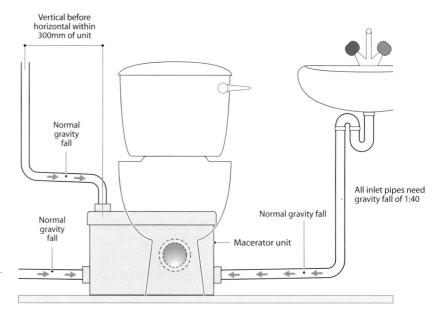

Vertical rise of outlet pipework

Discharge pipework

- Copper pipe or plastic solvent weld pipes are both suitable for the discharge pipework of a Saniflo macerator installation.

- If plastic piping is used it should be the solvent weld type and not push-fit. A continuous pipe such as Hep$_2$O can be used, but it is important to ensure that it is regularly supported to avoid any sagging or dipping in the pipe run, which could lead to poor performance.

For many of the Saniflo models a 22mm discharge is suitable. However, if a horizontal run exceeds approximately 10–12 metres, it is then advisable to increase the bore size of the pipework to 32mm. This will allow for easier drainage of the pipe.

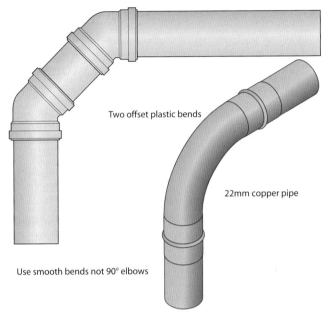

Two offset plastic bends

22mm copper pipe

Use smooth bends not 90° elbows

Discharge pipework

Changes of direction on outlet pipework

- Always use smooth bends and not knuckle type 90° elbows.
- If using copper, you can machine pull bends as this creates less frictional resistance.
- If using plastic solvent weld pipework then use two 45° bends in series to achieve the 90°.
- If using plastic, ensure you wipe off any excess solvent cement.
- Always remember to deburr any edges carefully to prevent the build-up of effluent at that point.
- Failure to observe these points could result in a narrowing of the pipe bore which will inevitably lead to blockages in the future.

Discharge pipe underground to a manhole

Copper or plastic pipes are suitable for above ground and underground installations provided the following criteria are adhered to:

- The 1:200 minimum fall is correctly laid.
- The ground above it is not subject to heavy wheel loads.
- The pipe is insulated to protect against frost.
- Where laid within 450mm of ground level, either a concrete casing or paving slab cover is protecting the pipe.

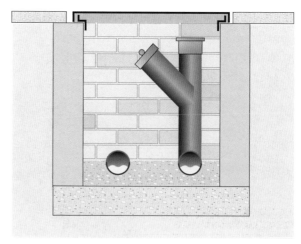

Below-ground connections

Installation options for a Saniflo macerator unit

It is normal practice to site the macerator unit directly behind the WC, taking care not to jam it against the pan itself. It is, however, possible to site the Saniflo a short distance further back (for example on the other side of the wall) by using an extension such as a Multikwik™ connector. In this situation, the extension should be no more than 150–200mm long. Extensions longer than this tend to attract blockages. Always check for leaks at joints. Never install the Saniflo unit underneath the floor.

Many installers tend to hide the cistern and Saniflo unit behind panels for aesthetic reasons. If this is the case always check that the macerator unit is accessible for removal for future maintenance. Full access to the jubilee clips securing the inlet and outlet pipework is also required.

Extended connections to the Saniflo

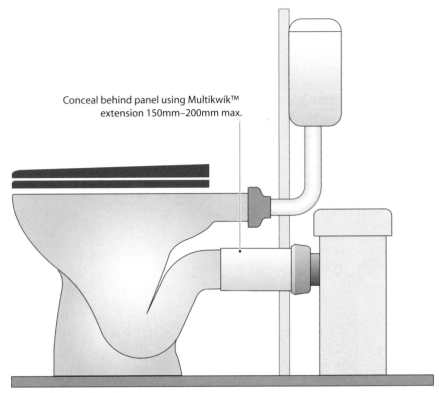

Conceal behind panel using Multikwik™ extension 150mm–200mm max.

Connections to Saniflow

Electrical connections

The correct way to make the electrical connection is with an unswitched fused connector fitted with a 5 amp fuse. The connection can be to a spur which is connected off a ring main circuit. The various Saniflo macerator units have motor load ratings from about 300 watts to 750 watts. Safe isolation is essential if you are working on any electrical appliance.

FUSE

Connect with unswitched fused spur with 5 amp fuse

Fused spur

Basic principles of operation

The principle of a macerator is as follows: a sealed plastic receptacle unit is attached to the horizontal outlet of a WC pan and the other to waste connections. Inside the unit is housed a motor and a pump. When the unit receives amounts of waste from basins or sinks or solids from a WC, a switch senses the new level of water entering the unit and in turn sends a signal for the rotating motor to operate.

The motor has stainless steel blades attached to the rotating spindle which breaks up any solids entering the macerating drum area. This transformed mass is then positively pumped to an outlet at the higher part of the unit and then into a vertical pipe, which after a minimum height then runs horizontally with a fall of a minimum of 1:200 to a soil stack.

Mechanical sequence of operation

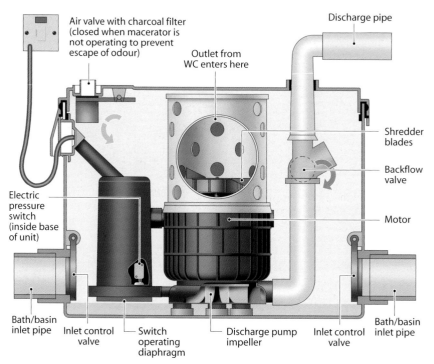

Macerator in starting position

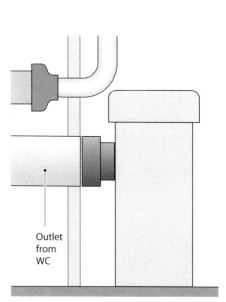

Side view of macerator unit

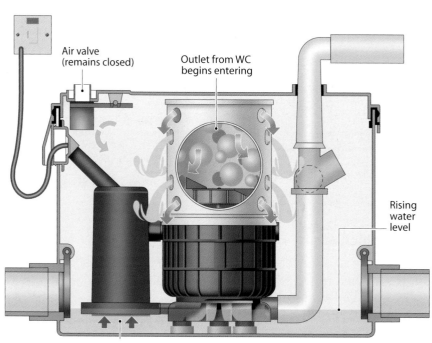

Macerator process beginning as toilet discharges

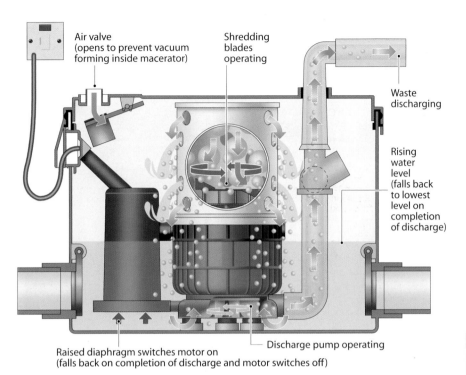

Air valve
(opens to prevent vacuum
forming inside macerator)

Shredding
blades
operating

Waste
discharging

Rising
water
level
(falls back
to lowest
level on
completion
of discharge)

Raised diaphragm switches motor on
(falls back on completion of discharge and motor switches off)

Discharge pump operating

A macerator shredding in process

External non-return flap valve

Is installed on the outlet of the macerator pipework and prevents the return of effluent into the unit.

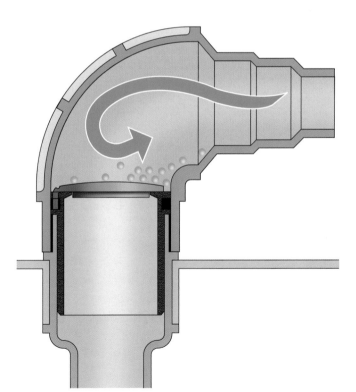

An external non-return flap valve – no discharge

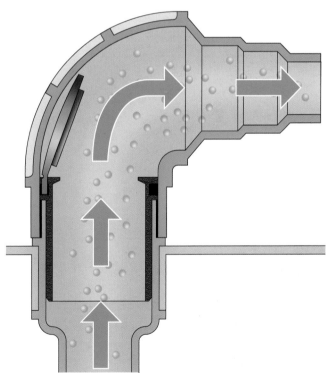

An external non-return flap valve – discharging

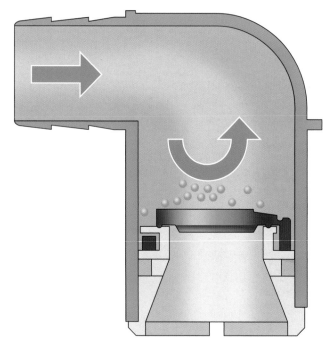

An external non-return flap valve closed

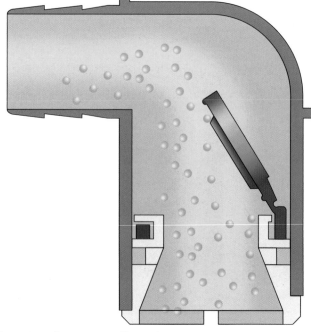

An external non-return flap valve open

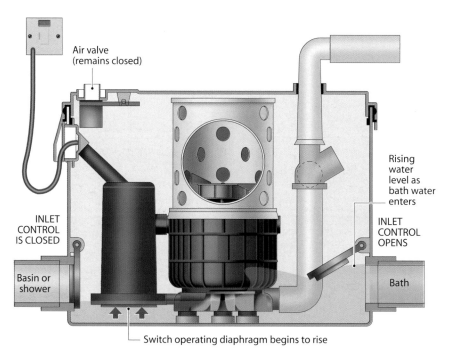

Air valve
(remains closed)

Rising
water
level as
bath water
enters

INLET
CONTROL
OPENS

INLET
CONTROL
IS CLOSED

Basin or
shower

Bath

Switch operating diaphragm begins to rise

A macerator cutaway

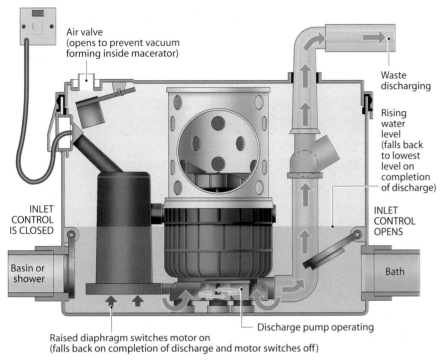

Air valve
(opens to prevent vacuum
forming inside macerator)

Waste
discharging

Rising
water
level
(falls back
to lowest
level on
completion
of discharge)

INLET
CONTROL
IS CLOSED

INLET
CONTROL
OPENS

Basin or
shower

Bath

Discharge pump operating

Raised diaphragm switches motor on
(falls back on completion of discharge and motor switches off)

A macerator cutaway, two valves closed

Maintenance and commissioning of a macerator

WC macerator

Once the macerator has been installed it is important to test it to ensure that it operates properly and clears all of the contents of the pan. Checks should be carried out to ensure that there are no leaks on any connection where the pan connects into the macerator or on the pipe run itself. Checking for leaks is especially important where there has been an extension to the outlet of a pan and where it travels through a partition to the macerator unit.

The customer should always be given a demonstration to see how the unit works and information on safe isolation of electrical and water supplies. A benchmark book should be signed by both the customer and the installing plumber, as well as any other commissioning material.

Macerators require maintenance and sometimes they need repair. Before carrying out any work like this, ensure that you have a discussion with the customer first to ascertain their interpretation of the problem.

This will equip you with essential knowledge to proceed. The manufacturer's instructions will usually provide a flow chart that will help with fault-finding.

SmartScreen Unit 305

Worksheet 3

Before any work starts on a macerator it is imperative that safe electrical isolation has been achieved before you carry out any work on one of these appliances. To ensure this, follow the steps below:

- Remove fuse from spur outlet.
- Turn off and lock MCB at consumer unit and leave a sign saying that the unit is locked.
- Keep any components capable of accidental reconnection to the electrical supply in a safe place on your person.
- Check the size of the fuse in the fused spur outlet. If there are discharge problems always visually check the installation outlet pipework to ensure there is only one lift and that the horizontal pipework afterwards has a fall.
- Check the clipping distance to ensure there are no dips if flexible pipework is fitted.
- Ensure that there is a sufficient gravity fall of at least 1:40 to the unit from the appliances.
- Sometimes customers require simple, not-to-scale drawings, to show how installation pipework can be altered to provide a solution. You may have to supply this.
- Any carbon air filters and NRVs may need inspecting and changing during a service. It's good to know the process in case this is necessary.

Turn on the appliance if safe to do so to check operation. Then diagnose problems in accordance with the manufacturer's flow chart, which could provide solutions to typical problems. For example:

- If a macerator ran for a long time after flushing the problem could be due to a blockage in the area of the pump located within the unit.
- If a pump failed to operate on a WC macerator after it had been flushed then the float switch could have a fault.
- If there was a slow discharge from a WC pan connected to a macerator with a pump working correctly, this could be caused by a blocked carbon air filter.

Sink waste disposal units

These units are installed under kitchen sinks and need a ready-made hole, 89–90mm in diameter, made in the sink to fit the unit. A standard 40mm trap will fit on the outlet of the waste disposal unit.

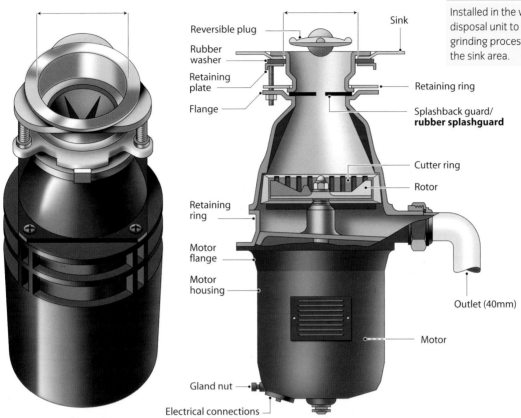

89mm (approximately) hole in sink to accomodate the unit

Reversible plug

Sink

Rubber washer

Retaining plate

Flange

Retaining ring

Splashback guard/ **rubber splashguard**

Cutter ring

Rotor

Retaining ring

Motor flange

Motor housing

Outlet (40mm)

Motor

Gland nut

Electrical connections

A sink waste disposal unit

Rubber splashguard

Installed in the waste section of a sink waste disposal unit to prevent debris from the grinding process from splashing back into the sink area.

Waste disposal units dispose of waste food and cooking products and discharge them into the drainage system. The cutting or grinding blades can deal with a large range of food matter including bones. The process turns anything in the unit into a paste solution and water flushes this into the drain via a 40mm waste outlet. The electric motor that turns the rotor where the blades are attached is located at the base of the unit. A sink housing one of these units requires a larger waste outlet than normal, approximately 89mm, and manufacturers usually supply this on the cutlery bowl. The motor on the unit should be connected to an electrical supply via the correctly sized fused spur outlet with a fuse appropriately sized in relation to the load (typically 10 amp).

Manufacturers often recommend that the circuit be protected with a 30mA RCD. The standard that relates to this appliance can be found in BS EN 60335-2-16: Specification for safety of household and similar electrical appliances.

Care should be taken when servicing such devices. It is important to ensure that you are trained and fully aware of the manufacturer's servicing procedures. The units should be supplied with a special tool to free the grinding blades should they become trapped. The device must have some form of accessible thermal trip cut-off device that will turn off the unit in the event of the blades jamming.

SUGGESTED ACTIVITY

Compare the advantages and disadvantages between waste water lifters and macerators in domestic and commercial sanitary installations.

SmartScreen Unit 305

Worksheet 2

A waste disposal unit fitted to the base of a sink unit

Fused spur outlet

Bonding

A bonding to the underside of a sink

It is important to check that earth bonding is connected to exposed metallic surfaces, such as sink units, especially when an electric device is fitted to it. Safe electrical isolation safety is always vital, especially when inspecting the operation of the mechanism before removing debris from the unit inlet on a maintenance visit.

Commissioning on sanitation systems

SmartScreen Unit 305
PowerPoint 3

By using the job specification and manufacturer's instructions during a visual inspection of a sanitary system, a plumber can verify that all complies with the original design and nothing has been changed.

Once the plumber is satisfied that the installation of a sanitary system is complete, it is important to check that all connections are properly fitted, for example checking that any push-fit spigots are completely engaged in the fitting socket and that any solvent welding is complete on waste and soil pipe joints.

It is essential that none of the joints or components leaks. Appliance pipework falls should be inspected and tested to confirm a smooth and efficient discharge. If a macerator is fitted make sure there are no push-fit connections on the discharge pipework.

Any WC cisterns, mechanisms should be adjusted to discharge so that they comply with requirements for low water energy consumption. Mixing valves should be tested to make sure they are operating at a safe temperature and the flow rates of showers and basins confirmed as being satisfactory.

Clips are often overlooked but they must be checked to confirm that they are properly anchored and spaced in accordance with the standards as their performance will be tested under load conditions.

Clips

If there are problems identified during the commissioning process, then an apprentice plumber should consult with their supervisor and seek guidance for a remedy. Quite often only an adjustment is required to a float-operated valve or temperature settings to a mixing valve. On some occasions there could be a more serious problem, such as very slow discharge from an appliance that previously performed normally. It could be that since the first fix some debris has entered a trap or a discharge pipe. It is possible that an improvised plug of compressed plastic has travelled down the soil stack and caused a major blockage affecting all the appliances that are connected. The solution would be to remove it via an access point on the soil stack.

Once the installation procedures of all the sanitary appliances to a new soil stack have been completed, soundness testing can begin. In the case of multi-storey property installations, testing of appliances on a floor-to-floor basis is required. The installation needs to be checked in accordance with BS 12056-2:2000 to ensure that there are no leaks as this will result in the ingression of foul odours into a property.

Air test a sanitary pipework system to industry requirements

SmartScreen Unit 305
Worksheet 2

The testing preparation

1 Start the process by filling all the traps with water and sealing the stack with drain plugs or drain testing bags. The excess water from the traps will accumulate at the lowest plug or bag to create a seal.

2 Fill a manometer, which is basically a small U-shaped tube calibrated in millimetres, with water and use this as the test instrument.

3 Next, connect a hose via a tee piece to one end of the manometer and the other hose to a hand pump.

4 Make sure the water in the manometer is level at zero.

5 Ensure that there is water in the traps.

6 Gently squeeze the hand pump until the water level in the gauge reaches 38mm and wait for 3 minutes.

7 If there is no drop seen on the gauge during that time then the system is sound.

8 If there is a drop then there is a leak somewhere and this can be detected by applying leak detection fluid to all of the joints while the system is under pressure and bubbling will reveal any leaks.

Always test the test equipment before use!

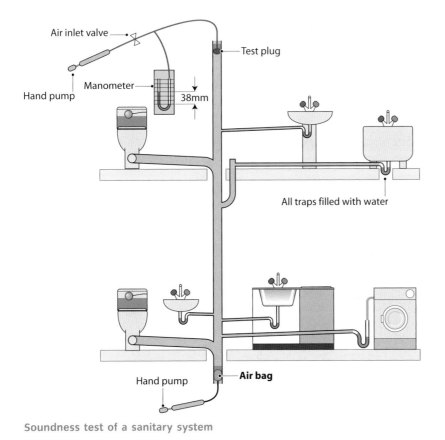

Soundness test of a sanitary system

Performance test sanitation systems to test for trap seal retention

Once a successful soundness test has been completed a **performance test** can be carried out. The purpose of the test is to ensure that after simultaneous operation of all the appliances connected to the same soil stack, the trap seal depths remaining should be at least 25mm.

Performance test

Carried out on sanitary systems to ensure that after simultaneous operation of the appliances connected to the same soil stack, the trap seal depths remaining should be at least 25mm.

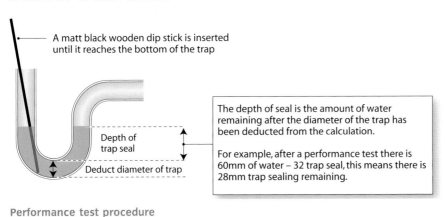

A matt black wooden dip stick is inserted until it reaches the bottom of the trap

Depth of trap seal

Deduct diameter of trap

The depth of seal is the amount of water remaining after the diameter of the trap has been deducted from the calculation.

For example, after a performance test there is 60mm of water – 32 trap seal, this means there is 28mm trap sealing remaining.

Performance test procedure

The performance testing procedure is as follows:

1 Check the depth of seal using a black dip stick and make a note.

2 Fill all the appliances to overflow level and discharge simultaneously.

3 Flush the WCs at the same time.

4 After all of the appliances have been discharged, check the traps again with a dipstick to ensure that the seal is not less than 25mm (carry out the procedure three times).

Testing for loss of trap seal

Testing for self-siphonage

It is important to check whether the pipework conveying the water is either too long or too small. A plug of water accumulates while it is discharging; this in turn creates a partial vacuum which sucks out the water from the trap upstream. This happens frequently on wash basins because of the speed of discharge and the small diameter of the pipe.

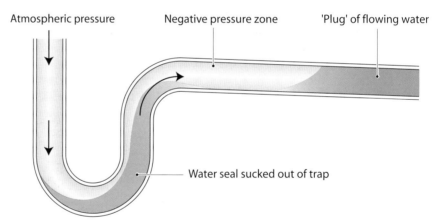

Self-siphonage in action

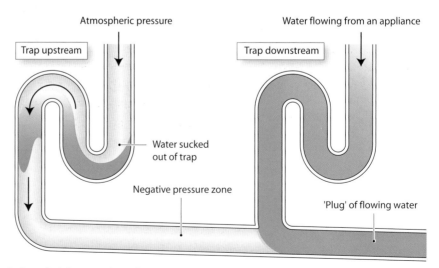

Induced siphonage in action

Testing for induced siphonage

This type of siphonage occurs to a passive water trap when water is discharged from other appliances downstream that are connected to the same branch pipework. Once again, a plug of water accumulates in the downstream appliance while it is discharging, and this in turn creates a partial vacuum which sucks out the water from the trap of the appliance upstream. This happens often when a wash basin is connected to the same waste branch as a bath. Therefore, connecting two appliances to the same waste branch should be avoided.

A gas pipe and WC problem

The procedure for notifying works carried out to the relevant authority

Once an installation is finished, the appropriate commissioning form requires completing and if an installer is not part of a self-certification scheme then the Local Authority Building Control department (**LABC**) should be informed.

LABC

Local Area Building Control.

However, if you are a member of a certification scheme and you have completed your commissioning paperwork, you have 30 days to submit your details. It is important to keep a record of all the tests that you have carried out as this will help in the event of a query at a later date and will help you diagnose any problems that may have occurred since the installation. Invariably you will also be installing sanitary fittings so the following forms may require completing.

Regulation 5.
Notification
5.-(1) Subject to paragraph (2), any person who proposes to install a water fitting in connection with any of the operations listed in the Table below-
(a) shall give notice to the water undertaker that he proposes to commence work;
(b) shall not begin that work without the consent of that undertaker which shall not be withheld unreasonably; and
(c) shall comply with any condition to which the undertaker's consent is subject.

TABLE

1. The erection of a building or other structure not being a pond or swimming pool.

2. The extension or alteration of a water system on any premises other than a house.

3. A material change of use of any premises.

4. The installation of-
(a) a bath having a capacity, as measured to the centre line of overflow, of more than 230 litres;
(b) a bidet with an ascending spray or flexible hose;
(c) a single shower unit (which may consist of one or more shower heads within a single unit), not being a drencher shower installed for reasons of safety or health, connected directly or indirectly to a supply pipe which is of a type specified by the regulator;
(d) a pump or water booster drawing more than 12 litres per minute, connected directly or indirectly to a supply pipe;
(e) a unit which incorporates reverse osmosis;
(f) a water treatment unit which produces a waste water discharge or which requires the use of water for regeneration or cleaning;
(g) a reduced pressure zone valve assembly or other mechanical device for protection against a fluid which is in fluid category 4 or 5;
(h) a garden watering system unless designed to be operated by hand; or
(i) any water system laid outside a building and either less than 750 mm or more than 1350 mm below ground level.

5. the construction of a pond or swimming pool with a capacity greater than 10,000 litres which is designed to be replenished by automatic means and is to be filled with water supplied by a water undertaker.

(2) This regulation does not apply to the installation by an approved contractor of a water fitting falling within paragraph 2, 4(b) or 4 (g) in the Table.

(3) The notice required by paragraph (1) shall include or be accompanied by-
(a) the name and address of the person giving notice, and (if different) the name and address of the person on whom notice may be served under paragraph (4) below;
(b) a description of the proposed work or material change of use, and
(c) particulars of the location of the premises to which the proposal relates, and the use or intended use of those premises;
(d) except in the case of a fitting falling within paragraph 4(a), (c), (h) or 5 in the Table above,
(i) a plan of those parts of the premises to which the proposal relates; and
(ii) a diagram showing the pipework and fittings to be installed; and
(e) where the work is to be carried out by an approved contractor, the name of the contractor.
(4) The water undertaker may withhold consent under paragraph (1), or grant it subject to conditions, by a notice served before the expiry of the period of ten working days commencing with the day on which the notice under that paragraph was given.
(5) If no notice is given by the water undertaker within the period mentioned in paragraph (4), the consent required under paragraph (1) shall be deemed to have been granted unconditionally.

Water undertaker notification

NOTICE OF INTENTION TO INSTALL WATER FITTINGS

I hereby give notice as required under Regulation 5 of the Water Supply (Water Fittings) Regulations 1999 that I intend to install water fittings as follows:

Intended installation date [   ]

Location of premises where work is to be done...
....

Use of the buildings to which the notice refers...
....

Description of proposed work/fittings...
....
....

Is plan of proposed installation included?   [Yes] [No]

Will there be a material change of use of the premises?   [Yes] [No]   if yes give details

Name of installer.. **Approved Contractor Number**..
....

Company name and address...
....

Name of person on whom the notice may be served (if different to above)..

and address..
....

Signed... **Date**...

To the customer: please keep this certificate safe, you may need to show it to an authorised water inspector.

Water Supply (Water Fittings) Regulations 1999

1: Installation of water fittings at: (insert name and address of premises where work has been undertaken)

Certificate of compliance

I certify that the work indicated below, carried out at the above premises complies with the requirements of the Water Supply (Water Fittings) Regulations 1999

2: Installation work carried out at the premises indicated by this notice	
the erection of a building or other structure, not being a pond or swimming pool	
the extension or alteration of a water system in premises other than a house	
a material change of use of premises	
the installation of:-	
a bath with a capacity, measured to the centre of the overflow, of over 230L	
a bidet with an ascending spray or flexible hose	
a single shower unit of a type specified by the regulator	
a pump or booster drawing more than 12 litres per minute from a supply pipe	
a unit that incorporates reverse osmosis	
a water treatment unit with waste water discharge or use of water for regeneration or cleaning	
a reduced pressure zone valve assembly or mechanical device for fluid category 4 or 5 protection	
an automatic garden watering system	
an outside water system laid less than 750 mm or more than 1350 mm below ground level	
an automatically filled pond or swimming pool with a capacity greater than 10,000L	

3: Name and address of contractor supplying this certificate

4:
Signature ....Date..

Certificate of compliance

Regulation 6.

Contractor's certificate
6.-(1)   Where a water fitting is installed, altered, connected or disconnected by an approved contractor, the contractor shall upon completion of the work furnish a signed certificate stating whether the water fitting complies with the requirements of these Regulations to the person who commissioned the work.

(2)   In case of a fitting for which notice is required under Regulation 5(1) above, the contractor shall send a copy of their certificate to the water undertaker.

Contractor's certificate

SmartScreen Unit 305
Worksheet 3

Handing over a completed system to the end user

Once all of the tests have been carried out satisfactorily, the system operates as planned and the work area, appliances and fittings are cleaned and ready for use, it is time to hand over to the customer. The customer will need to know how their newly installed system works and will need to be given clear information on how appliances such as macerators, waste water lifters and showers operate. A full demonstration of how they operate is required and advice on the limitations of an appliance's performance should be discussed in line with the manufacturer's instructions.

Handover to a customer

It is good practice to give the customer advice on self-maintenance, for example keeping shower heads clean. They will need to know what to do in an emergency so electrical and water services isolation should be identified and the customer shown how to operate them.

Benchmark book

A document that, when completed, verifies that the installation complies with the manufacturer's instruction, and relevant standards and regulations. When signed by the installer and customer it can be sent to the manufacturer to validate any warranty.

The manufacturer's instructions, along with their component guarantees and a fully completed **benchmark book**, plus compliance certificates and other documents such as commissioning records, should be signed by both the plumber and the customer. At this point recommended servicing and maintenance advice can be given as well as guarantees of workmanship and company details in the event of a problem in the future.

Designing rainwater systems

When designing a rainwater system, a survey of the property must be carried out and there must be a discussion with the customer about their requirements and choices. It could transpire that an existing installation may not be correctly installed. Therefore, it is beneficial to ask the customer about how the system has performed in the past.

SmartScreen Unit 305
Worksheet 5

When working on a new build or alteration, it is good practice to select some manufacturers' brochures to show the customer so they can select an aesthetically pleasing style. This can also help a plumber specify a suitable style as the discharge rates will be provided.

It is wise to establish the type of drainage for the premises and plan your system around whether or not it will be combined, separate or partially separate. If it is the latter check that any soakaway is fit for purpose.

A ground soakaway near a car park walkway, protected against foot traffic by a special grid arrangement

Sometimes a new building extension will require a rainwater system. This could be connected to an existing functioning system already installed on the premises. In this situation a re-calculation of the existing system may be required to estimate if the gutter size and outlets are sufficient to accommodate the additional flow rates caused by the new extension.

There are many documents which need to be consulted when designing or installing rainwater systems. This is because there are a range of restrictions in legislation to ensure that the water is efficiently collected and safely discharged from a building.

Approved Building Regulation Document H3:2002 rainwater drainage

Design and installation of rainwater systems:

- **BS EN 12056-3:2000** – Used along with the Building Regulations, it includes rainwater system design, outlet positions and rainfall intensity calculations.

- The manufacturer's instructions must be referred to during any installation.

The British Standard for PVCu eaves guttering and fittings is BS EN 607:2004

- **BS EN 122001:2000** – Covers rainwater piping systems for above ground external use. Most of the guttering systems used on domestic dwellings are made from unplasticised polyvinyl chloride (PVCu).

Calculating the size of a gutter

To assess the suitability of a gutter system to drain the roof on a building efficiently, the following factors need to be taken into consideration:

- the effective roof area to be drained
- rainfall intensity
- the flow characteristics of the gutter system
- the number and position of down pipes.

BS EN 12056-3:2000 measures rainfall intensity in l/s/m² for a two-minute storm event. It also has maps that give details of the rainfall intensity in areas around the country for periods between 1 and 500 years.

SUGGESTED ACTIVITY

The next time you visit the plumbing merchants, pick up some manufacturers' literature on rainwater systems and check out the range of styles, calculations and specifications for guttering and down pipes.

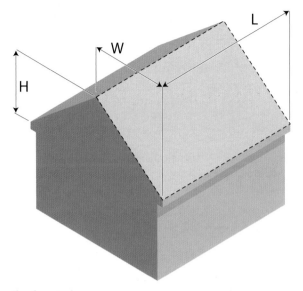

Roof area

The angle of the roof is a vital consideration when designing a guttering system. BS EN 12056-3 gives the following formula to work out a roof size:

Effective maximum roof area (allowance for wind)

$W + \dfrac{H}{2} \times L$ (length of roof) = area in m²

Where:

W = Horizontal span of slope

H = Height of roof pitch

L = Length of roof

Example 1

To calculate the area if a roof is 12m long, 7m wide and 3m high:

$7 + \dfrac{3}{2} \times 12 =$ **102m²** (area of roof)

Example 2

Calculate the area if a roof is 11m long, 6.5m wide and 4m high:

$6.5 + \dfrac{4}{2} \times 11 =$ **93.5m²** (area of roof)

The size of the roof directly relates to the size of the guttering required, so if the size of the roof increases so does the guttering and the discharge pipework. This principle also applies to the angle of the roof as the greater the angle, the faster the flow, which will increase the speed at which rainwater enters the gutter.

The rainwater system must therefore be accurately designed to adequately manage the predicted rainfall. The following table shows the factor which should be added to the roof area once the pitch of the roof is known.

Type of surface	Design in (m²)
Flat roof	Plan area of relevant portion
Pitched roof at 30°	Plan area of portion × 1.29
Pitched roof at 45°	Plan area of portion × 1.50
Pitched roof at 60°	Plan area of portion × 1.87
Pitched roof over 70° or any wall	Elevation area × 0.5

Multiplication factors for all roof pitches

The next stage is to include the factor for the pitch of the roof which can be selected from the table below.

Roof pitch	Factor	Roof pitch	Factor
10°	1.088	30°	1.288
12.5°	1.111	32.5°	1.319
15°	1.134	35°	1.350
17.5°	1.158	37.5°	1.384
20°	1.182	40°	1.419
22.5°	1.207	42.5°	1.459
25°	1.233	45°	1.500
27°	1.260	47.5°	1.547

Note: For roofs of 50° and above a factor of 1:600 may be used.

Table for roof pitch and factors

Roof pitch factor multiplications

By using the figures from Example 1 on the previous page, the multiplication factor for the pitch of the roof (as shown in the table) can be included in the new calculation.

Calculate the area if a roof is 12m long, 7m wide and 3m high.

$$7 + \frac{3}{2} \times 12 = \textbf{102m}^2$$

If the roof pitch was 45° then the roof area should be multiplied by 1.5.

$$102m^2 \times 1.5 = \textbf{153m}^2$$

A manufacturer's chart can now be used to select an appropriate gutter size for the roof.

Other roof area calculation methods

The area of a flat roof should be considered as the total plan area.

When a roof has a more complex layout with a range of spans and pitches then each individual area should be separately calculated.

In an alternative calculation offered by the Building Regulations, the length and span are multiplied and then multiplied again by a factor for the given pitch of the roof.

Width × length × (design factor for given roof angle)

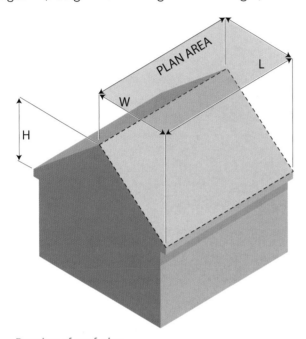

Drawing of roof plan

If the angle of the roof is known then we can calculate using the factor for the pitch as shown in the previous table.

Here is a worked example:

Example

What is the effective area if a roof is 6m long, 4m wide with a pitch of 45°?

The effective design area for 45° is 1.5 taken from the table on the previous page.

If the plan area of a 45° pitched roof measures 6m × 4m the effective area will be:

6 × 4 × 1.5 = **36m²**

Elevation of a roof

When calculating the effective area from an elevation and a different factor is used, the elevation area of the roof is the **W**idth × the **H**eight.

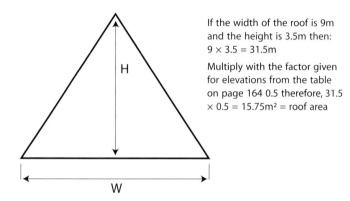

If the width of the roof is 9m and the height is 3.5m then:
9 × 3.5 = 31.5m

Multiply with the factor given for elevations from the table on page 164 0.5 therefore, 31.5 × 0.5 = 15.75m² = roof area

Elevation of a roof with a 75° pitch (not to scale)

Working out the size of a gutter

The size of the gutter is dependent upon the size of the roof area to be drained.

The effective roof area for flat roofs is different from that for pitched roofs and needs to be calculated.

The table below extracted from Part H of the Building Regulations shows that for pitched roofs, a greater 'run-off' or flow will be experienced and must be allowed for.

Sizing the gutter

In Example 1, 36m² was calculated as the effective area of our roof with an angle of 45°, so by using the table below* **a gutter size of 100mm diameter, a half round gutter** can be chosen along with a 63mm diameter downpipe.

Gutter sizes and outlet sizes			
Max. effective roof area (m²)	Gutter size (mm diameter)	Outlet size (mm diameter)	Flow capacity (litres/sec)
6.0	-	-	-
18.0	75	50	0.38
37.0	100	63	0.78
53.0	115	63	1.11
65.0	125	75	1.37
103.0	150	89	2.16

Note: Refers to **nominal half round eaves gutters** laid level with outlets at one end sharp-edged. Round-ended outlets allow smaller downpipe sizes.

Chart for gutter size

*The table should only be used for half round gutters with outlets at one end.

Gutter flow capacity

BS EN 12056-3 requires that only 90% of the gutter flow should be relied upon. It is also recommended by many manufacturers that gutters be fixed at this level as this enables the gutter to be fitted as high as possible while still ensuring that the correct relationship to the roof's edge is maintained. Careful consideration needs to be given to the position of rainwater outlets.

Centre outlets are more efficient than end outlets as the area that can be drained is almost double, with the result of reducing the possibility of down pipes on the system, saving time and money.

The fall of a gutter

Although some manufacturers say that gutters should be levelly installed, generally gutters should be laid so that they fall between 1–3mm/m. This is interpreted as a fall of 1:600 (25mm for every 15m). Although gutters are designed to discharge water when installed at a level position, a fall will greatly increase the flow capacity.

Another reason for the fall of 1:600 is so that it will ensure that the gutter will not fall too low at the end run. Brackets should be installed at a maximum of 1m intervals to ensure the gutter does not sway when filled with water.

Selecting a gutter type

There are a range of different gutter profiles produced today. These have varying capacities and come in a range of colours and materials. Manufacturers' literature will give specifications of individual gutter performances. You will find below a few examples.

Ogee

A popular Victorian style ornamental gutter design.

	Half round – used on many domestic properties
	High capacity – used on larger and steeper roofs where high volume and velocity of water enters the gutter
	Square section – good rainwater capacity. Used with square-sectioned rainwater pipes. Popular during the 1980s and 1990s
	Ogee (ornamental gutter) – popular Victorian style gutter design

Drawings of gutter profiles

SUGGESTED ACTIVITY

Use the method shown in the Approved Building Regulation Document H3 to work out the gutter and down pipe size for a roof 4.5m long × 3.1m wide with a 45° pitch.

Outlet positions

This is the part of the guttering system that acts as a connection for gutter pipework at both ends and as an outlet to the down pipe. The location of running outlets is often based on the location of the gullies for the surface water sewer, which are positioned around a dwelling and they can be identified in a building layout drawing.

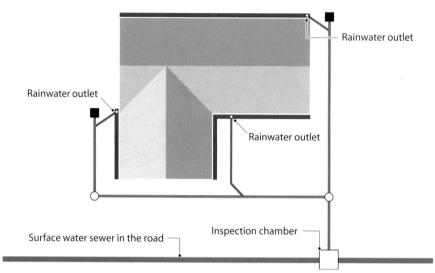

Building layout drawing

Running outlet positions

The guttering system will be more effective with more outlets located on the gutter as this will allow for a better balanced flow from the roof. Placing an outlet centrally rather than at the ends of a roof means that the outlet could accommodate a greater area of roof water run-off. The illustration that follows shows that the specific location of outlets can increase the effectiveness of a guttering system.

By dividing the expected flow rate of the roof by the flow rate of the outlet you can work out how many outlets you will need, so always check the manufacturer's literature as flow rates for outlets can vary.

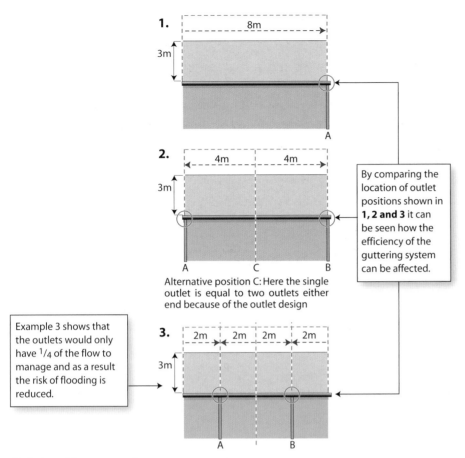

1. 8m / 3m / A

By comparing the location of outlet positions shown in **1, 2 and 3** it can be seen how the efficiency of the guttering system can be affected.

2. 4m / 4m / 3m / A / C / B

Alternative position C: Here the single outlet is equal to two outlets either end because of the outlet design

Example 3 shows that the outlets would only have ¹/₄ of the flow to manage and as a result the risk of flooding is reduced.

3. 2m / 2m / 2m / 2m / 3m / A / B

Outlet positions on roofs

Changes in direction

Changes of direction are unavoidable and they will affect the flow capacity of the gutter to discharge when the change of direction is in excess of 10°. A 90° angle will reduce the effectiveness of the flow by 15% and every other angle reduces the efficiency of the gutter even further.

This applies to angles located near the end of an outlet. Changes of direction effectively reduce the area of a roof that the gutter can usefully serve therefore always try to follow these principles when designing a gutter system:

- Try to install straight gutter runs which offer the maximum flow rate.
- Do not locate outlets near to changes of direction.
- Apply the maximum fall ratio where there are lots of bends.
- Install larger gutters where there a lot of changes in direction.

Conclusion

As a Level 3 plumber you will be expected to install and commission sanitary installations and their associated appliances, as well as analyse their problems. Once the principles of operation are understood and put into practice, the world of sanitation will prove to be an interesting, challenging and valuable aspect of the varied and diverse world of plumbing. Properly installed sanitary systems will help people enjoy the benefits of years of progress in design, plus promote hygiene and protect people from disease. This is an exportable skill and craft, as many countries around the world have benefitted from the excellent design and innovations of sanitary systems in the UK.

Test your knowledge questions

1   Name the Building Regulations that relate to sanitary pipework.

2   Which standard would give guidance for spacing requirements to enable people to move safely and comfortably in bathrooms?

3   Who should be informed when a new sanitary system is installed in a dwelling by a person who is not part of a certification scheme?

4   According to the Water Regulations, what is the flushing volume for multiple urinals?

5   Which item creates the watertight deal between the WC cistern and the pan on a close-coupled WC?

6   State the minimum distance that BS 6465-2:1996 recommends should be in front of a close-coupled WC.

7   When soundness and performance testing a sanitary discharge system, which standard should be referred to?

8   What are discharge units used to calculate?

9   On a ventilated branch system, what is the vent pipe size for a single appliance?

10 When installing a WC connection to a soil track, what distance is the danger zone for cross flow?

11 What is the main factor to consider when selecting a gutter for a dwelling?

12 How much trap seal should remain after a full performance testing procedure has been completed?

13 What needs to be checked if a pump fails on a WC macerator after it has been flushed?

14 What backflow prevention is used on a conventional wash basin?

15 Which Building Regulation Approved Document should be complied with for ventilation in bathrooms?

16 What could be the problem if a macerator ran for a long time after flushing?

17 An air admittance valve (AAV) would be unsuitable for a sanitary pipework installation if it included which component?

18 Describe the function of an air admittance valve.

19 What should the installer give to the client to verify that work has been tested and carried out to the correct standard when a new installation has been completed?

20 Which document verifies that the installation complies with the manufacturer's instruction, and relevant standards and regulations?

Assessment checklist

What you now know (Learning Outcome)	What you can do (assessment criteria)	Where this is found (page numbers)
1. Understand design requirements of above-ground drainage systems	1.1 State documents relating to sanitation and above-ground drainage systems and components	118–119
	1.2 Identify different types of above-ground drainage system types	121
	1.3 Explain the reasons for selecting above-ground drainage system types	121
	1.4 Describe design specifications of waste pipes	122–123
	1.5 Describe the design considerations of stub stacks	122–123
	1.6 Describe the operation of an air admittance valve	133
	1.7 Explain the benefits of waste valves (mechanical traps) compared with traditional water seal traps.	131
2. Know the requirements of installing sanitary appliances and associated drainage	2.1 Identify types of urinals	139–140
	2.2 Describe installation considerations of urinals	139–140
	2.3 Explain the spacing requirements of sanitary appliances	143–144
	2.4 Interpret documents relating to disabled accommodation	142
	2.5 Explain the importance of ventilation in bathrooms	144
	2.6 Describe design considerations of macerators	145
	2.7 Explain installation considerations of sink waste disposal units.	154
3. Understand commissioning and testing requirements of drainage systems	3.1 Explain the procedure for soundness testing above-ground drainage systems	157–158
	3.2 Explain the procedure of performance testing above-ground drainage pipework	157–158
	3.3 Describe the commissioning procedure for macerators	153–154
	3.4 Describe potential reasons for poor performance of drainage systems	157–158
	3.5 Describe common faults with macerators.	159–160
4. Be able to carry out commissioning and fault finding of above-ground drainage systems	4.1 Demonstrate performance testing of above-ground drainage systems	157–158
	4.2 Perform commissioning of macerators	153–154
	4.3 Diagnose waste pipe faults	159–160
	4.4 Diagnose macerator faults.	159–160

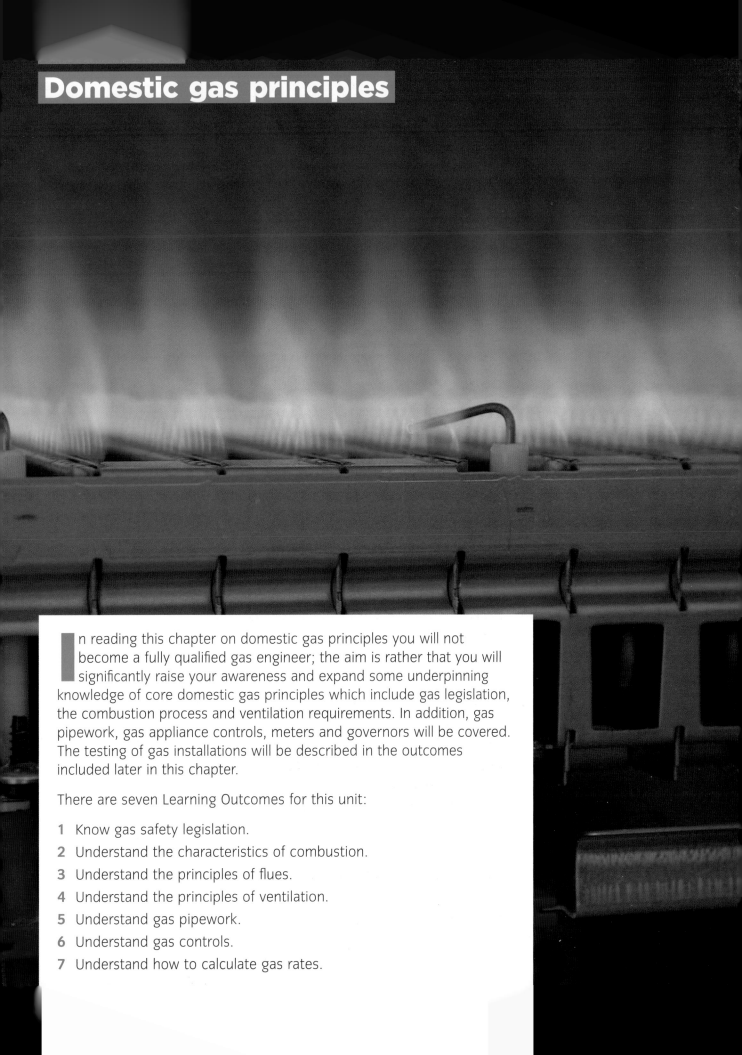

Domestic gas principles

In reading this chapter on domestic gas principles you will not become a fully qualified gas engineer; the aim is rather that you will significantly raise your awareness and expand some underpinning knowledge of core domestic gas principles which include gas legislation, the combustion process and ventilation requirements. In addition, gas pipework, gas appliance controls, meters and governors will be covered. The testing of gas installations will be described in the outcomes included later in this chapter.

There are seven Learning Outcomes for this unit:

1 Know gas safety legislation.
2 Understand the characteristics of combustion.
3 Understand the principles of flues.
4 Understand the principles of ventilation.
5 Understand gas pipework.
6 Understand gas controls.
7 Understand how to calculate gas rates.

Gas safety legislation (LO1)

There are six assessment criteria for this outcome:

1 State hierarchical responsibilities for the gas industry in Great Britain, Northern Ireland, the Isle of Man and Guernsey.
2 State the date the Gas Safety (Installation and Use Regulations) 1998 came into force.
3 State the competent persons citation.
4 Describe the three families of gas.
5 Describe the meaning of the term 'gas fitting'.
6 Define what constitutes work on a gas fitting.

Gas safety organisations

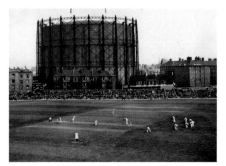

A gas holder overlooking a cricket match

CO

Chemical formula of carbon monoxide.

Ventilation

The process of supplying air to and removing air from a room, internal space, appliance, compartment or garage.

In the past, qualified gas engineers were requested to be members of an organisation called CORGI. This organisation was originally established in 1970 and operated a voluntary register of gas installers. The letters of the name CORGI stood for Confederation for the Registration of Gas Installers. The organisation was set up because of a gas explosion in 1968 which contributed to the partial collapse of a tower block in London called Ronan Point. When the Gas Safety (Installation and Use) Regulations were introduced on 31 October 1998, they stated that registration with CORGI was a legal requirement for any person or company that carried out work in relation to a gas fitting – Regulation 3(3).

Even though gas explosions do occur, the greatest danger to the public when using gas is from carbon monoxide (**CO**) and, as a result, much of the concern of gas safety legislation focuses on preventing appliances producing excessive amounts of CO because of inadequate **ventilation**, which can affect the complete combustion of gases. In addition the regulations also focus on the safe dispersal of products of combustion by effective flue systems.

On 1 April 2009 the **Gas Safe** Register became the new official gas registration body for the United Kingdom. On 1 April 2010 it became the official register for the Isle of Man and Guernsey. The Health and Safety Authority for each area requires by law that all gas engineers must be on the Gas Safe Register.

The Gas Safe Register aims to improve and maintain gas safety to the highest standards. The Gas Safe Register will make sure that all gas engineers on the Gas Safe Register endeavour to protect the public from any unsafe gas work through the national investigations team which tracks down anyone working illegally on gas work. It also carries out regular inspections of Gas Safe-registered engineers and offers advice and guidance to installers as well as assessing the quality of individual work. Gas Safe also has a goal to educate consumers and help raise their awareness of gas safety. In addition it investigates reports of unsafe gas work.

It produces a magazine called the *Registered Gas Engineer* which provides excellent technical articles and updates for registered installers. It also highlights bad practice and illegal activities that have been identified by its own investigation team, and examples of court cases are published. There are also photographs supplied by engineers who encounter illegal and dangerous examples of work carried out by unqualified persons, which could put the public at risk.

Gas Safety (Installation and Use) Regulations 1998 (GSIUR)

The Gas Regulations lie at the heart of all decisions that engineers will make when working on gas appliances and on pipework installations, and should be referred to throughout their working life. Everything comes back down to the regulations and, wherever possible, references will be made here to help contextualise the regulations within every-day working experiences and encounters of an engineer.

This outcome deals with the Gas Regulations and it is advisable to have a copy of the Gas Regulations to hand when reading this section. However, the breakdown in the brief description of each regulation is given as follows.

> 'The Gas Safety Installation and Use Regulations (GSIUR) 1998 deals with the safe installation, maintenance and use of gas systems, which include fittings, appliances and flues mainly in domestic and commercial premises. They generally apply to any gas as defined in the Gas Act 1986. The requirements include both natural gas and liquid petroleum gas subject to regulations and place responsibilities on a wide range of people including those who install, service, maintain or repair gas appliances as well as other gas fittings. Suppliers and certain landlords also come under the scope of the regulations.
>
> The enforcing authority for the GSIUR and other Gas Regulations in Great Britain, Northern Ireland, the Isle of Man and Guernsey is the Health and Safety Executive (the **HSE**).'

Background

The approved code of practice (ACOP) and guidance gives the user practical advice under the GSIUR. They have been drawn up in consultation with the Confederation of British Industry, the Trade Union Congress, local authorities, government departments, consumer organisations and the HSE. In the GSIUR publication, each

Gas Safe

Gas Safe is the official gas registration body for the United Kingdom, Isle of Man and Guernsey approved by the HSE.

GSIUR book cover

HSE

HSE (Health and Safety Executive) is the enforcing body for the GSIUR.

SmartScreen Unit 307

Handout 1

of the regulations is followed by the ACOP and then by guidance. The regulations are written in italic type, the ACOP in bold and any accompanying guidance in normal type.

The following summary will help give a synopsis of each of the regulations but the Gas Regulations (GSIUR 1998) must be referred to in detail throughout to give the reader a more thorough understanding of each of the regulations and to help them assess their particular application to gas work.

Summary of the regulations

Regulation 1 – Gives the date the regulations came into force which was:

31 October 1998

Regulation 2 – Defines important terms used in the regulations:

There are many important terms such as 'disconnecting and reconnecting a gas fitting'. (Only HSE-approved engineers should carry out this task.) For a qualified gas engineer the term 'work' in relation to a gas fitting includes any of the following activities:

Installing or reconnecting the fitting, maintaining, servicing, permanently adjusting, disconnecting, repairing, altering or renewing the fitting or purging it of gas. Where the fitting is not readily removable, changing its position and removing the fitting is considered work. However, there is an exclusion with regard to cookers inasmuch as a user can connect and disconnect the appliance hose connection from the self-sealing bayonet fitting in order to clean behind the appliance.

The definition of the gas fitting as stated by IGEM/G/4 Edition 2 is:

'Gas pipework, valves (other than the emergency control valve – **ECV**), regulators, meters, fittings, apparatus and appliances designed for use by consumers of gas for heating, lighting, cooking or other purposes for which gas can be used but it does not mean:

- Any part of the distribution main or service pipe
- Any part of the pipeline **upstream** of a distribution main or service pipe
- A gas storage vessel
- A gas cylinder or cartridge designed to be disposed of when empty.'

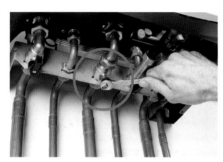
Adjusting a gas pipe fitting

KEY POINT

Removing or adjusting fittings on gas appliances is considered as work according to the GSIUR.

KEY POINT

Disconnecting a cooker hose to clean behind the appliance does not constitute work according to the GSIUR.

ECV

ECV is an emergency control valve used for the isolation of gas in an installation.

Upstream

This means before a given point which could for example be a gas meter. Therefore if an isolation valve were located upstream of a meter, it would mean it was situated on the pipework before the meter inlet.

The same document continues, stating that:

'The definition of work in relation to a gas fitting is any of the following activities carried out by any person whether they are an employee or not.

- Installing a fitting
- Maintaining, servicing, permanently adjusting, repairing, altering or renewing a fitting, or purging it of gas
- Changing the position of the fitting when it is not readily removable
- Removing a fitting.'

Regulation 3 – Requires that any gas engineer should be Gas Safe-registered.

Previously engineers and operatives had to be CORGI-registered but Gas Safe is the new organisation that registers gas engineers. Regulation 3(3) states that gas fitters are required to be a class of persons approved by the Health and Safety Executive to carry out gas work and be on the Gas Safe Register. In any event, people working on gas fittings must be competent to do so and this depends on a combination of training and experience. Needless to say, this regulation mentions that it is an offence for any person to pretend to be a registered member, ie the required class of person to carry out gas work.

The *Registered Gas Engineer* often highlights legal cases where people have falsified documents to claim they are Gas Safe-registered. The discovery of such offences often comes about when very poor and incompetent workmanship results in the public being endangered by exposure to the products of combustion, gas escapes and even fire.

Regulation 4 – States that it is the duty of an employer or self-employed person requiring work to be done on a gas fitting to take reasonable steps to ensure that any person carrying out the work on their behalf is Gas Safe-registered. As previously mentioned, this means they are a class of person approved by the HSE and therefore deemed to be competent to carry out any such work.

Regulation 5 – Requires that installers check that any fitting is suitable for the purpose for which it is to be used, which means every part of it is of good construction, made of a sound material and of adequate strength and size to secure safe use for the gas it is designed to carry. The use of lead and non-metallic fittings is prohibited in new gas work installations although there is still some lead work in existence, especially at meter locations and, providing this pipework is still in good condition and shows no signs of damage, then it can be connected onto.

This logo can be seen on vehicles of Gas Safe engineers (Gas Safe Register is a registered trademark of the HSE and is used under licence)

Gas Safe Register card

KEY POINT

No person shall carry out any work in relation to the gas fitting or gas storage vessel unless they are competent to do so – GSIUR Reg 3(1).

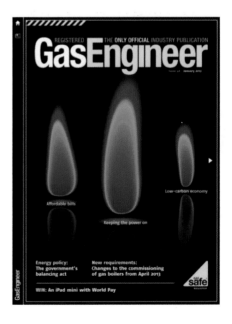

Documents being checked

Lead pipe on the outlet of a meter

Plastic push-fit cap which is not fit for purpose on gas installations and is RIDDOR reportable

This regulation also emphasises that any work carried out on a gas fitting or storage vessel should comply with the appropriate standards and be carried out in a manner that does not endanger people. It emphasises that, apart from connectors to readily removable appliances such as Bunsen burners, non-metallic pipe should only be used within buildings if is sheathed in metal to minimise the risk of gas escaping should that pipe should ever fail.

An installer must therefore ensure that any fitting installed is of a good construction, made of a sound material and of an adequate strength and size.

Copper capillary fittings, commonly used on domestic gas pipework

Regulation 6 – States measures to be taken by any engineer working on a gas fitting against the risk of gas release and the requirement to seal any gas ways and then retest for gas tightness once the work is complete. The regulation mentions the danger of searching for gas escapes with naked flames and the associated risks of ignition and explosion.

Engineers must ensure that any gas that could be released does not constitute a danger to anyone. In addition, the regulation emphasises the risks associated with smoking or sources of ignition if a gas way is exposed.

Regulation 7 – Requires any gas fittings to be protected from damage including corrosion and from any blockage by a foreign body, for example dirt or dust.

Open-ended copper gas pipe which is classified as immediately dangerous (ID) and RIDDOR reportable to the HSE

Pipework should be properly and effectively supported and installed to avoid any undue risk of damage

Regulation 8 – Prohibits any alteration to the premises by which a gas fitting or storage vessel no longer complies with the regulations. This also applies to work carried out on a gas fitting or any associated flue or ventilation systems which could result in danger to any persons.

Regulation 9 – Requires that the emergency control is provided when gas is first supplied to premises. It also requires that a notice is posted adjacent to the control whenever a control itself is not next to the meter. The notice must describe the safety procedure in the event of a gas escape.

Regulation 10 – Requires that electrical continuity is maintained during any work on a gas fitting to avoid any danger.

It is important to ensure that bonding clips are in good condition and the cross-sectional area of the bonding cable is 10mm² minimum

The usual method of connecting bonding clips is upstream first, then **downstream**.

Regulations 11–12 – Requires that gas meters are installed in such a way so as not to impede the escape of people from a premises. It also specifies requirements for the construction of certain gas meters. There are requirements to avoid electrical hazards and facilitate inspection and maintenance for pipe connections, gas **tightness testing** and purging of meters.

Downstream

This means after a given point which could for example be a gas meter. Therefore if an isolation valve were located downstream of a meter, it would mean it was situated on the pipework after the meter inlet.

Tightness test

A test to ascertain if a gas installation has any leaks.

KEY POINT

Equipotential bonding must be installed on the pipework a maximum of 600mm from the outlet of the meter and before the first tee.

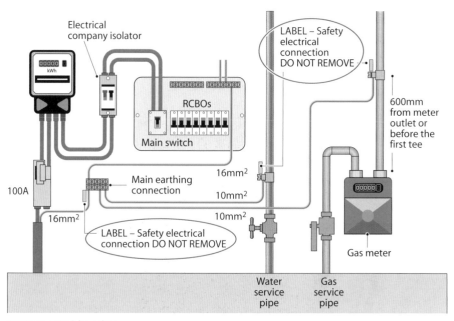

Equipotential bonding

Full ¼ turn movement of ECV lever impeded by obstruction; in addition the lever incorrectly falls to the 'on' position

Regulation 13 – Specifies requirements for meter housings in respect of the safe disposal of gas in the event of an escape, avoidance of combustion of materials and the provision of keys to enable the customer to access the ECV.

Regulation 14 – Stipulates protection arrangements to maintain gas pressures within safe operational limits. This mainly relates to LPG storage tanks or certain cylinder configurations. This regulation also gives details of the requirements for sealing of regulators on the meters and prevention of any unauthorised interference.

Meter regulator seal removed

Meter regulator seal intact

Emergency notice on a gas meter

Regulation 15 – Requires an emergency notice to be posted on the primary meter. This notice is to clearly state the procedure to be carried out in the event of a gas escape.

An extra notice may also be required which shows the position of the emergency control valve.

Regulation 16 – Prohibits the installation of any prepayment meter as the primary meter in certain cases. It also specifies requirements for the provision of notices for primary meters where gas is supplied to more than one secondary meter. Details are also specified in situations where a primary meter has been removed.

A prepayment meter is not permitted to be the primary meter

Regulation 17 – Requires any person who supplies or permits gas to be supplied through a primary meter to a secondary meter, such as a landlord, to display at a required position a notice which shows the configuration of the gas system.

Regulation 18 – Requires that gas pipework is to be installed in a safe position in relation to other pipes, drains, cables and electrical apparatus. It also requires that any engineer installing gas pipework to the meter must inform the responsible person of the requirement of equipotential bonding.

Electrical switch located too close to gas pipework

Regulation 19 – States the restrictions and protective measures for any gas pipe passing through a solid wall, cavity wall, floor or building foundations. Ducts and voids that accommodate installation pipework are required to be ventilated adequately. It also gives special conditions where pipework that is supplied to a living-flame-effect fire may be run in the wall cavity such that the appliance itself must operate with the fanned flued system and be installed within the inner leaf of a cavity wall.

No one shall install any installation pipework under the foundations of a building or in the ground under the base of a wall or footings unless adequate steps are taken to prevent damage to the installation pipework in the event of the movement of those structures or the ground.

Regulation 20 – Requires installation pipework to be installed to avoid impairing the structure of fire resistance of the building.

Regulation 21 – Requires a receptor to be fitted to an installation pipework where liquid or solid deposits may occur, for example from wet gas.

Regulation 22 – Specifies requirements for gas tightness testing after any work has been completed on installation pipework. It also requires that any such pipework be purged and then capped off. This applies whether or not gas is supplied to a premises.

Regulation 23 – Requires installation pipework that is not part of the premises or dwelling to be clearly marked and colour-coded to identify that it is carrying gas.

Tightness test to IGE/UP/1B/Ed3

KEY POINT

IGE/UP/1B/Ed3 is the normative document which gives up-to-date details on tightness testing.

Large bore gas pipe coloured yellow ochre

Regulation 24 – Requires that valves should be fitted in certain installation pipework and a system diagram be provided especially for use by the emergency services when the pipework exceeds certain specified sizes for supplying buildings with two or more floors.

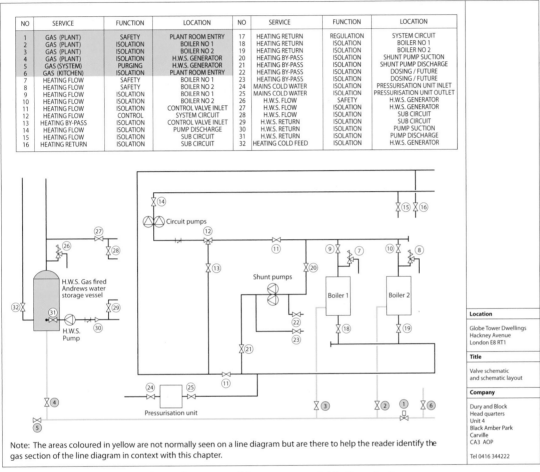

NO	SERVICE	FUNCTION	LOCATION	NO	SERVICE	FUNCTION	LOCATION
1	GAS (PLANT)	SAFETY	PLANT ROOM ENTRY	17	HEATING RETURN	REGULATION	SYSTEM CIRCUIT
2	GAS (PLANT)	ISOLATION	BOILER NO 1	18	HEATING RETURN	ISOLATION	BOILER NO 1
3	GAS (PLANT)	ISOLATION	BOILER NO 2	19	HEATING RETURN	ISOLATION	BOILER NO 2
4	GAS (PLANT)	ISOLATION	H.W.S. GENERATOR	20	HEATING BY-PASS	ISOLATION	SHUNT PUMP SUCTION
5	GAS (SYSTEM)	PURGING	H.W.S. GENERATOR	21	HEATING BY-PASS	ISOLATION	SHUNT PUMP DISCHARGE
6	GAS (KITCHEN)	ISOLATION	PLANT ROOM ENTRY	22	HEATING BY-PASS	ISOLATION	DOSING / FUTURE
7	HEATING FLOW	SAFETY	BOILER NO 1	23	HEATING BY-PASS	ISOLATION	DOSING / FUTURE
8	HEATING FLOW	SAFETY	BOILER NO 2	24	MAINS COLD WATER	ISOLATION	PRESSURISATION UNIT INLET
9	HEATING FLOW	ISOLATION	BOILER NO 1	25	MAINS COLD WATER	ISOLATION	PRESSURISATION UNIT OUTLET
10	HEATING FLOW	ISOLATION	BOILER NO 2	26	H.W.S. FLOW	SAFETY	H.W.S. GENERATOR
11	HEATING FLOW	ISOLATION	CONTROL VALVE INLET	27	H.W.S. FLOW	ISOLATION	H.W.S. GENERATOR
12	HEATING FLOW	CONTROL	SYSTEM CIRCUIT	28	H.W.S. FLOW	ISOLATION	SUB CIRCUIT
13	HEATING BY-PASS	ISOLATION	CONTROL VALVE INLET	29	H.W.S. RETURN	ISOLATION	SUB CIRCUIT
14	HEATING FLOW	ISOLATION	PUMP DISCHARGE	30	H.W.S. RETURN	ISOLATION	PUMP SUCTION
15	HEATING FLOW	ISOLATION	SUB CIRCUIT	31	H.W.S. RETURN	ISOLATION	PUMP DISCHARGE
16	HEATING RETURN	ISOLATION	SUB CIRCUIT	32	HEATING COLD FEED	ISOLATION	H.W.S. GENERATOR

Circuit pumps

H.W.S. Gas fired Andrews water storage vessel

H.W.S. Pump

Shunt pumps

Boiler 1

Boiler 2

Pressurisation unit

Location

Globe Tower Dwellings
Hackney Avenue
London E8 RT1

Title

Valve schematic
and schematic layout

Company

Dury and Block
Head quarters
Unit 4
Black Amber Park
Carville
CA3 AOP

Tel 0416 344222

Note: The areas coloured in yellow are not normally seen on a line diagram but are there to help the reader identify the gas section of the line diagram in context with this chapter.

Line diagram to be displayed clearly on a wall in a commercial boiler plant room

Regulation 25 – Gives interpretations of flues and gas operating pressures:

'A flue pipe means a pipe forming a flue but does not include the pipe built as a lining into either chimney or gas appliance ventilation duct.'

'Operating pressure in relation to a gas appliance means the pressure of gas at which it is designed to operate.'

A typical large commercial boiler plant room

Regulation 26 – Requires that any gas engineer who installs a gas appliance ensures that it is safe to use and is not connected to the gas supply if it cannot be used safely. It also requires that any second-hand appliance is in a safe working condition for further use. It gives details on how work on an appliance should maintain safety standards. It also highlights requirements for the examination of an appliance after the work has been completed and notification of any defects given to the owner or the user.

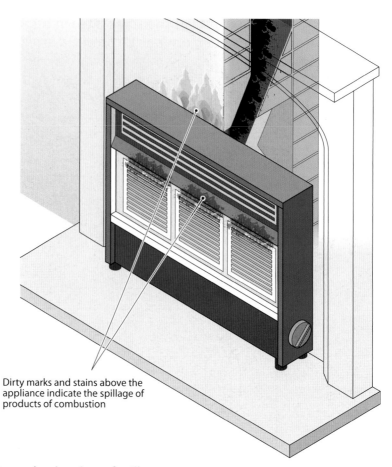

Dirty marks and stains above the appliance indicate the spillage of products of combustion

Appliance showing signs of spillage

Often referred to in industry as the FAGS rule (flues, air, gas, safety), the following is an interpretation of the GSIUR Regulation 20(6) Para 9:

'The engineer should check the effectiveness of any flue, the supply of combustion air and the operating pressure of the gas or heat input or where necessary both and its operations so as to ensure it is safe-functioning. For example a flued domestic gas appliance such as the boiler shall only be connected to the gas supply with a permanently fixed rigid pipe and never a flexible hose.'

Regulation 27 – Requires any flue to be fit for use, suitable and in a proper condition for the safe operation of the appliance it serves. It also requires that any power-operated flue system will **interlock** to turn off the appliance if the draught fails. There is also a requirement to examine the flue to ensure that it is installed in safe position. It also gives details of methods to prevent **spillage**.

Regulation 28 – Requires a gas appliance to be installed in a position that is readily accessible for operation inspection and maintenance.

Interlock

To terminate the gas supply to an appliance by a safety device when, for example, a fan in a flue system fails to operate.

Spillage

Signs of the products of combustion around an area, typically of an appliance, which should have discharged properly via a flue.

KEY POINT

Minimum clearance distances for operation inspection and maintenance purposes are usually specified by the manufacturer's instructions when installing an appliance.

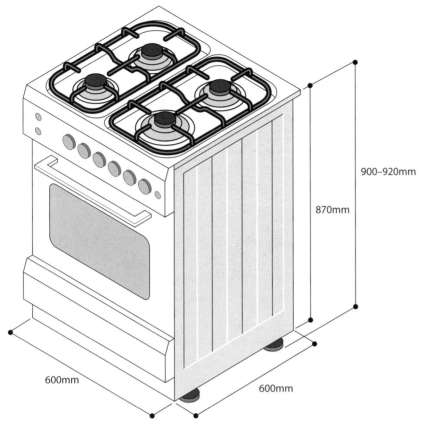

900–920mm

870mm

600mm

600mm

Manufacturers provide specific appliance dimensions which an engineer requires to correctly plan and install an appliance

Regulation 29 – Requires that the installer of any gas appliance leaves the manufacturer's instructions with the owner or occupier where the appliance is installed.

Regulation 30 – Prohibits the installation of certain gas appliances in specified rooms unless the appliance is a room-sealed type.

For example, no one shall install a gas appliance of more than 12.7kW input (14kW gross) in a sleeping area unless the appliance is room-sealed and incorporates a safety control-designed shutdown before there is a build-up of a dangerous quantity of products of combustion in the room.

Regulation 31 – Prohibits the installation of suspended appliances unless the installation pipework is capable of supporting the weight of the appliance and any associated fittings and pipework.

Regulation 32 – Specifies requirements for interlocking of automatic flue dampers and their inspection. It states that any manual flue damper in a domestic installation is prohibited and should either be removed or fixed in the fully open position.

Gas installer referring to manufacturers' technical literature before installation

Regulation 33 – Specifies requirements for testing gas tightness and examining appliances, flues and ventilation, and any action required when adjustments are necessary where gas appliances are installed at a time when gas is being supplied to the premises. It also gives details related to manufacturers' instructions.

Regulation 34 – Requires a responsible person, for instance an occupier or owner of the premises, typically a landlord, not to use or permit the use of any unsafe gas appliance. Any engineer who discovers unsafe service pipework or fittings must report this information to the responsible person or, if they are not present, to the gas supplier or transporter.

Regulation 35 – Requires an employer or self-employed person to ensure any gas appliance, flue or installation pipework installed at a place of work is controlled and maintained in a safe working condition.

Regulation 36 – Requires landlords in specified circumstances to ensure the safe maintenance of gas appliances, flues and installation pipework installed in their premises. It requires that annual safety checks are carried out and records are kept, and on some occasions displayed, regarding all of the inspected and tested appliances. It also requires that landlords ensure that no gas fittings, such as certain instantaneous water heaters, are or have been fitted in any room which is used as a sleeping accommodation since the regulations came into force. This also applies to any room that has been converted into a bedsit.

A label to identify an unsafe appliance must also be accompanied by a written record. All labels and report documents must be signed and dated with the gas engineer's registration details and/or location of the particular fault

Regulation 37 – Specifies action to be taken by gas suppliers and persons responsible for the premises in the event of an escape of liquid petroleum gas and/or the emission of carbon monoxide from any associated appliance or flue.

Regulation 38 – Requires protective measures as stipulated by the gas transporter to be taken by the consumer where gases used with the plant (such as a compressor or engine) could cause dangerous fluctuations or changes of pressure in the gas supply or where other gases such as compressed air could be induced into the supply.

Regulation 39 – Exceptions as liability.

This regulation provides certain exceptions as to liability under which a person is not deemed to be guilty of an offence where they can show that they took reasonable steps to prevent the contravention of the GSIUR.

Regulation 40 – Exemption certificates.

This regulation enables the HSE to grant exceptions. The intention is to use its power only in exceptional circumstances, usually to deal with variations to the regulations arising from technological or innovative changes that could not have been foreseen.

Regulation 41 – Revocation and amendment.

This regulation deals with proposed amendments to other related regulations.

Families of gas

There are three families of fuel gases that have been internationally agreed based on the Wobbe index or **Wobbe number**, which is used to compare the combustion energy outputs of different compositions of fuel gases in an appliance when it is operating.

- **Family 1** – Manufactured gases previously known as town gases and derived from coal. They can also be derived from oil feedstock (a derivative of coal tar processing) and sometimes manufactured gas can include LPG/air mixtures.
- **Family 2** – Natural gases, typically hydrocarbons, predominantly methane, which come from wellheads in the North Sea and Morecambe Bay and can also be imported from other countries.
- **Family 3** – Liquefied petroleum gas (LPG), which is generally composed of propane, butane or a mixture of those gases.

Wobbe number

Sometimes known as the Wobbe index, this is used to compare the combustion energy outputs of different compositions of fuel gases.

Combustion (LO2)

There are eleven assessment criteria for this outcome:

1. State the characteristics of combustion for natural gas and liquid petroleum gas.
2. State the combustion process.
3. Describe complete and incomplete combustion.
4. Identify the causes of incomplete combustion in gas appliances.
5. State the visual signs of incomplete combustion.
6. Identify stoichiometric ratios of natural gas and liquid petroleum gas.
7. Compare the difference between net and gross kW output.
8. Describe the characteristics of flame type.
9. Explain the dangers of carbon monoxide (CO).
10. State the symptoms of carbon monoxide poisoning.
11. State the actions to reduce the risk of carbon monoxide poisoning.

This outcome deals with the combustion of natural gas, which is mainly 'methane' (CH_4), and liquid petroleum gas (LPG), eg propane (C_3H_8) and butane (C_4H_{10}), and its aim is to ensure that the principles of combustion are fully understood to ensure gas safety.

The Gas Regulations in Regulation 26(9) lay down mandatory duties on gas users and operatives to ensure that correct combustion takes place when operatives are working on gas appliances.

When assessing the combustion performance of domestic appliances, a visual survey of the flame picture will usually be sufficient to detect if complete combustion is taking place.

SmartScreen Unit 307
PowerPoint 1

Gascoseeker™ mark 2 showing the Lower Explosive Limit (LEL) measurement mode

IS

IS means intrinsically safe, ie apparatus in which no spark or any thermal effect, which is produced under prescribed test conditions, is capable of causing ignition of a given explosive mixture. Therefore, a Gascoseeker™ must be IS as it is used to measure the ratio of gas in air.

Gas characteristics

Odour

Natural gas (NG) and LPG have no easily discernible natural odour. Therefore an odourant is added to help identify if there is any gas present in the air. The chemical originally used for this purpose was called tetrahydrothiophene although diethyl sulphide and ethyl or butyl mercaptan are now more commonly used. Only a tiny amount is used to give the gas a recognisable smell. The strength of the smell in itself cannot be used to assess actual volume of gas in the air. Therefore precise instruments must be used to determine if there is an explosive mixture present in a given area or if that limit is in danger of being reached. These instruments must be regularly calibrated and be intrinsically safe (**IS**), which means that when they are in use they will not create a spark which could ignite an explosive mixture of gas.

Toxicity

The toxicity of a gas means whether it is poisonous and could cause death if inhaled.

Many years ago town gas (family 1) used to be processed from coal and in its natural state produced carbon monoxide (CO). Inhaling it could lead to death as the CO replaced oxygen in the bloodstream and the organs of the body would become poisoned.

The composition of coal gas varied in accordance with the type of coal used and the temperature of the carbonisation process. However, typical figures were hydrogen 50%, methane 35%, carbon monoxide 10% and ethylene 5%, meaning that carbon monoxide was present in the gas even before it was burnt. The ethylene produced a luminous flame and was used in gas mantles earlier in the twentieth century to provide lighting on the street and in houses.

Typical gas light in dwelling circa 1900

Gas engineer servicing a street light

Gas street lighting – this period style lighting is still in operation in some parts of London

Natural gas (family 2) does not contain CO and is therefore non-toxic. However, if incomplete combustion occurs during the burning process of natural gas then CO can be produced. Therefore, it is important when carrying out work on any gas appliance that you check that the products of combustion can be adequately removed and sufficient air is provided for complete combustion. It is also important to ensure that heat input and ventilation to the appliance are correct.

In any event, if natural gas is allowed to build up in a confined space, it can displace oxygen in the air and can present a risk of suffocation.

Calorific value (CV)

When gas burns it gives off heat and this energy is called its **calorific value** (CV). This gives an indication of the heating power or amount of heat that is released when complete combustion of a specific volume of gas is achieved. The calorific value of, for example, natural gas in the UK is typically measured in the SI unit of megajoules per cubic metre (MJ/m^3) and its CV is between 37.5 and 43.0 MJ/m^3 gross. The CV of natural gas varies very slightly in each part of the UK because the gas is derived from different sources. Up-to-date information about the CV of the gas being supplied is printed on consumers' domestic gas bills.

> **KEY POINT**
>
> Gas family 1 contains CO.

> **Calorific value**
>
> Energy factor measured in MJ/m^3 when gas burns and gives off heat.

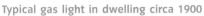

Gas summary			Gas account		
Last reading	This reading	Gas used	Cost split	Charges	Meter:
Tariff - Standard Gas / Monthly Direct Debit					
15/06/11 9770 Actual	30/09/11 9833 Estimate	Calorific Value 39.200 63 (100s cubic feet) = 1985 kWh	first 174 at 7.253p next 1811 at 2.656p	£12.62 £48.10	
PC * 30/09/11 9833 Estimate	05/12/11 9959 Estimate	Calorific Value 39.300 126 (100s cubic feet) = 3981 kWh	first 1296 at 8.297p next 2685 at 3.086p	£107.53 £82.86	
		Cost of gas used this period		£251.11	
'M' Number	3063131305	VAT at 5% on £251.11		+ £12.55	
Correction Factor	1.022640	Total gas charges this period		£263.66	

Your meter reading

* **Price Change**
Please note - there's been a price change during this bill period. We've split your fuel usage over the different prices.

Excerpt from a typical energy bill showing the current calorific value of the gas supplied to a dwelling

SmartScreen Unit 307
Handout 2

The CV of natural gas is measured continually by National Grid using process gas chromatographs which separate natural gas into its constituent compounds (methane, ethane, carbon dioxide, etc) and then measure the CV amount of each gas to end up with a very accurate and reliable figure in accordance with international gas standards. All domestic customers and most industrial customers are billed on the basis of the daily CV averages for the charging area in which their premises are situated.

Gross calorific value is the amount of heat obtained from gas during the complete combustion process. This includes water vapour. Some of the heat is trapped in this water vapour and is referred to as latent heat. This latent heat is lost through the flue when it discharges the products of combustion to atmosphere. Condensing boilers capture or reclaim much of the latent heat and, as a result, adds to the overall efficiency of such appliances. Because of the drop in temperature in the flue gases during this condensing process, it turns back from vapour into a liquid at about 55°C which is known as the dew point and condensate is formed – hence the term 'condensing appliances'.

BS 5440-1:2008 explains the conversion calculation of gross and net as follows.

> 'NOTE 5 – The data in this British Standard refers to heat input expressed in terms of **net calorific values** (CV) with conversion given for natural gas gross CV quoted in brackets where appropriate. The ratio of gross heat input to net heat input is approximately 1.11 for natural gas propane and butane. For example, conversion of 9kW input based on gross CV for natural gas to the equivalent net CV input is as follows.
>
> net input = 9.0 ÷ 1.11 = 8.1kW'

Gross calorific value, therefore, is the amount of heat obtained from gas during the complete combustion process which includes water vapour (latent heat); net calculations do not include this latent heat and accordingly take away about 10% from a gross figure to end up with a net figure.

Specific gravity (relative density)

Every substance has weight or mass and this includes gas. For various reasons it is necessary to compare the mass of gases and this is done by a comparison of their densities. The density of a substance is the mass of a given volume such as kilograms per cubic metre (kg/m^3). When comparing a liquid or a solid the standard is water and has been given the figure 1; when comparisons are made for gas the standard is air. Dry air has a specific gravity of 1 and all

---

Gross calorific value

The amount of heat obtained from gas during the complete combustion process which includes water vapour (latent heat).

Net calorific value

The amount of heat obtained from gas during the complete combustion process excluding latent heat.

KEY POINT

The calorific value of gas changes periodically depending on where it is sourced. This value is always printed by the supplier on energy bills.

gases are compared to this. The relationship between the density of a given substance and the density of the standard, ie 1, is known as the relative density or the specific gravity (SG).

Natural gas is less dense and lighter than air (1) with a density of 0.58 and therefore will tend to rise if released into the atmosphere. LPG, ie propane (approximately 1.5) and butane (approximately 2), is more dense and therefore heavier than air and as a result will fall to the ground if present in air. The different fuel gases which are used today differ greatly in their individual properties. Therefore any appliances designed to burn on natural gas would not be suitable for LPG without some modification.

Flame speed

The speed at which a flame travels while it is mixed with air is critical to the end result at the burner.

The flame speed of natural gas is 0.36m/s and that of propane 0.46m/s.

Gas needs to be ignited correctly before it will burn continuously. Each gas has its own individual ignition temperature which must be reached before combustion can be achieved.

Natural gas 704°C

Propane   482–540°C

Butane   410–470°C

A typical burner comprises an injector and a burner bar. The purpose of the injector is to inject gas into the mixing tube of the burner at correct speed in order to entrain air to create the appropriate air–gas mixture to complete combustion at the burner ports. The sizing of the injector is critical because even with the same pressure applied, different sizes of injector orifices will affect the heat input of an appliance. For this reason manufacturers mention in the literature that when servicing an appliance, you should never use a metallic object to clean the orifice of an injector. This is because the use of metals which are harder than the injector can enlarge or distort the shape of the injector orifice.

Some injectors have single holes while others are composed of several holes.

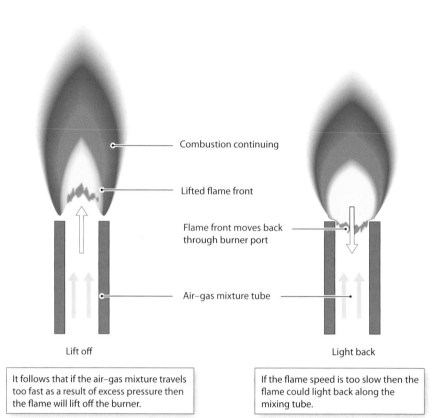

Combustion continuing

Lifted flame front

Flame front moves back through burner port

Air–gas mixture tube

Lift off

Light back

It follows that if the air–gas mixture travels too fast as a result of excess pressure then the flame will lift off the burner.

If the flame speed is too slow then the flame could light back along the mixing tube.

Injectors

Flammability limits

If a room were absolutely full of natural gas with no air present and a source of ignition was introduced then there is no possibility of the gas igniting. Gas requires a proportion of air to create an explosive mixture.

The ratio of gas to air for natural gas to ignite is between 5 and 15% approximately.

- 5% is the lower explosive limit (LEL).
- 15% is the upper explosive limit (UEL).

Therefore if the same room mentioned above had between 5 and 15% of gas present in air and a source of ignition was introduced then combustion would occur.

LPG has lower limits of flammability than natural gas, and concentrations in the air between 2 and 10% for propane and 1.8 and 9% for butane could result in an explosive mixture.

An adjustable air inlet port on the primary inlet of a burner which allows for correction of the flame picture

Wobbe number

A Wobbe number or index gives an indication of the heat output from a burner when a specific gas is used. The amount of heat released at a burner will depend on the amount of heat in the gas as determined by the calorific value (CV). The rate at which the gas is burned is crucial. This depends on the size of the burner injector, the gas pressure and its relative weight, all of which correspond to how easily the gas can pass through the injector to the burner.

The Wobbe number links two sets of information to create a number: first, the calorific value and the specific gravity, which can be variable and, second, the injector size and the gas pressure, which are fixed because of the design of the appliance (which can only be changeable by adjustment carried out by a gas engineer for example).

If the calorific value (CV) is divided by the square root of the specific gravity (SG), the Wobbe number will be obtained.

Example

$$\text{Wobbe number} = \frac{CV}{\sqrt{SG}}$$

For example the Wobbe number for natural gas is

$$\frac{38.5 \text{MJ/m}^3 \text{ (CV)}}{\sqrt{0.58} \text{ (SG)}} = 50.55$$

Families of gases

There are different families of gas and because of their different CVs and SGs they have a varied range of Wobbe numbers.

Families of gas and their respective Wobbe numbers

Family	Wobbe number range (approx)	Gas type
1	23–29	Town gas (manufactured)
2	47–54	Natural
3	72–87	LPG

Combustion

In order to understand the gas combustion process some basic understanding of chemistry is required. Combustion is in fact a chemical reaction which requires three essential elements:

- fuel
- oxygen
- ignition.

The effect of these elements will create an exothermic reaction, in other words, heat. The main products of combustion (**POCs**) generated from this reaction are carbon dioxide (CO_2), carbon monoxide (CO)* and water vapour (H_2O). It is important to keep levels of carbon monoxide (CO) to a minimum.

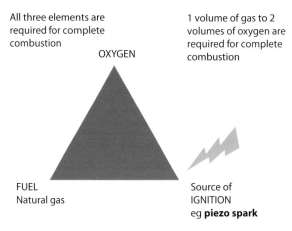

All three elements are required for complete combustion

OXYGEN

1 volume of gas to 2 volumes of oxygen are required for complete combustion

FUEL
Natural gas

Source of
IGNITION
eg **piezo spark**

The ignition temperature of natural gas is 704°C

Combustion triangle for natural gas

*Invariably there can be very low parts per million (PPM) readings of CO for even the newest and cleanest-burning appliances, but often no CO reading shows up, as the amount of CO is so minimal. Only combustion would show the presence of CO.

Air requirements for the complete combustion of natural gas:

$$CH_4 \quad + \quad 2O_2 \quad = CO_2 \quad + \quad 2H_2O$$
1 volume + 2 volumes = 1 volume + 2 volumes

As with all equations both sides must balance.

POCs

POCs stands for Products of Combustion which are produced during the combustion process of gas.

Piezo spark

These ignition are commonly found on space heaters and older style boilers. Piezo ignition uses the principle of piezoelectricity, which is the electric charge that accumulates in some materials in response to high pressure. The devices consist of a small, spring-loaded hammer which, when a button is pressed, hits a quartz crystal which in turn deforms and produces a high voltage and the resultant spark ignites the gas typically located at the pilot port of an appliance.

KEY POINT
Natural gas is composed of 90% methane.

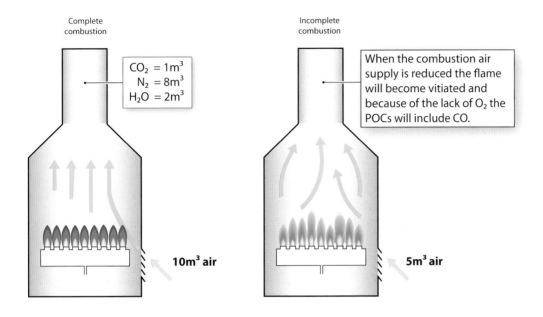

A comparison of two appliances showing the effect of the reduction of primary air in the combustion process (approximate figures)

Stoichiometric combustion

The term **stoichiometric combustion** means perfect combustion and is only ever achievable in laboratory conditions.

To create perfect complete combustion 1 volume of natural gas (mainly methane) must react with 2 volumes of oxygen. In normal living environments, particulates such as hair and dust and contaminants like oils and vapours are induced into the air intake of an appliance during the combustion process and affect the quality of the combustion process; this means that the stoichiometric mixture cannot be achieved.

Air

Air is made of many different gases. Nitrogen is the largest constituent of air and is an inert gas because it cannot affect the combustion process. Oxygen, however, is an essential component of combustion and creates an explosive mixture with a gas such as natural gas which is mainly composed of methane.

Stoichiometric combustion

Combustion involving the exact proportions of air and gas required to create complete combustion.

Constituents of air

Gas	Chemical symbol	Percentage (%)
Oxygen	O_2	21
Nitrogen	N_2	78
Other gases		1

Constituents of natural gas

Natural gas	Chemical symbol	Percentage (%)
Methane	CH_4	90
Ethane	C_2H_6	5.3
Nitrogen	N_2	2.7
Propane	C_3H_8	1
Carbon dioxide	CO_2	0.6
Butane	C_4H_{10}	0.4

The table above shows the gases that make up natural gas. It can be seen that natural gas is mainly composed of methane as is described in the GSIUR.

Comparison of the properties of gases

Property	Unit value	Natural gas	Propane	Butane
Specific gravity	1 (Air)	0.58	1.5	2
Gross calorific value	MJ/m^3	38.5	95	121.5
Air/gas ratio	vol/vol	9.8:1	23.8:1	30.9:1
Wobbe number	MJ/m^3	47–54	72–87	72–87
Flammability limits	% gas in air	5–15	2–10	2–9
Ignition temp	°C	704	530	500
Flame speed	m/s	0.36	0.46	0.38

By referring to the comparison chart it can be seen that LPG requires a different ratio of air to gas to create complete combustion when compared with natural gas. One volume of propane requires 23.8 volumes of air while butane requires 30.9.

Combustion process

When dealing with domestic gas appliances the gas typically enters the burner through an injector. The size of the injector orifice and the burner pressure are very important as the right amount of air needs to be drawn in through the primary air port to create the correct air–gas mixture in the mixing tube and eventually the burner itself. Once the flame is ignited it requires secondary air to sustain complete and proper combustion.

When a qualified engineer inspects and services such burners they will look out for any type of obstruction inside the mixing tube or blockages that could affect the combustion process. Lint and other blockages can cause lift-off, especially if the retention ports are affected. Lighting back of the flame could also occur if the primary air ports or mixing tube are blocked.

The perforated lint arrestor located at the primary air inlet is partially blocked with airborne debris and particles which make up lint

Flame retention

Natural gas has a slower flame speed than manufactured gas and retention ports are built into the burner bar to prevent the flame from lifting. Close examination of cooker hotplate burners will reveal small retention ports below the larger burner ports.

KEY POINT

If dirt and debris are allowed to build up on a burner bar then the retention ports can become blocked, and flame lift and incomplete combustion can occur.

A primary air port showing the location of the injector on a boiler burner assembly. The section of the burner shows large ports for the main flame and smaller ports which are the retention ports to keep the flame stable and prevent it from lifting

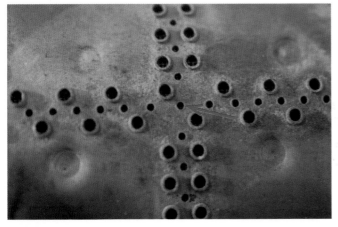

Retention ports

Pre-aerated flame

Air is entrained in the mixing tube before ignition.

Post-aerated flame

Air is drawn for combustion from the surrounding air once the flame is lit often resulting in a loose yellow floppy flame.

Pre

Means 'before'.

Flame pictures

When gas and oxygen are burned in a mixture, a chemical reaction takes place and a flame is produced. This happens when a mixture of gas and air is heated to its ignition temperature.

There are two main types of flame relevant to the combustion process and they are **pre-aerated** and **post-aerated**.

A **pre**-aerated flame is the most common type used in domestic gas appliances. This is where some of the air required for combustion is pre-mixed in a tube before it is ignited at the outlet such as the burner. The air that is provided is called primary air.

A pre-aerated flame is smaller than a post-aerated flame but both give off the same amount of heat. The pre-aerated flame burns with a well-defined inner cone inside the outer mantle.

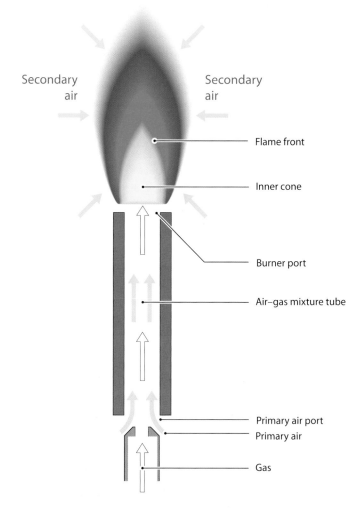

Pre-aerated flame

Four major components make up a pre-aerated burner. They are the primary air port, injector, mixing tube and the burner incorporating the flame ports

A **post**-aerated flame takes its air for combustion from the surrounding atmosphere after the gas leaves a pipe or tube and has a luminous appearance. In other words, all of the air for the combustion process is provided once a gas leaves the burner ports.

Post

Means 'after'.

An example of a luminous loose yellow floppy flame

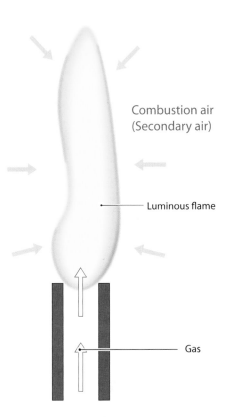

Post-aerated flame

The post-aerated flame which receives secondary air only for combustion will result in a loose yellow, floppy flame. Similarly a pre-aerated flame with the primary air port blocked will also produce the same result

Overgassing and undergassing

The correct gas operating pressure for an appliance is stated in the manufacturer's instructions and can also be located on the appliance data plate. When testing or servicing an appliance the gas pressures should always be checked and adjusted accordingly. If too much gas is applied to an appliance mixing tube which has a fixed air port, then the required volume of air will be reduced accordingly and incomplete combustion is likely to occur. If the gas pressure is too low, then insufficient air will be entrained into the mixing tube and this will again produce incomplete combustion, typically evident by a loose floppy flame.

Flame front

Once the air–gas mixture has travelled through the mixing tube and is being ignited at the injector, the place where the unburnt gas stops and the flame begins is called the flame front.

The shape of the flame front is often conical but this does depend on the actual burner design and this is the point where the speed of the gas is the same as the flame speed.

The amount of primary air will determine the shape of the flame front: more air will help create a flatter and noisier flame at the burner and less air tends to produce a longer flame front.

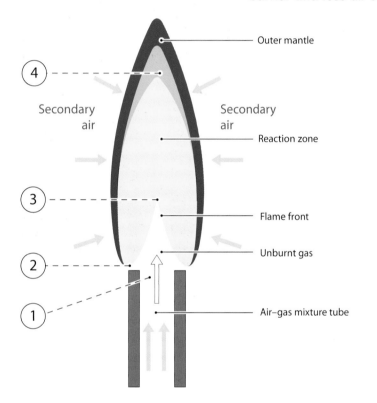

4: This is the outer mantle and the hottest part of the flame where combustion is completed. Temperature begins to fall here as heat is lost to ambient air.

3–4: This is the reaction zone and as more air is drawn in the mixture weakens further.

2–3: This is the zone of the flame up to the top of the inner cone which forms the actual flame front. The temperature of the mixture rises quickly here and is weakened because of the induced air resulting in some unburned gases remaining.

1–2: This is at the top of the burner and burner port. Just inside this opening is where the temperature of the air–gas mixture begins to rise.

Flame front

Flame impingement

Flame impingement occurs when flames impede one another on a gas burner bar and, as a result, change their individual shape. This problem can be caused by debris falling onto the burner bar from a rusty or dirty heat exchanger or by a build-up of soot. Whenever a flame comes in contact with a colder surface and the inner cone of a pre-aerated flame is broken, then unburnt gases will be released and, as a result, the combustion process will become much worse.

Flame chilling

Flame chilling can occur when a flame makes contact with an object and the temperature of the flame is consequently reduced. The gases will be lowered below their normal ignition temperature and incomplete combustion will occur. Chilling can also occur when a flame is affected by a draught or other sources of cold air.

Sooting on top of a flueless water heater

A post-aerated yellow floppy flame with its primary air port partially blocked resulting in incomplete combustion and the potential hazard of the creation of sooting on an appliance

Sooting

The poor performance of a flame could lead to soot deposits appearing within an appliance or even the flue. If a flame picture is yellow, loose and floppy, this indicates that there is a lack of air in the combustion process and, as a result, incomplete combustion is occurring causing CO to be produced. Carbon (soot) in itself is not dangerous but when a flame touches a surface then the carbon is deposited onto it and this can manifest itself in the form of dust or hard lumps.

Burners are often completely removable from the appliance for the purposes of inspection and cleaning and there are metal locators incorporated into the design housing to enable the correct location and alignment of the burner. If there is an error in the refitting of the burner into its correct location, then incomplete combustion and resultant sooting can occur, especially if the flame from the burner touches any surface within the appliance. This problem is often therefore caused by poor alignment of a burner located within a heat exchanger.

If the deposits gather around the passages of the heat exchanger then the combustion process degenerates as the secondary air is reduced and soot is then carried upwards and adheres to the flue. This in turn narrows the diameter of the outlet which will eventually lead to the unwanted event of spillage of POCs into a building.

Alcohols are present in the combustion process but during incomplete combustion these become aldehydes. They are identifiable by their smell and can cause irritation to the eyes.

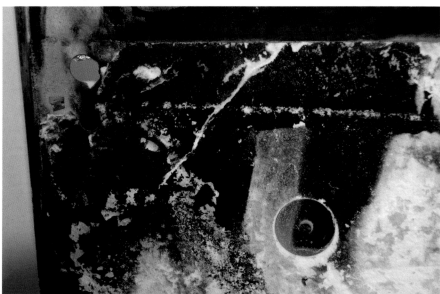

Soot deposits on a panel from a boiler heat exchanger location, the result of incomplete combustion

Vitiation

Vitiation means lack of oxygen. If the atmosphere from where the gas draws its air supply for combustion becomes vitiated the result will be incomplete combustion.

Vitiation

Lack of oxygen.

Vitiation can occur if the purpose-provided ventilation within a dwelling is insufficient or has become blocked. If the products of combustion spill back into the room where the appliance is located then the atmosphere will also become vitiated. Blockages of the flueways within an appliance create a vitiated environment and result in incomplete combustion identifiable by a loose and floppy flame picture. Ventilation and flues will be covered in more detail in Learning Outcome 4 in this chapter.

Staining and damp

When inspecting appliances an engineer frequently comes across staining around the primary flue area where it is connected to the appliance or perhaps around a gas fire or even on the casing of a gas appliance. Sometimes dampness is evident on brickwork which is in close proximity to the flue of an appliance. These stains and signs of dampness are typical indications that products of incomplete combustion have not travelled to the flue terminal and the atmosphere as they are designed to do but instead are entering the building. This indicates an immediately dangerous situation for whomever is in the area when the appliance is in operation and potentially puts them at risk of carbon monoxide poisoning.

Linting

Linting of a gas appliance means that a pre-aerated burner can become blocked or choked by a combination of dust and fibres present in the atmosphere from where the air for combustion is drawn. Lint comprises fats, oils, wool, hair, dust and fibres from man-made materials such as terylene. Lint will collect in primary burner ports, burner ports and gauzes and this interferes with the combustion process as it restricts primary aeration. As a result some **open-flued** appliances such as back boiler units (**BBU**) have lint arresters incorporated into their design to prevent such a problem occurring.

> **Open flue**
>
> A flue that is open to the room where the appliance is fitted and relies on heat from the combustion process to create an updraught to evacuate the products of combustion. Often called natural draught.
>
> An open flue typically comprises a primary flue, draught diverter, secondary flue and terminal.

> **BBU**
>
> BBU means back boiler unit which is a boiler located in a builder's opening with a flue which discharges up an existing chimney. They often have integral space heaters fitted at the front of them and are commonly situated in a lounge or living room of a dwelling.

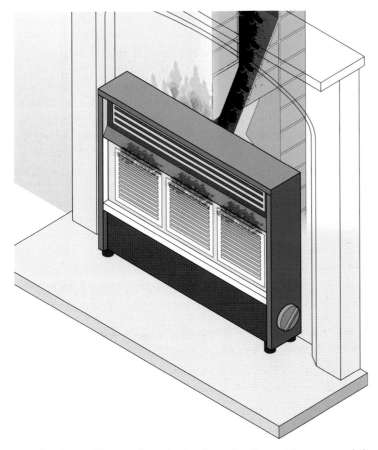

Appliance showing evidence of products of combustion spillage around the case

Over a period of time staining can be produced around an appliance because of incomplete combustion occurring due to a lack of primary air. This damaging process will continue and can then prevent the safe dispersal of POCs by blocking off flue ways and heat exchangers with the resultant forcing of particles of carbon to deposit outside the appliance. Evidence of this type of hazard signifies that the set-up is immediately dangerous and the cause must be fully investigated and remedied before the appliance can be used again.

Carbon monoxide (CO)

Carbon monoxide is the deadly and invisible by-product of incomplete combustion.

It has no colour, taste or smell and if it is inhaled the effects on the human body are immense and, depending on the amount of CO being produced and the duration of exposure, in the worst case scenario can prove fatal within a few minutes.

The human body takes in oxygen through the lungs and transports it around the body in haemoglobin within red blood cells. However, CO binds more easily with haemoglobin than oxygen. This preferential binding leads to displacement of oxygen, and so starves the tissues of oxygen.

The effects of CO on the body

Volume % CO in air	Volume % CO in blood	How this adversely affects the body
0.01	0–15	**After 2 to 3 hours** – Slight headache
0.02	1–30	**After 2 to 3 hours** – Increased headache, dizziness and feeling sick
0.05	30–50	**Within 1 to 2 hours** – Strong headache, nausea and palpitations
0.15	50–55	**Within 30 minutes** – Severe headache, dizziness and nausea
0.3	55–60	**Within 10 minutes** – Severe headache – convulsions and increased breathing rate with dizziness and nausea
0.6	70–75	**Within 1 or 2 minutes** – Severe symptoms leading to death within 15 minutes
1	85–90	**Within 1 to 3 minutes** – Immediate symptoms – death

Actions required to help prevent CO developing

Regular servicing of appliances which will include inspecting and cleaning of primary air ports, burner bars and heat exchangers will help to prevent the build-up of deposits which can lead to incomplete combustion.

A calibrated flue gas analyser should be used to confirm that an appliance is operating safely and efficiently. It should be used in conjunction with setting up burner pressures and gas rates in accordance with the manufacturer's instructions.

Sometimes a flue can become blocked and a spillage and flue flow test will help detect any such problem. If a chimney or flue requires cleaning then it is recommended that a qualified Gas Safe chimney sweep should carry out the work and produce a report on the condition of the chimney and any remedial work required.

CO detectors are excellent devices which can help warn people in order to prevent accidents. Some devices can be installed to activate an interlock which will isolate a gas appliance when predetermined levels of CO are detected. BS 7967 Part 1:2005 describes these devices as electrically operated gas detection apparatuses designed for continuous use to give a warning alarm in the event of a hazardous accumulation of CO. Just like smoke detectors, these devices are becoming more readily available in the market and, as a result, more visible in people's homes. Many devices are battery-powered which gives versatility in where to locate them. They should always be installed in accordance with the manufacturer's guidelines.

A flue gas analyser is often used in the process of servicing gas appliances. It can also be used to detect the presence of CO in a room, especially when a flueless appliance like a cooker is operating in an area such as a domestic kitchen. The operation, range and scope of flue gas analysers are identified in BS 7967.

It is essential that gas appliances are serviced regularly in accordance with the manufacturers' instructions to ensure and sustain their safe, efficient and economic operation. Through careful routine maintenance many problems can be identified and anticipated, and by setting up the correct gas pressures, then testing with a calibrated combustion analyser, the performance of the appliance can be verified.

> **KEY POINT**
>
> The combustion of natural gas is mentioned in the GSIUR Regulation 26(9) which states that an operative should examine:
> - the effectiveness of any flue
> - the supply of air for combustion
> - the operating pressure or heat input of any appliance
> - the capacity of the appliance to function correctly.

> **KEY POINT**
>
> It is recommended that appliances should be regularly serviced and/or inspected by Gas Safe engineers to ensure their safe and efficient operation.

Domestic CO detector

A hand-held flue gas analyser

Principles of flues (LO3)

There are eight assessment criteria for this outcome:

1 State the primary purpose of flues.
2 Explain the working principles of different flue types.
3 Distinguish different flue types in relation to flue categories.
4 Identify flue terminal positions in accordance with BS 5440 Part 1.
5 Describe flue component parts.
6 State the factors that can influence flue performance.
7 Explain how to carry out a flue flow test.
8 Explain how to carry out a spillage test.

The aim of this outcome is to identify the primary purpose of a flue when connected to a gas appliance and to describe and distinguish the working principles of different flue types in relation to their individual categories. Throughout this section details of the components of a flue and terminal positions will be shown as well as factors that can influence the performance of a flue. It is essential that any person working on an appliance knows how to carry out a spillage and flue flow test and this process is made clear in this outcome.

The purpose of flues

SmartScreen Unit 307
PowerPoint 2 and Handout 4

The purpose of a flue is to safely and effectively remove the products of combustion from, in this instance, a gas-burning appliance. BS 5400 Part 1:2008: Installation and maintenance of flues and ventilation for gas appliances of a rated input not exceeding 70kW net (1st, 2nd, and 3rd family gases) adopts the terminology used in EN 15287 and describes a flue as 'a passage for conveying combustion products to the outside air'. A chimney is described in this standard as 'a structure surrounding a flue or flues'. A terminal is identified as 'a fitting fitted to the chimney outlet'.

Manufacturers' instructions take precedence whenever standards conflict regarding the design or installation requirements of a flue system.

Flue types

Flue types are divided into three basic categories:

Category letter	Type of appliance
A	Flueless
B	Open-flued
C	Room-sealed

These categories are then further divided by the addition of a second number which identifies if the flue is natural draught or has a fan, and if the fan is located upstream or downstream of a heat exchanger. Manufacturers' instructions and appliance data plates will give details on what type of flue or flue variations appliances are designed for.

Flue types

A – flueless, B – open-flued, C – room-sealed.

Flue type	Category letter with first digit	Flue of chimney design	Natural draught identified by the second digit	Fan downstream of heat exchanger identified by the second digit	Fan upstream of heat exchanger identified by the second digit
Flueless	A	Not applicable	A_1	A_2	A_3
Open-flued	B_1	With draught diverter	B_{11}	B_{12}	B_{13}
	B_2	With draught diverter	B_{21}	B_{22}	B_{23}
Room-sealed	C_1	Horizontal balanced flued inlet with air ducts to outside air	C_{11}	C_{12}	C_{13}
	C_2	Inlet and outlet ducts connect to a common duct system in SE-duct for multi-appliance connections	C_{21}	C_{22}	C_{23}
	C_3	Vertical – balanced flue and inlet ducts to outside	C_{31}	C_{32}	C_{33}
	C_4	Inlet and outlet connections to U-duct system for multi-appliance system	C_{41}	C_{42}	C_{43}
	C_5	Unbalanced flue or inlet air ducted system	C_{51}	C_{52}	C_{53}
	C_6	Appliance purchased with a flue or air inlet ducts	C_{61}	C_{62}	C_{63}
	C_7	Vertical flue to an outlet which takes its air from a loft space	C_{71}	C_{72}	C_{73}
	C_8	Flue connected to a common duct system which takes an air supply from outside making it an unbalanced system	C_{81}	C_{82}	C_{83}

Type A₁ – flueless appliance

A flueless appliance takes the air required for combustion from the room where it is situated and discharges its products of combustion into the same area.

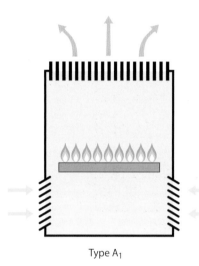

Type A₁

Flueless natural draught

A typical example of flueless single-point water heater

Type B₁ – open-flued appliance

An open-flued appliance also takes the air required for combustion from the room in which it is situated but discharges its products of combustion to the outside air via a flue system.

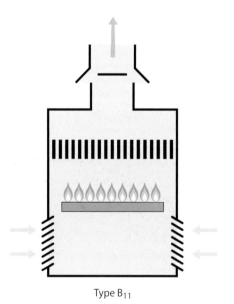

Type B₁₁

Open-flued natural draught with draught diverter

Draught diverter on a floor-standing open-flued boiler

Type C₁ – room-sealed appliances

A room-sealed appliance takes its air for combustion from the outside and it discharges its products of combustion to the outside.

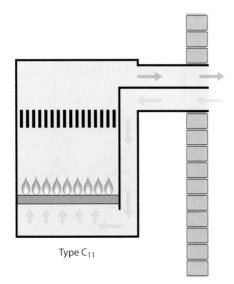

Type C_{11}

Horizontal balanced flue/inlet air ducts to the outside air – natural draught

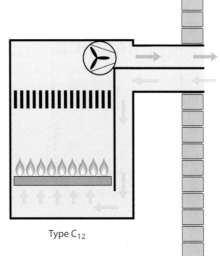

Type C_{12}

Room-sealed with fan downstream of the heat exchanger

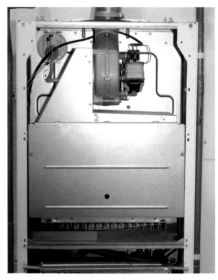

Type C_{12} appliance with case removed (fan downstream)

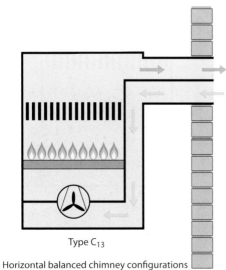

Type C_{13}

Horizontal balanced chimney configurations

Horizontal balance flue/inlet air ducts to outside air with the fan located upstream of the heat exchanger

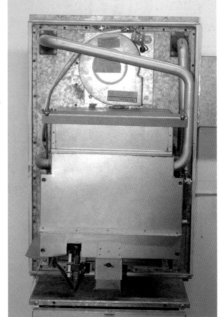

Type C_{13} appliance with case removed (fan upstream)

With Type C_{13} flues the case of the appliance is under pressure. Therefore checking the integrity of the seal is of paramount importance for safe and efficient operation of the appliance.

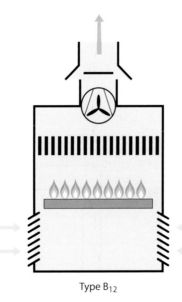

Type B$_{12}$

A type B$_{12}$ open-flued appliance with fan downstream of the heat exchanger

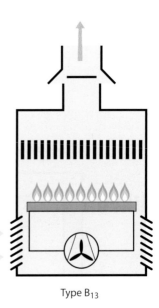

Type B$_{13}$

A type B$_{13}$ open-flued appliance with fan upstream of the heat exchanger

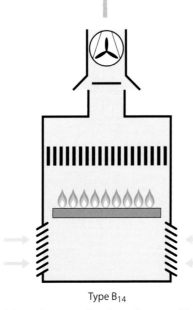

Type B$_{14}$

A type B$_{14}$ open-flued appliance with fan downstream of the draught diverter

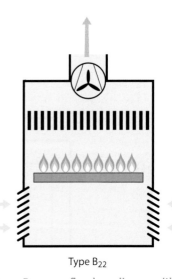

Type B$_{22}$

A type B$_{22}$ open-flued appliance without a draught diverter with a fan downstream of the heat exchanger

Vertex flue

A special type of C$_{72}$ flue arrangement which takes its air for combustion from the roof space which is ventilated in accordance with the manufacturer's instructions.

Air vent

A non-adjustable purpose-provided arrangement which is designed to allow permanent ventilation to an appliance.

A more recent method of removing products of combustion is the **vertex flue** system.

The type of flue seen in the image on the next page is called a vertex C$_{72}$ and it takes its air for combustion from the loft area rather than from the outside like other room-sealed balanced flues. The critical distance above the finished floor level (FFL), which could simply be joists in this case, in the loft area to the underside of the air inlet is 300mm. In addition, the measurement would need to be at least 150mm above any insulation and the measurement in both cases is taken from the bottom openings of the **air vent**. A cage is fitted around the air intake to prevent the ingress of foreign bodies and debris which could create incomplete combustion. It is also advisable to fit a bird guard to the terminal to prevent blockages.

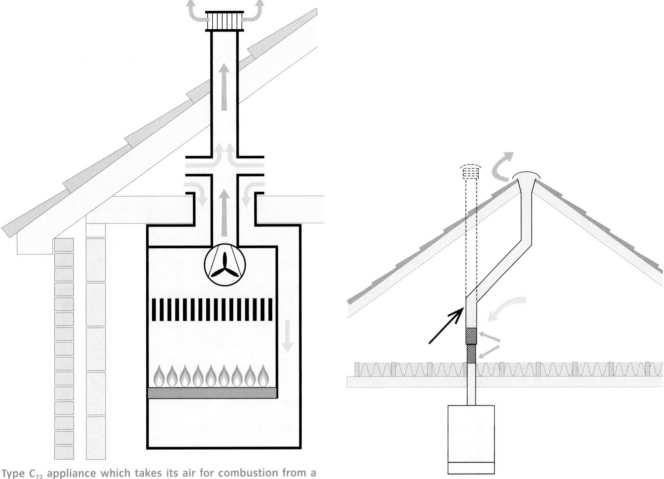

Type C$_{72}$ appliance which takes its air for combustion from a specially vented roof space

Type C$_{72}$ flue also known as vertex type flue

Components of an open flue

There are four components to an open flue:

- The primary flue, which provides a route for the products of combustion (POCs) from the heat exchanger.
- A draught diverter, which admits air to dilute the discharging flue gases and provides a means of diverting downdraught into the combustion chamber. It prevents excessive flue pull which could affect the combustion process.
- A secondary flue, which transports the POCs to the terminal.
- The flue terminal, which safely discharges the POCs to atmosphere – therefore its location is critical.

If there is no draught diverter incorporated in this type of system it is called a 'closed flue'.

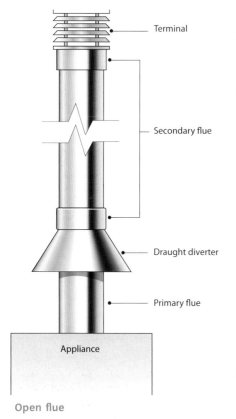

Terminal

Secondary flue

Draught diverter

Primary flue

Appliance

Open flue

The operation of the downdraught diverter is shown below and it can be seen that when functioning properly a draught diverter will entrain air to dilute the products of combustion. However, in adverse conditions it has the provision to divert any downdraught away from the heat exchanger to avoid incomplete combustion taking place.

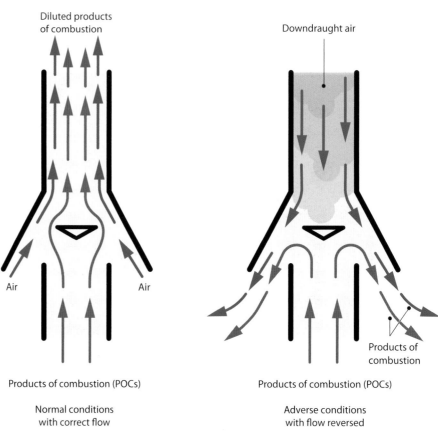

Diluted products of combustion

Downdraught air

Air

Air

Products of combustion

Products of combustion (POCs)

Products of combustion (POCs)

Normal conditions with correct flow

Adverse conditions with flow reversed

It is therefore essential that an open-flued appliance operates correctly. A check for the safe operation of such a flue can be achieved by carrying out spillage and flue flow tests.

Spillage testing

A smoke match or smoke-emitting device can be used to check the performance of a flue and manufacturers' instructions must be adhered to when carrying out a test. After an appliance has been running for about five minutes a smoke match is placed at the edge of a draught diverter while the appliance is operating. Any smoke emitted from the match should be drawn up into the flue to confirm that the flue is operating correctly. If any smoke is blown back into the room this would indicate spillage of products of combustion. Testing the appliance again after the appliance has had a time to heat up for a further 10 minutes is the next step, but if it continues to fail after another attempt then further investigation should be carried out to identify the problem and urgent remedial action taken. If the problem cannot be identified then the person responsible must be advised that the appliance is immediately dangerous and should not be left connected to the gas supply until the problem is remedied.

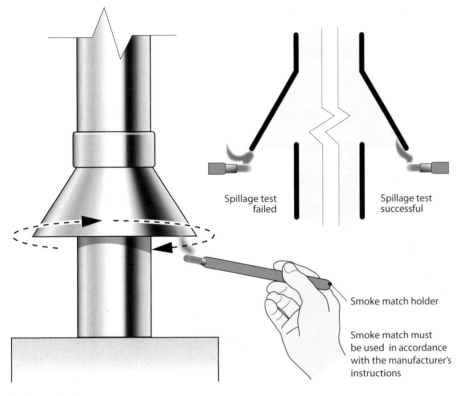

Spillage test failed

Spillage test successful

Smoke match holder

Smoke match must be used in accordance with the manufacturer's instructions

A smoke match holder is typically made from an 8 or 10mm copper tube which is formed at one end to secure the stem of a match, thereby protecting the fingers of the engineer from the radiated heat of a working appliance

Spillage testing

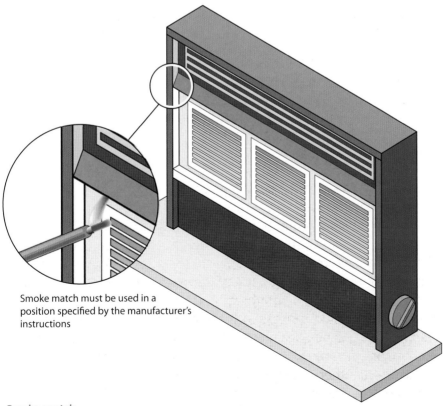

Smoke match must be used in a position specified by the manufacturer's instructions

Smoke match

A space heater is a popular domestic appliance, often open-flued, and it typically uses an existing chimney, formerly designed for a solid flue application such as a coal fire, to discharge the products of combustion. Once the manufacturer's instructions have been consulted, ensure that all doors and windows in the room are closed. Make sure all adjustable vents are in the closed position. If there are any fans they must be turned on and any passive stack ventilation should be in the open position. In addition, if there are any other open-flued appliances in the same area they should also be turned on when the test is carried out. BS 5440 Part 1:2008 also advises the installer to switch off any mechanical ventilation supply to the room other than that which provides combustion air to the appliance.

Space heater

Once the space heater has been running for about five minutes, the test should follow the same procedure as mentioned previously. However, on the drawing on the previous page a smoke match is placed in a location designated by the manufacturer because any other location may result in what appears to be a failed test. The precise location of the test is therefore critical and is specified in the manufacturer's instructions.

If there are any fans located in an adjoining room then the spillage test should be repeated with the door to that room left open. The idea is to carry out the test in the worst case scenario to ensure safe discharge of POCs at all times.

If the spillage test fails then leave the appliance running a while longer and retest.

If it still fails then switch off any fan in the vicinity and see if this is causing the problem.

Another solution would be to open a window in the same room to see if it allows smoke to be drawn in. If it does, then the problem is insufficient ventilation and the area of the opened window will determine the amount of extra ventilation required.

Typically a 50cm^2 vent allowing free air from outside into the area can solve the problem.

Extractor fan

Opened window allowing free air to enter room where appliance is located

A failed spillage test could also indicate a partially or fully blocked flue or appliance spigot. A poor terminal location or an incorrect terminal could also cause spillage problems.

Dirty marks and stains above the appliance indicate the spillage of POCs which presents an immediately dangerous (ID) situation. If the situation cannot be remedied, then, with the owner's permission, the appliance must be isolated and capped off, appropriate warning labels attached and the problem documented.

Flue flow test

The purpose of a flue flow test is to determine if a flue or chimney is able to sustain an updraught in order to safely discharge the POCs from an appliance. A smoke pellet which can produce a minimum volume of 5m^3 of smoke in 30 seconds is used to carry out such a test.

Sometimes smoke pellets with a dye are used to precisely locate known faults but before any type of flue flow test is carried out it is advisable to test with a smoke match to ensure there is the potential for a satisfactory test.

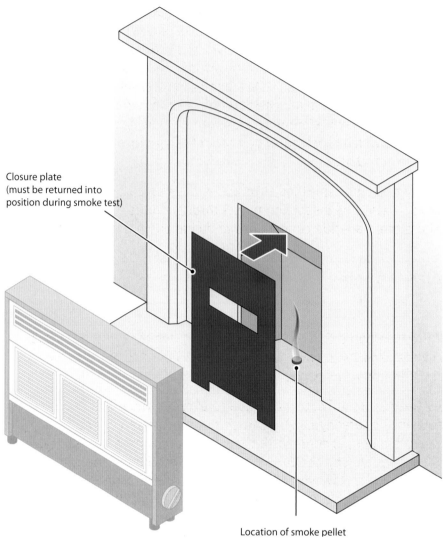

Closure plate
(must be returned into
position during smoke test)

Location of smoke pellet

Flue flow test

Ensure that all windows and doors to the room are closed. Sometimes the introduction of heat from a blowlamp can help improve updraught.

Locate a smoke pellet at the base of the flue, typically a builder's opening (see page 221), and light it. If there is normally a space heater in the location then cover the opening with the metal closure plate during the test.

Flue flow test procedure

If smoke can be seen discharging from the correct terminal and there is no smoke in the room of the test, or in any other room or area where the flue or chimney travels, especially the loft space, then a successful test has been achieved. It is worth noting that a smoke test is very subjective and is intended to establish that a specific chimney serving an appliance has sufficient integrity that it can safely remove the products of combustion when the appliance is working.

Sometimes flue flow tests must be carried out with the appliances in situation. In this scenario the smoke pellet is carefully located under the appliance and lit once the appliance is turned off. Often the whole length of the flue cannot be visually inspected, especially in the case of a flexible liner installed in brick-built chimneys, and the flue flow test will give an indication of the integrity of the system. A metallic chimney system may show some small signs of leakage from the joints which represent a permitted leakage rate of a certified chimney product.

If a rigid flue system is installed and is covered by boxing then there should always be inspection points throughout its route especially where there are flue connections and changes of direction exist.

Conditions that can affect the performance of a flue while testing

It must be noted that weather conditions, the temperature of the chimney and the combination of materials used to construct a chimney can all influence a smoke test.

Sometimes a pre-heating of a flue to simulate the effect of an appliance operating can be carried out by using a common blowtorch and, in some instances, the process may need to be applied for as long as 30 minutes before the chimney performs as it was intended. However, a blowtorch does not provide a representative volume of heat into a chimney which is consistent with an appliance when it is operating. If the flue continues to fail after extended application of heat then more investigation and testing processes should be carried out to remedy the situation and these can be found in BS 5440 Part 1:2008.

> **KEY POINT**
>
> It is essential that the seal on the primary flue spigot is inspected to ensure there is no leakage of products of combustion (POCs).

Open flue types

The flue type for an open-flued system can be one of the following:

- rigid single-walled
- rigid double-walled (twin-walled) with or without insulation
- flexible single- or double-walled (twin-walled).

Single-walled flues

Single-walled flues are usually connected by a socket and a spigot with the socket facing uppermost. They can be made from stainless steel or vitreous enamel, and older flues were made from cement and even asbestos. Single-walled flues are not suitable for external installations or even in uninsulated loft spaces as cold temperatures affect the flue performance.

> **KEY POINT**
>
> Any open flue under 10" requires a flue terminal.

Stainless steel flue pipe

Vitreous enamel flue pipe

Old asbestos-style 4" (100mm) flue pipe

Double-walled flues

A double-walled or (twin-walled) metal chimney should be installed with the internal socket facing uppermost. Whenever bayonet joints are utilised then the full twist movement process should be applied to ensure that the joint is complete and secure. They provide thermal protection during the conveyance of flue gases. This is achieved by the air gap between the inner and outer walls. Some flues have insulation in this space.

Whenever a double-walled metal chimney is connected to an appliance or chimney fittings and components, then an appropriate adaptor should be used. Similarly, when the connection of different makes of metal chimneys are carried out, it is recommended that the chimney manufacturer's recommended adaptor is used. With all applications of flue connection, it is essential that the appliance manufacturer's instructions be followed. Double-walled metal chimneys are mainly made from stainless steel or zalutite outer shells and stainless steel or aluminum inner shells. To avoid condensation no external run of twin-walled flue pipe insulated with an air gap should exceed 3m.

When installing flues, fittings and components, unless the manufacturer specifically gives permission and details, then metal chimney components or fittings should not be cut. Each individual section must be examined before assembly is completed and any sections that have damaged joints or other internal damage should not be used.

Never improvise a connection or adapt a flue. Always consult the manufacturer's instructions. Connections to primary flues and secondary flues can be made up with proprietary components such as heat-resistant rope and fire cement, for example, and these should always be checked for integrity when testing and inspecting the operation of an appliance. Creative ideas can lead to leaks and fires on gas installations.

Not to current standard. This is an unusual and illegal way to connect a flue

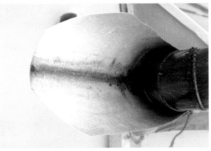

An improvised method of removing the build-up of condensate and aldehydes from a flue – this allows leaks from poor jointing and is an immediate hazard and potentially dangerous to the user (any broken seal on a flue connection within a building is considered ID)

Flexible flue liners

A flexible flue-liner is fitted to the primary flue outlet of a fire/back boiler unit (BBU) and from there it travels within an existing chimney to a terminal. At the point where it enters the base of the chimney a register plate must be installed to prevent secondary flue pull. In the same way, it must be sealed at the top of the chimney with a sealing plate where it connects with the terminal. A typical way of sealing the **annular space** between the chimney and the flexible flue liner is with the use of mineral wool.

Annular space

The required 25mm gap between any hot surface of a flue and any combustible materials when travelling through a floor in a dwelling.

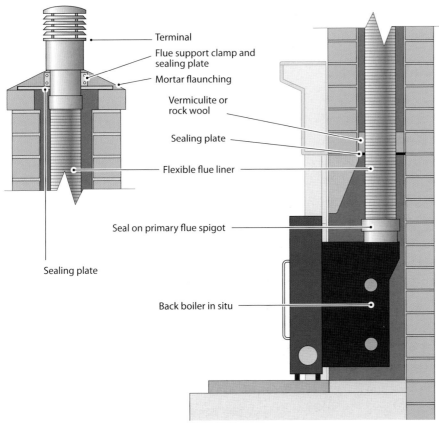

A sectional view of a typical back boiler installation in a builder's opening

BS 5440 Part 1 states that under normal operating conditions, a correctly installed metallic liner conforming to BS 715:1989, BS 715:1993 or BS EN 1856-2 should operate safely for at least the operational lifespan of an appliance, which is normally 10 to 15 years.

Traditional chimneys

KEY POINT

Aerials can affect the performance of a flue in the same way as a tree that is located too close to a terminal or even a wind turbine that operates nearby.

The above picture shows a traditional chimney with a range of different terminals. Some are suitable, but others, such as the half-round ones, are there purely to ventilate a decommissioned stack in order to prevent condensation and are not fit for use as flue terminals. When carrying out a flue flow test, an engineer should always check to ensure that the flue terminal is not restricted or impeded by any adjacent obstruction such as a TV aerial.

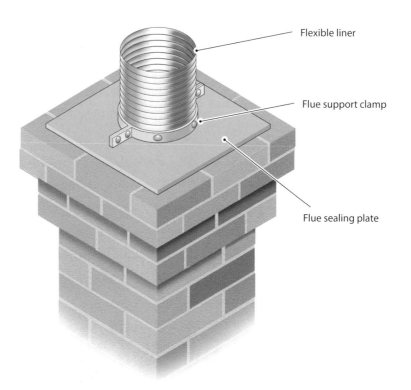

Flexible liner

Flue support clamp

Flue sealing plate

When installing a flexible flue within a traditional chimney, the chimney pot must often be removed and a sealing plate installed to prevent secondary flue pull

Flue terminals

The design of flue terminals has changed over the years and many of the older styles are no longer fit for use. Terminals should always be fitted to flue outlets up to 170mm diameter. Above that dimension they are not considered necessary unless there is a risk of birds nesting.

An old-style flue terminal which is no longer fit for use

Builder's opening

If a solid fuel appliance was previously installed in a builder's opening then the chimney should be cleaned and inspected by a Gas Safe-registered chimney sweep and any flue damper removed or permanently fixed in the fully open position. The base of a traditional class I chimney is called the builder's opening and this is where the products of combustion are discharged via the spigot of the space heater as shown below. There is a lintel at the top of the fireplace and a chairbrick at the rear which sometimes requires removing if it impedes the flow of the products of combustion from the spigot, as there should be no obstruction or surface within 50mm. The appliance should have a non-combustible hearth at the base of a thickness no less than 12mm.

A flue type and location which is no longer fit for use

KEY POINT

Any installation which has previously used a solid fuel appliance must have the chimney swept and tested if an open flued space heater is to be installed. Any obstructions such as flue dampers should be either removed or fixed in the fully open position.

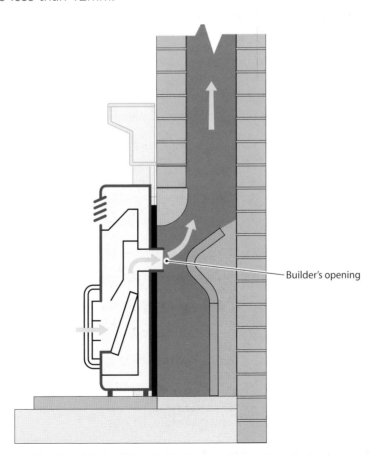

Builder's opening

Builder's opening with a gas fired space heater installed

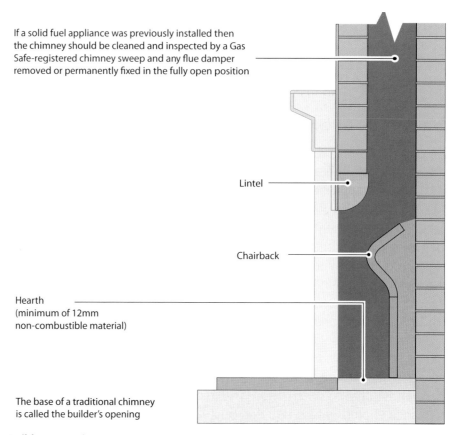

If a solid fuel appliance was previously installed then the chimney should be cleaned and inspected by a Gas Safe-registered chimney sweep and any flue damper removed or permanently fixed in the fully open position

Lintel

Chairback

Hearth
(minimum of 12mm
non-combustible material)

The base of a traditional chimney
is called the builder's opening

Builder's opening

Void volume (catchment space)

At the base of the builder's opening is the area where the appliance is located known as the 'void volume'. The dimensions of the area behind the appliance are critical when determining the suitability of an installation and the table below gives guidance on different types of application determined on individual type and previous usage of a chimney.

The void volume is determined by the length × width of the opening × the distance below the appliance spigot. The spigot of the appliance must not be less than 50mm from any obstruction and must protrude at least 12mm past the closure plate. In any event the manufacturer's instructions will give specific installation details which could differ from the British Standard.

Chimney type/ circumstance	Void volume (litres)	Spigot height (mm)
Unlined brick	12	250
Lined brick – new/unused/used with gas	2	75
Lined brick – previously solid fuel/oil	12	250

Chimney type/ circumstance	Void volume (litres)	Spigot height (mm)
Flue block – new/unused/used with gas	2	75
Flue block – previously solid fuel/oil	12	250

The above chart derives from the British Standards.

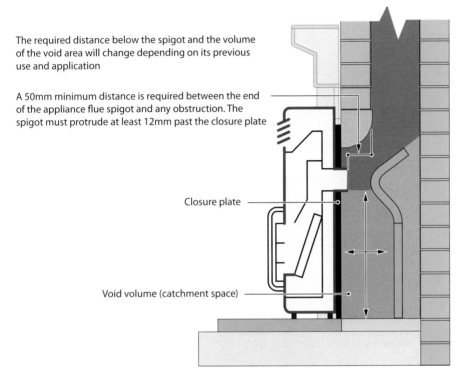

The required distance below the spigot and the volume of the void area will change depending on its previous use and application

A 50mm minimum distance is required between the end of the appliance flue spigot and any obstruction. The spigot must protrude at least 12mm past the closure plate

Closure plate

Void volume (catchment space)

Catchment area

Terminal guards

Flue terminal guards should be installed on balanced flue appliances if the underside flue is less than 2m from the ground. There should be a minimum of a 50mm space between the guard and any hot surface of the flue terminal. The purpose of this guard is to protect anyone from coming in contact with the hot surface. The appliance terminal shown to the right is a Type C_{11} and this sort of installation is commonly found on balcony walkways in houses of multiple occupation.

A typical guard installed on a balcony to protect from people from hot surfaces. The guard has a 50mm distance from the flue terminal surfaces

Although the circular flue shown on the next page has a terminal guard, there are other considerations as BS 5440 Part 1:2008 gives precise information about the location of flues in respect to openings to a building. While this installation might have been acceptable when it was installed, it may not comply with the new standard. An engineer must test and assess the performance of a flue to ensure that it operates without causing a risk to anyone. If the appliance operates without POCs entering a building then it could be considered 'not to current standard' (NCS). **Engineering judgement** is essential and in some instances this installation could be classified as 'at risk' (AR). If POCs did enter the building then the appliance would be 'immediately dangerous' (ID).

On open flues where there is evidence that a chimney is used for nesting by birds, squirrels or other wildlife, or if any such problem is known of in the vicinity, then a suitable guard or terminal should be fitted to the chimney to prevent entry of these creatures. This is especially important in areas where birds such as jackdaws are known to roost.

A chimney should be inspected and reinforced if required before fitting a guard to ensure that it can support such a fitting. Once a terminal guard has been installed the appliance should be checked for spillage to ensure that POCs are being effectively cleared during the combustion process.

Circular flue. An engineer must determine the status of such an installation in relation to the current standards and the manufacturers' instructions

Engineering judgement

This is a technical decision which is based on the competence of a person who has an appropriate combination of technical education, training and practical experience in the specific field of work. Competence in specific areas of gas work is verified by assessments of an engineer's theoretical and practical knowledge at an independent nationally approved ACS gas centre, and then registration with the HSE approved Gas Safe register.

Brewer™ Birdguard

A birdguard fitted on a new installation

The Brewer™ Birdguard as shown above is suitable for gas, oil or solid fuel systems. It prevents the entry of birds and can be installed in chimney pots with a diameter of 150–250mm.

Square birdguards are designed to fit an internal pot size of 6–10" square and have a strap fixing suitable for gas, oil or solid fuel systems. This guard protects from birds nesting and the entry of rain and other debris. Both of the terminal guards have versions that are suitable for gas and are designed to BS 5871:2005 requirements.

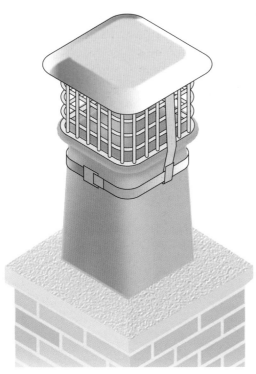

Square birdguard

Flue blocks

As with a conventional flue, there are several components that make up a flue block system. There are some key points to consider to enable safe and effective operation of such a flue. For example, the minimum cross-sectional area of new chimneys should be no less than 16,500mm^2 and any angle build into an offset should be no greater than 30°.

Flue blocks are designed to save space within living areas and are built into the fabric of the building. They form part of the structure and are staggered and bonded into a standard pattern.

When a gas fire or a fire/back boiler unit is to be connected to the chimney then the chimney manufacturer's starter or recess block(s) that are appropriate for that particular appliance type must be fitted at the base of the chimney along with a lintel or cover block. Sometimes an engineer must deal with the temperature transfer from an appliance to the building next to it and a **cooler plate** located at the rear of the appliances could help solve this problem. In addition flue block chimneys should not be directly faced with plaster, or plaster cracking might occur.

BS 5440 Part 1:2008 explains that flue blocks are more resistive to the flow of flue gases than metal chimneys of the same cross-sectional area. In addition, any mortar extrusions where joints are made will increase resistance even more. Internally extruded mortar should be removed and coring should be carried out through the

Flue blocks can be jointed with mortar or a special caulking compound

Cooler plate

A device used behind an appliance in a flue block installation to prevent the unwanted transfer of heat from the appliance.

erection to remove all extrusions and droppings. Previously engineers used a small canvas bag of sand which was lowered on a rope from the top of the chimney to remove any excess mortar.

When connecting a metal chimney component to a flue block chimney, the manufacturer's transfer block should be used. Any metal chimney component connected to such a block should not project into the flue such that it restricts the cross-sectional area of the flue. When connecting a gas fire to the base of a flue block chimney there should be a debris collection space below the spigot.

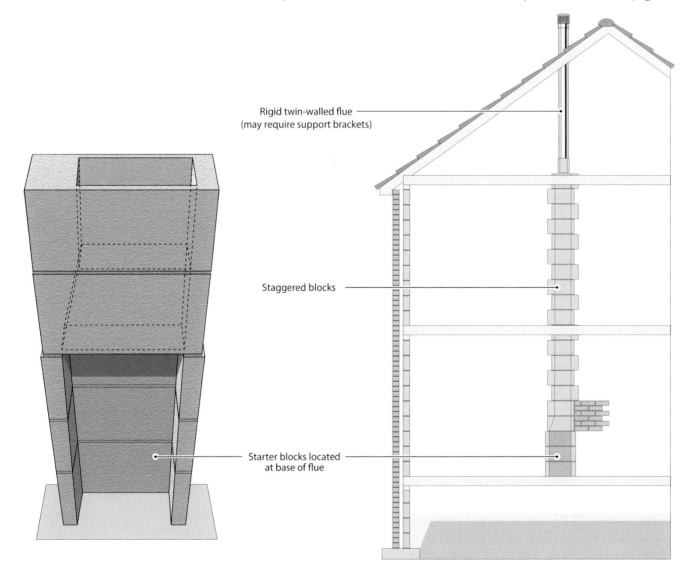

Rigid twin-walled flue (may require support brackets)

Staggered blocks

Starter blocks located at base of flue

Flue blocks

Ridge terminals

Often flues terminate at ridge terminals which are located at the highest part of the roof. It is important that they are located at 1500mm away from any adjacent structure which is higher than the ridge vent position. In addition if the vent has openings on all four sides, it is essential that they should be positioned so that they are a minimum of 300mm from other such ridge terminals. It is important that ridge terminals are located so that the connected flue pipe will be at least 50mm from any combustible materials such as roofing timbers.

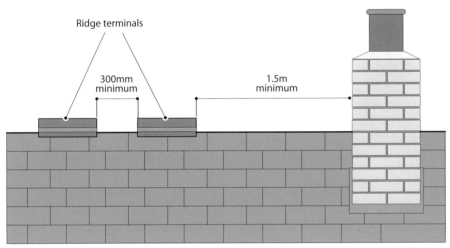

Siting for ridge terminals

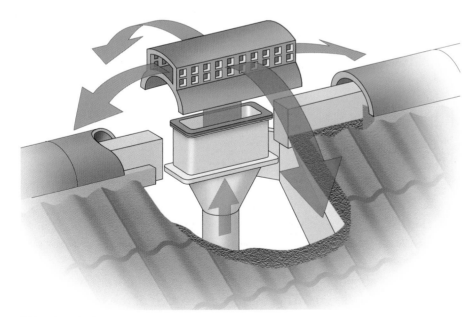

Ridge terminal

Ridge terminals are located on the highest point of an angled roof and provide a convenient and unobtrusive means of discharging flue gases. It is important that if they are installed in series, they are no less than 300mm apart.

Key design considerations for locating flue terminals for open-flued appliances

The location of the terminal of a flue is critical to ensure the safe dispersing of POCs. BS 5440 Part 1 states the dimensions that must be adhered to, to help achieve good flue performance. Therefore, when locating a flue externally, an engineer must assess the effect that small wind turbines and TV aerials may have on the operation of a flue. Climatic conditions such as very warm weather can also affect flue performance.

Wind can also adversely affect the operation of a flue. Therefore careful consideration is required when siting a flue. Similarly, locating a flue terminal near an obstruction can affect its performance.

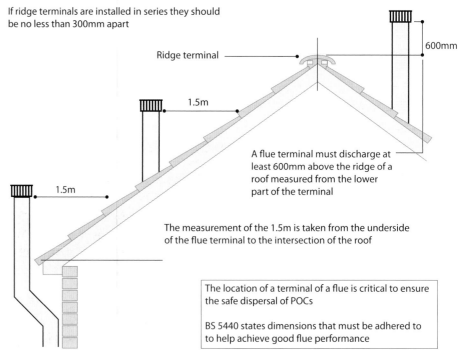

If ridge terminals are installed in series they should be no less than 300mm apart

Ridge terminal

600mm

A flue terminal must discharge at least 600mm above the ridge of a roof measured from the lower part of the terminal

1.5m

1.5m

The measurement of the 1.5m is taken from the underside of the flue terminal to the intersection of the roof

The location of a terminal of a flue is critical to ensure the safe dispersal of POCs

BS 5440 states dimensions that must be adhered to to help achieve good flue performance

Recommended flue terminal locations for open-flued appliances in accordance with BS 5440 part 1:2008

In the image above, a measurement of 1.5m is taken from the underside of the flue terminal to the intersection of the roof which is shown by the horizontal arrows.

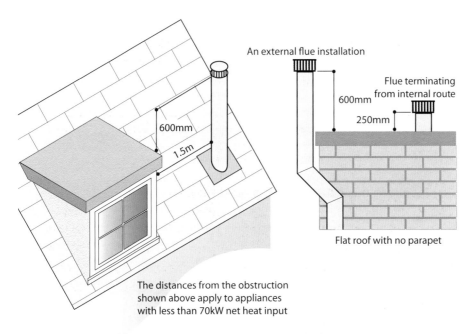

An external flue installation

Flue terminating from internal route

600mm

250mm

600mm

1.5m

Flat roof with no parapet

The distances from the obstruction shown above apply to appliances with less than 70kW net heat input

It is essential the POCs do not re-enter the building. Therefore the precise location of the flue is critical and must be followed by testing to ensure safe operation

Key design considerations on open-flued installations

BS 5400 Part 1 advises that an open-flued boiler should allow a minimum of 600mm from the outlet of the boiler to the first bend on the flue. There is a maximum of two bends allowed; any bends should be 45°. No 90° bends should be used.

Whenever a single-walled flue passes through a combustible material there should be an annular space of 25mm around the circumference of the flue. BS 5440 Part 1:2008 emphasises that for a single-walled metal chimney, the 25mm is measured from the outside surface and for a double-walled metal chimney the 25mm is measured from the outside surface of the inner liner.

Where passing through a combustible wall, floor or roof (other than a fire compartment wall or floor) a suitable method would be to use a non-combustible sleeve enclosing the metal chimney with a 25mm air space.

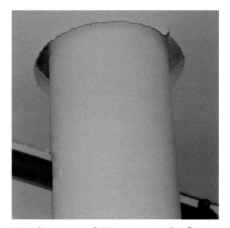

Annular space of 25 mm around a flue

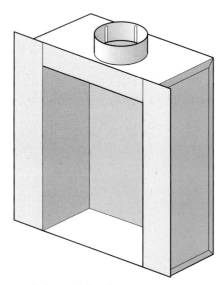

Typical metal flue box to BS 715

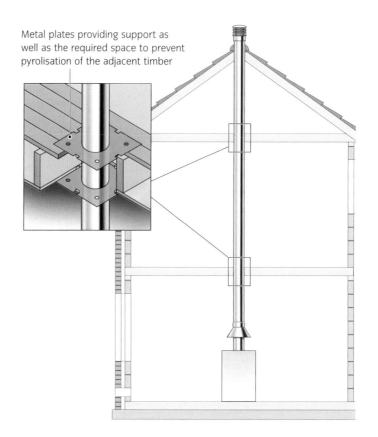

Metal plates providing support as well as the required space to prevent pyrolisation of the adjacent timber

Ideally a flue should be supported with a metal plate which keeps it in position as well as providing the required space around the circumference of the flue

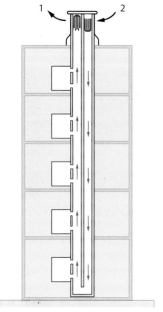

1 Combustion products
2 Air inlet

U-duct system

Flue boxes

Whenever there is no existing brick-built or flue block chimney in a dwelling, a space heater or gas appliance can still be installed using the versatile metal flue box system. This will provide a safe fireproof housing for the appliance and enable the safe removal of products of combustion. The construction of a gas flue box should conform to BS 715.

A flue box should only be used to accommodate a fire where it has been identified as being suitable for such use by the appliance manufacturer and/or the flue box manufacturer.

Shared flue systems (U-duct and SE-duct)

U-duct systems

A U-duct system is suitable for use with appliance flue types C_2 and C_4 which are both room-sealed. U-ducts operate on the principle of air for combustion being drawn down from the top of the building via a vertical duct next to a venting duct which is connected to it at the base.

SE-duct systems

An SE-duct system is suitable for use with appliance flue types C_2 and C_4. The air for combustion is taken from ground level and then travels via a vertical duct which rises up through the building and discharges at roof level. The combustion air for the appliances is taken from a horizontal duct which is run from one side of the building to the other or by means of a single inlet duct located at a zone of neutral pressure beneath the vertical duct itself.

The arrows in the figure to the right indicate the location of the special room-sealed appliances. Labels must be attached to each of the appliances to let the engineer know that it forms part of a shared flue system.

Labels for air inlets

All of the air inlet grilles and the duct base itself must be labelled to indicate the purpose of the duct and give information regarding who is responsible for the building.

BS 5440 Part 1 emphasises that only a C_2 appliance can be connected to a SE-duct or U-duct chimney (where the flue duct and air supply duct of the appliance are connected into the same common duct of the system) in accordance with the manufacturer's installation instructions. In addition the standard goes on to state that only a C_4 appliance should be used with the shared flue chimney where the flue duct and the air supply of the appliance are connected to separate common ducts of the shared chimney.

The replacement of appliances can be carried out as long as the rated input of the new appliance is not greater than the existing one.

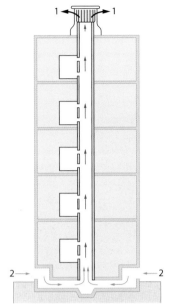

1 Combustion products
2 Air inlet

Note: This version incorporates a horizontal duct run from one side of the building to another

SE-duct system

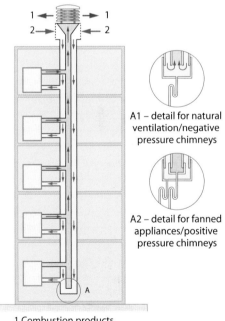

A1 – detail for natural ventilation/negative pressure chimneys

A2 – detail for fanned appliances/positive pressure chimneys

1 Combustion products
2 Air inlet

Shared flue system chimney

Ventilation (LO4)

There are eight assessment criteria for this outcome:

1 State the reference documents to be used for gas appliance air ventilation requirements.

2 State the reasons for providing ventilation to gas appliances.

3 Describe requirements for air vents.

4 Define adventitious allowance.

5 Calculate ventilation requirements for different flued appliances.

6 Calculate ventilation requirements for flued appliances in compartments.

7 Calculate vents in series for more than one room.

8 Describe ventilation requirements for multiple appliances.

To fully understand the requirement for ventilation you must first examine the combustion process as explained in Learning Outcome 2.

SmartScreen Unit 307

Handout 3

The aim of Learning Outcome 4 is to identify the normative reference documents that are used for air ventilation requirements for gas appliances and give the reasons for providing ventilation for gas appliances.

Vents and air bricks: through wall vent (left), floor vent (middle) and air brick (right)

Adventitious air

Air that comes in from the outside, typically through gaps in windows or doorways in a particular area and which is estimated to equate to about 35cm² of free air.

The individual requirements for air vents will also be covered and **adventitious air** explained. Calculations for room compartment ventilation will be explained for different flued appliances as well as ventilation requirements for multiple appliance installations. In the absence of manufacturers' instructions BS 5440 Part 2:2009 should be referred to when calculating ventilation requirements.

When natural gas is burned it requires oxygen to create complete combustion. Therefore, when an appliance such as an open-flued boiler is located in a dwelling, it must have sufficient air to burn properly and the supply of air is commonly provided via a vent located on an outside wall of the property. If inadequate ventilation is provided in this situation then the atmosphere could become vitiated (lacking in oxygen). This could lead to the formation of carbon monoxide in the room and the appliance will cease to function properly and become dangerous.

It is therefore essential to remove the products of combustion efficiently via a flue (covered in Learning Outcome 3) and provide a permanent air supply to the appliance.

The normative document that gives guidance and advice on ventilation is BS 5440 Part 2:2009. It covers appliances of up to 70kW in permanent dwellings. Building Regulations Approved Document J gives information which must be complied with and manufacturers' instructions must always be referred to when installing or inspecting appliances.

SmartScreen Unit 307
PowerPoint 3

Reasons for ventilation

An adequate supply of air is essential for the safe operation of gas appliances. Inadequate ventilation will lead to incomplete combustion and carbon monoxide being produced.

Ventilation is also required to dissipate heat and provide cooling. In addition it aids the removal of condensation by providing air changes within a room.

Ventilation also provides relief air to overcome the effects of mechanical extraction and fans on the performance of open-flued gas appliances.

Ventilator requirements

BS 1179-6 defines an air vent as a non-adjustable purpose-provided arrangement designed to allow permanent ventilation. IGEM/G/4 edition 2 defines ventilation as the movement of air and its replacement with fresh air due to the effects of wind, temperature gradients or any artificial means, for example fans or extractors. A simple vent should provide a grille or louvre on both ends of the smooth and uninterrupted duct. An engineer will have to measure the free area of a ventilator or louvre.

The free area is described in BS 5440 Part 2:2009 as the unobstructed cross-sectional area of a grille, louvre or duct which is calculated as the sum of the cross-sectional areas of all unobstructed apertures measured through the plane on the minimum area and at right angles to the air flow within the apertures. In other words, an engineer has to check that there are no blockages and, if checking a terracotta brick, the engineer must measure from the smallest orifice. There are tools available to assess the free air of existing vents.

Stainless steel gauge to measure openings in air vents

The stainless steel gauge shown is used to measure the size of the slots and enable the engineer to calculate the area of ventilation provided by a vent where this information has not been marked on the components. The gauge is stepped in increments of 1mm and can measure vent slots from 5mm to 10mm. The size of the opening can be calculated by pushing the gauge into the vent slot until it stops and then taking note of the markings on the exposed calibrated steps of the gauge which give the vent size in millimetres. Sometimes the use of a stainless steel rule is required to measure the size of slots and apertures whenever the free area is not marked on a vent.

The Gas Safety Installation and Use Regulations (GSIUR)

The GSIUR state that operatives must not install a gas appliance unless it can be used without being a danger to any other person. Therefore an engineer must ensure that a permanent supply of air is available for the appliance which is sufficient for complete combustion and for the purposes of cooling if it is installed in a compartment or cupboard.

Ventilation categories

Ventilation is required for all the categories below but is calculated in a different way for each individual situation:

- flueless appliances
- open-flued appliances
- open-flued appliances located in a compartment
- room-sealed appliances located in a compartment.

Adventitious ventilation

Buildings admit draughts from the outside and this is called 'adventitious ventilation' which equates to about $35cm^2$ of free air. When air for combustion is calculated, $5cm^2$ is required for each kW of gas used, which in effect means the first 7kW of the input rating of a gas appliance can be deducted. It is worth noting that because of the advancement of draught reduction in many new buildings, adventitious allowance may be reduced because of highly effective draught proofing incorporated into the building structure or design.

> **Example**
>
> A 16kW open-flued boiler is installed in a room.
>
> 16kW − 7kW = 9kW
>
> Ventilation for 9kW = 9kW × $5cm^2$ = **45cm²**
>
> A vent providing 45cm² of free air should therefore be located on an outside wall to provide air supply for combustion.

If an open-flued appliance is installed in a compartment then adventitious air is never deducted from the calculation.

Similarly the same rule applies to flueless appliances such as cookers or to open-flued decorative fuel effect (DFE) gas fires, unless the DFE manufacturer states otherwise.

Decorative fuel effect gas appliances are covered in BS 5871 Part 3 which states that they require $100cm^2$ of ventilation unless manufacturers' instructions (**MI**) differ.

MI

MI means manufacturers' instructions.

A grate for a decorative fuel effect gas fire

Example of ceramic coals

Ceramic coals fitted in a grate in accordance with the manufacturer's specific coal picture arrangement

A DFE in operation showing the decorative fuel effect

A tumble dryer also usually requires 100cm^2 and this depends on the room size where it is located. A fire/back boiler unit (BBU) will require a minimum of 100cm^2 unless the manufacturer's instructions (MI) state otherwise.

Gross and net

When working out your ventilation requirements, calculate either in gross or net. Gross is the higher heating value which takes into account the latent heat of the vaporisation of the water in the combustion process, whereas net assumes that the latent heat of the water in the fuel has not been recovered. Therefore when calculating in net allow 5cm^2 per kilowatt input and for gross allow 4.5cm^2 per kilowatt input.

- To convert gross to net, divide by 1.11.
- To convert net to gross, multiply by 1.11.

A gas appliance such as a back boiler unit will have a data plate which gives technical details about the rating and performance of the boiler. It can be seen on the data plate shown on the next page that the maximum heat input of the appliance is 21.8kW.

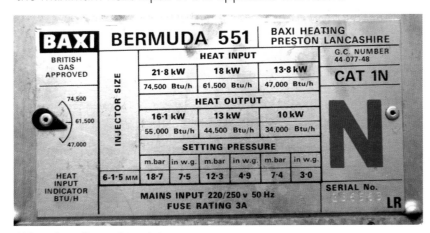

Old Baxi appliance data plate

Because this is an older appliance, which is evident because of the BTU/H indicator on the left-hand side of the plate, the maximum input must be converted from gross to net.

The calculation is:

21.8kW ÷ 1.11 = 19.64kW net

Therefore the ventilation required is:

19.64kW − 7kW = 12.64kW

$12.64kW \times 5cm^2 = \textbf{63.2cm}^2$

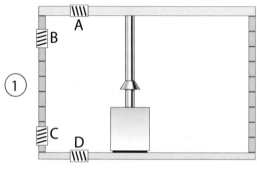

In a room

One vent required in either position A, B, C or D direct to outside air. (5cm²/kW of rated heat input above 7kW)

Ventilation options for open-flued appliances in a room or internal space

Compartment ventilation

A compartment is an enclosure designed to house a gas appliance. This will require high- and low-level ventilation unless the manufacturer's instructions state otherwise. The purpose of vents located on an **appliance compartment** is to provide air for complete combustion, to enable the correct operation of the flue and for appliance cooling. There is no adventitious air allowance in compartments.

Appliance compartment

An enclosure specifically designed or adapted to house one or more gas appliances.

If an appliance is to be installed in a compartment then the following rules must be adhered to:

- Both of the air vents should communicate with the same room or space.
- Vents must be located at both the lowest and highest practicable locations within the compartment.
- Both of the air vents must be on the same wall to the outside.
- If a compartment contains two or more appliances, the aggregate maximum input rating of both of them must be added together when calculating vent sizes.
- Range-rated appliances must be calculated using their maximum input rating.
- There should be 75mm clearances around the front, the sides, and above and below an appliance situated in a compartment unless the manufacturer's instructions state otherwise.

- An appliance compartment should never be used for storage purposes because of the risk of fire and blocking of air vents.

Small rooms such as cloakrooms and WCs are not usually considered as compartments but just like small appliance compartments they can be susceptible to vitiation which is caused by a downdraught. In addition heat loss from appliances can cause high ambient temperatures to occur. Therefore an engineer should carefully assess such installations and decide whether or not to treat them as compartments and install the required ventilation.

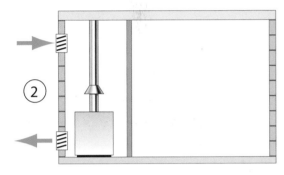

In a compartment

Ventilated direct to outside air $10cm^2/kW$ of rated heat input at low level and $5cm^2/kW$ of rated heat input at high level

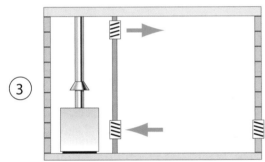

In a compartment

Ventilated via a room or internal space $20cm^2/kW$ of rated heat input at low level and $10cm^2/kW$ of rated heat input at high level. The room is ventilated as in 1 on the previous page

Compartment ventilation for open-flued appliances

Calculation examples

If we calculate the ventilation requirement for an open-flued appliance of 15kW input installed in a compartment with vents facing externally we would use the formula of multiplying the lower vent by $10cm^2$ times the kilowatt input of the appliance and the higher level multiplied by $5cm^2$.

Therefore:
$10cm^2 \times 15kW = \mathbf{150cm^2}$ at the lower level
$5cm^2 \times 15kW = \mathbf{75cm^2}$ at the higher level

If the vents in the compartment face internally then the following equation applies: input rating of the appliance times $20cm^2$ for the lower vent and $10cm^2$ for the higher vent.

Therefore:
$20cm^2 \times 15kW = \mathbf{300cm^2}$ at the lower level
$10cm^2 \times 15kW = \mathbf{150cm^2}$ at the higher level

Ventilation in series for open-flued appliances

Sometimes open-flued appliances are located some distance away from an outside wall and in order to provide air for combustion it will be necessary to install ventilation via another wall between the appliance and the outer wall. This method is called installing air vents 'in series' and the following rules must be adhered to.

- When venting through one wall to an appliance then the internal vent will need to be the same size as the one located on the outer wall.

- If venting through more than one room the internal vents need to be 50% bigger than the external vent.

- If air is provided from the outside air as shown in the example below then both internal and external vents remain the same size.

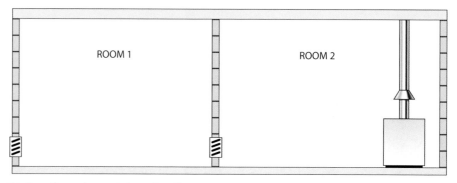

Venting through one internal wall

In the situation shown below the external air vent number 1 remains the same but both internal vents 2 and 3 are 50% bigger than the external vent.

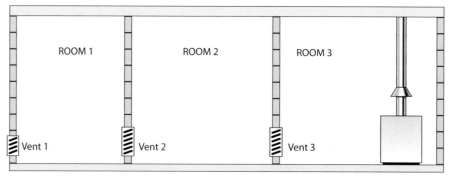

Venting through two internal walls

In the image below vents A and B are sized for the compartment as normal in accordance with the maximum input rating of the appliance. However, both internal vents 2 and 3 are still required to be 50% bigger than vent 1.

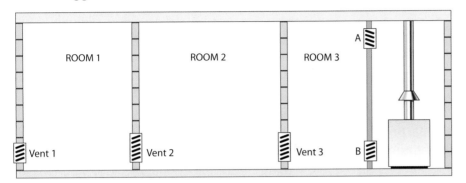

Venting through two internal walls and into a compartment

Ventilation calculations for room-sealed appliances

Room-sealed appliances do not require air for combustion as they receive this air from the outside via the special ducts in the flue which are balanced to atmospheric pressure and the appliance itself is sealed from the effects of the room – hence the term room-sealed. The reason the air is needed is for cooling and to keep the appliance operating at its designed temperature.

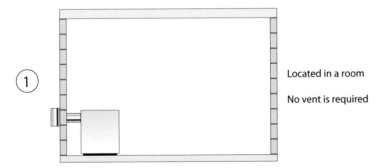

Located in a room

No vent is required

When room-sealed appliances are installed in compartments, ventilation is required for cooling only and is provided from vents located at both high and low level at the greatest possible vertical distance apart to encourage a convective flow.

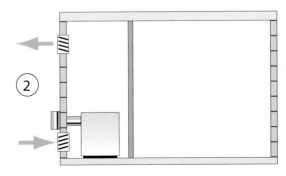

Compartment

If the appliance is ventilated to outside air then 5cm²/kW of free air ventilation is required

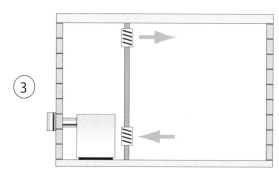

③ **Compartment**

Ventilated via a room or internal space 10cm²/kW of rated heat input at both high and low level

Many manufacturers now state that ventilation is not required for compartment installations because of the low surface temperature of their room-sealed boilers. The correct operating temperature of an appliance relates directly to its performance and the following information is essential to maintain optimum performance.

It is important for the purposes of cooling not to exceed air temperatures of:

- 25°C up to 100mm from finished floor level (FFL)
- 32°C at 1.5m above FFL
- 40°C at 100mm below and up to ceiling level.

Vents and grilles

- Ventilation must allow free air to pass and vents should not be closable.
- The air cannot be taken from bath or shower rooms.
- Vents should not incorporate any gauzes or screens.
- Air vent openings should be not be larger than 10mm and no smaller than 5mm.
- Air vents located externally should be located so that they will not become blocked.
- Air vents located on internal walls should not be fitted any higher than 450mm.
- An air vent should never penetrate a protected shaft or stairway.
- Vents can be made from a range of materials such as terracotta, plastic, brass and aluminium.

Plastic vents such as the one shown to the left are installed through a wall using a core drill. The free area for combustion is printed on the vent and in this case it is 34cm² which will be sufficient for a rated input of an open-flued appliance of 13.8kW. This is calculated as follows. If the input of the appliance is 13.8kW then 7kW is deducted, because of adventitious air, leaving a total of 6.8kW. This figure is then multiplied by 5cm² per kilowatt which results in a free air requirement of (5cm² × 6.8kW) 34cm².

A plastic vent

Sometimes a more aesthetically pleasing style of vent similar to the brass one shown to the right may be required to complement a design within a dwelling, but in any event the free air rating of the fitting will still be shown on its surface.

An engineer should always verify the free air admitted through a vent and this should preferably be marked on the vent. While inspecting a vent it can sometimes be seen that the space between two vents has become blocked either by debris or even intentionally by an owner to prevent unwanted draughts. Therefore the removal of the outer cover of the vent may be required.

A brass vent

As a practical solution to the problem of customers blocking vents, an innovative device which incorporates baffles to reduce the effect of draughts has been developed. However, recent tests have shown that the vent may not always produce the required amount of air for combustion. Therefore a spillage test should always be carried out when one of these devices is installed.

The brown plastic terracotta part will be located on the external wall to blend with brickwork; the free air volume of the device is then protected with ducting which incorporates a baffle system and the device eventually terminates with a white plastic vent inside the building.

A black hole ventilator ducted typically through a cavity wall

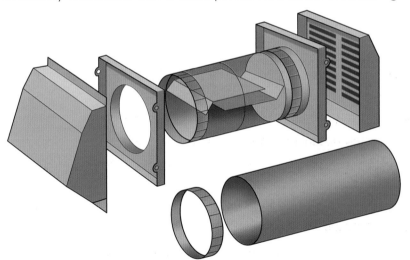

A circular option incorporating a baffle system to fit a cored hole through a wall

High- and low-level vents should be located at the greatest vertical distance apart.

If a duct comes from high level, the duct should terminate below the level of the burner. It is not acceptable to duct from low to high level.

On louvre doors the total free area should be equal to that of the calculated high- and low-level vents.

A typical louvre door as shown in the image to the right requires the gap between each of the louvres to be measured individually by the engineer to calculate the free air that can pass through them.

A louvre door

An internal vent for compartment or door ventilation

A heavy-duty external vent

Vents for compartments

Compartments containing gas appliances should be labelled accordingly.

> **IMPORTANT**
> **DO NOT BLOCK THIS VENT.**
> **DO NOT USE FOR STORAGE.**

Typical example of label to be fixed on a cupboard

The purpose of vents located on an appliance compartment is to provide air for complete combustion, to enable the correct operation of the flue and for appliance cooling.

Internal vents for compartments

The fitting on the top left is a typical example of a plastic face fitting compartment or door ventilator. It can be used internally or externally and this vent has a free area of 306cm².

External vents for compartments

The vent shown to the left is a face fit heavy-duty ventilator which is for use on exterior walls where strength and security are important.

An external vent can be constructed from a range of materials and be of various sizes which are sufficient for the requirements of the appliance or appliances installed in the compartment.

Ducting requirements

A duct which connects two air vents should be no longer than 3m in length and should have no more than two 90° bends in the design. Ducting size should be increased by 50% for each extra part or section after every 3m. Flexible ducting should not be used as this could cause sagging low points and the potential for condensation to form.

> **KEY POINT**
>
> Ducting runs, where unavoidable, should be kept to a minimum of not more than 3m in length.

> **KEY POINT**
>
> Hit-and-miss vents can be opened or closed therefore they are not suitable for the combustion ventilation of gas appliances.

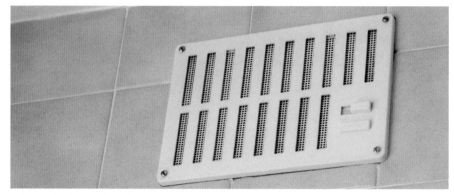

A hit-and-miss vent with gauze

The image on the previous page shows a hit-and-miss type vent with gauze. This should never be used as a means of ventilation for gas appliances because it can be adjusted to close all ventilation and, even if it were permanently left open, the gauze, which is never acceptable as a vent component, could become blocked, thereby reducing any air passing through into the room.

Flueless ventilation requirements

When setting up flueless ventilation:

- Ventilation must be provided directly from outside and it should be possible to open a window or a hinged panel in the same room in accordance with the Building Regulations.
- Ventilation can only be conveyed from one room to another if it is ducted.
- There must be sufficient room volume and there are restrictions on maximum input ratings of a flueless appliance.
- Smaller rooms will need increased purpose-provided ventilation.
- Manufacturers' instructions must always be adhered to.
- Flueless space heaters are constrained by W/m^3 of room volume and individual appliance rated input. Manufacturers' instructions will give guidance on specific appliance installation requirements.

Flueless ventilation guidance (selected section)

Type of appliance	Maximum rated input limit (net)	Room volume (m³)	Permanent vent size (cm³)	Openable window or equivalent also required
Domestic oven, hotplate, grill or any combination thereof	None	< 5	100	Yes
		5 to 10	50^2	
		> 10	Nil	
Instantaneous hot water heater	11kW	< 5	Installation not permitted	Yes
		5 to 10	100	
		> 10 to 20	50	
		> 20	Nil	

Note: If the room or internal space containing these appliances has a door which opens directly to the outside, then no permanant opening is required.

The full guide to the minimum permanent opening free area for flueless appliances can be found on Table 6 of BS 5440 Part 2:2009.

Flueless ventilation calculation

If, for example, a flueless water heater of 10kW net were located in a room measuring 2m × 2m × 2.4m, the total volume of the room would be 9.6m³. By referring to the flueless ventilation guidance it can be seen that if the room was between 5 and 10m³, then 100cm² ventilation would be required, as well as an openable window or equivalent such as a hinged panel. If a domestic cooker were located in the same room it would require a permanent vent and 50cm² with an openable window or equivalent. Details, guidance and ventilation requirements for other flueless appliances are given in Table 6 in BS 5440 Part 2:2009.

Intumescent air vents

Intumescent air vents

An intumescent vent contains a substance which swells when exposed to heat and blocks the free air opening which will help prevent the spread of smoke in a fire.

Intumescent air vents are special types of air vents that are designed to close in the event of a fire to stop the spread of smoke and fumes. It is important to check the vents to ensure the correct free air space. BS 5440 Part 2:2009 describes them as an assembly specified for preventing the spread of fire, consisting of a metal louvre or grille with an intumescent block secured behind it which incorporates a latticework of holes to provide continuous ventilation but which will expand and close in the event of extreme heat build-up such as in a fire. When fitted to doors the assembly usually has a louvre or grille on both sides.

Multi-appliance installations

Internal space

An indoor space not classified as a room because it is either a hall, passageway, stairway or landing.

Where a room or an **internal space** contains more than one gas appliance then the air vent free airs should be calculated from the greatest of the following:

- the aggregate maximum rated heat input of all flueless space heating appliances
- the aggregate maximum rated heat input of all open-flue space heating appliances*
- the greatest maximum rated heat input of any other type of appliance in the same area, for example, this could be an oil boiler.

* There is an exception to the second point when there is a situation where the interconnecting wall between two rooms has been removed and, as result, the room contains only two similar chimneys each fitted with a similar gas fire of an individual rating less than 7kW. In this situation an air vent may not be required.

Example

A room or an internal space contains:

- three gas appliances with a volume of 9m^3
- an open-flued boiler with an input of 25kW gross
- a flueless water heater with an input of 11kW net
- a balanced flue cooker of 28kW input net.

We must first work out the individual ventilation requirements of each appliance.

Open-flued boiler:
25 ÷ 1.11 = 22.52 (converting gross to net)
22.52 − 7 = 15.52 (removing allowance for adventitious air)
15.52 × 5 = 77.6cm^2 (multiplying the final figure by the factor of
                  5cm^2 to find out air required)

By referring to the flueless ventilation guidance it can be seen that the flueless water heater will require 100cm² plus an openable window.

A balanced flue cooker of 28kW input will require no ventilation.

Therefore a **100cm²** vent would be the correct size with the addition of an **openable window** in this instance.

Effects of fans

Warm air heater fans, fans in flues of open-flued appliances, ceiling (paddle) fans, room extractor fans, externally ducted tumble dryers, cooker hoods and fans used for extracting radon gas all can potentially reduce the ambient pressure to an appliance and therefore adversely affect the operation of a flue; they should therefore be operated during spillage testing. The spillage test will involve first testing with the fan off and then testing with any fan on to assess the performance of the appliance. Where applicable the fan to be tested should operate in both directions. An engineer must make an engineering judgement based on specific testing procedures.

BS 5440 Part 2 suggests that that 50cm^2 extra free air space added to the existing air space will usually solve any problems with spillage from gas appliances that is related to ventilation problems. Once the extra ventilation has been provided then the appliance should be tested again for spillage. Spillage testing is dealt with in Learning Outcome 3.

KEY POINT

When a fan is deemed to be causing the spillage of an open-flued appliance, BS 5440 Part 2 suggests that an additional 50cm² be added, then the system tested again.

Radon gas

In areas where radon gas has been identified as a problem, ventilation should not be taken from the space below the ground floor level, for example by use of a floor vent.

No design for ventilation for gas appliances should in any way interfere with the remedial measures that may already be in place to prevent radon gas entering the habitable part of a building.

When testing for spillage, any extraction systems should be turned on and running.

Passive stack ventilation

Passive stack ventilation is a ventilation system using ducts from the ceiling of a room to terminals on the roof. It operates by incorporating the principles of the natural stack effect. This means movement of air due to difference in temperature between inside and outside and the effect of the wind passing over the roof of the dwelling. This system is becoming popular in new dwellings but under no circumstances should it be used for ventilating gas appliances.

Domestic gas pipework (LO5)

There are six assessment criteria for this outcome:

1 Describe the requirements for gas pipework.
2 Describe materials used in internal gas pipework.
3 State common gas pipework faults.
4 Calculate pipe sizing for domestic natural gas installations.
5 Identify tools required to undertake domestic let-by and tightness testing.
6 State the procedure for domestic let-by and tightness testing.

This outcome is about gas pipework and the aim is to explain the basic requirements for gas pipework and describe the tools and materials that are used in internal pipework installation. The outcome will show good practice and give examples of common basic pipework faults. Pipe-sizing will also be explained as well as how gas installations are tested for tightness and let-by.

Installation pipework

SmartScreen Unit 307
PowerPoint 4

Installation pipework is commonly known as the carcass and the term is specifically applied to pipework in a new house when it is under construction. Gas installation pipework should be carried out in accordance with BS 6891:2005+A2:2008 and must also comply with the Gas Safety Installation and Use Regulations (GSIUR 1998) and the Building Regulations.

The most commonly used materials for pipework for gas installations are steel pipes of a medium weight in accordance with BS 1387 and light gauge copper tubes in accordance with BS EN 1057. The choice of a particular pipe is determined by a range of factors which include the need for mechanical strength or ability to resist impact or damage, the need for protection from types of corrosion, aesthetic considerations such as the appearance of pipe runs and in the end overall cost which includes fittings and labour.

Copper capillary fittings

The present standard for the installation of low-pressure gas pipework of up to 35mm (R1¼) in domestic premises (for second family gas) is BS 6891:2005+A2:2008. The Gas Safety (Installation and Use) Regulations 1998 (GSIUR) state that installation pipework means any pipework for conveying gas for a particular consumer and any associated valves or other gas fittings. Service pipes or pipework, a pipe in a gas appliance or a valve attached to a storage container or cylinder are not included in this definition.

Steel fittings

Installation pipework materials

Copper capillary or solder ring fittings are suitable for domestic installations but not all fluxes are suitable for the soldering process.

Low carbon steel is best for resisting mechanical damage. A tapered **BSPT** thread fits into a parallel thread socket to form a seal. Hemp should not be used.

PE (polyethylene) pipework is mainly used for underground supplies. If part of it does enter a house it must be protected against UV. It can be joined by compression or fusion welding.

BSPT

Stands for British Standard pipes and British Standard pipe threads, and relates to the type of thread we use on screwed low carbon steel pipes and fittings. Although the pipe is measured in mm, it is universally referred to in imperial measurements, eg ½-inch BSPT (½-inch British Standard pipe thread).

Press fit type fittings suitable for gas. Geberit Mapress™ bend 90° on the left and Geberit Mapress™ coupling on the right

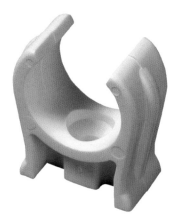

Corrugated stainless steel tubes (CSST) require special fittings

Corrugated stainless steel tube (CSST) has the same resistance as copper. It requires special fixings but can be adapted to fit any other pipe used for gas installation.

Rigid stainless pipework is suitable for both natural gas and LPG. It can be connected with a special press fitting tool.

Gas fittings are identified by a clear yellow mark and incorporate yellow internal O-rings. A pressing indicator on the pipe-fitting fabricating tool will help to achieve a successful joint – if the joints are not properly sealed they will leak. There are versions for other mediums such as water and they are colour-coded accordingly.

Pipework support

The chart below is derived from BS 6891:2005 and shows the maximum intervals for pipe support for rigid steel and copper and corrugated stainless steel pipework in gas installation.

Maximum intervals for pipe support

Material	Nominal size	Interval for vertical run (m)	Interval for horizontal run (m)
Steel (rigid)	Up to DN15 (R½)	2.5	2.0
	DN20 (R¾)	3.0	2.5
	DN25 (R1)	3.0	2.5
Copper and corrugated stainless	Up to 15mm A_1 and DN15 A_1 22mm A_1 and DN22 A_1 and above	2.0 / 2.5	1.5 / 2.0

It is important that pipework is adequately supported in order to prevent pressure on connections and to withstand mechanical impact. If broken or damaged clips are identified, they should be replaced as they offer very little effective support. The selection of pipe supports is very important as an open-ended plastic pipe fitted to a horizontal pipe on a ceiling can be less secure than a closed clip or a munsen ring which supports the whole circumference of the pipe.

Open-ended snap-on clip

Locking clip

Yellow clips are an innovative way to identify a gas pipe

A munsen ring with its base is connected with 10mm threaded studding which is cut to size on site

Munsen ring base

Buried pipework

BS 6891:2005 emphasises that installation pipework should not be installed under the foundations of a building nor in the ground under the base of the wall or footings unless adequate steps are taken to prevent any damage to the pipework in the event of the movement of those structures or the ground. Pipe fittings that conform to BS 7838 and compression fittings should not be buried in the ground. The use of fittings in these situations should be kept to a minimum and where it is practical and aesthetically acceptable, bends should be incorporated in the design rather than elbows.

A cover of 40mm below concrete slabs in an area where people walk or 375mm below any open ground or drives will be enough to prevent mechanical damage to buried gas pipework.

> **KEY POINT**
>
> The maximum spacing distance for pipe supports for a horizontal run of 15mm copper pipe-carrying gas is 1.5m and the maximum interval for a vertical run is 2m.

> **KEY POINT**
>
> If pipework is buried under a driveway, the cover should be a minimum of 375mm from the surface.

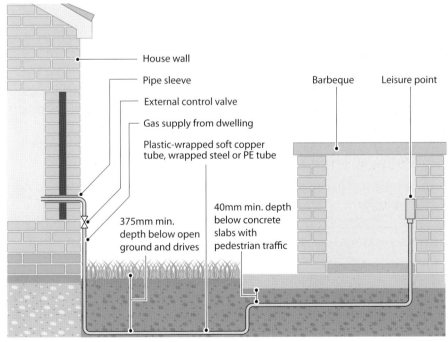

- House wall
- Pipe sleeve
- External control valve
- Gas supply from dwelling
- Plastic-wrapped soft copper tube, wrapped steel or PE tube

Barbeque   Leisure point

375mm min. depth below open ground and drives

40mm min. depth below concrete slabs with pedestrian traffic

External appliance installation

Great care should be taken to protect pipework which is buried in screed from mechanical damage. Generally a minimum cover of 25mm from the surface will be sufficient.

KEY POINT

The minimum depth of cover for pipework buried in screed is 25mm.

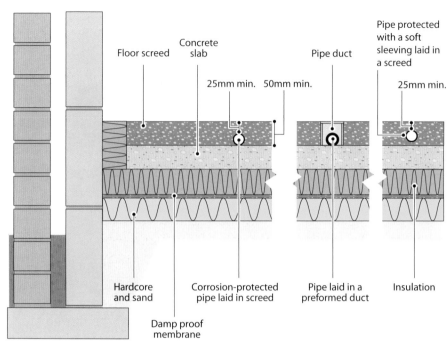

Protecting pipework

A buried low carbon steel gas pipe which is too close to an electric cable and fused switch

BS 6891:2005 explains that when installation pipes are not separated by electrical insulating material they should be spaced at least 150mm away from electricity meters and any associated excess current controls as well as electrical switches, sockets, distribution boards or consumer units. In addition, gas installation pipework should be spaced at least 25mm away from electricity supply and distribution cables.

Pipework in ducts

BS 6891 states that vertical and horizontal ducts which contain installation pipework should be ventilated to ensure that any minor gas leakage* that could occur does not cause the atmosphere within the duct to become unsafe. However, this level of ventilation would not clear a major gas escape which could arise from a damaged gas pipe.

*A minor gas leak represents an amount of gas which would remain undetected by a normal tightness test.

A duct may run freely through a number of storeys within a building or take the form of an enclosure at each storey level.

Cross-sectional area of duct (m²)	Minimum free area of each opening (m²)
Not exceeding 0.01	0
> 0.01 and < 0.05	Cross-sectional area of duct
> 0.05 and < 7.5	0.05
Exceeding 7.5	1/150 of the cross-sectional area of the duct

Derived from Table 3, BS 6891:2005

Where ducts are continuous then ventilation can normally be achieved by the provision of an opening which is sized in accordance with the table shown on the previous page.

A duct which has a small cross-sectional area of 0.01m² or less with a total volume of less than 0.1m³ is considered to be adequately ventilated by the adventitious air and therefore no additional opening will be required.

The normal fire resistance period of a duct for buildings of not more than three storeys is 30 minutes.

External and internal risers

When inspecting houses of multiple occupation, always ensure that a means of emergency isolation is as nearby as is practical to the entry of each flat. Where buildings contain flats and maisonettes, pipework should be fire-stopped as it passes from one floor to the next unless it is enclosed in its own protected shaft. Any such shaft must be ventilated at the top and the bottom with outside air. Whenever installation pipes emerge from a continuous duct and enter a flat or maisonette they should be fire-stopped at the point of entry. Thermal movement of the pipework should be considered in the design without compromising the integrity of the fire-stopping protection.

KEY POINT

In houses of multiple occupation, the practical location of an individual emergency control valve and fire-stopping of any associated gas pipework which enters each property should always be ensured during installation and checked whenever an engineer inspects such a dwelling.

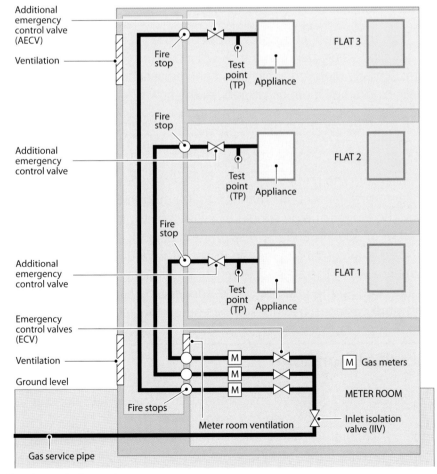

Fire-stopped pipework

Pipe-sizing

Nominal pipe sizes (mm)		Length of pipe (m)						Discharge (m³/h)
Copper	CSST							
BS EN 1057	BS 7838	3	6	9	(12)	15	20	
15	15	2.9	1.9	1.5	1.3	1.1	0.95	
(22)	(22)	8.7	5.8	4.6	(3.9)	3.4	2.9	
28	28	18	12	9.4	8	7	5.9	
35	35	32	22	17	15	13	11	

Extract from the pipe-sizing chart in Table 1 of BS 6891:2005+A2:2008 which gives maximum lengths of straight horizontal copper and CSST pipes runs and their volumes with a maximum of 1mbar differential pressure drop across the installation for gases with a relative density of 0.6 (air = 1) (Steel and PE pipe have been omitted from the table)

By referring to the table above, a simple calculation can be made. For example, it can be seen that the volumes of gas can be increased by using a larger pipe size over a similar length. If a boiler required 3.9m³/h of gas and was located 12m from the outlet of the gas meter it can be seen from the table that a 22mm copper or CSST pipe would suffice. As with any pipe-sizing, bends and tees will increase the equivalent pipe length. Similarly pipework which has been creased, flattened or is partially blocked with debris will reduce the flow of gas to an appliance.

One of the biggest problems with gas pipework installation is undersizing. Many appliances incorporate a 15mm isolation valve but it can never be assumed that the supply pipework size to the appliance from the meter should be the same diameter as the fitting. Manufacturers' instructions mention that although the fitting is 15mm, the length of pipe should be restricted to, for example, a maximum of 300mm and the rest of the pipework should be calculated in accordance with the British Standard. The documentation in the appliance benchmark books ensures that pressure-reading the gas rate of the appliance is carried out to confirm the correct pipework size has been installed.

Electrical bonding

An engineer should always ensure that there is adequate bonding applied to the outlet pipework of a gas meter. The bonding conductor should be 10mm² and it should be attached no more than 600mm from the outlet or before the first tee.

Whenever removing gas pipework, temporary continuity bonding should be applied.

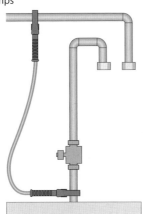
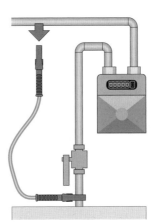

Temporary bonding clamps

(A) A temporary bond must be fitted before any part of the system is disconnected

(B) Carry out the work only while the temporary bond is connected

(C) When the work is completed remove the DOWNSTREAM clip first

Application of temporary continuity bonding

Electrical bonding

Although a temporary bonding cable is applied here it will not be effective as it is attached to a plastic condensate discharge pipe

The temporary bonding application shown here is now correctly installed

Common pipework faults

When inspecting gas installations, pipework faults are quite common and the following are just a few examples of what could be found during a day's work.

Leaking pipework

Bubbles on the screw test point are a sign of gas escaping and could be the result of forgetfulness, but if this were identified during an inspection after a report of a smell of gas, it would certainly be an indication that a tightness test had not been carried out when someone was previously working on the installation. The GSIUR states that any leak left on gas pipework is immediately dangerous (ID) and is Riddor-reportable.

Leaking pipework

LDF

A special fluid used to help find leaks on pipework and fittings as bubbling will occur if applied to an area where there is an escape of gas.

Two examples of poor practice. The copper gas pipe on the left is unsleeved and the pipe on the right is sleeved but not sealed and the sleeve is not sealed to the fabric of the building

KEY POINT

A sleeve such as steel would be suitable to protect a gas pipe travelling through a wall.

Flattening of copper tubes is an unacceptable method of sealing pipework

Open ended copper tube on gas installation

Therefore, whenever a joint has been disturbed, always check with **leak detection fluid (LDF)** afterwards and test when the fitting is under pressure.

Sleeving and sealing

The sleeving of a pipe travelling through a wall must be able to contain gas and should be sealed at one end only so that any escaping gas discharges to the atmosphere rather than collecting within the building or a cavity wall. There should also be sealing around the sleeve itself to prevent any discharging gas from reentering the building. No unprotected pipe should travel through a cavity wall.

Sleeving solutions

The drawings below show some practical and efficient ways to sleeve a gas pipe that is travelling through walls.

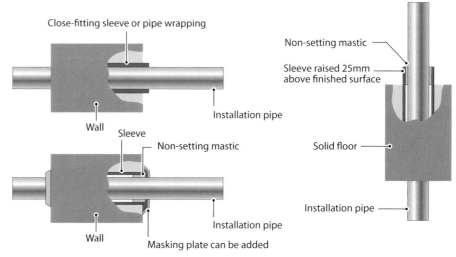

Pipework solutions

Flattened joints

The method of terminating a copper tube shown to the left involves flattening the end of a pipe and is unacceptable on gas pipework installations. It does not incorporate an approved and appropriate fitting at the end of the pipe which would enable the installation pipework section to be fully purged of air.

Open ends

An open end left on a gas pipe on an installation is considered immediately dangerous (ID) and RIDDOR-reportable. The image to the left shows an open end of a 15mm section of copper tube but similarly an isolation valve installed on gas-filled pipework which is uncapped or plugged would represent a similar risk because of the potential for it being opened.

Inappropriate use of a fitting

The cooker appliance flexible hose in the image to the right is used incorrectly to connect to rigid copper pipes. Similarly an appliance such as a fire/back boiler unit should never be fitted with a flexible hose.

Inappropriate materials

Plastic-capping of gas installation pipework is not allowed and is considered immediately dangerous (ID) and RIDDOR-reportable. Even though the pressure of gas is much lower than the typical operating pressure of water, for which these type of fittings are designed, there is no guarantee that they will be gas-tight or that components won't break down over a period of time because of their exposure to gas.

Plastic caps should never be used on gas pipework even as a temporary measure in an attempt to protect pipework from the ingress of dirt.

Lead may be found on existing installations but cannot be installed on a new gas pipework installation.

Cooker hose incorrectly used to connect pipework

Inappropriate plastic cap used to seal gas pipe work (ID and RIDDOR reportable)

A typical instance where a lead pipe has been installed on the meter connection on an older gas system

Equipotential bonding

There should be a 10mm² cross-sectional area (CSA) of bonding conductors permanently installed within 600mm of the outlet on gas meter pipework or before the first tee connection, whichever is closer.

There is no equipotential bonding on the meter outlet pipework

The movement of an emergency control valve (ECV) lever impeded by an obstruction

KEY POINT

A compression fitting on a gas pipe should not be fitted under floorboards where there is limited access to them.

SmartScreen Unit 307
PowerPoint 5 (Part 2)

Restricted movement

Another problem may be when an emergency control valve (ECV) has restricted movement and therefore cannot open fully because of an obstruction.

Installation pipework

The process of notching and drilling of timber floors is a common everyday job for the engineer who installs gas and any associated pipework. The reason why there are set limits regarding the location depth and size of notch or hole is to ensure that the joist is not weakened or damaged by any such action.

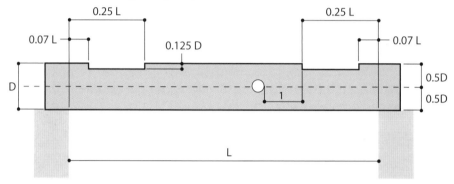

Limits for the notching and drilling of solid timber floor joists

Tightness and let-by testing of natural gas

A tightness test is a test to ascertain if a gas installation has any leaks while a let-by test determines if gas is escaping through the ECV (emergency control valve). The new standard for domestic gas tightness testing is IGE/UP/1B/Ed3 and this normative document includes some changes to the test procedure which are highlighted in this outcome.

The basic tools required to work on gas fittings include a manometer with a tube, leak detection fluid, a flat-bladed screwdriver, a stopwatch and a dry lint-free cloth.

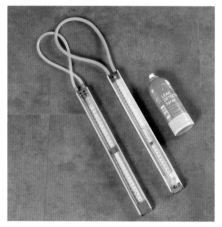

Manometers with leak detection fluid

Flat-bladed screwdriver

Stopwatch

Lint-free cloth

Test equipment

Always ensure that your test equipment is in good condition and clean so that readings can be clearly seen, thereby enabling an accurate test to take place.

A manometer with staining making accurate reading of the meniscus difficult

A clean manometer enabling a clear, accurate reading of the meniscus to be taken

Tightness testing – visual survey

It is essential that a gas installation is visually inspected before progressing with a gas tightness test. In the image on the right, the engineer is checking the label on the meter to confirm supplier details and emergency numbers are up to date and correct. Any label or notice fitted to a gas installation must be accurate and precise. Out-of-date information should be updated to the current regulations and standards.

An engineer carrying out a visual inspection of a gas installation

The regulator in the image on the right does not have a seal and this must be reported to the gas provider as it poses a risk to the occupiers of the dwelling. Any increase or decrease of the pressure could cause a hazard at the point of use of the customer's gas appliances. It can be seen that the information shown on the regulator states that there is a maximum pressure of 75mbar at the inlet with an operating pressure of 21mbar. This regulator can also pass 6m³/h of gas.

Meter label

ECV

ECV stands for the emergency control valve and, in some instances, is called the MECV, which means the meter emergency control valve.

Inspection of CSST pipework and labelling

Let-by test

A test to determine if gas is escaping through the ECV (emergency control valve).

When testing the system, it is essential that the lever of the valve falls to the 'off' position as shown because this will indicate that the whole of the system is isolated from this point. Following on in this outcome, we will see in more detail that a **let-by test**'s purpose is to confirm that the ECV lever, while in this position, is gas tight and not 'letting by' or leaking gas into the pipework.

The corrugated stainless steel tube (CSST), commonly known as the anaconda, is labelled showing the correct direction of the lever.

Beginning the tightness test procedure (in accordance with IGE/UP/1B/Ed3)

STEP 1 A slotted screwdriver of the correct size is used to remove the test nipple on the meter.

STEP 2 If spanners are used there is a possibility of overtightening and this could break the test nipple inside its housing. Therefore a slotted screwdriver is often considered the most appropriate tool for the job.

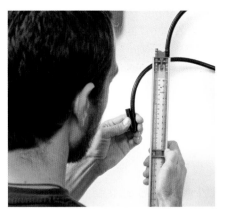

STEP 3 Before a tightness test takes place it is important to check the equipment to ensure that it is working properly; otherwise an inaccurate test could occur.

STEP 4 The engineer admits water into the manometer and ensures that the level of the water in both legs is set at zero. The slider at the rear of most gauges allows some adjustment in order to achieve this. Air pressure can then be admitted to raise the level of water in the manometer to around 20mbar and the end of the hose is nipped together to form a temporary seal. If the pressure remains stable it would indicate that the instrument is accurate and suitable for test purposes.

Once the engineer considers it safe to do so and the manometer is attached to the test point of the meter, the lever valve can be slowly opened to begin the tightness test.

KEY POINT

A tightness test is carried out by an engineer to check the integrity of a gas pipework installation. A water-filled manometer is typically used and the test is carried out in accordance with IGE/UP/1B/Ed3.

KEY POINT

Manometers, electronic gauges and hoses should be tested before tightness testing.

Operating an ECV

A slow steady hand movement is required to operate the ECV to avoid overshooting the required pressure and even creating possible regulator lock-up with the added potential of water rapidly discharging from the open end of the manometer.

Attaching the hose to the test point

Damaged hose causing a leak and making testing impossible

When attaching the hose to the test point it is important that a visual check on the integrity of the hose is carried out, as hoses can perish and split over a period of time, as can be seen in the image on the right above.

Let-by test

The purpose of the let-by test is to check the integrity of the valve to see if it is leaking when in the closed position.

To carry out the test:

1 Remove the test nipple and carefully attach the manometer hose to the test point.

2 Slowly open the ECV and raise the pressure in the manometer to between 7mbar and 10mbar. It is important to read the level of the meniscus of the water at eye level.

3 When the pressure has reached 7–10mbar, close the ECV and test the pressure for one minute.

4 If there is any **perceptible rise** (0.25mbar – or two decimal places on an electronic meter) during that period it would be deemed that there is a let-by from the ECV.

5 If it is safe to do so, loosen the connection downstream on the ECV and spray leak detection fluid on the exposed inner valve to see any evidence of leakage.

6 If leakage is confirmed, inform the gas supplier who will repair or replace the valve.

The purpose of the stabilisation test is to ensure that a temperature rise or fall in the pipework does not adversely affect the tightness test reading.

Once a successful let-by test has been achieved, for example if there was no perceptible rise on the manometer, then raise the pressure to 20–21mbar by slowly opening the ECV. Once the pressure has been reached, close the ECV and test for one minute.

The purpose of the tightness test is to test the integrity of a gas installation.

Once a successful temperature stabilisation test has been achieved, retain or readjust the pressure of 20–21mbar and proceed with the tightness test for two minutes. Record any movement of the gauge. Any pressure drop detected should be checked against the permissible drops which are shown in IGE/UP/1B/Ed3 2012, Table 3 and in the table on page 261.

Note: Care should be taken not to exceed the test pressure as any increase over 23mbar could lead to lock-out of the regulator and a false reading could result.

Perceptible movement

Movement detected by the eye of the engineer while testing is considered to be 0.25mbar on a manometer and two decimal places on an electronic gauge.

Timing the let-by test for one minute

KEY POINT

0.25mbar on a manometer and two decimal places on an electronic gauge are considered 'perceptible'.

Stabilisation test

KEY POINT

There is no permissible pressure drop on a new system.

Tightness test between 20 and 21mbar to comply with the IGE/UP/1B/Ed3

After a satisfactory tightness test, always check the test nipple for any gas escape with leak detection fluid when the system is repressurised.

It is important to wipe off any residue of leak detection fluid with a lint-free cloth as this will prevent corrosion of metals. Never use washing-up liquid solution to test for leaks as the residue will cause corrosion to metal parts.

Tightness testing/permissible pressure drops on existing systems

The information below is derived from IGE/UP/1B/Ed3 2012, Table 3 and shows the maximum permissible pressure drops allowed providing there is no smell of gas.

Type of installation

Meter designation	Pipework diameter	Maximum permissible pressure drop
No meter – AECV only (eg a flat)	$\leq$ 28mm	8mbar
	> 28mm $\leq$ 35mm	4mbar
Ultrasonic $\leq$ 6m^3/h (eg electronic E6)	$\leq$ 28mm	8mbar
	> 28mm $\leq$ 35mm	4mbar
Diaphragm $\leq$ 6m^3/h (eg U6, G4)	$\leq$ 28mm	4mbar
	> 28mbar	2.5mbar
Diaphragm $\leq$ 6m^3/h $\leq$ 16m^3/h (eg U16, G10)	$\leq$ 35mm	1mbar

Key $\leq$ less than or equal to, $\geq$ greater than or equal to, > greater than

During a tightness test there may be a pressure drop and by referring to the above table an engineer can determine if it is acceptable providing there is no smell of gas.

There is no permissible pressure drop allowed on any new gas installation.

Tightness test summary

Here is a review of the tightness test procedure:

- Different types of meter permit pressure drops when testing providing there is no smell of gas.
- Electronic gas meters require calibration every 12 months to ensure they produce accurate readings.

- A tightness test means that the installation pipework and the appliances up to the gas valve are included.

- When testing pipework only, there is no permissible leakage.

- Even after a successful tightness test, sometimes components such as gas valves on appliances can leak gas during operation. If this happens then check the component with leak detection fluid to find and repair the source of the leak.

The tightness testing procedure on installations of pipework up to 35mm is covered in IGE/UP/1B/Ed3 2012.

For larger pipework, eg 42mm or with systems containing over $0.035m^3$ of gas, the testing procedures are covered in IGE/UP/1A.

Air test

An air test is a test using the medium of air. It can be undertaken before the installation is connected to a live gas supply, tightness tested and purged with fuel gas. Air is introduced into the pipework with a hand bellow connected via a tube to a tee pipe. At the tee, the two other connections are connected via individual hoses to a test point on the gas pipework system and to a manometer. The test is carried out to the same pressures as a tightness test with gas, with one minute allowed for stabilisation and two minutes for the tightness test. The let-by test of the ECV is not required. If a regulator is connected then care should be taken not to over-pressurise as meter lock-up could occur.

Controls (LO6)

SmartScreen Unit 307
PowerPoint 6

There are three assessment criteria for this outcome:

1 Identify gas controls.
2 Describe the operation of principal gas controls.
3 Describe common faults in gas controls.

The aim of this outcome is to enable the learner to identify and describe the operation of the principal gas controls and give details of some common faults.

Flame rectification

Flame rectification utilises the ability of a flame to conduct electricity. It converts an AC current to DC and turns off the gas supply to an appliance if the flame goes out.

The purpose of the gas control is to provide a safe and manageable supply of gas to an appliance. The types of controls which are installed on gas appliances vary and range from a basic on–off plug tap to a more sophisticated **flame rectification** process.

Gas tap

A **gas tap** is the most simple of gas controls but, unless it is maintained, it can cause problems. For example, if the plug taper type tap is not properly greased it could become stiff and let by gas.

Gas tap

A manually operated device which can be operated by either a lever or knob to isolate or allow gas to flow.

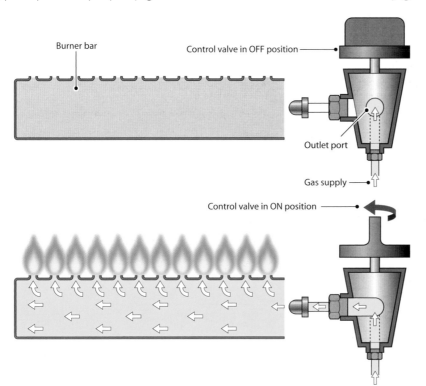

Gas taps: ball ¼ turn (top) and plug taper type (bottom)

A simplex burner consists of one injector and is typically found on space heaters

The simplex burner operates by allowing the amount of gas distributed across the whole of the burner bar to be determined by incremental turning of the control knob to achieve the desired heat output.

The duplex burner operates by allowing a predetermined amount of gas to be distributed to a central burner via one injector while the other section of the burner is supplied by the other injector. The sectional area of the burner bar can therefore be served by the operation of the control knob which incorporates precisely located ports dedicated to each injector to supply each section in order to achieve the desired heat output.

KEY POINT

The stiff operation of a control tap could perhaps cause a problem for an elderly person trying to operate a gas fire or a cooker control knob. Therefore an engineer should be able to lubricate and service these valves to remedy the problem. Stiff controls indicate the drying out of lubrication and could cause an immediately dangerous situation when located on a burner rail of a cooker hob. This problem can be caused by the ambient heat from a leaking door seal on an oven located below the burner rail.

A maintenance task being carried out on a float rail on a cooker which houses the control taps for individual burners, oven and grill

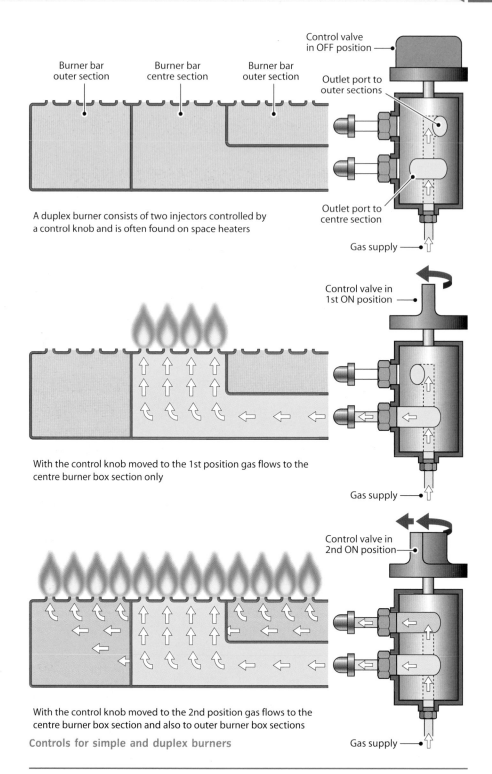

Burner bar outer section

Burner bar centre section

Burner bar outer section

Control valve in OFF position

Outlet port to outer sections

Outlet port to centre section

Gas supply

A duplex burner consists of two injectors controlled by a control knob and is often found on space heaters

Control valve in 1st ON position

With the control knob moved to the 1st position gas flows to the centre burner box section only

Gas supply

Control valve in 2nd ON position

With the control knob moved to the 2nd position gas flows to the centre burner box section and also to outer burner box sections

Controls for simple and duplex burners

Gas supply

Cooker safety cut-off valve

A cooker safety cut-off valve prevents cooker hob burners being used when a closedown lid is closed.

There are three basic types:

- A cut-off device which turns off the gas supply and is not resettable, which means, when the lid is opened again, unlit gas returns to the burners, as shown in the illustration on the next page.

- A closedown lid which turns off the gas supply and which then requires resetting by manually pushing a button usually located at the back of the appliance.

- A more sophisticated type which turns off the gas taps to the hob as the lid is lowered – the gas supply to the hob remains off if the lid is raised again.

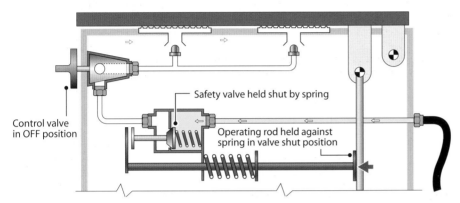

Cooker lid closed therefore isolating gas supply to hob burners

A cooker lid in the closed position with the safety cut-off device located at the front of the image

A lever-operated shut-off valve is operated by the 90° lever action of the raising and lowering of a cooker lid. The illustration above shows the lid in the closed position and the gas supplied, shown in yellow, via the hose into the appliance terminates where the valve seating is closed by the action of the spring.

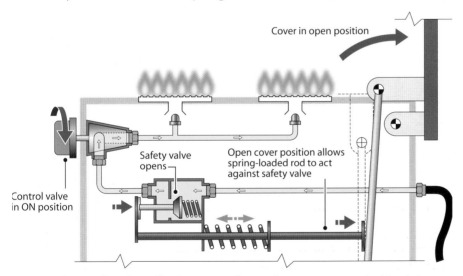

Cooker lid open therefore allowing gas to flow to burners once control knob is opened

A cooker lid shown in the open position

When the lid is raised, the lever action of the attached rod opens the gas valve by pushing the chamfered component off its seating against the reciprocating pressure of the spring. This allows gas to flow to the burner control taps where the user can operate the hob and control the flow of gas to each individual burner.

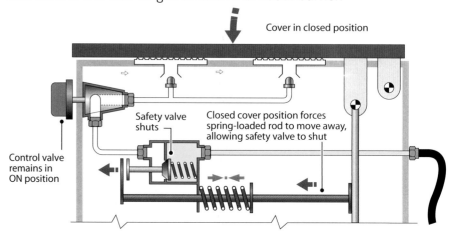

Cooker lid closed showing the action of SSOV

Mechanical thermostat

The main aim of a thermostat is to maintain safety in the event of overheating and to sustain even temperatures during the heating and cooking process. The thermostat can be either primary or secondary control.

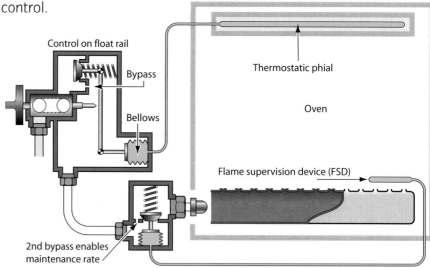

Mechanical thermostat located in a domestic oven

In liquid-filled oven thermostats, the temperature range is selected by the user at the control knob which is connected to the spindle, which operates the gas inlet cock, the temperature setting and, in more modern appliances, an oven ignition micro-switch.

The thermostat body contains a flexible diaphragm (bellows) and valve control mechanism, which is contained in a gas chamber that travels to the burner via the diaphragm-controlled main valve and a **bypass**, which is located between the chamber and the outlet.

The bypass is very important, as it allows a maintenance rate of gas to the burner during the cooking process. For example when the oven has reached the required temperature the bellows' closing action will cause the main port to the burner to close, leaving only a small amount of gas to travel via the bypass.

Once the gas has travelled to the burner, there is another bypass which allows a small flame to be lit. This flame provides the maintenance rate which is always present as long as the thermostat is turned on.

The small flame heats the phial which is located over the burner and causes the liquid within it to expand and open the bellows, which in turn allows the full rate of gas to enter the burner. This is the **flame supervision device** of the oven. It is important therefore that the phial is located in the correct position; otherwise, if it is out of range of the flame, the flame will remain at the maintenance rate. If the phial were in the correct position during this process and there were no main flame, it would indicate that the phial, capillary tube or valve itself had failed.

Flame supervision device

Flame supervision device is a gas control valve which is incorporated in the gas supply to a burner. Its purpose is to isolate the supply of gas if no flame is detected, eg if a pilot light is extinguished this will cause the valve to close via a thermocouple on a thermoelectric valve.

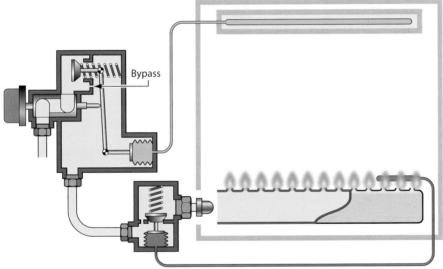

Low flame activated phial being heated which will expand liquid in bellows

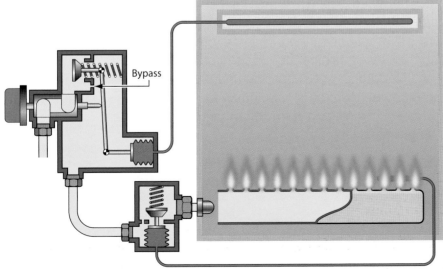

Bellows open which allows full flame at the burner

In the previous image, the main flame is lit as the bellows on the oven flame supervision device (FSD) have responded to the expanded liquid from the phial via the capillary tube and opened the valve.

When the oven has reached the temperature preset on the control knob, the liquid oven thermostat phial expands and the bellows respond by pushing the mechanism within the valve to close the gas inlet port. Gas is still present because the valve is open but it can only travel through the bypass port. This small volume of gas travels to the inlet of the burner and produces a low maintenance rate which keeps the food in the oven at the required temperature. If the bypass were blocked with grease then the oven would go out at this stage of the cooking process as no gas would be available to supply the burner.

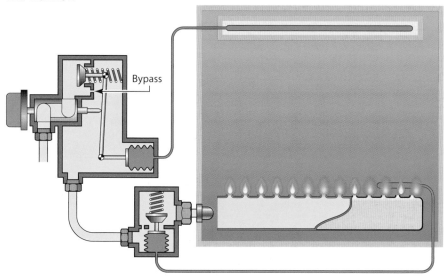

Low maintenance flame keeps the burner alight via bypass

The image above shows that the oven has reached the preset temperature and the low maintenance rate flame is provided by the gas which passes through the bypass orifice at the top of the main oven thermostat valve. When the temperature drops to a predetermined level within the cooker, the liquid in the phial contracts and reduces the pressure on the thermostat bellows, allowing more gas to the burner to increase the heat within the oven and thereby sustaining the required cooking temperature for the food. This process of expansion and contraction of the oven thermostat continues to provide an even cooking temperature until the oven control knob is turned off and the burner flame extinguished.

Bimetallic strip

These devices are no longer used as flame supervision devices but can be found on older appliances.

A bimetallic strip works on the principle that two dissimilar metals are attached to one another forming a strip which in this instance (in the image to the right) is then bent into a loop shape. When a pilot flame comes in contact with the bimetallic strip the two dissimilar metals expand at different rates and the loop bends as it moves. One part of the loop is attached to a rod which in turn is connected to the seating of a gas valve and while there is heat on the bimetallic strip, it will allow gas to pass. When the heat is removed, the loop will return to its original shape, pulling the rod back to its original position resulting in the closing of the gas valve.

Bimetallic strip

Over time these devices harden and distort and, as a result, lose their original shape and level of performance which can lead to dangerous let-by of gas at the appliance.

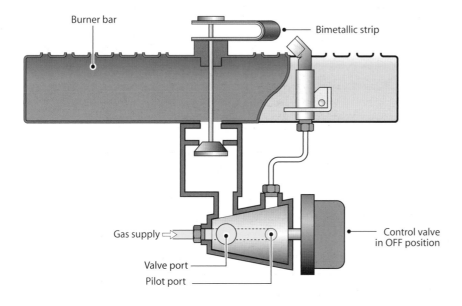

Appliance OFF

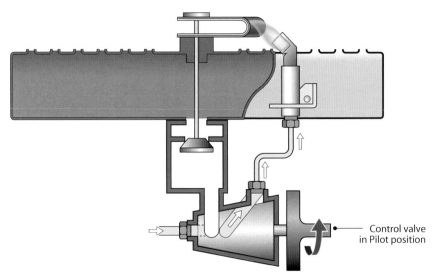

Pilot ON position and gas flows to pilot injector

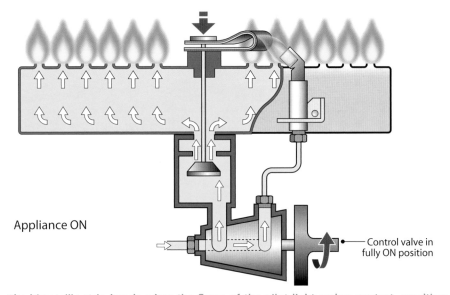

Appliance ON

The bimetallic strip bends when the flame of the pilot light makes contact, resulting in the main valve opening to allow gas to the burner box

The drawing above shows a pilot flame heating a bimetallic strip located close to an appliance burner bar. The end of the strip is connected to a rod which controls the travel of a valve on a seating. There is a control tap located at the gas supply inlet to the appliance, which will allow gas to travel to the burner bar once the tap is opened.

Control knob showing OFF, Pilot, and ON positions.

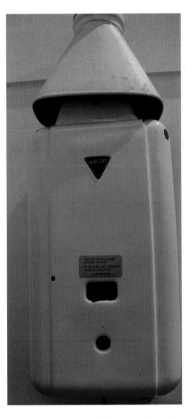

A typical older-style open-flued water heater incorporating a bimetallic strip

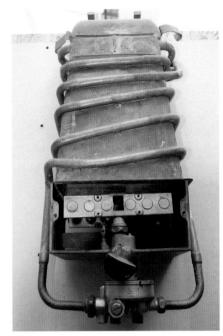

View of an older water heater with bimetallic strip with its casing removed

The drawing on the previous page illustrates the movement of the bimetallic strip by application of heat from the pilot which moves the rod and lifts the valve from its seating. When the control tap is opened, gas, shown in yellow, travels to the burner where it is ignited by the pilot flame.

The image on the previous page shows the control section for an appliance which uses a bimetallic strip. The pilot has a separate tube coming from the main gas control and is protected with a gauze which acts as a lint arrestor. The main body of the valve transports the gas from the inlet once the appliance is turned on. The bimetallic strip is located behind the rectangular opening on the burner.

Label on an older-style water heater. Note that open-flued appliances are no longer allowed in bathrooms

Thermoelectric devices

These devices work on the principle that when heat from the pilot is applied to the tip of a thermocouple, a small electrical voltage is created. This signal energises a small electromagnet which in turn holds open the gas valve while the sprung plunger, which was manually holding the valve open, returns to its original position, making the valve ready for use.

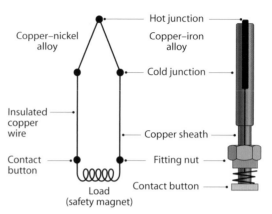

Components of a thermocouple

A thermocouple

A thermocouple is a component often found on a multifunctional gas valve and is located at the point where the pilot flame emerges from the outlet which is positioned next to a burner. From the point when the pilot flame initially envelopes the tip (12mm area) of the thermocouple (hot junction), it takes about 20 seconds maximum to energise the contact button which is attached to the magnetic part of the flame supervision device, located on the gas valve. This sequence is known as the thermocouple **pull-in time**.

Testing a thermocouple

The pilot flame produces a heat temperature of 650 ± 50°C at the hot junction. This in turn creates a small DC voltage across the cold junction. The minimum voltage required to energise the magnet in the flame supervision device is 15mV DC, which means gas can flow via the solenoid to the burner when energised by a signal from the appliance thermostat. If the pilot flame is interrupted, the magnet in the flame supervision device is de-energised and no gas can flow to the burner. The maximum time it takes to stop the flow of gas is 60 seconds on domestic boilers and this is known as the **drop-out time**.

Pull-in time

Pull-in relates to the time it takes a thermocouple, when heat is applied to it from a pilot flame, to energise an electromagnet within a thermoelectric device.

Drop-out time

Drop-out time refers to the time it takes for an electromagnet to de energise after heat has been removed from the tip of the thermocouple, eg when a pilot light is extinguished.

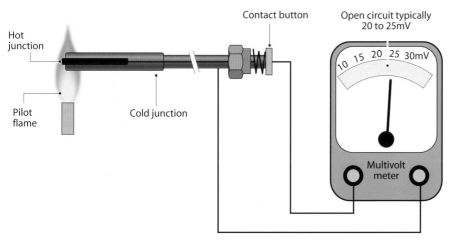

Multivolt meter measuring millivolts signal from thermocouple enveloped by pilot flame

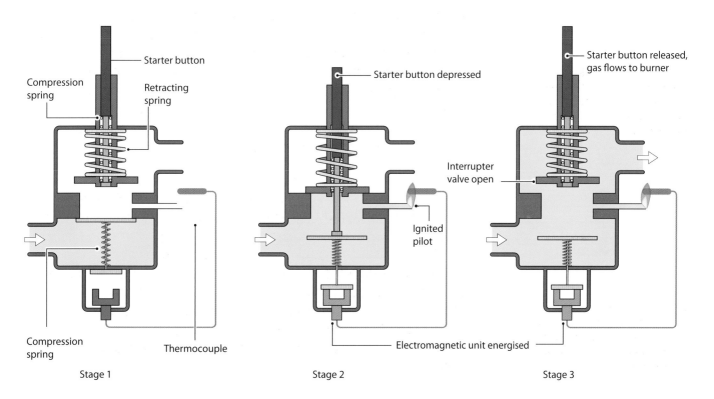

Manual sequence of operation of thermoelectric valve

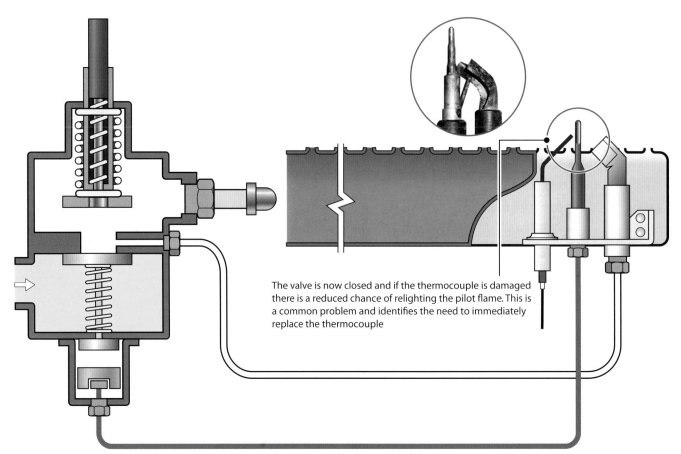

The valve is now closed and if the thermocouple is damaged there is a reduced chance of relighting the pilot flame. This is a common problem and identifies the need to immediately replace the thermocouple

Stage 1

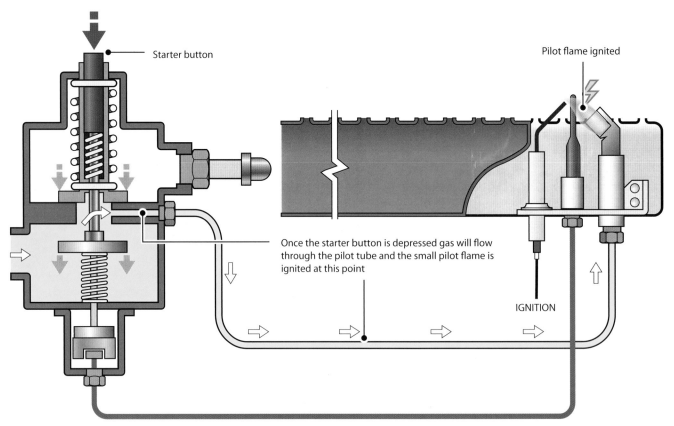

Starter button

Pilot flame ignited

Once the starter button is depressed gas will flow through the pilot tube and the small pilot flame is ignited at this point

IGNITION

Stage 2 – Pilot lit

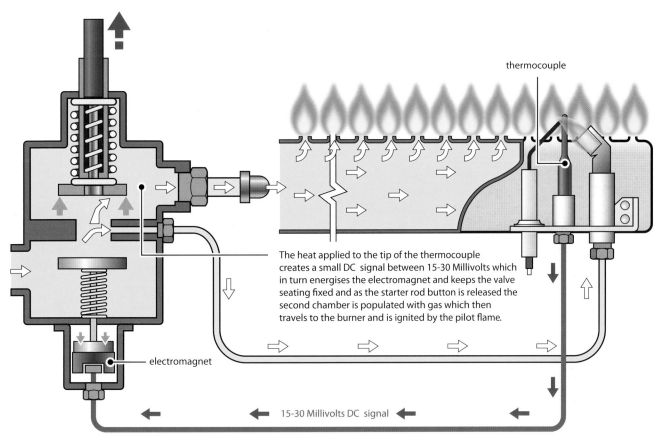

thermocouple

The heat applied to the tip of the thermocouple creates a small DC signal between 15-30 Millivolts which in turn energises the electromagnet and keeps the valve seating fixed and as the starter rod button is released the second chamber is populated with gas which then travels to the burner and is ignited by the pilot flame.

electromagnet

15-30 Millivolts DC signal

Stage 3

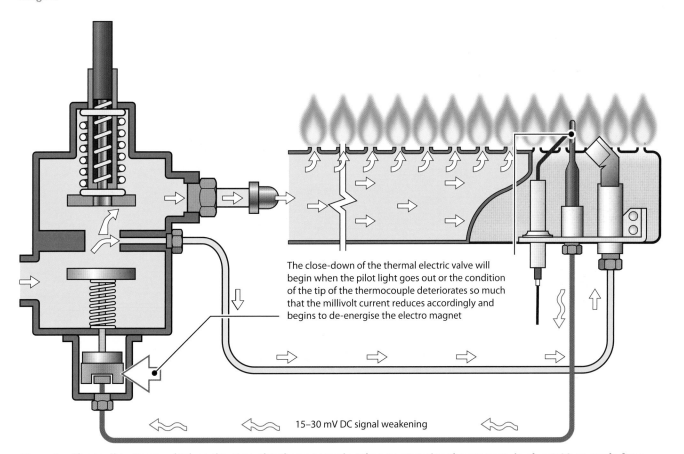

The close-down of the thermal electric valve will begin when the pilot light goes out or the condition of the tip of the thermocouple deteriorates so much that the millivolt current reduces accordingly and begins to de-energise the electro magnet

15–30 mV DC signal weakening

Stage 4 – The 'pull-in time', which is the time the thermocouple takes to energise the magnet, is about 20 seconds for a domestic boiler

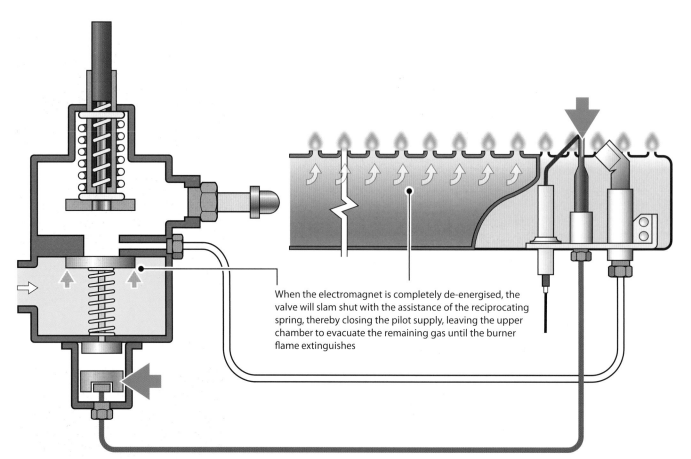

When the electromagnet is completely de-energised, the valve will slam shut with the assistance of the reciprocating spring, thereby closing the pilot supply, leaving the upper chamber to evacuate the remaining gas until the burner flame extinguishes

Stage 5 – The 'drop-out time', which is the time for the magnet to de-energise once the pilot flame is extinguished at the tip of the thermocouple, is a maximum of 60 seconds for a domestic boiler

The tip of a thermocouple with signs of pitting

KEY POINT

A damaged thermocouple tip could cause an appliance to turn off or prevent the pilot light from staying lit.

KEY POINT

A loose nut at the connection between the thermocouple and the gas valve can also cause an appliance to fail during operation or prevent the pilot from staying alight.

Whenever a thermoelectric device is inspected it is important to check the condition of the tip of the thermocouple as, over a period of time, the component will deteriorate. If any pitting or damage is detected at the tip of the thermocouple, it should be replaced as there is a likelihood that it will fail and the appliance will not be able to light. The thermocouple makes contact with the gas valve where the thermoelectric device is located and it is attached to the valve housing by a screw-in nut. If this nut is loose then the appliance will fail to light or will experience intermittent failure during its operation. There needs to be a good firm contact at the valve and the pilot flame should envelope the tip of the thermocouple by about 12mm to ensure a trouble-free operation.

Regulator

The image on page 277 shows a regulator which is typically found on the inlet of domestic U6, E6 and G4 gas meters.

This regulator is capable of working in an inlet pressure of 75mbar, stepping down to 21mbar for working pressure within the dwelling. They can pass a volume of 6m^3 per hour. The seal should always be intact on the meter regulator and if it is found to be removed or tampered with, then it should be reported immediately to the gas supplier.

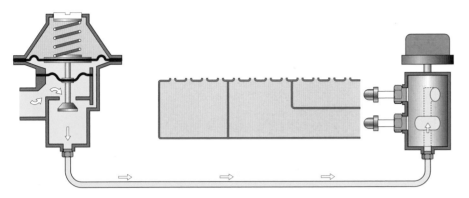

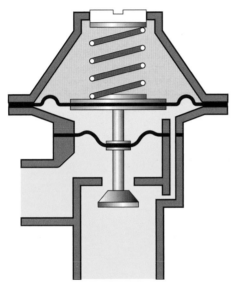

A pressure regulator located upstream of control valve on an appliancer

Regulator

A smaller in-line appliance regulator typically found on older appliances

Large commercial solenoid gas valve

Solenoid gas valve

A solenoid gas valve is a device which is controlled by an electrical circuit often from an electric thermostat located on a boiler. The energy from this circuit then creates an electromagnet which in turn holds open the valve so that gas will then flow. When the circuit to the solenoid valve is de-energised, the valve slams shut and closes the gas supply to the burner.

Solenoid valves come in all shapes and sizes and the one shown above is a slam-shut valve (SSV), which is located on the incoming main of a 50mm gas supply pipe.

The solenoid valve shown on the previous page is cutaway for demonstration purposes. It is incorporated into a multi-functional gas valve. Part of the protective insulation has been removed to show the copper windings. This **multifunctional** valve has two solenoids: one for the pilot and the other for the main burner.

Solenoid gas valve cutaway

KEY POINT

Diaphragms are moving parts and, through wear and tear, can split or perforate. This can be identified on a regulator by the smell of gas escaping through the breather hole at the top of the control.

Multifunctional

This means several functions are incorporated into one device such as gas valve, typically a regulator, flame supervision device or solenoid.

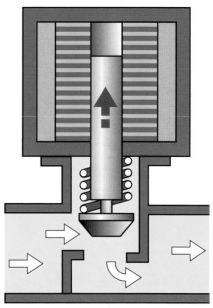

A solenoid valve in the closed position, which means there is no power to the solenoid from a control device such as an electrical thermostat

A solenoid valve in the open position because the armature is energised by an electric signal. This can be either an AC or a DC current

Electrical thermostat

An electrical thermostat operates by using electrical circuits which are operated by either mechanical or electronic means, which in turn control the flow of gas to an appliance to obtain a predetermined temperature level.

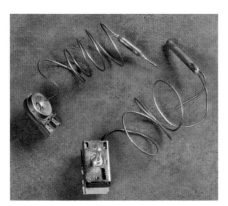

Two electrical thermostats, on the left is a high limit thermostat and on the right is a boiler control thermostat.

A thermistor located in a pocket of a boiler heat exchanger

Electrical thermostat

With an **electrical thermostat**, the control knob is calibrated to achieve a range of temperatures by adjusting its travel to and from the contacts. The phial is located in the pocket of the boiler heat exchanger.

Electrical thermostat and overheat device

The two components shown in the images to the left control the operating temperature of a gas boiler. Both controls work on the principle of expanding liquid contained in the phial being transferred by a capillary tube to bellows, which make contact with a switch.

The component at the top is an overheat thermostat with a reset button. The one below is the boiler thermostat with calibrated control which, when in situ, is operated via a knob which is located on the spindle.

The following illustrations show an electrical thermostat used in conjunction with a solenoid gas valve.

The control knob is calibrated to achieve a range of temperatures by adjusting its travel to and from the contacts

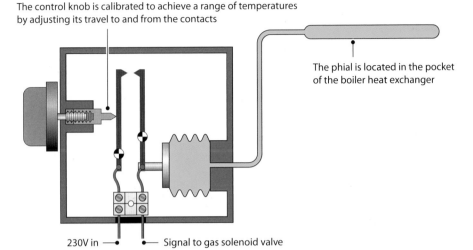

The phial is located in the pocket of the boiler heat exchanger

230V in —•   •— Signal to gas solenoid valve

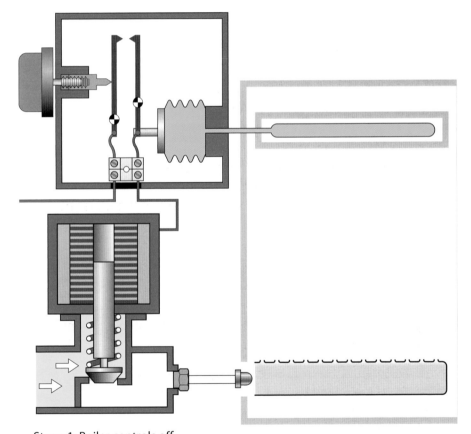

Stage 1: Boiler controls off

An electrical thermostat used in conjunction with a solenoid gas valve

When an electrical signal travels from the domestic central heating control system, its first destination is the boiler thermostat. If the boiler is calling for heat then the two contacts within the thermostat will meet and send the signal to the gas solenoid which will open the port within the valve so that gas will flow to the burner.

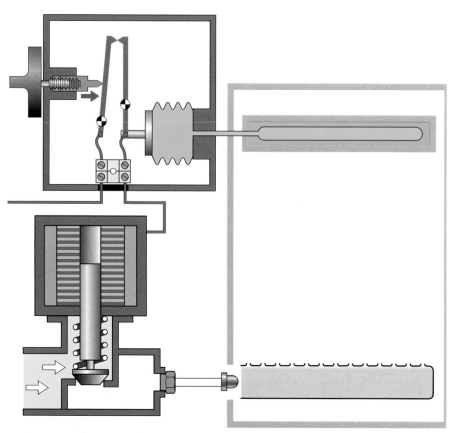

Stage 2: Boiler control on – signal sent to solenoid valve

The solenoid valve is receiving the electrical signal from the thermostat because the contacts are made

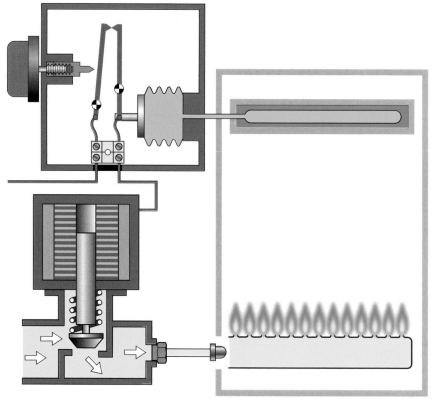

Stage 3: Boiler control on – signal sent to solenoid valve – gas flows to burner

The solenoid is energised and lifts off the valve seating, allowing gas to flow to the burner

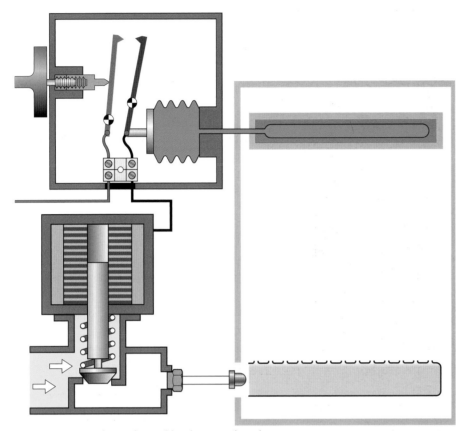

Stage 4: Signal to solenoid broken – valve closes

With the contacts separated, the electrical signal to the solenoid valve is terminated

When the signal is terminated from the thermostat to the solenoid valve, it will slam shut and the gas will stop flowing to the burner. The solenoid will be activated again once there is a call for heat from the thermostat. This process will continue for the duration of the timed heating cycle originating at the programmer. Similarly a room thermostat can interrupt the signal to the boiler during the heating cycle when the ambient temperature in the room has been reached.

A typical control sequence on a modern domestic heating installation would be as follows:

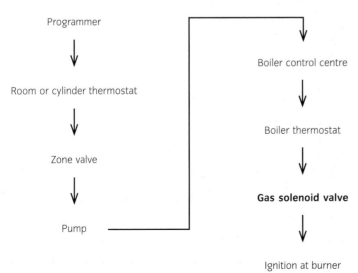

Gas solenoid valve

This is a device which is controlled by an electrical circuit often from an electric thermostat located on a boiler. The energy from the circuit then creates an electromagnet which in turn holds open a valve so that gas will flow. When the circuit to the solenoid valve is de-energised, the valve slams shut and closes the gas supply to the burner.

A multifunctional valve found on a modern boiler

A multifunctional valve located on a floor-standing Gloworm Hideaway boiler

Multifunctional gas valve

This control device typically comprises a pressure regulator, a flame supervision device and a solenoid valve. In addition it can also include other components such as a filter at the inlet of the valve as well as pressure points to check the inlet and operating pressure. Sometimes it can incorporate a pilot adjustment screw.

Multifunctional gas valves are commonly found on boilers and have pressure test points to confirm the inlet and the burner operating pressure of the appliance.

The plug on the left sends electrical power to the unit and the circular white knob next to it is the thermostat control. On the far right is the thermoelectric knob which is marked for each individual stage of the lighting process. This is depressed and held down while the pilot is lit which sends a signal to energise the electromagnet as explained earlier in the outcome. The black knob on the left is the button for the piezo ignition device which sends a spark signal to the pilot area to create a flame.

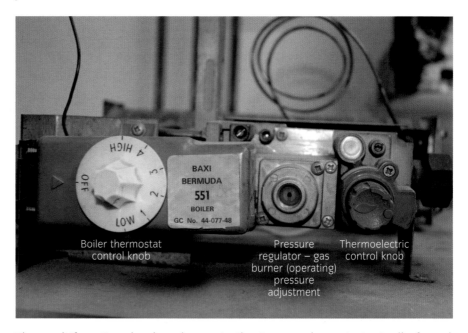

Boiler thermostat control knob

Pressure regulator – gas burner (operating) pressure adjustment

Thermoelectric control knob

The multifunctional valve shown in the image above is typically found on an older back boiler unit. This one shows the regulator in the middle. The knob on the far left is the thermostat and the one on the far right is the knob to initiate the thermoelectric process.

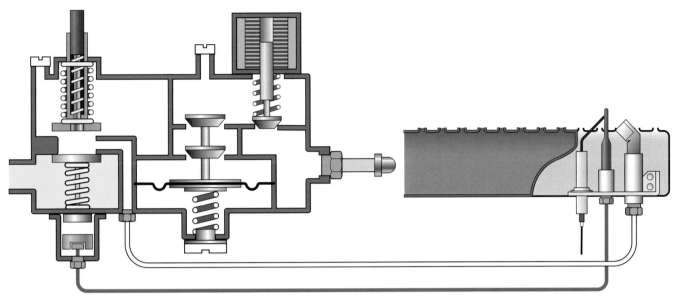

A multifunctional control valve stage 1. Appliance off, no pilot lit

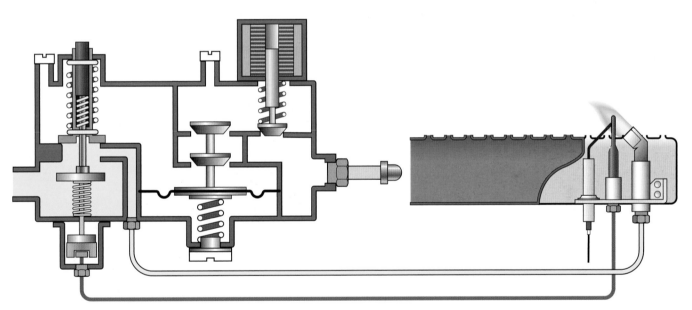

A multifunctional control valve stage 2. Pilot on

The illustration in stage 2 shows the thermoelectric button being depressed during the stage of lighting the pilot.

Once the flame has enveloped the thermocouple, a signal of about 25–30 millivolts is sent to the electromagnet. The button or plunger can then be released as the magnet has pulled in and is held tight against the spring-loaded plate which now opens the gas inlet port, meaning that gas can travel within the body of the valve.

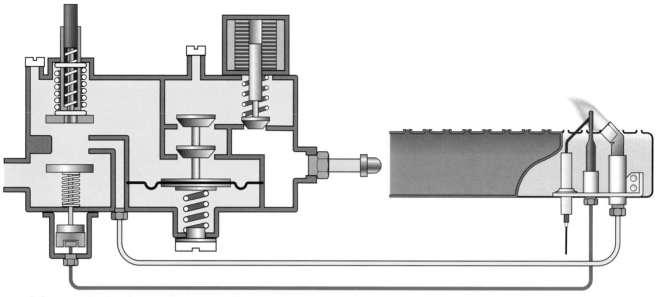

A multifunctional control valve stage 3. Regulator under pressure

The regulator is in position to allow gas to travel to the burner once the solenoid is energised.

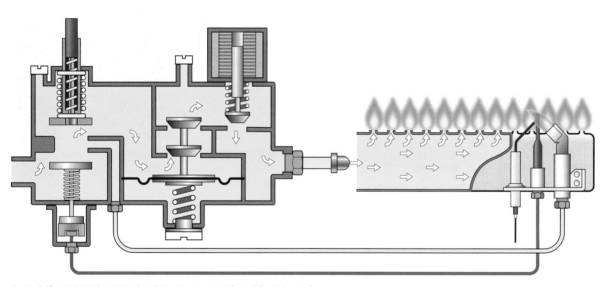

A multifunctional control valve stage 4. Solenoid activated

The solenoid is now energised and open because of a signal sent from the boiler thermostat. Gas can now flow to the burner and will be ignited by the pilot flame.

Once the thermostat is satisfied, the electrical signal to the solenoid will be terminated and this will then close the valve and the supply of gas to the burner will stop. When there is a call for heat, the whole process will begin again.

The typical sequence of operation originates at the boiler thermostat where the electrical connection from the central heating control system is located. The thermostat will either send or stop the electrical power to the solenoid which controls the flow of gas to the burner.

Vitiation-sensing device

This device is also known as an oxygen depletion device and an atmospheric sensing device. Vitiation means lack of oxygen in the air. The control shown in the image to the right is installed on a space heater. It operates on the principle that when there is no oxygen present, a flame will hunt in search of it. As a result, it will lose contact with the tip of the precision pilot thermocouple, resulting in the thermoelectric process dropping out and causing the flow of gas to the burner to stop.

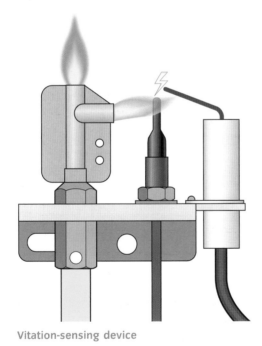

Vitation-sensing device

When the flame envelops the thermocouple, the pilot will remain alight because the small millivolt signal sent from the heated tip of the thermocouple will energise the electromagnet which keeps the gas port open.

Vitiation-sensing device

Vitiation-sensing devices are often fitted to space heaters and other open-flued appliances. They respond to any lack of oxygen (O_2) in the air (vitiation). The precision pilot flame will lift off the tip of the thermocouple in search of oxygen which will cause the termination of the millivolt signal to the electromagnet on the thermoelectric flame supervision device.

Vitiation-sensing device located on a space heater. The right-angle port on the pilot burner is designed to enable the flame to envelope the tip of the thermocouple

An engineer blocks the air inlet port to the pilot to simulate the effect of the oxygen reduction. This is evident from the yellow flame rising upward and not enveloping the thermocouple

If there is a lack of oxygen in the room, the flame which envelopes the thermocouple will begin to lift or hunt for more oxygen. As explained in the combustion section in Learning Outcome 2, when a flame lacks oxygen in the combustion process, it will change from a well-formed picture to being loose, floppy and yellow in colour. Because the flame lifts off the tip of the thermocouple, the small millivolt signal generated by the application of heat will reduce and de-energise the electromagnet, which will in turn shut off the supply of gas to the burner.

There are many variations and applications of oxygen depletion devices and one common method is shown in the image to the left.

Flame rectification

Flame rectification is used as a flame supervision on many boiler designs. It works on the principle of utilising a flame as a conductor and passing a current through it. If there is a flame present, a signal can pass through it and back to a control box and then the boiler ignition sequence can begin. This means that if there is no flame there will be no ignition.

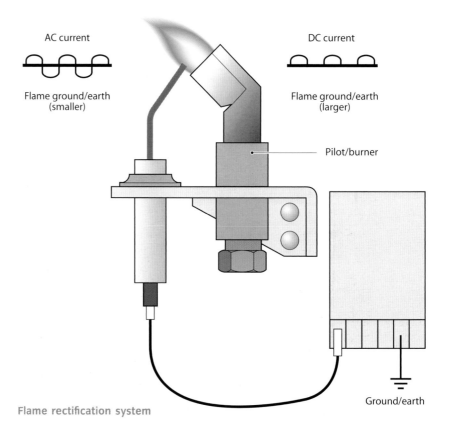

Flame rectification system

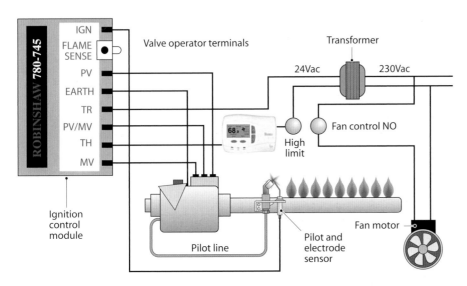

Pilot ignition on a flame rectification system

Flame rectification systems operate on the principle that a flame can conduct and rectify a small electric current

There is a probe attached to the burner that transmits a current from the control box, creating a spark and in turn causing a flame on the burner to light.

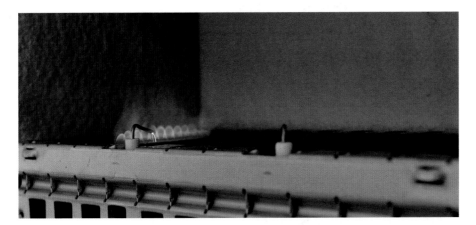

The current is then conducted by the flame and passes through it, becoming a half-wave rectified AC via the earth route of the metal mass of the burner. It then travels back to the control box where the solenoid valve is opened at the gas valve, allowing gas to flow to the burner. In this way the main flame is established.

Pressure differential valve

Venturi principle

A Venturi operates on the principle that by reducing the bore of a water pipe for example, the flow of water will increase in velocity after that point. The process is similar to putting a finger over the end of a hose pipe or nipping the end of it which results in increased velocity.

Pressure differential valves

The image to the left is a pressure differential valve. It is found in instantaneous hot water heaters and combination boilers. It comprises a diaphragm with a rod connected to it which opens the flow of gas to a burner when the diaphragm rises and vice versa. The valve works on the **Venturi principle** and the integrity of the neoprene diaphragm is essential for efficient operation.

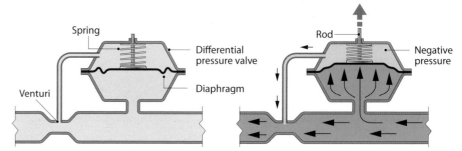

When there is no water flowing through the water pipe there will be equal pressure on both sides of the diaphragm and there will be no movement

When water flows, ie the hot water tap is turned on, the diaphragm will lift because the pressure is reduced at the top of the valve because of the negative pressure created at the Venturi. This is the differential pressure which creates the movement of the diaphragm within the valve

Pilot assembly with thermocouple and spark igniter

The image to the left shows a typical pilot assembly, located on the front of the boiler. On the left-hand side is a pilot tube, in the centre is the spark electrode and on the right-hand side is the thermocouple connection.

The image below it shows a section of the pilot assembly on the inside of an appliance, with the pilot shroud, the spark igniter and the thermocouple next to the burner.

Rod-type thermostats

The principle of a rod-type thermostat is based on the coefficient of expansion between two dissimilar metals. The thermostat comprises

Pilot flame enveloping the tip of a thermocouple

an outer tube of brass or copper with an inner rod of invar steel which is fixed at one end of the brass tube.

The end of the brass tube is anchored to the valve body, which ensures that expansion can take place in one direction only. Brass will expand much faster than invar steel and, as a result, when it does expand after being exposed to the heat from the oven, the fixed invar steel is pulled in the same direction as the brass tube.

When the oven heats up and expansion takes place, the invar steel rod will move off its seating and the spring action of the control knob section will push the valve to the closed position. As the flow of gas gradually reduces there must be sufficient gas provided to maintain the correct temperature within the oven and this is called the maintenance rate or a holding rate. This is the minimum amount of gas required to achieve continuity of the cooking process. This is achieved by a bypass port, which is incorporated into the body of the valve and allows this minimum volume of gas to travel to the burner when the valve is held firmly against its seating, preventing the main flow of gas to the oven burner.

This stage of the operation occurs when the oven has reached its preset temperature, determined by the setting of the control knob which is calibrated to control the travel of the valve during the duration of cooking. When the oven requires more heat, the whole process is reversed and the invar rod will then return to its original position, pushing against the control spring to allow gas to flow to the burner via the open gas way.

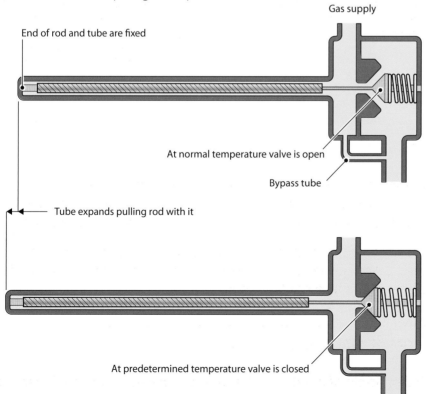

Invar steel rod oven thermostat

In this rod thermostat a bypass is included which will allow sufficient gas to the burner to achieve the maintenance rate which is the low rate of gas required to sustain the cooking process once the thermostat has reached its set temperature. This process occurs when the rod has expanded and pulls the valve component onto its seating.

The illustration on the previous page shows the invar steel rod secured at one end inside the brass tube which is then secured to the body of the valve. Therefore, as the brass tube expands it pulls the invar rod with it, resulting in the closing of the valve.

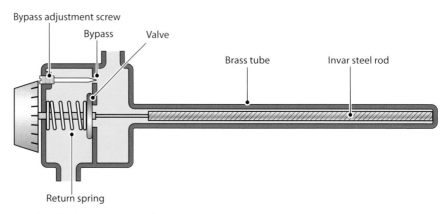

A rod and tube type oven thermostat with a bypass

The illustration above shows the adjustable bypass screw which allows different rates of gas to the burner to sustain the maintenance rate once the appliance has reached temperature and the expanded rod closes the main flow of gas. If the bypass port becomes blocked, the oven will go out once it has reached temperature and the cooking cycle will terminate.

Zero governor

Zero governors are devices often found on forced draught appliances and condensing boilers. The governor is designed so that the gas pressure is reduced to atmospheric pressure which is zero. There is then negative pressure at the outlet side of the valve via the balancing diaphragm, which means that the correct amount of gas can flow and mix proportionally with the air at the burner to achieve excellent combustion. These valves are incorporated into many modern appliances and typically operate in conjunction with the variable speed of the appliance fan via the appliance control board. When there is a high demand, the fan speeds up in accordance with the differential pressure created within the zero governor valve. Similarly, low demand equates to a low fan speed. Zero governors are also known as 'air gas ratio valves' as they increase efficiency by controlling excess air to the appliance burner.

Maxtrol zero governor

Zero governors

These devices are also known as 'air gas ratio valves'. They are often installed on condensing boilers to increase efficiency by controlling excess air to the appliance burner.

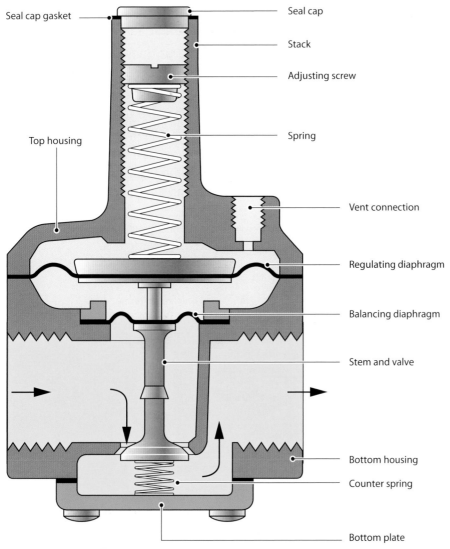

Seal cap gasket

Seal cap

Stack

Adjusting screw

Top housing

Spring

Vent connection

Regulating diaphragm

Balancing diaphragm

Stem and valve

Bottom housing

Counter spring

Bottom plate

Cutaway section of zero governor

Relay valve

A relay device is no longer found on domestic appliances. One of the last boilers on which it could be found on was the Potterton Diplomat. In days gone by, relay valves were used to control the gas lamps used to light up homes before the advent of electricity. They are still used on some commercial catering equipment. They require no electricity to work and operate on the principle of differential pressure.

The following sequence explains the typical operation of a relay valve.

1   A weep pipe supply is connected from the weep connection port in the upper diaphragm housing of the valve.

2 This supply is then controlled by a gas thermostat or by a combination of an electrical thermostat and a solenoid valve.

3 The weep supply should be routed to a position where it can be ignited with ease such as to a pilot burner.

4 When the thermostat is open, the pressure is reduced above the diaphragm which causes the diaphragm valve to rise and then open.

5 When the thermostat closes, the pressure above and below the diaphragm valve is equalised and the weight of the valve itself causes it to fall and in turn close the valve.

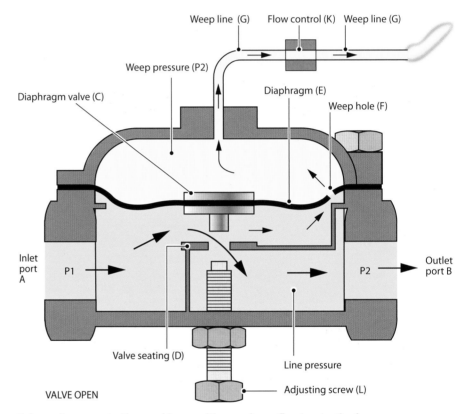

Relay valve open in the working position and gas flowing to the burner

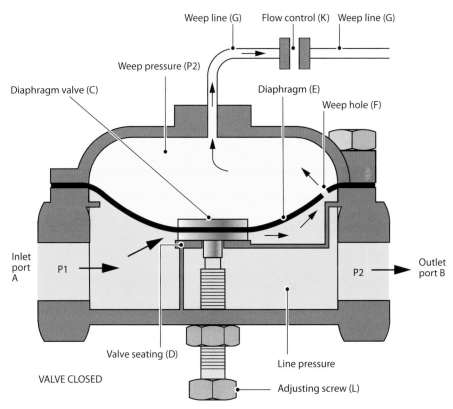

Weep line (G) Flow control (K) Weep line (G)

Weep pressure (P2)

Diaphragm valve (C)

Diaphragm (E)

Weep hole (F)

Inlet port A P1

Outlet port B P2

Valve seating (D)

Line pressure

VALVE CLOSED

Adjusting screw (L)

Relay valve in the closed position and no gas flowing to the burner

In the figure on the previous page, the valve is in the open or working position. The gas enters at the inlet port (A) at the line pressure (P1) which is sufficient to lift the diaphragm (E) and diaphragm (C) to allow gas to flow through to the outlet port (B). A small quantity of gas passes through a weep hole (F) in the diaphragm to the top of the valve and out through a weep line (G) via a flow control (K), which could be a gas thermostat or a solenoid valve, which in turn is connected to a time switch. It then continues through a further weep line which is burned safely at a pilot or a main burner.

The weep pressure (P2) is lower than the line pressure as gas is allowed to escape through the weep line and it exerts very little pressure on the diaphragm.

In the second figure, the valve is shown in the closed position. The flow control has closed and the weep gas pressure (P2) therefore builds up to the line pressure (P1). There is now an equal pressure on both sides of the diaphragm and the controlling force is now the weight which is located on the diaphragm valve (C) and thus gravity will ensure that the valve closes back onto the seat (D), which in turn cuts off the gas to the outlet port.

When the flow control re-opens, the pressure (P2) will reduce and the valve will lift to the open position as the line pressure (P1) is greater. If the adjusting screw (L) is screwed in, the diaphragm valve will be held off the valve seating and this can be adjusted to give the desired low fire rate at the burner. This will revert to the normal opening sequence when the flow control is re-opened.

These types of valves need to be mounted horizontally because of the role that gravity plays in their operation.

Relay valves were sometimes used in the past for domestic gas lamp lighting installations found in older dwellings. Old-style gas lamps such as the ones shown on the previous page are still specially made for historic buildings.

Gas rates (LO7)

There are two assessment criteria for this outcome:

1 State the typical calorific value for natural gas.
2 Calculate gas rates of natural gas appliances with imperial and metric meters.

Gas-rating

The main purpose of **gas rating** is to confirm that an appliance is operating properly and in accordance with the manufacturer's technical instructions. If the stated working pressure to the appliance is correct then this test will confirm if the appliance is consuming the correct amount of gas in relation to the stated operating pressure. The outcome of the test will give an indication of the correct size and condition of the injector.

If an injector is too small or partially blocked, the volume of gas passed will be less than stated in the manufacturer's instructions and on the appliance data plate. If the volume of gas is more than expected, then the injector could be too large or worn.

If too much gas is being passed then the appliance could be overgassing and there are dangers of the flame on the burner being too large and the possibility of impingement, ie the flame touching the surfaces of surrounding metal surfaces causing flame chilling and, in the end, production of carbon monoxide. If the flame is too large and the volume of gas too great in relation to the amount of air available then incomplete combustion would occur.

Similarly if the gas rate is too low, apart from the appliance not operating efficiently, in extreme situations this could create lightback into the burner.

When carrying out gas rating in domestic premises, you may come across both **metric meters** and **imperial meters**. Although the purpose of the test remains the same, the means of calculating the volumes will be different.

Safety shut-off valve (SSOV)

The SSOV is attached to the lid lever mechanism of a cooker and will turn off the gas supply to the hob burners when the lid is lowered.

An injector at the inlet of a burner bar

Gas rating

Measuring the volume of gas consumed by an appliance when at operating temperature.

KEY POINT

The burner pressure could be identified as being correct in accordance with the manufacturer's literature but the actual volume of gas being consumed could be different from that which is stated in the literature. This could be the result of a wrongly sized burner injector.

Metric meter

This type of meter measures the volume of gas passed in cubic metres per hour (m^3/h).

Imperial meter

This type of meter measures the volume of gas passed in cubic feet per hour (ft^3/h).

Gas-rating using metric meters

The meter displayed on the right shows 12.216 which means $12m^3$ and 216 litres of gas have been consumed by the appliances connected to the system.

During a gas-rating test only a very small amount of gas will be measured over a two-minute period. Once the appliance reaches its operating temperature the meter reading is then confirmed and recorded while the appliance is working. After two minutes the reading is taken again. For example, if we take the meter reading of $12.216m^3/h$ in the first image as the first reading and $12.260m^3/h$ as the second reading after two minutes then the volume of gas can be calculated.

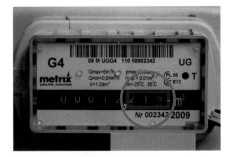

A metric meter

An imperial meter

$$\begin{array}{l} 12.260m^3/h \text{ (2nd reading)} \\ - \ 12.216m^3/h \text{ (1st reading)} \\ \hline = \ \mathbf{00.044m^3/h} \text{ (volume of} \\ \quad \text{gas passed in 2 minutes)} \end{array}$$

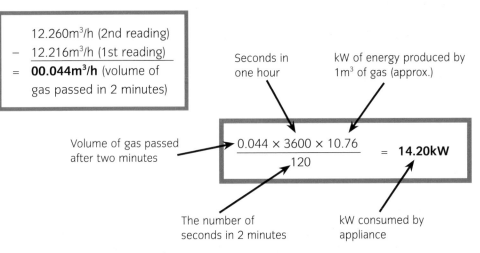

Seconds in one hour

kW of energy produced by $1m^3$ of gas (approx.)

Volume of gas passed after two minutes

$$\frac{0.044 \times 3600 \times 10.76}{120} = \mathbf{14.20kW}$$

The number of seconds in 2 minutes

kW consumed by appliance

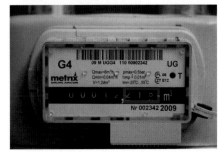

A digital measurement display on a G4 meter

Once the calculations are complete they can be compared with the manufacturer's instructions to assess if it they are acceptable. In the manufacturer's technical data permissible tolerances to any reading will be given.

In addition to gas rating many manufacturers require that a combustion analysis is carried out to confirm the efficiency of the appliance in accordance with their specifications.

Gas-rating using imperial meters

An older-style domestic U6 imperial meter will pass the same maximum volume of gas per hour as its metric counterpart such as a G4 or E6 which is $6m^3$. Instead of measuring m^3/h, on an imperial meter the volume is measured in cubic feet per hour (ft^3/h). Once the appliance has reached its operating temperature and the burner pressure is established, a reading can then be taken from the dial.

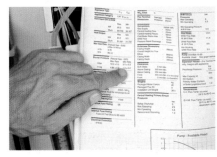

A manufacturer's technical data being used to assess the correct performance of an appliance

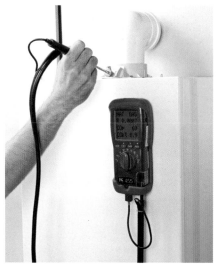

A combustion analyser being used on a fanned draught gas boiler and its purpose is to verify the efficiency of an appliance once the correct gas rate has been identified

Measurement display on an imperial U6 meter. The pointer on the dial needs to complete one full revolution to have passed 1ft³ of gas

British thermal units (BTU)

An imperial method of measuring energy. There are 1055.06 joules in a British thermal unit. To convert BTUs to kW divide by 3412.

Megajoule (MJ)

A joule is a small unit used to measure energy named after Dr James Joule. This unit is incorporated into the larger megajoule as it is a more useful unit to work with. There are 3.6MJ in a kilowatt hour (kW/h).

Process of measuring how much gas is being consumed by an appliance connected to an imperial meter

STEP 1 By taking a reading from the pointer on the meter and then checking the time it takes to complete one revolution of the dial, a volume of gas consumed can be measured. Note the digit 5 to the left of the dial.

STEP 2 The pointer shows that 0.5ft³ has been consumed at this stage

STEP 3 Finally the pointer completes one revolution of the dial and this shows that one 1ft³ of gas has been consumed. Note that the digit to the left of the dial has now moved from 5 to 6 confirming the measurement of gas.

Comparing imperial and metric units

Under the imperial system different units are used for different kinds of energy.

- Heat energy is measured in **British thermal units (BTUs)** or therms.
  - 1BTU equals 1,055J approximately.
  - In the SI system (System International) energy is measured in joules (J). A joule is a small unit and the **megajoule (MJ)** is a more practical size.
  - The unit used for gas charges in the UK is kW/h.
  - Electrical energy is measured in kilowatts per hour (kW/h).

There are many conversion charts from metric to imperial and vice versa. Here are just a few.

1 kilowatt = 3.6MJ/h = 3,412BTU/h

Therefore to convert BTUs to kilowatts, divide by 3,412.

When gases burn they produce heat energy and the calorific value (CV) indicates the heating power. This means the number of heat or energy units that can be obtained from a measured volume of gas. When measuring CV in System International (SI) units, megajoules per cubic metre are used (MJ/m^3). In the UK the CV of natural gas is about $39.5MJ/m^3$, although this does vary and is printed on every consumer's gas bill.

Before April 1992 the calorific value of gas used to be measured imperially which meant it was measured in therms.

1 therm = 105.5MJ
1MJ = 947.8BTU

Once the pointer has taken the time to complete one revolution of the dial then the gas rate can be calculated.

For example if it took 38 seconds to pass $1ft^3$ of gas the following calculation applies.

SmartScreen Unit 307

PowerPoint 7

$$\frac{3600 \times 1040^*}{38} = \frac{3744000}{38} = 98526 \text{BTU/h}$$

$$98526 \div 3412 = 28.87 \text{kW (gross)}$$

$$28.87 \div 1.1 = \textbf{26kW net}$$

*1040 is the imperial CV of gas measured in BTUs.

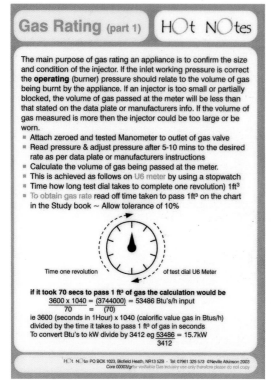

Gas rating imperial

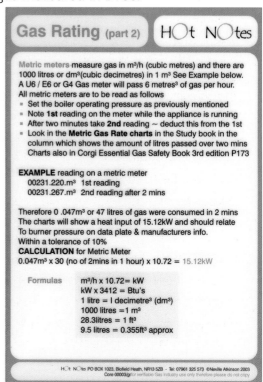

Gas rating metric

Simple memory aids such as Hot Notes can help an engineer to recall essential processes during testing. Smaller concise information could be more convenient to the qualified engineer than taking out a larger manual to refer to when working on appliances.

Conclusion

This chapter is just an introduction to give you an awareness of the world of gas. Hopefully this learning will encourage you to pursue work experience opportunities with a registered Gas Safe company to gain your professional ACS qualifications in this specialist plumbing craft category.

Test your knowledge questions

1   At what distance from the roof of a car port should a flue terminal from a room-sealed fanned draught boiler be positioned?

2   What is the minimum cover for gas pipework below a soil surface?

3   When tightness testing an existing installation which includes 22mm and 15mm pipework and a U6 meter and where the volume is less $0.35m^3$, providing there is no smell of gas, what is the maximum permitted pressure drop over a two-minute period?

4   How much ventilation would an open flued space heater of 7kW input (net) require if it were located in a room?

5   A steel pipe used for gas needs to comply with which standard?

6   What size of additional vent does BS 5440 Part 2:2009 recommend as a solution to overcome the spillage of POCs from an appliance?

7   What distance should ridge terminals be spaced from one another if their design incorporates openings on all sides?

8   A balanced flued terminal located less than 2m from the FFL should be fitted with which component?

9   If the annular space between a flue liner and a brick-built chimney were not sealed, what effect could this have on the performance of the flue?

10 The route of a flue or chimney should always be positioned at the highest point of a roof with a pitch in excess of 45° to prevent what problem from occurring?

11 If a type C_{12} appliance developed a blocked flueway, what could occur?

12 What should be located as near as practical to the entry of each flat in a multi-storey building and supplied with gas via an internal riser?

13 How would you categorise an appliance with a horizontal balanced flue inlet with air ducts to the outside?

14 If the flue terminal of a 13.5kW input natural draught room-sealed appliance were located below an opening in a wall, what distance between these two points would have to be ensured to avoid the ingress of POCs into a building?

15 Name the normative document which would identify the correct tightness procedure if an installation had an internal volume in excess of $0.35m^3$ and included a U16 meter.

16 How much ventilation is required for a flueless water heater with an input of 10.3kW located in a utility room which is 1.8m W × 2.5m L × 2.55m H?

17 If the flue terminal of a 29kW fanned draught room-sealed appliance were located above an opening in a wall, what distance between these two points would have to be ensured to avoid the ingress of POCs into a building?

18 What should be considered when installing gas pipework in close proximity to other services?

19 If someone explained they thought they were in contact with CO, what advice should be given?

20 What is the minimum depth of a gas pipe located beneath a screed?

Assessment checklist

What you now know (Learning Outcome)	What you can now do (assessment criteria)		Where this is found (page number)
1. Know gas safety legislation	1.1	State hierarchical responsibilities for the gas industry in Great Britain, Northern Ireland, the Isle of Man and Guernsey.	174–175
	1.2	State the date the Gas Safety (Installation and Use Regulations) 1998 came into force.	176
	1.3	State the competent persons citation.	177
	1.4	Describe the three families of gas.	187
	1.5	Describe the meaning of the term 'gas fitting'.	176
	1.6	Define what constitutes work on a gas fitting.	177
2. Understand the characteristics of combustion	2.1	State the characteristics of combustion for natural gas and liquid petroleum gas.	192
	2.2	State the combustion process.	194
	2.3	Describe complete and incomplete combustion.	201–207
	2.4	Identify the causes of incomplete combustion in gas appliances.	201–207
	2.5	State the visual signs of incomplete combustion.	201–207
	2.6	Identify stoichiometric ratios of natural gas and liquid petroleum gas.	196
	2.7	Compare the difference between net and gross kW output.	235
	2.8	Describe the characteristics of flame type.	198
	2.9	Explain the dangers of carbon monoxide (CO).	204
	2.10	State the symptoms of carbon monoxide poisoning.	204
	2.11	State the actions to reduce the risk of carbon monoxide poisoning.	205
3. Understand the principles of flues	3.1	State the primary purpose of flues.	206
	3.2	Explain the working principles of different flue types.	206–211
	3.3	Distinguish different flue types in relation to flue categories.	207
	3.4	Identify flue terminal positions in accordance with BS 5440 Part 1.	225–227
	3.5	Describe flue component parts.	227
	3.6	State the factors that can influence flue performance.	217
	3.7	Explain how to carry out a flue-flow test.	215–217
	3.8	Explain how to carry out a spillage test.	212–215

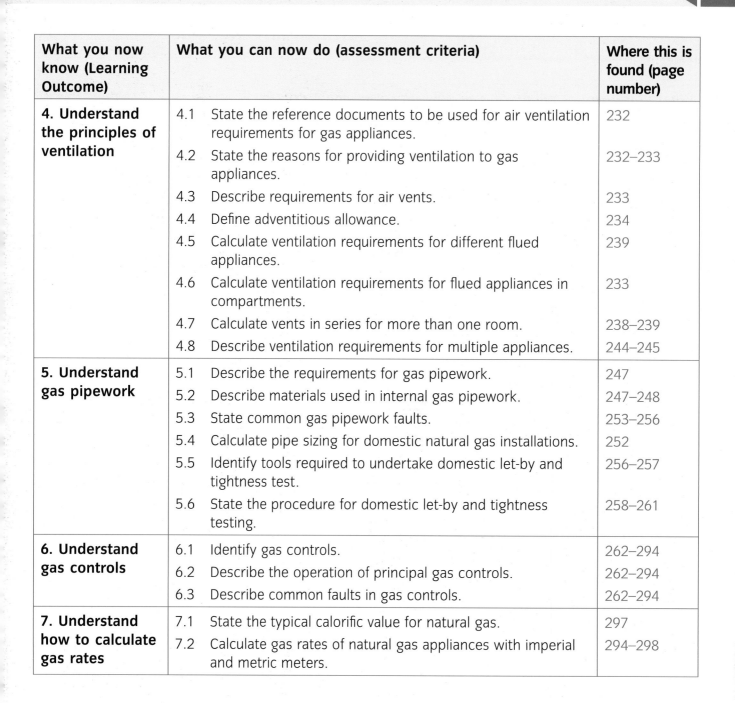

What you now know (Learning Outcome)	What you can now do (assessment criteria)		Where this is found (page number)
4. Understand the principles of ventilation	4.1	State the reference documents to be used for air ventilation requirements for gas appliances.	232
	4.2	State the reasons for providing ventilation to gas appliances.	232–233
	4.3	Describe requirements for air vents.	233
	4.4	Define adventitious allowance.	234
	4.5	Calculate ventilation requirements for different flued appliances.	239
	4.6	Calculate ventilation requirements for flued appliances in compartments.	233
	4.7	Calculate vents in series for more than one room.	238–239
	4.8	Describe ventilation requirements for multiple appliances.	244–245
5. Understand gas pipework	5.1	Describe the requirements for gas pipework.	247
	5.2	Describe materials used in internal gas pipework.	247–248
	5.3	State common gas pipework faults.	253–256
	5.4	Calculate pipe sizing for domestic natural gas installations.	252
	5.5	Identify tools required to undertake domestic let-by and tightness test.	256–257
	5.6	State the procedure for domestic let-by and tightness testing.	258–261
6. Understand gas controls	6.1	Identify gas controls.	262–294
	6.2	Describe the operation of principal gas controls.	262–294
	6.3	Describe common faults in gas controls.	262–294
7. Understand how to calculate gas rates	7.1	State the typical calorific value for natural gas.	297
	7.2	Calculate gas rates of natural gas appliances with imperial and metric meters.	294–298

UNIT 308
Career awareness in building services engineering

By enrolling and working towards your 6035 qualification you have already shown your commitment to becoming employed in the building services industry, but now is the time to take the next step towards getting a job within the sector. This unit is designed to help you with your own career development, setting goals to help realise your plans.

There are two Learning Outcomes for this unit:

1 Understand how to plan for careers in building services engineering.
2 Understand the requirements to become a qualified operative in building services engineering.

Plan for careers in building services engineering (LO1)

There are eight assessment criteria for this outcome:

1 To support career planning.

2 Describe elements of career planning.

3 Describe documents to support career development.

4 Explain the principles of goal-setting.

5 Describe how to set goals.

6 Define the different roles in building services engineering.

7 Explain opportunities for progression within building services engineering.

8 Describe types of employment.

SmartScreen Unit 308
PowerPoint 1

Career planning helps realise your ambitions. A plan helps you focus on what you should be doing to start a new career or progress in the career you are in. Planning needs time and careful consideration to make your career happen rather than you letting your career happen to you.

In order to plan a career you will need to be able to identify the support available to you.

Resources to help you include:

■ The internet (career guidance sites, and industry sites of employers you might want to apply to).

■ Professional bodies/organisations such as the National Career Guidance Service.

■ Educational support and guidance, such as your college careers advisor.

■ Role models – people in the industry that you admire and could ask for advice on how they've got to where they are.

■ Networking – through attending industry events or asking to be introduced to people who might be able to help you through advice or contacts within companies that are recruiting.

■ Job centres and recruitment agencies.

The internet is a logical and easy place to look for sources of information to support career planning. However, resources found on the internet should always be read carefully in the light of the original purpose of the website or blog and the actual benefit you can glean from them. For example, many websites relate just to overseas employment or specific sectors. Before relying on such information, make sure it is relevant to your needs.

The most useful sites for career planning are generally those provided by UK government departments or agencies sponsored to promote career awareness. The National Careers Service, at http://nationalcareersservice.direct.gov.uk, provides general advice and career-planning information. (It is funded in association with the European Social Fund and is provided on behalf of the Department for Business Innovation and Skills.)

Once you have determined your career path, the National Careers Service website can provide useful information in a general context, including information on government support and guidance. Depending on circumstances, individuals may be able to seek government funding support for certain retraining.

Specific requirements and qualifications need to be researched from relevant trade organisations, competent person registration schemes, etc. There are many UK Accreditation Service (UKAS) accredited awarding bodies that provide support and guidance to trainees and to those already qualified wishing to keep themselves up to date and maintain their own continuing professional development (CPD). If you are already qualified in a specific trade or profession, your professional institution will have a recognised development programme, criteria for meeting their requirements, a mapping process and access to mentors so you can complete the process.

Elements of career planning

There is a vast amount of information designed to support you through the stages of planning your career and seeking a job. This includes:

- goal-setting
- curriculum vitae (CV)
- personal statements
- covering letters
- SMART targets
- SWOT analysis.

A candidate in discussion with a career officer

Goal-setting

A goal is an outcome that an individual or organisation is trying to reach. It is likely to be quite general and long range; it can look quite idealistic and doesn't include all the practical details of exactly what is required and when it is required by. An example of a goal could be to have a complete career change within the next five years. This may be not fully detailed but that goal is the starting point in the planning process.

When setting your goal make sure you can answer the four questions that begin with W: What, Where, Who, and When?

- What position do I want?
- Where will I find relevant information?
- Who will I contact?
- When will I make contact?

You should also know the difference between a specific goal and a vague goal. For example, there is a big difference between saying, 'I would like a job' and 'I would like to be an apprentice plumber.' You may also like to set a goal of contacting a certain number of companies a week. This is then measurable.

So, if you want to attain anything of significance, you must sit down and define what you really want, put it in writing, develop a real plan, and lay out the guidelines for completion. There's no better way to accomplish a really strong desire than a well-written plan.

Set out your goals

Break your goals into short term, medium term and long term. The short- and medium-term goals can be thought of as stepping stones to the long-term goal.

For example:

In one year's time I want to have …
In five years' time I want to be …
In ten years' time I want to be able to …

Curriculum vitae (CV)

How you write your CV and covering letter is up to you, but there are some basic rules to follow if you want to create the best impression.

You should include a summary of your educational and academic background, and skills you have demonstrated. You should also include any interests, hobbies and work experience. An example CV is provided below:

SUGGESTED ACTIVITY

Define your own short-, medium- and long-term goals.

KEY POINT

A curriculum vitae (CV) can be literally translated as 'course of life'. This provides an overview of a person's experience and other qualifications. A CV is typically the first item that a potential employer encounters regarding a job seeker. CVs are often used to screen applicants in order to shortlist them for an interview.

CURRICULUM VITAE: John Jones

PERSONAL DETAILS

Name	John Jones
Date of birth	11 November 1991
Address	1 Market Street
	Any Town
	Any City
	AB12 3CD
Mobile	0799 321654
Email	john.jones@interweb.co.uk

Personal statement

I am currently working as a personal care and support carer. I always worked hard at school and was head boy in my last year. I believe this shows I have maturity and a sense of responsibility. My school results show I am able to pass examinations. I believe I would be an excellent trainee plumber.

SCHOOL EDUCATION

2003–2008   Any Town High School
             School Road
             Any Town
             AD12 3CE
             Telephone: 01789 567123

Qualifications obtained

Subject	Level	Grade achieved	Date achieved
Maths	GCSE	A	July 2008
English Language	GCSE	A	July 2008
English Literature	GCSE	A	July 2008
Science	GCSE	A	July 2008
Additional Science	GCSE	C	July 2008
Spanish	GCSE	B	July 2008
Geography	GCSE	C	July 2008
Media	GCSE	A	July 2008
Drama	GCSE	B	July 2008

Example CV

SUGGESTED ACTIVITY

Go to National Careers Service and download and complete a CV. https://nationalcareersservice.direct.gov.uk/advice/getajob/cvs/Pages/default.aspx

Most employers would expect to receive a curriculum vitae along with a covering letter outlining your suitability for the position that you are applying for.

Personal statement

A personal statement is a short summary of your key skills and experience that you should put at the top of your CV. It is vital to spend time getting this right, as many employers will often use this statement to decide whether or not to read the rest of your CV. The best advice is to keep it short: your personal statement should be just a few lines or bullet points, around 50–100 words.

> **Example of a personal statement**
>
> I am a conscientious, punctual, reliable, hardworking person capable of working alone or as part of a team and able to adapt to different work environments.

Covering letter

A covering letter accompanies a CV (and/or completed application form). It is an opportunity to highlight what is in your CV and to provide any real examples to support your ability to do the job.

SMART targets

SMART targeting is an acronym for the five steps of Specific, Measurable, Attainable, Relevant and Time-based targets and is one of the most effective tools used to achieve a desired goal.

SMART targets can be a useful tool to help you in your career path.	
S Specific	What is the task to be done?
M Measureable	What evidence could be used to show if and how well the task has been done?
A Attainable	Is the task possible?
R Relevant	Why is this target important?
T Time-based	Are review dates built in to check progress?

SmartScreen Unit 308

Worksheet 1

SWOT analysis

When planning your career, the first thing to look at is what you can already do. Ask yourself, 'What am I already good at or do I have an aptitude for?' It may be that you already have a number of skills and qualifications that are transferrable to a new career. A useful self-analysis tool is SWOT analysis.

SWOT is an acronym for Strengths, Weaknesses, Opportunities, Threats. It is a planning tool used to understand the strengths, weaknesses, opportunities and threats involved in a project or in a business. It involves identifying the internal and external factors that are either supportive or unfavorable to achieving that objective.

	Positive factors	Negative factors
Internal	Strengths • example • example • example • example	Weaknesses • example • example • example • example
External	Opportunities • example • example • example • example	Threats • example • example • example • example

SmartScreen Unit 308
Worksheet 2

Different roles in building services engineering

Building services engineering is made up of four key industries:

- electrotechnical
- plumbing and domestic heating
- heating and ventilating
- air conditioning and refrigeration.

There are many optional career pathways within the building services engineering sector. The pathways that you have prepared for in your studies include:

- installation electrician
- heating and ventilation service and maintenance engineer
- plumber
- heating and ventilation installation engineer
- refrigeration engineer
- maintenance electrician ductwork installer
- air-conditioning engineer.

Typical roles within building services

Plumber

Plumbing and domestic heating is a responsive and continually developing industry. The plumber is responsible for the installation of complex cold and hot water systems, sanitation, heating systems and domestic fuel burning appliances such as gas, oil or solid fuel boilers. In recent years environmental technologies have been integrated within the industry and the modern tradesperson now undertakes a huge variety of jobs, including:

- installing and maintaining central heating systems, hot and cold water systems and drainage systems
- installing, commissioning and maintaining solar water heating, rainwater harvesting or grey water recycling systems
- installing and maintaining gas, oil and solid fuel appliances, including biomass.

Installation electrician

An installation electrician is responsible for the installation of power, lighting, fire protection, security and structured cabling. They may also maintain modern electrical systems and the equipment they serve to ensure effective and efficient operation.

Heating and ventilation engineer

A heating and ventilation engineer installs complex heating equipment and pipework systems to exact design specifications within large buildings such as office blocks, hospitals, schools, etc.

Ductwork installer

A ductwork installer is responsible for the installation of complex ductwork and ventilation systems to exact design specifications within large buildings.

Refrigeration engineer

A refrigeration engineer may install, service and maintain systems and equipment that control and maintain the quality, temperature and humidity of air within modern buildings. Another aspect of the job may be to install, service and maintain refrigeration and environmental technology systems throughout the UK in places such as supermarkets, hospitals, food-processing and research establishments.

These are just a few of the many roles within the building services industry which may lead to different pathways in your chosen career. For example, you may progress into a supervisory role either within the same company or a different company. You may wish to become involved in the design and estimating of large-scale projects. There are many people who have started apprenticeships and progressed to running their own businesses or you may wish to go into education and train others. The opportunities available within the industry are many and varied and all are attainable.

Types of work in building services engineering

The industry itself is also varied in its different forms of work, which include:

- contract work
- consultancy
- subcontraction
- casual labour.

Contract work

This means you are providing a service/labour to another company under terms specified within an agreement. It could mean you don't work regularly for an employer but are self-employed.

Consultancy

Once a lot of experience and qualifications have been attained, there are opportunities for consulting work. A consultant is a professional who provides expert advice in a particular area, for example, in:

- hot water
- cold water
- central heating
- underfloor heating
- renewables.

Subcontractor

A subcontractor is a person or company that is hired by a main contractor to perform a specific task as part of an overall project and is normally paid for the services by the main contractor. A building company that doesn't have its own plumber may subcontract the plumbing work out.

Casual labour

This can be part-time, piece or temporary work, which means someone looks for and accepts any type of work within their skill sector. They are not part of the permanent workforce.

The requirements to become a qualified operative in building services engineering (LO2)

There are five assessment criteria for this outcome:

1 Describe specific requirements for career choices in building services engineering.
2 Identify the areas in building services that run the Competent Person Scheme.
3 Define the term 'Competent Person Scheme' (CPS).
4 Identify the renewal requirements for being part of the Competent Person Scheme.
5 Describe the consequences of not being part of the Competent Person Scheme when working in building services engineering.

Becoming highly skilled in your own craft will be your first priority but over time you may wish to explore some form of supervisory responsibilities.

Opportunities for progression within the sector include: supervisor, manager, business owner, sideways moves to different crafts, assessor/trainer, designer, surveyor, estimator, apprenticeship, engineer and director.

SmartScreen Unit 308

PowerPoint 2

To progress in any trade you will need to achieve your qualifications and gain experience alongside the qualification. It is important to have thought about your career path and to have set yourself attainable goals in the short, medium and long term.

As you progress, you may need to become a 'competent' person. This means you have been trained, tested and passed in a certain area of work. A certificate is given that states you are competent to carry out work in that area.

Competent persons

The Competent Person Scheme was introduced by the Department of Communities and Local Government (CLG) to enable companies to self-certify plumbing and heating works that fall under the scope of Building Regulations. Self-certification provides a much more cost-effective route compared with the alternative of notifying work through local building control bodies.

Areas for competency include:

- gas
- electrics

KEY POINT

The Competent Person Scheme applies the principles of self-certification and is based on giving people who are competent in their field the ability to self-certify that their work complies with the Building Regulations without the need to submit a building notice and thus incurring local authority inspection costs or fees.

- unvented water G3
- cold water
- oil
- solid fuel
- environmental technologies
- health and safety.

Gas

The Gas Safe Register is the official gas registration body for the United Kingdom, the Isle of Man and Guernsey, appointed by the relevant health and safety authority for each area. By law all gas engineers who are actively working on gas installations must be on the Gas Safe Register. Registration must be renewed every five years.

The Gas safe register

Electrics

The NICEIC (the National Inspection Council for Electrical Installation Contracting) Competent Person Scheme (CPS) allows registered installers who are competent in their field to self-certify certain types of building work as compliant with the requirements of the Building Regulations in England and Wales.

Unvented hot water G3

The Approved Building Regulations Document G (Section G3) requires that an unvented hot water system with a capacity of more than 15 litres should be installed and commissioned by a competent person who is a member of the Competent Person Scheme. This allows the self-certification of certain types of work and provides exemption from notification under the Building Regulations.

> **KEY POINT**
>
> It is a legal requirement to be registered with the appropriate body prior to carrying out any work. If the requirements of the scheme are not met the operative may face fines, imprisonment or loss of licence to practise.

Cold water

The approved plumber has been given a very useful concession in that he/she may start work without notification or prior consent on certain types of work, provided he/she issues the customer (and for some types of work the water supplier) with a certificate of compliance when the work is completed. This can save up to ten days of waiting for the water supplier's consent and reduces the paperwork of notification.

Oil

OFTEC (the Oil-firing Technical Association for the Petroleum Industry) was formed in 1991 and replaced the former Domestic Oil Burner Equipment Testing Association (DOBETA), an organisation formed after the enforced split of Shell-mex and BP in the early 1970s.

OFTEC also administers a Competent Person Scheme and encourages those working in the oil-firing industry to become registered. Becoming registered with OFTEC allows installers to self-certify installation work without the need to have it checked by local authority building control (where applicable).

Solid fuel

HETAS (the Heating Equipment Testing and Approval Scheme) is the official body recognised by the government to approve biomass and solid fuel domestic heating appliances, fuels and services including the registration of competent installers. HETAS administers a competent person scheme which will allow competent persons to self-certify installations work.

Environmental technologies

Competence in renewable technologies is becoming more important as environmental issues come to the forefront. Training in these areas is offered under the 'environmental' heading but more specific training is offered by independent manufacturers of these technologies. These include both environmental care and renewable energies.

Health and safety

The Construction Skills Certification Scheme (and the resultant CSCS card) proves competency in site health and safety, and is a requirement for any site work. Working on a building site requires that an operative is in possession of a current Competent Person Scheme card.

Test your knowledge questions

1 Identify two sources of information that could help you with career planning.

2 What is the purpose of a personal statement?

3 Identify four items that could be included in a CV.

4 In SWOT analysis, what do the letters SWOT stand for?

5 What are SMART targets?

6 Name three job roles in building services engineering.

7 What is a subcontractor?

8 How often must an operative renew their Gas Safe registration?

9 What regulations do people need to comply with under the Competent Person Scheme?

10 An approved plumber may start work without notification or prior consent on certain types of plumbing systems, provided they issue which type of certificate?

Assessment checklist

What you now know (Learning Outcome)	What you can now do (assessment criteria)	Where this is found (page number)
1. Understand how to plan for careers in building services engineering	1.1 Identify resources to support career planning.	304
	1.2 Describe elements of career planning.	305–306
	1.3 Describe documents to support career development.	307–309
	1.4 Explain the principles of goal-setting.	307–308
	1.5 Describe how to set goals.	307
	1.6 Define the different roles in building services engineering.	309
	1.7 Explain opportunities for progression within building services engineering.	309–311
	1.8 Describe types of employment.	311
2. Understand the requirements to become a qualified operative in building services engineering	2.1 Describe specific requirements for career choices in building services engineering.	307–312
	2.2 Identify the areas in building services that run the Competent Person Scheme.	312–314
	2.3 Define the term 'Competent Person Scheme' (CPS).	312
	2.4 Identify the renewal requirements for being part of the Competent Person Scheme.	312
	2.5 Describe the consequences of not being part of the Competent Person Scheme when working in building services engineering.	312

Unit 302

1   Customer needs
    Building layout
    Sustainability of the system
    Energy efficiency
    Environmental impact
    Fuel source.

2   Approved Document M.

3   Sustainable design is the practice of increasing the efficiency of energy, water and materials usage of a building whilst reducing, over the life of the building, the impact of the building on the environment and human health.

4   The British Standards provide guidance on interpreting and following regulations.

5   Letters
    Emails
    Faxes.

6   A quotation is a fixed price and cannot vary. An estimate is not a fixed price but can go up or down.

7   200 x 20   = 4000 litres for hotel guests
    7 x 30   = 210 litres for restaurant guests
    4000 + 210   = **4210** litres total cold water storage

8   Accumulators can be situated anywhere within a property but it must be remembered that the higher the accumulator is positioned above the incoming supply, the more the pressure will drop – by 0.1 bar for every metre the accumulator is raised.

9   Stratification is where the hot water 'floats' on the layer of colder water entering the storage vessel. The hot water sits in temperature layers with the hottest water at the top of the storage cylinder, gradually cooling towards the bottom.

10 $(8 + \frac{4}{2}) \times 12 =$ **120m²**

11 a) From direct solar radiation, in other words direct sunlight
    b) From the surrounding warm air.

12 a) Top, bottom, same end or TBSE
    b) Top, bottom, opposite end or TBOE
    c) Bottom, bottom, opposite end or BBOE (the most common arrangement in domestic heating systems).

13 $$\frac{\text{SHC x litres of water x temperature difference } (\Delta t) \times \text{boiler efficiency}}{\text{Time in seconds x 100}}$$

    SHC   = 4.19
    Litres of water   = 200
    Δt = 56
    Time in seconds   = 7200 (2hrs)
    Boiler efficiency = 92%

    $$\frac{4.19 \times 200 \times 56 \times 92}{7200 \times 100} = 5.99\text{kW}$$

14 The legal right to cancel a contract after the customer signs it.

15 a) Good design
    b) Good planning
    c) Good installation
    d) Correct commissioning and setting up procedures.

16 1:100.

17 225 litres.

18 Excessive noise.

19 30 loading units.

20 0.38 litres/second.

Unit 305

1 Part H1 (H in Northern Ireland).

2 BS 6465.

3 Local Authority Building Control.

4 7.5lts per hour per permission.

5 Doughnut or rubber seal (washer).

6 600mm.

7 BS EN 12056.

8 The size of the soil stack.

9 25mm.

10 200mm.

11 The roof area.

12 25mm.

13 The float switch.

14 AUK2 air gap.

15 Part F.

16 Blockage in the area of the pump within the unit.

17 An interceptor trap.

18 Allows air in if the pressure fluctuates, but does not let foul air out and prevents trap seal loss through pressure changes – self- or induced siphonage.

19 Commissioning records of the installation.

20 Benchmark book.

Unit 307

1 200mm.

2 375mm.

3 4mbar.

4 0cm^2.

5 BS 1387.

6 50cm^2.

7 300mm.

8 Terminal guard.

9 A secondary flue effect identifiable by spillage of POCs.

10 Downdraught.

11 Vitiated air would develop leading to incomplete combustion.

12 ECV on inlet pipework.

13 C$_{11}$.

14 600mm.

15 IGE/UP/1A.

16 50mm^2 plus an openable window.

17 300mm.

18 Critical distances should be adhered to so that it can be installed safely.

19 Move to the outside air and then seek medical advice.

20 25mm.

Unit 308

1 Two of the internet, the National Career Guidance Service, college careers advisor and job centres.

2 A personal statement is the short summary of your key skills and experience.

3 Any of academic background, interests, hobbies, work experience, covering letter and personal statement.

4 Strength, weakness, opportunity and threats.

5 Specific, measurable, attainable, relevant and time-based.

6 Any of plumber, electrician, heating engineer, refrigeration engineer and ductwork installer.

7 A subcontractor is a person or company that is hired by a main contractor to perform a specific task as part of an overall project.

8 Every five years.

9 Building Regulations.

10 A certificate of compliance.

GLOSSARY

A

abrade To scrape or wear away.

abutment The junction between a pitched roof and a vertical wall.

acceleration A measure of the rate at which a body increases its velocity.

acceleration due to gravity The rate of change of velocity of an object due to the gravitational pull of the earth.

acetylene (C$_2$H$_2$) A flammable gas used in conjunction with oxygen for welding.

acrylonitrile butadiene styrene (ABS) A type of thermoplastic used for waste pipes, soil pipes, underground drainage, gutters and rainwater pipes. Can be solvent welded.

Acts of Parliament These create new laws or change an existing one.

adhesion The way that water tends to stick to whatever it comes into contact with.

adventitious air Air that comes in from the outside, typically through gaps in windows or doorways in a particular area and which is estimated to equate to about 35cm^2 of free air.

air admittance valve Allows air into a stub stack to prevent the loss of trap seals.

air bag An inflatable bag which is inserted into a soil stack to create an airtight seal while carrying out a soundness test.

air changes The amount of air movement within a building.

air gap A physical unrestricted open space between wholesome water and possible contamination.

air separator A fitting designed to correctly position the feed and vent pipes on a central heating system to ensure that the neutral point is automatically built into the system.

air temperature The temperature of the air within a building.

air velocity The speed at which air travels through a building.

air vent A non-adjustable purpose-provided arrangement which is designed to allow permanent ventilation to an appliance.

alloy A mixture of two or more metals.

alternating current (AC) An electrical current that reverses its direction of travel constantly and uniformly throughout the circuit.

ambient This relates to the feeling of surroundings or atmosphere. For example, the ambient temperature of the liquid inside a cylinder, or even the ambience of a nightclub.

ampere The unit of electrical current.

annealing A process that involves heating copper to a cherry-red colour and then quenching it in water. This softens the copper tube so that the copper can be worked without fracturing, rippling or deforming.

annular space The required 25mm gap between any hot surface of a flue and any combustible materials when travelling through a floor in a dwelling.

anodic corrosion protection A form of corrosion protection that uses a sacrificial anode to distract the corrosion away from vulnerable parts of the system.

anodising Coating one metal with another by electrolysis to form a protective barrier from corrosion.

anti-gravity valves A valve used in older central heating systems to stop unwanted gravity hot water circulation. Often called a dumb ball valve.

appliance compartment An enclosure specifically designed or adapted to house one or more gas appliances.

Approved Codes of Practice (ACoP) Documents giving practical guidance on complying with the Regulations.

aquifers Water-bearing rocks below the earth's surface.

arcing Electricity flowing through the air from one conductor to another – it can produce visible flashes and flames.

architect The designer of a building or structure.

artesian wells and springs Water that rises from underground water-bearing rock layers under its own pressure.

asbestos A naturally occurring fibrous material that has been a popular building material since the 1950s, now known to cause serious and fatal illness.

atmospheric pressure The amount of force or pressure exerted by the atmosphere on the earth and the objects located on it.

atom A fundamental piece of matter made up of three kinds of particles called subatomic particles: protons, neutrons and electrons.

audit To conduct a systematic review to make sure standards and management systems are being followed.

automatic bypass valve A spring-loaded valve used on fully pumped heating systems; it is designed to automatically open when other paths for water flow begin to close.

automatic urinal flushing cistern Used to flush urinals.

B

back boiler A boiler made from a non-ferrous metal that is situated behind a real fire. Used with a direct cylinder.

back siphonage A vacuum that can suck water backwards causing contamination of the water supply.

backflow The flowing of water in the wrong direction due to loss of system pressure.

backflow prevention device A mechanical device, usually a fitting, designed to prevent contamination of water through backflow or back siphonage.

backflow protection Protection of contamination of water through backflow or back siphonage.

banjo-type bath waste fitting A type of waste fitting fitted to a bath that connects an overflow to the waste trap.

barbed shanked nail A nail with grooves cut into the shank. This makes the nail difficult to pull out once it has been driven into the wood.

batch feed boiler A solid fuel boiler where the fuel is fed by hand.

BBU Means back boiler unit which is a boiler located in a builder's opening with a flue which discharges up an existing chimney. They often have integral space heaters fitted at the front of them and are commonly situated in a lounge or living room of a dwelling.

batter or slope The angle in relation to the horizontal surface, of the trench walls of an excavation, to prevent the walls collapsing.

benchmark book A document that, when completed, verifies that the installation complies with the manufacturer's instruction, and relevant standards and regulations. When signed by the installer and customer it can be sent to the manufacturer to validate any warranty.

Bernoulli's principle Bernoulli's principle states that when a pipe is suddenly reduced in size, the velocity of the water increases but the pressure decreases. The principle can also work in reverse. If a pipe suddenly increases in size, the velocity will decrease but the pressure will increase slightly.

bill of quantities (BOQ) A document used in tendering in the construction industry in which materials, parts and labour (and their costs) are itemised. It also (ideally) details the terms and conditions of the construction or repair contract and itemises all work to enable a contractor to price the work for which he or she is bidding.

biomass Any plant or animal matter used directly as a fuel or that has been converted into other fuel types before combustion.

black water Water and effluent from WCs and kitchen sinks that can only be treated by a water undertaker at a sewage works.

blackheart fittings A type of fitting for low carbon steel pipe with a tapered female thread.

boiler cycling This happens when a heating system has reached temperature, and the boiler shuts down. A few minutes later the boiler will fire up again to top up the temperature as the system loses heat, and after a few seconds shuts down again. This constant firing up and shutting down as the system water cools slightly wastes a lot of fuel energy.

boreholes Man-made wells that are drilled directly to a below-ground water source.

Boyle's law A gas law that states that the volume of a sample of gas at a given temperature varies inversely with the applied pressure.

branch ventilating pipe Used on the ventilated branch discharge system of sanitary pipework to ventilate excessively long waste pipe runs.

British thermal units (BTU) An imperial method of measuring energy. There are 1055.06 joules in a British thermal unit. To convert BTUs to kW divide by 3412.

BS 1566-1:2002 The British Standard for copper indirect hot water storage cylinders.

BS 6700:2006+A1:2009 The main British standard for the installation of hot and cold water installations in dwellings.

BS 7671 The national standard to which all wiring, industrial or domestic, should conform.

BS 8000-13:1989 The Code of Practice for the workmanship on site relating to the installation of sanitation systems.

BS EN 12056-3:2000 The British and European Standard for the installation of rainwater and guttering systems.

BS EN 12056-5:2000 The British and European Standard for the installation of sanitary pipework.

BS EN 12588:2006 The British and European Standard for rolled (milled) sheet lead.

BSP or BSPT Stands for British Standard pipes and British Standard pipe threads, and relates to the type of thread we use on screwed low carbon steel pipes and fittings. Although the pipe is measured in mm, it is universally referred to in imperial measurements, eg ½-inch BSPT (½-inch British Standard pipe thread).

building control officer Responsible for ensuring that regulations on public health, safety, energy conservation and disabled access are met.

Building Regulations Approved Document F: Ventilation Document dealing with indoor air quality to ensure buildings are properly ventilated.

Building Regulations Approved Document H3 The main document concerning the installation of rainwater discharge systems.

Building Regulations Approved Document L: Conservation of fuel and power: 2010 (Part J in Scotland and Part F in Northern Ireland) Document controlling the insulation values of building elements, the heating efficiency of boilers, the insulation and controls for heating appliances and systems together with hot water storage, lighting efficiency and air permeability of the structure.

building services engineer Designer of the internal services within the building such as heating and ventilation, hot and cold water supplies, air conditioning and drainage. Many building services engineers are members of the Chartered Institution of Building Services Engineers (www.cibse.org).

Bypass Bypass ports are often located within a valve such as an oven thermostat and allow a small amount of gas to supply the burner when the oven has reached the required temperature, thereby sustaining the correct oven temperature during its cooking cycle. This is also called the maintenance rate. If a bypass port or screw becomes blocked, the oven will go out when it reaches the preset temperature.

C

calorific value Energy factor measured in MJ/m^3 when gas burns and gives off heat

capillary attraction The process where water (or any fluid) can be drawn upwards through small gaps against the action of gravity.

capillary fitting A fitting for copper tubes that uses the principle of capillary attraction to draw solder into the joint when heated.

carbon footprint The amount of carbon dioxide released into the atmosphere as a result of the activities of a particular individual, organisation or community.

Carbon Trust An independent, non-profit organisation set up by the UK government with support from businesses to encourage and promote the development of low-carbon technologies.

carburising flame A sooty flame containing too much acetylene.

carcinogenic A substance that causes cancer.

celsius (°C) A common unit of temperature that has as its zero point (0°C) the temperature at which water will freeze.

Central Heating System Specifications (CHeSS) 2008 CE51 Produced by the Building Research Energy Conservation Support Unit (BRECSU) to create a set of common standards for energy efficiency which domestic heating installers and manufacturers should work towards.

centralised hot water systems Those systems where the source of hot water is sited centrally in the property for distribution to all of the hot water outlets.

centre to centre Measuring from the centre line of one pipe to the centre line of another so that all the tube centres are uniform. This ensures that the pipework will look perfectly parallel because all of the tubes will be at equal distance from each other.

ceramic discs Two thin close-fitting, slotted ceramic plates that control the flow of water from a tap.

chamfer To take off a sharp edge at an angle. If we chamfer a pipe end, we are taking the sharp, square edge off the pipe.

Charles's law A gas law discovered by Jacques Charles which states that the volume of a quantity of gas, held at constant pressure, varies directly with the Kelvin temperature.

chased In the case of pipework or cables, this means fitted inside a cut made in a wall.

chlorine A chemical added to water for sterilisation purposes.

cistern A vessel for storing cold water that is only subjected to atmospheric pressure.

civil engineer Designer of roads, bridges, tunnels, etc that may be required.

clerk of works (CoW) An architect's representative on site. He or she ensures that the building is constructed in accordance with the drawings while maintaining quality at all times.

Climate Change Act 2008 Sets a target for the UK to reduce carbon emissions to 80% below 1990 levels by 2050.

CO Chemical formula of carbon monoxide.

coal A heavy hydrocarbon that releases high content of sulphur dioxide and carbon dioxide when burnt.

cohesion The way in which the water molecules 'stick' together to form a mass rather than staying as individuals.

coke Produced by heating coal in an oven which reduces both sulphur and carbon dioxide content. Known as a smokeless fuel.

combination boiler A boiler that supplies both instantaneous hot water and central heating from the same appliance.

combined cooling, heat and power (CCHP) Uses the excess heat from electricity generation to achieve additional building heating or cooling.

combined heat and power (CHP) A plant where electricity is generated and the excess heat generated is used for heating.

combined storage and feed cistern Stores water for the domestic hot water system and the indirect system of cold water to the appliances, wash hand basin, bath, WC, washing machine, etc.

combined system A system of below-ground drainage where both rainwater and foul water discharge into the same drain.

combustible Able to catch fire and burn easily.

combustion A chemical reaction in which a substance (the fuel) reacts violently with oxygen to produce heat and light.

commissioning The process of bringing a system or appliance into full working operation through a system of checks to ensure correct operation to the design specification.

communication pipe A pipe connecting the water main to the customer's external stop valve. Owned by the water undertaker.

competent person Recognised term for someone with the necessary skills, knowledge and experience to manage a specific area of work.

Competent Persons Scheme Members of CPS must follow certain rules to ensure that their work complies with Building Regulations.

compliance The act of carrying out a command or requirement.

compression Back pressure of air created by water discharging down a soil pipe travelling up the stack blowing the water out of the traps.

compression fitting A mechanical fitting that requires tightening with a spanner to make a watertight joint.

compressive strength The maximum stress a material can sustain when being crushed.

condensation A process where steam turns to water.

condensing boiler A boiler that extracts all usable heat from the combustion process, cooling the flue gases to the dew point. The collected water is then evacuated from the boiler via a condensate pipe.

conduction Heat travelling through a substance with the heat being transferred from one molecule to another.

conductivity The property that enables a metal to carry heat (thermal conductivity) or electricity (electrical conductivity).

Construction (Design and Management) Regulations 2007 The principal piece of health and safety legislation specifically written for the construction industry.

contamination The introduction of a harmful substance to an area.

Control of Asbestos Regulations 2006 Legally enforceable document prohibiting the importing, supplying and use of all forms of asbestos.

Control of Lead at Work Regulations 2002 Legally enforceable document that applies to all work which exposes any person to lead in any form whereby the lead may be ingested, inhaled or absorbed into the body.

convection Heat transfer through the movement of a fluid substance, which can be water or air.

cooler plate A device used behind an appliance in a flue block installation to prevent the unwanted transfer of heat from the appliance.

corrosion Any process involving the deterioration or degradation of metal components.

COSHH COSHH is an acronym that stands for 'Control of Substances Hazardous to Health'. Under the COSHH Regulations 2002, employers have to prevent or reduce their employees' exposure to substances that are hazardous to health.

coulomb The SI unit of electrical charge, equal to the quantity of electricity conveyed in one second by a current of 1 ampere.

creep A term that is used to describe the effects of thermal movement whereby the lead fails to return to its original position after expansion has taken place.

cross-connection When one fluid category connects with another, for example, within a mixer tap.

cuprous chloride corrosion This occurs because the chloride ions present in sodium hypochlorite solution are very aggressive when in contact with copper and copper alloys, due to the fact that the chloride can form an unstable film on the inside of the pipe. This means that even small amounts of chlorine can cause corrosion problems with copper piping.

Data Protection Act 1998 Gives people the right to know what information is held about them.

delivery note A document that lists the type and amount of materials that are delivered to site.

deposition The process whereby steam turns directly to ice.

dew point The temperature at which the moisture within a gas is released to form water droplets. When a gas reaches its dew point, the temperature has been cooled to the point where the gas can no longer hold the water and it is released in the form of water droplets.

dezincification A form of selective corrosion (often referred to as de-alloying) that happens when zinc is leached out of brass.

direct current (DC) An electrical current where the polarity or direction of the electron flow never reverses.

direct hot water storage cylinder A hot water storage vessel that does not contain a heat exchanger.

direct system of cold water A cold water system where all cold water outlets are connected to the main cold water supply.

Disability Discrimination Act 1995 Applies to companies that employ over 20 people. They are required to accommodate the needs of the disabled.

discharge units Discharge units are used to calculate the size of a soil stack.

district heating A system for distributing heat generated in a centralised location for residential and commercial heating requirements.

Domestic Building Services Compliance Guide 2010 Lays down rules for minimum boiler energy efficiency requirements. Often abbreviated to DBSC Guide.

double-feed indirect hot water storage cylinder A hot water storage vessel that contains a heat exchanger in the form of a coil or an annular.

downstream This means after a given point which could for example be a gas meter. Therefore if an isolation valve were located downstream of a meter, it would mean it was situated on the pipework after the meter inlet.

ductility A mechanical property that describes by how much solid materials can be pulled, pushed, stretched and deformed without breaking.

duty holder The person in control of a danger.

downstream This means after a given point which could for example be a gas meter. Therefore if an isolation valve were located downstream of a meter, it would mean it was situated on the pipework after the meter inlet.

drop-out time Refers to the time it takes for an electromagnet to de energise after heat has been removed from the tip of the thermocouple, eg when a pilot light is extinguished.

dynamic pressure The pressure of water while it is in motion.

economy 7 electricity A UK tariff that provides for seven hours of cheaper-rate electricity, usually between 1 am and 8 am in the summer and 12 am and 7 am in the winter (although times may vary between regions and suppliers).

ECV An emergency control valve used for the isolation of gas in an installation.

effort arm In mechanics, the arm where the force is applied.

electrical thermostat An electrical thermostat operates by using electrical circuits which are operated by either mechanical or electronic means which in turn controls the flow of gas to an appliance to obtain a predetermined temperature level.

electrolyte A fluid that allows the passage of electrical current, such as water. The more impurities (such as salts and minerals) there are in the fluid, the more effective it is as an electrolyte.

elevation A drawing showing one side of a building.

Enabling Act An enabling Act allows the Secretary of State to make further laws (regulations) without the need to pass another Act of Parliament.

end feed fitting A capillary fitting for copper tubes that requires solder to be fed into it during the soldering process.

Energy Performance of Buildings (Certificates and Inspections) (England and Wales) Regulations 2007 States the requirements for clients and landlords to produce energy performance certificates when buildings are constructed, rented out or sold.

Energy Saving Trust (EST) An independent non-profit organisation set up after the 1992 Rio 'Earth Summit' that attempts to reduce energy use in the UK.

Engineering judgement This is a technical decision which is based on the competence of a person who has an appropriate combination of technical education, training and practical experience in the specific field of work. Competence in specific areas of gas work is verified by assessments of an engineer's theoretical and practical knowledge at an independent nationally approved ACS gas centre, and then registration with the HSE approved Gas Safe register.

Equality Act 2010 Implemented by the Equality and Human Rights Commission (EHRC) to provide a single legal framework with clear, streamlined law that will be more effective at tackling disadvantage and discrimination.

equilibrium This term can relate to keeping the air pressure even within a sanitary system so that any negative pressure or pressure fluctuation does not cause the trap seal to be lost and allow the ingress of foul air into a building.

equipotential bonding A system where all metal fixtures in a domestic property such as hot and cold water pipes, central heating pipes and gas pipes, radiators, stainless steel sinks, steel and cast iron baths and steel basins are connected together through earth bonding so that they are at the same potential voltage everywhere.

erosion corrosion Corrosion that occurs in tubes and fittings because of the fast-flowing effects of fluids and gases.

erroneous Incorrect.

estimate A costing for a piece of work that is not a fixed price but can go up or down if the estimate was not accurate or the work was completed ahead of schedule.

expansion vessel A vessel divided by a membrane with air one side and water the other that allows the expansion of water to take place safely.

external non-return flap valve Is installed on the outlet of the macerator pipework and prevents the return of effluent into the unit.

F

fan-assisted boiler A boiler that uses a fan to evacuate the products of combustion.

fascia bracket A clip for securing a gutter to a fascia board.

fatality Death.

feed and expansion cistern Used to feed a vented central heating system and also allows expansion of water into the cistern when the system is hot.

feed cistern Holds only the water required to supply the hot water storage vessel.

ferrous metal A metal that contains iron and is susceptible to corrosion through rusting.

filling loop A method of filling sealed central heating systems directly from the water main.

fireclay A malleable clay used for heavy-duty sanitary appliances.

flame arrester A device fitted to lead welding equipment to prevent a dangerous situation known as flame blowback.

flame rectification Flame rectification utilises the ability of a flame to conduct electricity. It converts an AC current to DC and turns off the gas supply to an appliance if the flame goes out.

flame supervision device A gas control valve which is incorporated in the gas supply to a burner. Its purpose is to isolate the supply of gas if no flame is detected, eg if a pilot light is extinguished this will cause the valve to close via a thermocouple on a thermoelectric valve.

flange A projecting flat rim or collar, which is designed to strengthen or attach to another object. Flanges can also be found on large industrial pipe installations.

flashings A term given to a small weathering, usually at an abutment.

flow rate The amount of fluid or gas that flows through a pipe or tube over a given time.

flue types A – flueless, B – open-flued, C – room-sealed.

fluid category A method of water classification from 1 to 5 according to its potential level of contamination, with 5 being the most dangerous.

flushing valve A method of flushing a urinal and WCs fitted in industrial premises using water direct from the mains supply without the need for a cistern.

flux A paste used to clean oxides from the surface of copper and to help with the flow of solder into the fitting.

footing a ladder Standing with one foot on the bottom rung, the other firmly on the ground.

force The influence on an object which, acting alone, will cause the motion of the object to change. It is measured in newtons (kgm/s^2).

forced draught Any flue that uses a fan to help evacuate the products of combustion.

fossil fuels Formed by anaerobic decomposition of buried dead carbon-based plants, these fuels are known as hydrocarbons and release a high carbon dioxide content when burnt.

Freedom of Information Act 2000 Gives people the right to ask any public body for all the information they have on any subject.

frequency factors A variable that should be used when determining the pipework system flow rate based on the frequency of use of sanitary appliances for different building functions.

fully pumped heating systems A heating system where both hot water circulation and central heating are pumped by a central heating circulator.

G

galvanic corrosion Corrosion that occurs when two dissimilar metals are in contact with each other in the presence of an electrolyte, usually water.

Gantt chart Otherwise known as a programme of work, it is used on site to illustrate dates and lengths of time to complete particular jobs. It includes start and finish dates, labour and materials required and overall progress.

gas rating Measuring the volume of gas consumed by an appliance when at operating temperature.

Gas Safe Gas Safe is the official gas registration body for the United Kingdom approved by the HSE.

Gas Safety (Installation and Use) Regulations 1998 These cover the safe installation, maintenance and use of gas and gas appliances in private dwellings and business premises, aimed at preventing carbon monoxide (CO) poisoning, fires and explosions.

gas solenoid valve This is a device which is controlled by an electrical circuit often from an electric thermostat located on a boiler. The energy from the circuit then creates an electromagnet which in turn holds open a valve so that gas will flow. When the circuit to the solenoid valve is de-energised, the valve slams shut and closes the gas supply to the burner.

gas tap A manually operated device which can be operated by either a lever or knob to isolate or allow gas to flow.

gradient curve A method of determining the fall of a 32mm waste pipe.

granular soils Gravel, sand or silt (coarse-grained soil) with little or no clay content. Although some moist granular soils exhibit apparent cohesion (grains sticking together forming a solid), they have no cohesive strength. Granular soil cannot be moulded when moist and crumbles easily when dry.

gravity feed boilers A solid fuel boiler where the fuel is automatically fed to the fire bed via gravity.

greywater recycling A method of collecting water used for bathing from baths, showers and wash basins and using it for other purposes such as WC flushing.

gross calorific value The amount of heat obtained from gas during the complete combustion process which includes water vapour (latent heat).

guard rails Erected to stop a person falling from a scaffold.

gutter profile The shape of a gutter when viewed from the side.

H

hardness The property of a material that enables it to resist bending, scratching, abrasion or cutting.

hazard Anything with the potential to cause harm (eg chemicals, working at height, a fault on electrical equipment).

hazardous substance Something that can cause ill health to people.

hazardous waste Waste that is harmful to human

health, or to the environment, either immediately or over an extended period of time.

Health and Safety at Work Act 1974 The principal piece of legislation covering occupational health and safety in the UK.

health and safety file A document held by a client by which health and safety information is recorded and kept for future use.

Health and Safety Inspectors Persons employed by either the Health and Safety Executive or the local authority to enforce health and safety legislation.

heat exchanger A device or vessel that allows heat to be transferred from one water system to another without the two water systems coming into contact with each other. The transfer of heat takes place via conduction.

heat pumps An electrical device with reversible heating and cooling capability. It extracts heat from one medium at a low temperature (the source of heat) and transfers it to another at a high temperature (called the heat sink), cooling the first and warming the second.

hertz (Hz) The SI unit of frequency, measuring the number of cycles per second in alternating current.

hit-and-miss vents Can be opened or closed therefore they are not suitable for the combustion ventilation of gas appliances.

Home Energy Conservation Act (HECA) 1995 Places obligations on local authorities to draw up plans to increase domestic energy efficiency in their area by 30% over 10–15 years.

hopper A container.

hopper head A large bucket type fitting for collecting rainwater from two or more rainwater pipes.

hot work Work that involves actual or potential sources of ignition and carried out in an area where there is a risk of fire or explosion (eg welding, flame cutting, grinding).

HSE HSE (Health and Safety Executive) is the enforcing body for the GSIUR.

HTC fuse This is a special type of fuse used on printed circuit boards.

humidity The amount of moisture in the air.

hunt To cycle on and off unnecessarily with even a slight drop in temperature.

hydroelectric power Electricity generated by turbines driven by the gravity movement of large amounts of water.

hydro-pneumatic A pressure intensifier that enables generation of great force.

I

ice Water in its solid state when subjected to temperatures below its freezing point.

immersion heater A hot water heater that uses an electrical heating element to heat the water. Controlled by a thermostat.

impeller A rotor used to increase the pressure and flow of a fluid.

imperial meter This type of meter measures the volume of gas passed in cubic feet per hour (ft³/h).

independent boiler A freestanding boiler, usually solid fuel.

independent scaffold A scaffold that does not require the building to support it because it has two rows of vertical standards.

indirect system of cold water supply A cold water system where only the kitchen sink is connected to the mains cold water supply. All other cold water outlets are fed from a protected cistern.

induced siphonage An appliance causing the loss of trap seal of another appliance connected to the same waste pipe.

instantaneous hot water systems A system of hot water supply that heats cold water directly from the cold water main via a heat exchanger. There is no storage capacity.

integral solder ring fitting A capillary fitting for copper tubes with a ring of lead-free solder in the joint.

interlock To terminate the gas supply to an appliance by a safety device when, for example, a fan in a flue system fails to operate.

internal space An indoor space not classified as a room because it is either a hall, passageway, stairway or landing.

IS Means intrinsically safe, ie apparatus in which no spark or any thermal effect, which is produced under prescribed test conditions, is capable of causing ignition of a given explosive mixture. Therefore, a Gascoseeker™ must be IS as it is used to measure the ratio of gas in air.

J

job specification A description of the installation that is being quoted for, complete with the types of materials and appliances that the installation must contain.

joule Unit of heat. 4.186 joules of heat energy (equals one calorie) is required to raise the temperature of 1g of water from 0°C to 1°C.

jumper plate A circular plate that holds a tap washer in place. It can be fixed or loose depending on the type of tap in which it is fitted.

K

kelvin (K) A unit of temperature where the lowest point, 0 Kelvin, corresponds to the point at which all molecular motion would stop. 0 Kelvin is −273° Celsius or absolute zero.

kerosene fuel oil (grade C2 28-second viscosity oil to BS 2869) A medium hydrocarbon liquid fuel. It is a residual by-product of crude oil, produced during petroleum refining. It has a high carbon content and is clear or very pale yellow in colour.

kinetic ram guns A device that uses a pump action to create compressed air which is discharged down sanitary pipework to remove blockages.

L

LABC Local Area Building Control.

ladders Used to gain access to scaffolds or light work at high levels. There are three main classes: 1, 2 and 3.

latent heat A change of state as a result of temperature rise.

LDF (leak detection fluid) A special fluid used to help find leaks on pipework and fittings as bubbling will occur if applied to an area where there is an escape of gas.

lead welding A type of fusion welding to join two sheets of lead.

***Legionella* bacteria (*Legionella pneumophila*)** Bacteria that breed in stagnant water. They can give rise to a lung infection called Legionnaire's disease, which is a type of pneumonia.

legislation A law or group of laws that have come into force. Health and safety legislation for the plumbing industry includes the Health and Safety at Work Act and the Electricity at Work Regulations.

let-by test A test to determine if gas is escaping through the ECV (emergency control valve).

level When pipework is perfectly horizontal.

lever A rigid object that can be used with a pivot point or fulcrum to multiply the mechanical force that can be applied to another, heavier object.

liability A debt or other legal obligation to compensate for harm.

liquid petroleum gas (LPG) The generic name for the family of carbon-based flammable gases that are found in coal and oil deposits deep below the surface of the earth. They include propane, butane, methane and ethane.

local authority Ensures that all works carried out

conform to the requirements of the relevant planning and building legislation.

local company A company that will send you a bill for electricity usage.

localised hot water systems Systems of hot water supply that are installed at the place where they are needed.

locking out A process by which a thermostat protects a boiler from overheating by shutting it down when a temperature of around 85°C is reached. High limit thermostats are manually resettable by pushing a small button on the boiler itself.

low-pressure, open-vented central heating systems A central heating system that is fed via a feed and expansion cistern and contains an open-vent pipe.

low-surface-temperature radiator (LST) A radiator designed to give full heat output whilst being cooler to the touch.

low-water-content boiler A boiler that contains only a small amount of water for quick water heating.

lubricant A substance, often a liquid or a grease, introduced between two moving surfaces to reduce friction.

M

malleability The property of a material, usually a metal, to be deformed by compressive strength without fracturing.

manifold A manifold, in systems for moving fluids or gases, is a junction of pipes or channels, typically bringing one into many or many into one.

manual handling The movement of items by lifting, lowering, carrying, pushing or pulling by human effort alone.

MCB (miniature circuit breaker) A type of fast-reacting, resettable fuse.

megajoule (MJ) A joule is a small unit used to measure energy named after Dr James Joule. This unit is incorporated into the larger megajoule as it is a more useful unit to work with. There are 3.6MJ in a kilowatt hour (kWh).

meter A display that enables a local company to take readings for your bill.

metric meter This type of meter measures the volume of gas passed in cubic metres per hour (m^3/h).

MI Means manufacturers' instructions.

microbiological contamination Contamination by microscopic organisms, such as bacteria, viruses or fungus.

microbore system A central heating system using very small pipework, usually 8mm and 10mm, to feed the heat emitters.

molecule The smallest particle of a specific element or compound that retains the chemical properties of that element or compound.

momentum Trap seal loss caused when a large amount of water is suddenly discharged down the trap of an appliance.

multifunctional This means several functions are incorporated into one device such as gas valve, typically a regulator, flame supervision device or solenoid.

multi-point hot water heater A water heater that serves more than one hot water outlet.

N

national grid The network of high-voltage cables that carries electricity around the country – pylons carry the cables well out of the way of the public.

natural gas A light hydrocarbon fuel found naturally wherever oil or coal has formed. Predominantly contains five gases – methane, ethane, butane, propane and nitrogen.

naphthas A derivative of coal tar processing which can be utilised to provide a commercial gas.

near miss Any incident that could, but does not, result in an accident.

neutral water Water that is neither hard nor soft and has a pH value of 7.

net calorific value The amount of heat obtained from gas during the complete combustion process excluding latent heat.

newton A unit of measurement of force (kgm/s^2).

nogging A term often used on site to describe a piece of wood that supports or braces timber joists or timber-studded walls. They are particularly common in timber floors as a way of keeping the joists rigid and at specific centres, but they can also be used as supports for appliances such as wash hand basins and radiators that are being fixed to plasterboard.

non-ferrous metal Metals that do not contain iron.

non-rising spindle Mainly found in taps, a non-rising spindle is connected to a hexagonal barrel holding the washer. It does not rise when the tap is opened.

nuclear A type of power station that uses atomic energy to produce steam to drive the turbines.

O

ogee A popular Victorian style ornamental gutter design.

ohm The unit of electrical resistance.

one-pipe central heating system A simple ring circuit of pipework to and from the boiler and as such, there are no separate flow and return pipes.

open flue A flue that is open to the room where the appliance is fitted and relies on heat from the combustion process to create an updraught to evacuate the products of combustion. Often called natural draught. An open flue typically comprises of a primary flue, draught diverter, secondary flue and terminal.

open-vented central heating system A system fed from a feed and expansion cistern in the roof space that contains a vent pipe, which is open to the atmosphere.

open-vented direct hot water storage system A hot water storage system containing a direct cylinder.

open-vented hot water system A system fed from a cistern in the roof space that contains a vent pipe which is open to the atmosphere.

open-vented indirect hot water storage system A hot water storage system containing an indirect type cylinder.

outriggers Tubes or special units that connect to the bottom of tower scaffolds at the corners, giving a greater overall base measurement.

overflow pipe A method of warning of float-operated valve malfunction.

overheads On a building site, costs that include those of the site office and site/administration staff salaries.

oxygen (O_2) A very powerful oxidising agent used in gas form with acetylene when welding.

P

parallel threads A screw thread of uniform diameter used on fittings such as sockets.

parasitic circulation When hot water is pumped through one pipe below the radiators, then back to the tank for re-heating.

partially separate system A system of below-ground drainage where the foul water and some of the rainwater discharges into the foul water drain and all other rainwater discharges in a rainwater drain or soakaway.

pathogenic Causing disease.

peat A poor quality fossil fuel that has a high carbon content but much less than coal with large amounts of ash produced during combustion.

permanently hard water Water that contains magnesium and calcium chlorides and sulphates in the solution. Cannot be softened by boiling. Alkaline, with a pH value above 7.

permitted Being allowed to do something.

permit to work A document that gives authorisation for named persons to carry out specific work within a nominated time frame.

perceptible movement Movement detected by the eye of the engineer while testing is considered to be 0.25mbar on a manometer and two decimal places on an electronic gauge.

performance test Carried out on sanitary systems to ensure that after simultaneous operation of the appliances connected to the same soil stack, the trap seal depths remaining should be at least 25mm.

personal protective equipment (PPE) All equipment, including clothing for weather protection, worn or held by a person at work, which protects that person from risks to health and safety.

photovoltaic A method of generating electricity from the power of the sun. Also known as solar arrays.

piezo spark These ignition are commonly found on space heaters and older style boilers. Piezo ignition uses the principle of piezoelectricity, which is the electric charge that accumulates in some materials in response to high pressure. The devices consist of a small, spring-loaded hammer which, when a button is pressed, hits a quartz crystal which in turn deforms and produces a high voltage and the resultant spark ignites the gas typically located at the pilot port of an appliance.

pitting corrosion This is the localised corrosion of a metal surface. It is confined to a point or small area and takes the form of cavities and pits. Pitting is one of the most damaging forms of corrosion in plumbing, especially in central heating radiators, as it is not easily detected or prevented. Copper tube, although not a ferrous metal, is relatively soft and can suffer from pitting corrosion if flux residue is allowed to remain on the tube after soldering.

planned preventative maintenance Planned maintenance, usually to a schedule, so that systems and equipment can be serviced and checked at regular intervals to ensure optimum performance.

Planning Officer Responsible for processing planning applications, listed building consent applications and conservation area consent applications.

plumb When pipework is perfectly vertical.

POCs Stands for Products of Combustion which are produced during the combustion process of gas

polybutylene A type of thermoplastic used to manufacture pipes for cold water, hot water and central heating systems.

polyethylene A type of thermoplastic used to manufacture mains cold water pipes.

polypropylene A type of thermoplastic used to manufacture cold water cisterns, WC siphons and push-fit waste and overflow pipe.

polyurethane foam A sprayed form of insulation applied to hot water storage cylinders.

portable appliance testing (PAT) A method of testing portable electrical appliances and tools to ensure that they are safe to use.

post Means 'after'.

post-aerated flame Air is drawn for combustion from the surrounding air once the flame is lit often resulting in a loose yellow floppy flame.

potable Pronounced 'poe-table'. It comes from the French word *potable*, meaning drinkable.

power shower A cistern-fed shower mixing valve that uses a boosting pump to increase flow rate and pressure.

pre Means 'before'.

pre-aerated flame Air is entrained in the mixing tube before ignition.

predetermined Decided in advance.

press-fit fittings Fitting for copper tubes that require a special electrical press tool, which crimps the fitting onto the tube to make a secure joint.

pressure Defined as force per unit area. It is measured in pascals (newtons per square metre – N/m2).

pressure jet burner An oil burner found on oil-burning central heating boilers that atomises the fuel prior to combustion.

pressure relief valve A safety valve that safeguards against over-pressurisation by allowing excess water pressure to safely discharge to drain.

primary open safety vent A pipe on a central heating system that is open to the atmosphere to provide a safety outlet should the system overheat.

primary ventilated stack A system of sanitary pipework that relies on all the appliances being closely grouped around the stack and therefore does not need an extra ventilating stack.

private water supply Drinking water source which is not provided by a licensed water undertaker.

propane (C3H8) A flammable gas that is heavier than air. One of the five principal gases in natural gas.

proprietary trench support A specially designed support to prevent trench collapse.

PTFE tape PTFE stands for polytetrafluoroethylene. It is a tape used to make leak-free joints in copper and low carbon steel installations.

Pull-in time Relates to the time it takes a thermocouple, when heat is applied to it from a pilot flame, to energise an electromagnet within a thermoelectric device.

pure metal Derived directly from the ore and containing very little in the way of impurities.

push-fit fittings Simple push-on fittings for copper tubes or polybutylene pipe.

putlog scaffold A scaffold that is not self-supporting and has only one row of vertical standards.

Q

quantity surveyor A financial consultant or accountant who advises as to how a building can be constructed within a client's budget.

quotations A fixed price for a job, which cannot vary.

Q_{ww} Waste water flow rate.

R

radiation Heat transfer as thermal radiation from infrared light, visible or not, which transfers heat from one body to another without heating the space in between.

rafter bracket A bracket fixed to the roof members of a dwelling for securing a gutter when no fascia board is available.

rainwater cycle A natural process where water is continually exchanged between the atmosphere, surface water, ground water, soil water and plants. The scientific name is the hydrological cycle.

rainwater harvesting A method of collecting rainwater and using it for other purposes such as WC flushing.

refrigerant Fluorinated chemicals that are used in both liquid and gas states to create both heating and cooling effects.

regulations Rules, procedures and administrative codes set by authorities or governmental agencies to achieve an objective. They are legally enforceable and must be followed to avoid prosecution.

relative density The ratio of the density of a substance to the density of a standard substance under specific conditions.

Reporting of Injuries, Diseases and Dangerous Occurrences Regulations 2013 (RIDDOR) Places a legal duty on employers, the self-employed and people in control of work premises to report some work-related accidents, diseases and dangerous occurrences.

repose The angle to the horizontal at which the material in the cut face is stable and does not fall away. Different materials have different angles of repose, for example, 90° for solid rock and 30° for sand.

residual current device (RCD) A fast-reacting type of fuse that detects fluctuations in current flow.

resistance arm In mechanics, the arm where the load is concentrated.

resistance to earth Opposition of a conductor to a current flow.

retro-fitting Adding installations to systems that did not have these when manufactured.

reverse osmosis A water filtration process whereby a membrane filters unwanted chemicals, particles and contaminants out of the water.

reversed central heating return system A central heating system where the return travels away from the boiler in the same direction as the flow before looping around to be connected to the return at the boiler.

ridge terminals These are located on the highest point of an angled roof and provide a convenient and unobtrusive means of discharging flue gases. It is important that if they are installed in series, they are no less than 300 mm apart.

rising spindle Mainly found in taps, a rising spindle is connected to the washer and jumper plate. It rises as the tap is opened.

risk The chance (large or small) of harm actually being done when things go wrong (eg risk of electric shock from faulty equipment).

risk assessment A detailed examination of any factor that could cause injury.

rodding point A place where the drain or section of drain can be accessed to clear blockages.

room-sealed appliance An appliance where the combustion process and flue gas evacuation is sealed from the space where the boiler is fitted. These can be natural draught or forced draught.

RPZ valve A reduced pressure zone valve is a backflow protection device used to protect a category 1 fluid from fluid category 4 contamination.

rubber splashguard Installed in the waste section of a sink waste disposal unit to prevent debris from the grinding process from splashing back into the sink area.

saddle The top piece of an abutment flashing.

safety shut-off valve (SSOV) The SSOV is attached to the lid lever mechanism of a cooker and will turn off the gas supply to the hob burners when the lid is lowered.

sand cast lead sheet Lead sheet produced by traditional casting on a bed of sand.

sealed, pressurised central heating systems A central heating system fed directly from the cold water main and incorporating an expansion vessel.

secondary circulation A method of hot water circulation to prevent dead legs of cold water in hot water systems.

SEDBUK The Seasonal Efficiency of Domestic Boilers in the United Kingdom. A list of boiler efficiency ratings.

self-siphonage Water from a sanitary appliance, usually a wash basin discharging a plug of water, which creates a partial vacuum in the waste pipe between the plug of water and the water in the trap. This then pulls the water from the trap.

semi-gravity heating system A system of central heating where the hot water circulation is via gravity and the heating is pumped.

semi-permeable Allowing passage of certain small particles, but acting as a barrier to others.

sensible heat A temperature rise without a change of state.

separate system A system of below-ground drainage where rainwater and foul water discharge into separate drainage systems.

service pipe A pipe that connects the external stop valve to the dwelling.

shear strength The stress state caused by opposing forces acting along parallel lines of action through the material. The action of ripping or tearing.

short circuit A short circuit is an overcurrent which is the result of a fault between two conductors which have a different potential under normal operating conditions. This situation could occur because of damage from impacting condition or from poor system design or modification.

sick building syndrome (SBS) A combination of ailments associated with an individual's place of work or residence.

single-feed self-venting indirect hot water storage cylinder A hot water storage vessel that contains a heat exchanger that uses air entrapment to separate the primary water from the secondary water.

single point hot water heater A hot water heater that

serves only one outlet. Also known as a point-of-use water heater.

siphonic WC pan A WC pan that uses a vacuum to clear the contents of the pan.

soakaway drain A specifically designed and located pit, sited away from the dwelling, which allows the water to soak away naturally to the water table.

soaker A small piece of code 3 lead used as part of an abutment weathering on a plain tiled or slated roof.

soft water Water with a high content of carbon dioxide (CO_2). Acidic, with a pH value below 7.

soil stack The lower, wet part of a sanitary pipework system, which takes the effluent away from the building.

solar collector Used with solar hot water heating, the solar collector collects the sun's warmth and transfers it, through a heat exchanger, to the hot water storage vessel.

solar thermal Technology that utilises the heat from the sun to generate domestic hot water supply.

solenoid valve A solenoid valve operates with the aid of an electromagnet. When electricity is supplied to the electromagnet of the valve, the valve becomes magnetised and snaps open, allowing water to flow. Once the electricity has been switched off, the valve is no longer magnetised and a spring snaps the valve shut.

specific heat capacity The amount of heat required to change a unit mass of that substance by one degree in temperature. Measured in kJ/kg/°C.

spigot Another name for the plain end of a pipe. If the fitting we buy has a plain pipe end, we call this a spigot end.

spillage Signs of the products of combustion around an area, typically of an appliance, which should have discharged properly via a flue.

S-plan central heating system A fully pumped heating system that uses two two-port zone valves.

stagnation Where water has stopped flowing.

Statute A major written law passed by Parliament.

steam Water that has undergone a change of state in the presence of heat.

stoichiometric combustion Combustion involving the exact proportions of air and gas required to create complete combustion.

storage cistern Designed to hold a supply of cold water to feed appliances fitted to the system.

stratification This describes how the temperature of water varies with its depth. The nearer the water is to the top of the cistern, the warmer it will be. The deeper the water, the colder it will be. This tends to occur in layers, whereby there is a marked

temperature difference from one layer to the next. The result is that water quality can vary, with the warmer water near the top being more susceptible to biological growth such as *Legionella pneumophila* (the bacterium causing Legionnaires' disease).

structural engineer Calculates the loads (wind, rain, the weight of the structure itself) and the effects of the loads on the structure.

stub stack system A system of sanitary pipework where an air admittance valve replaces the vent pipe.

sublimation A process in which ice passes directly to steam.

substation A building fitted with electrical apparatus that converts voltages from low to high or high to low.

surface water drain Used to collect rainwater and discharge it away from a dwelling directly to a water course, river or stream.

surveyor The person responsible for ensuring that the Building Regulations are followed in the planning and construction phases of a new building and extensions and conversions to existing properties.

swarf Fine chips of stone, metal, or other material produced by a machining operation.

system boiler A central heating boiler that contains an expansion vessel and pressure relief valve in a single unit.

T

tampering Interfering with something that you are unauthorised to touch.

tapered threads A standard thread cut onto the ends of pipes and blackheart malleable, male fittings to ensure a watertight, gastight or steamtight joint. The tube tightens the further it is screwed into the fitting.

temper The temper of a metal refers to how hard or soft it is.

temporary continuity bonding Provides a continuous earth to prevent an electric shock in the event of any electrical fault while removing or replacing metal pipework.

temporary hard water Water that contains minerals such as calcium carbonate (limestone). Can be softened by boiling. Alkaline, with a pH value above 7.

tensile strength A measure of how well or badly a material reacts to being pulled or stretched until it breaks.

terminal The entry of a cable to a fixed position where it is known to terminate/fix.

tightness test A test to ascertain if a gas installation has any leaks.

thermal A type of power station that uses coal to produce steam to drive the turbines.

thermal envelope The part of a building that is enclosed within walls, floor and roof, and that is thermally insulated in accordance with the requirements of the Building Regulations.

thermistor A resistor that varies with temperature.

thermocouple A connection between two different metals that produces an electrical voltage when subjected to heat.

thermo-mechanical cylinder control valves A non-electrical method of controlling secondary hot water temperature. Works in a similar way to a thermostatic radiator valve.

thermometer A device for measuring temperature.

thermoplastic A type of plastic made from polymer resins that becomes liquid form when heated and hard when cooled.

thermosetting plastics Rigid plastics, resistant to higher temperatures than thermoplastics.

tightness test A test to ascertain if a gas installation has any leaks.

toe board A board placed around a platform or a sloping roof to prevent personnel or materials from falling.

torque The property of force that is exhibited when an object rotates around its axis.

tower scaffold A small, temporary structure for holding workers and materials during the construction or repair of a building. They can be static or mobile.

toxic Poisonous.

trade foreman The leader of tradesmen on site. For instance, a plumbing foreman is the plumber who is running the plumbing installation on site. The plumbing supervisor would have many sites to visit, and each one would have a plumbing foreman.

tripping Turning off, or breaking of a circuit, as a result of a fault occurring.

turbidity Turbidity refers to how clear or cloudy water is as a result of the amount of total suspended solids it contains – the greater the amount of total suspended solids (TSS) in the water, the cloudier it will appear. Cloudy water can therefore be said to be turbid.

two-pipe central heating system A system having two pipes, a flow and a return, which are connected to the boiler.

underfloor heating A method of using concealed underfloor pipework to warm a dwelling.

units of power These are read as kWh (kilowatts per hour).

unplasticised polyvinyl chloride (PVCu) A type of thermoplastic used for waste pipes, soil pipes, underground drainage, gutters and rainwater pipes. Can be solvent welded.

upstream This means before a given point which could for example be a gas meter. Therefore if an isolation valve were located upstream of a meter, it would mean it was situated on the pipework before the meter inlet.

unvented hot water storage systems Systems fed directly from the cold water main that are not open to the atmosphere and contain an expansion vessel or expansion bubble.

vaporising burner An oil burner found on some oil-fired appliances that warms the fuel to vaporise it prior to combustion.

velocity The measurement of the rate at which an object changes its position.

vent stack The upper part of a sanitary pipework system that introduces air into the system to help prevent loss of trap seal.

ventilated discharge branch system A sanitary pipework system used on larger installations where there is a risk of trap seal loss because the waste pipe lengths are excessive.

ventilation The process of supplying air to and removing air from a room, internal space, appliance, compartment or garage.

Venturi boost mixing valves A shower valve using the principle of a venturi tube for mixing hot and cold water to produce a showering temperature.

Venturi principle A Venturi operates on the principle that by reducing the bore of a water pipe for example, the flow of water will increase in velocity. The process is similar to putting a finger over the end of a hose pipe or nipping the end of it which results in increased velocity at that point.

Venturi tube A pipe that is suddenly reduced in size creating a reduction in pressure but an increase in velocity, in accordance with Bernoulli's principle.

vertex flue A special type of C_{72} flue arrangement which takes its air for combustion from the roof space which is ventilated in accordance with the manufacturer's instructions.

vitreous china Clay material with an enamelled surface used to manufacture bathroom appliances.

vitiation Lack of oxygen.

vitiation-sensing device Vitiation-sensing devices are often fitted to space heaters and other open-flued appliances. They respond to any lack of oxygen (02) in the air (vitiation). The precision pilot flame will lift off the tip of the thermocouple in search of oxygen which will cause the termination of the millivolt signal to the electromagnet on the thermoelectric flame supervision device.

volt The unit of electrical potential.

waste carrier's licence A licence required by the local authority for anyone transporting waste materials.

Waste Management Duty of Care Code of Practice Legislation that aims to ensure that producers of waste take responsibility for making sure that their waste is managed without harm to human health or to the environment.

water A compound constructed from two hydrogen atoms and one oxygen atom. The most abundant compound on earth. It can be fresh water or saline (salt) water.

water course A river, stream or other flowing natural water source.

Water Supply (Water Fittings) Regulations 1999 These relate to the supply of safe, clean, wholesome drinking water to properties and dwellings, specifically targeting the prevention of contamination, waste, undue consumption, misuse and erroneous metering.

water undertaker A water company in the UK. A supplier of treated, wholesome water.

watt SI unit for power. It is equivalent to one joule per second (1J/s), or in electrical units, one volt ampere (1V·A).

wavering out Trap seal loss caused by wind blowing across the top of a vent stack.

WC cistern Used to flush a WC.

whiteheart fittings A type of fitting for low carbon steel pipe with a parallel female thread.

wind turbine A method of generating electricity from a turbine connected to a large propeller driven by the wind.

Wobbe number Sometimes known as the Wobbe index, this is used to compare the combustion energy outputs of different compositions of fuel gases.

working drawings All plans, elevations and details needed by a contractor and trades to complete a building.

Y-plan central heating system A fully pumped heating system that uses one three-port mid-position valve.

Z

zero carbon fuel A fuel where the net carbon dioxide emissions from all the fuel used is zero.

zero governors These devices are also known as 'air gas ratio valves'. They are often installed on condensing boilers to increase efficiency by controlling excess air to the appliance burner.

INDEX

NOTES